THE COMPLETE HANDBOOK FOR COLLEGE WOMEN

PRAISE FOR THE BOOK

"Weinberg's advice is sound and based on not only practical experience, but on her own good judgment. The suggested readings and resources sections will provide a tremendous boost to women hoping to get the most out of their college experience."
—Sidonia M. Dalby, Associate Director of Admission, Smith College,
co-author of *The Transfer Student's Guide to Changing Colleges*

"One of the most comprehensive resources around. It will be mandatory for all my staff members and strongly recommended for all our new students. THE COMPLETE HANDBOOK FOR COLLEGE WOMEN addresses all the issues with which I have seen college women struggle. This is the handbook no one should be without."
—Folly Patterson, Assistant Dean of Students, Scripps College

"THE COMPLETE HANDBOOK FOR COLLEGE WOMEN? It belongs on every woman's bookshelf in between 'Our Bodies, Ourselves' and 'What Color Is Your Parachute.' Essential!"
—Allison Wildridge, * Associate Director of Residence Life for Student Development,
The College of William and Mary

"An ambitious, comprehensive, and personal guide which is as useful for college-bound seniors and undergraduates as it is informative for parents and college counselors. One of the few, if not the only one, of its kind—it covers an array of 'life issues' thus making it an important complement to a student's academic pursuits."
—Bekki Lee, Associate Dean of Students, Amherst College

"I like the way it seems to predict my questions and answers them in a non-threatening manner. I also like that it speaks to different audiences rather than assuming that the reader is white. It addresses difficult and sophisticated issues in a down-to-earth and straightforward manner. It has taken me four years to even figure out what the questions are—and it addresses them."
—Clara Shin, Smith College, Class of '92

"This handbook addresses literally every aspect of college life. I noticed its constant reference to the traditionally 'taboo' issues—homosexuality, AIDS, alcohol consumption. Any woman entering college is liable to be confronted with any one of these issues. This guide prepares you for the confrontation."
—L'Ornya Bowie, Howard University, Class of '91

"It touches on so many points that I understand now that I am a senior. If I had been clued in to some of these things *before* going to college, I think that, as a whole, my college experience would have been enriched. Had I gotten a headstart with the information it presents, I would have been aware of what to expect and not have to play so many guessing games my first year!"
—Jennifer Ahlstrom, Towson State University, Class of '92

THE
COMPLETE
HANDBOOK
FOR
COLLEGE
WOMEN

*Making the Most of
Your College Experience*

CAROL WEINBERG

NEW YORK UNIVERSITY PRESS

NEW YORK AND LONDON

Grateful acknowledgment is made to the following for granting permission to quote from copyrighted material: quotation from Peter Adair, Janet Cole, and Veronica Selver, "Absolutely Positive," PBS television program, "Point of View," November 1991; quotation from Becky Birtha, "A Sense of Loss," in *For Nights Like This One*, copyright © 1983 by Becky Birtha, reprinted by permission of Frog in the Well; quotation from Barbara Ehrenreich, "Welcome to Fleece U.," in *The Worst Years of Our Lives: Irreverent Notes from a Decade of Greed*, copyright © 1981, 1985, 1986, 1987, 1988, 1989, 1990 by Barbara Ehrenreich, reprinted by permission of Pantheon Books; quotation from Harvey Fierstein, *Torch Song Trilogy* (New York: Gay Presses of New York, 1981), copyright © 1978, 1979 by Harvey Fierstein; quotation from Jodie Foster, Academy Award acceptance speech, 1989, copyright © 1989 by Academy of Motion Picture Arts and Sciences; quotations from Ellen Goodman, "Carolyn Keene: Bringing Up Nancy Drew," and "The Double Standard," both in *Keeping in Touch*, copyright © 1985 by The Washington Post Company, reprinted by permission of Summit Books, a division of Simon & Schuster, Inc., and The Washington Post Company; quotation from Audre Lorde, *Sister Outsider*, reprinted by permission of Crossing Press; quotation from Gwyneth Ferguson Matthews, *Voices from the Shadows: Women with Disabilities Speak Out*, reprinted by permission of Women's Press; quotations from Mark Medoff, *Children of a Lesser God*, copyright © 1980 by Westmark Productions, Inc., reprinted by permission of the author and Dramatists Play Service, Inc.; quotation from Cherríe Moraga, "The Welder," in *This Bridge Called My Back: Writings by Radical Women of Color*, copyright © 1981, 1983 by Cherríe Moraga and Gloria Anzaldúa, reprinted by permission of Kitchen Table: Women of Color Press; quotation from Holly Near, *Fire in the Rain . . . Singer in the Storm*, copyright © 1990 by Holly Near, reprinted by permission of William Morrow & Co., Inc.; quotation from *New Current*, Smith College, April 1987, reprinted by permission; quotation from Gail Sausser, "Hello, I Am a Lesbian," in *Lesbian Etiquette*, copyright © 1986 by Gail Sausser, reprinted by permission of Crossing Press; quotation from Ntozake Shange, *for colored girls who have considered suicide/when the rainbow is enuf*, copyright © 1975, 1976, 1977 by Ntozake Shange, reprinted by permission of Macmillan Publishing Company and Methuen London Ltd.; quotation from Veronica A. Shoffstall, *After a While*, copyright © 1971 by Veronica A. Shoffstall; quotation from *Smith Alumnae Quarterly*, Summer 1991, reprinted by permission; quotations from Gloria Steinem, *Outrageous Acts and Everyday Rebellions*, copyright © 1983 by Gloria Steinem, copyright © 1984 by East Toledo Productions, Inc., reprinted by permission of Henry Holt and Company, Inc.; quotations from Wendy Wasserstein, *Bachelor Girls*, copyright © 1984, 1985, 1986, 1987, 1988, 1990 by Wendy Wasserstein, reprinted by permission of Alfred A. Knopf; quotations from Wendy Wasserstein, *The Heidi Chronicles and Other Plays*, copyright © 1990 by Wendy Wasserstein, reprinted by permission of Harcourt, Brace & Company; quotations from Mitsuye Yamada, "Invisibility Is an Unnatural Disaster: Reflections of an Asian American Woman," in *This Bridge Called My Back: Writings by Radical Women of Color*, copyright © 1981, 1983 by Cherríe Moraga and Gloria Anzaldúa, reprinted by permission of Kitchen Table: Women of Color Press.

New York University Press
New York and London

Library of Congress Cataloging-in-Publication Data
Weinberg, Carol.
The complete handbook for college women : making the most of your
college experience / Carol Weinberg.
p.   cm.
Includes bibliographical references and index.
ISBN 0-8147-9266-9.—ISBN 0-8147-9267-7 (pbk.)
1. Women—Education (Higher)—United States—Handbooks, manuals,
etc.   2. Women college students—United States—Life skills guides.
3. College student orientation—United States—Handbooks, manuals,
etc.   I. Title.
LC1756.W45   1994
376'.65'0973—dc20   94-2245
                          CIP

New York University Press books are printed on acid-free paper,
and their binding materials are chosen for strength and durability.

Manufactured in the United States of America

10   9   8   7   6   5   4   3   2   1

To
Dana, Megan, Adam, and Allison—
college students of the future,
and all the students
who have taught me,
and continue to teach me,
so much.

Contents

ɞ

Acknowledgments

I would like to thank the many colleagues who read early chapters of this book, provided feedback, and helped me to gather reactions from students: Phil Adams, Liz Anderson, Sally Baum, Kim Bennett, Donna Bourassa, Liz Carr, S. E. Chase, Cindy Coulson, Rev. Becky Dinan, Rev. Hugh Flesher, Kerrie Harthan, Carrie Hemenway, Jenny Jackson, Dr. Les Jaffe, Judy Jones, Lisa Norbury Kilian, Mim King, Rabbi Yechiael Lander, Marianne Leedy, M. J. Maccardini, Susie Margulis, Ginny Mayer, Folly Patterson, Connie Peterson, Pam Peterson, Rev. Bill Rich, Sharon Rust, Jen Tyne, Allison Wildridge, and Teresa Scott Woods.

I am also indebted to the many students who read chapters, offered feedback, or shared their own experiences: Jennifer Ahlstrom, Jane Allen, Amber Alonso, Kim Armstrong, Angela Baldwin, Laila Barrouk, Kelly Bivans, Nicole Black, Beth Bolyn, Mona Bond, L'Ornya Bowie, Patricia Brooks, Lisa Brown, Heather Cleary, Jennifer Cognard, Alison Conn, Jennifer Conn, Sîan Cotton, Susan Cross, Nilanjana Dasgupta, Jeanine Della Rocco, Keisha De Loatch, Virginia Easter, Jennifer Eyrich, Shawne Fischer, Katherine Footracer, Lori Fraker, Concessa Freinek, Sophie Godley, Elizabeth Gough, Juliet Habjan, Mary Hallet, Mehrunissa Hamid, Jennifer Harris, Felicia Heywood, Beth Hicks, Debra Hindman, Heather Hobson, Cathy Hogan, Jeanne Huger, Susan Ingram, Sharon Ishikawa, Leigh Jerner, Sandra Johnson, Coyote Karrick, Christina Kay, Alex Keany, Rebecca Ketron, Angela Kim, Eleanor Kim, Mary Kim, Natasha Kirjanov, LeeAnn Koenig, Jennifer Larter, Sarah Lazare,

E. Hayden Lemly, Denise Lilly, Mary Lindquist, Jennifer Ludwick, Greta Lundsgaard, Lina Macri, Jocelyn Manuel, Ronda Mink, Susan Murphy, Jennie Nyulasi, Lisa Olcese, Felicia Otchet, Renee Paschyn, Alyson Payne, Erica Reich, Satya Rhodes-Conway, Kira Scanlan, Ayse Sercan, Clara Shin, Shaida Sira, Lisa Slavid, Laura Spear, Lisa Tatum, Rebecca Wilusz, Cynthia Wilkerson, and Tracey Young.

Thanks to the always helpful, unbelievably patient staff at the Baltimore County Public Library, especially the Perry Hall Branch.

The original casts of *Les Misérables* and *Miss Saigon* provided inspirational musical accompaniment for me and my word processor. Bravo.

I greatly appreciate the energy and enthusiasm that Niko Pfund, Jennifer Hammer, and Despina Papazoglou Gimbel of New York University Press put into this project from start to finish.

My special thanks to Joan Keyser for generously giving me a home and workspace that allowed me the time and the freedom to pursue this project.

Finally, I'm tremendously grateful to my friends and especially my family—my late father, Stan, my mother, Alice, Sandy and Kin, Stu and Lisa, Susie and Peter, and my aunt Sue—who always offer great encouragement and support.

Some Notes on Terminology

I have consciously made some choices about terminology in writing this book. First, I have generally either used gender-neutral words or referred directly to women in order to focus on the population for whom this book is written.

Second, word choice can have a powerful influence over a woman's view of herself. For this reason, I've chosen to use stronger and more active terms such as "survivor" rather than weaker and more passive terms such as "victim."

There has been much discussion about the appropriate terms to use in referring to specific groups. I've tried to respect the right of people to name themselves rather than be named by others. Thus, while there are still differences among individuals within any group about the name they prefer to use, I've used terms that my research and experience have taught me are preferred by most, though not necessarily all, group members.

THE COMPLETE HANDBOOK FOR COLLEGE WOMEN

Introduction

I have wanted to write this book for women for a long time—to give you a head start as you enter college and a resource throughout your years there. Parts of what you read here will be helpful to you before you arrive on campus; other ideas will have more meaning as you encounter new people, experiences, and parts of yourself.

Life is increasingly complicated for students in college today. The media is talking more openly about issues such as sexual harassment, acquaintance rape, incest, eating disorders, and codependency. These behaviors have always existed but have not always been acknowledged or considered acceptable to discuss. As many long-held silences continue to be broken, more women are recognizing personal issues they need to confront. Some of these experiences occur at college; others surface there after having gone unrecognized for years. Even if you never have these experiences yourself, you're likely to encounter them, for your roommates, hallmates, or friends may have confronted them or may be dealing with them now.

The college population will continue to change over the next few decades as students come from increasingly diverse backgrounds and lifestyles. It's important to understand and value those differences as well as to recognize and appreciate similarities. Too often the needs of some women have been minimized or even ignored on college campuses. I hope that every college woman will find herself somewhere in these pages.

Academics are obviously a priority at college, but personal growth is equally important, and that is the emphasis of this book. Most college catalogues set out clear expectations about academic preparation for admission—so many years of English, social studies, math, etc. Much less is said about how you can prepare for the more personal experiences of living with others on a college campus. This book is an effort to fill in that gap.

Community living in college residence halls provides many exciting opportunities to learn about yourself and others. That learning can also be confusing and even frightening at times. I want to tell you about the things I've learned and let recent and current college students tell you about their experiences. Some of what you read in the chapters ahead will confirm what you already know; some of it may make you uncomfortable. If you can think about difficult issues before you actually encounter them, however, you'll be better prepared if and when they arise. In addition to the material offered in this book, be sure to familiarize yourself with the specific policies, offices, and resources on your own college or university campus.

Most of the chapters in this handbook begin with basic background information, sometimes including terminology about the specific issue or explaining potential sources of misunderstanding. In some chapters that cover several related topics (e.g., "Taking Care of Yourself" and "Sexuality"), this information is incorporated later in the chapter. When you live at college, you don't live in a vacuum; you often become part of others' lives and they become part of yours. Each chapter therefore describes specific examples of how you may encounter the issue on campus and suggests ways to respond. Many chapters are written to speak to different populations—to those of you who have more personal experience with an issue, lifestyle, or background, and to those of you who may, as yet, have more limited knowledge. Reading each full chapter will help all of you begin to understand and appreciate others' experiences as well as your own. Suggestions about where to look for help, both on and off campus, are also presented.

Finally, each chapter offers a variety of suggestions for ways to educate yourself, at your own pace, in the ways you prefer to learn. Each chapter (except chapter 11) has a bibliography listing helpful resources—nonfiction books, anthologies, biographies, poetry, plays, and novels. Many chapters include lists of magazine articles and other educational materials and sources of information, as well as the names and addresses of organizations that offer assistance. Popular culture also provides opportunities for learning. The annotated lists of films, videos, TV shows, and plays can help you explore topics through the media. Unless otherwise noted, the entries in these listings refer to movies. Most movies are also found on video, as are a number of the made-for-TV movies included. Where movies are based on books, that's noted in case you prefer to read the original source.

There is a powerful connection between what we have learned to think about women, how we feel about ourselves, and whether we give power away to others or take control over our own choices and lives. I hope this book provides you with support, challenges, and resources to keep or reclaim that power and make the most of your college experience.

· · ·

> I am the welder.
> I understand the capacity of heat
> to change the shape of things.
> I am suited to work
> within the realm of sparks
> out of control.
>
> I am the welder.
> I am taking the power
> into my own hands.
> —Cherríe Moraga, "The Welder" [1]

· · ·

A FINAL THOUGHT

You will find that the words and ideas of recent students are incorporated throughout this book. Your generation of college students can play a similar role in future editions. I'd like to hear from you.

- Are there any topics that you feel should be discussed more fully?
- Are there any additional issues that should be included?
- Do you have suggestions about books, movies, or other resources to add to the "Educating Yourself" sections?
- Are there any personal quotations or stories that you'd like to share with college women who will follow you? (If you send any personal quotations or stories, please indicate whether you are willing to have

us print them, in whole or part, in future editions of *The Complete Handbook for College Women*.)

Please send suggestions and comments to Carol Weinberg, c/o New York University Press, 70 Washington Square South, New York, NY 10012-1091. Thank you.

ONE

Arrival: Independence, Freedom, and Responsibility

I've been to more college commencements than I can count. A few were my own, but most were at schools where I worked. It's usually a hot day in May, and the audience is filled with parents, grandparents, brothers, sisters, partners, and children of graduating seniors. They fan themselves with programs and strain their necks trying to see everything. The seniors march in wearing identical caps and gowns, arguing about whether the tassel should start out on the right or the left side of their caps. There's also always one person who trips on the way up to the stage—my mom was kind enough to pass along that piece of information to me just before I walked across the stage at my elementary school graduation.

I always feel a mixture of excitement, relief, pride, and nostalgia at these ceremonies. I watch students I have come to know over the years. They cross the stage, shake hands with the president of the college, and take their diplomas. Some students have tears in their eyes, some raise a clenched fist in victory, some are beaming with happiness, and yes, someone usually trips. As I watch, I always think about the four or more years that have passed since these students entered the college. I see them change in so many ways. I often wish I had videotaped them arriving on their first day and could show them that tape now, so they could appreciate how self-reliant they have become. The process is easier for some and harder for others, but those who see it through are ready to take their next steps with a strong sense of who they are and what they can accomplish.

Picture yourself in your college residence hall the first night of your first semester. You may have arrived alone by public transportation or been driven by your family or friends. Your room is cluttered with boxes, books, and suitcases waiting to be unpacked. Chances are you're sharing the room with at least one other student. Perhaps you hit it off right away and are already talking to one another as if you've been friends for ages. Or you may be sizing one another up uneasily, wondering what the college was thinking when it paired you as roommates and how you're ever going to make it through the year.

The hall is full of other students, many of them also new to the campus. Someone may be asking around to see who wants to take a trip into town, or downtown, or to another college to see what's going on. Someone else wants to talk about classes and selecting courses. Another person is knocking on doors and taking orders for a run to the local store. Still another group is already forming in one room, or sitting out in the hall, talking and listening to music.

There are signs all over the hall advertising different clubs, organizations, activities, and parties. Some of the names are familiar to you; others aren't:

- Glee Club Auditions
- Join the College Republicans
- Black Students' Alliance Meeting
- AIESEC Wants You
- Gay, Lesbian, Bisexual Alliance Get-Together
- Interfaith Council Brunch
- Party with the Pre-Law Society

You have a copy of the orientation schedule, so you know what events and meetings are set up for the next few days. There may be upperclass students designated as orientation advisors or "big sisters," but for the most part it will be up to you to be where you need to be and do what you need to do.

Colleges differ in how much support and structure they provide for you. Some assume you are an adult from the moment you arrive. They'll expect you to follow instructions and meet requirements and deadlines without being reminded. You'll be responsible for your own choices and decisions. "I didn't know" or "I didn't read it" won't be acceptable excuses. There will be faculty and staff advisors available to you as resources, but you'll generally need to seek them out.

Other schools assume that you are an "adult-in-the-works." They'll provide varying degrees of support services to educate you about your responsibilities as a student. There may be seminars or credit classes to help you adjust to college life, explore your strengths, and identify resources available at the institution.

Some colleges have more concrete rules and don't give students all of the freedom found at other institutions. These rules can range from specific course requirements to curfews in the residence halls to restrictions on specific behaviors such as drinking.

ENCOUNTERING AND RESPONDING TO THIS ISSUE

· · ·

"In the fairy tales on my shelves, girls waited to be rescued from their sleep or their cinders by princes. . . . But Nancy Drew rescued herself. Nancy Drew solved problems. Nancy Drew behaved the way a child of nine wants to believe she will behave at eighteen: sensibly, competently, independently."

—Ellen Goodman, "Carolyn Keene: Bringing Up Nancy Drew" [1]

· · ·

People react differently to the freedom they find at college. For some of you the idea of being responsible for yourself may be what you've been looking forward to for a long time. Your parent or parents are not right there with you. Your choices, both academic and personal, are basically yours to make. The wealth of possibilities can also feel overwhelming, as can the advice you receive from many sides—home, old and new friends, your own curiosity.

Upon arrival at college, most students have little experience living on their own and being responsible and accountable for themselves. Perhaps your parents tried to protect you from being hurt, or maybe they gave you freedom and responsibility but the choices available to you were limited. Think about your own particular style of decision making, what you need in the way of information, structure, and support, and how to seek those out.

Get to know your own decision-making process. Are some kinds of decisions easier for you to make than others? For example, do you have a good method for choosing courses each semester but struggle for hours to decide which movie to go see? Why? Is it easier for you to make decisions similar to those you've made successfully in the past? What are the hardest decisions for you to make and why? For example, do you worry about choices that conflict with your parents' values, or those that may make you less popular with your friends? How realistic are your expectations of yourself? Do you expect more than you can really accomplish right away? Can you set priorities for yourself? This may mean making choices and not being able to do everything you want. You may need to choose, for example, between spending time working at a campus job to help defray some of your expenses or doing volunteer research with a professor to build your academic contacts and experience in your major.

If you need more structure and direction than your college provides, consider creating some of that structure yourself. Sometimes it can take as little as telling an advisor or a staff member that you need more direction from them or that you need them to be more clear. The worst that can happen is that they can't provide it for you, but perhaps they can refer you to someone who can.

Learn how to set your own goals and develop action plans. The resources described in the next section of this chapter include some places to look for help in building those skills. It could help to keep a written journal to sort out your thoughts and ideas. If you have to explain to yourself in writing what you're trying to understand, you may see patterns in the way you deal with various situations. Learn to expand on your strengths and develop strategies to overcome your limitations.

Academic Life

"What's your major?" You'll probably hear that question a million times—before you get to college, the first few weeks you're there, whenever you meet new people, when you go home for vacation. Many students don't know right away what they want to major in. Others change their minds one or more times during the course of their college experience. A premed major, for example, may discover that she can't stand the chemistry she needs to pursue that major, or she may find herself more excited by some other field. Your choice of academic major is one of the biggest decisions you'll make at college. If you make it too early in your academic career, you could narrow your learning experiences before it's necessary. Take the time to explore a variety of possibilities and make good use of advice from faculty members and academic advisors. If you're interested in a particular field that has not traditionally been open to many women, don't let that deter you. Find an advisor or mentor who is open to considering *all* the opportunities for you.

Each semester you will be responsible for selecting your courses and planning your schedule. Depending on the requirements at your college, you'll probably have some flexibility in choosing classes, instructors, and sections. Think about challenging yourself each semester without taking on more than you can handle. Consider some courses that are new and different, and look for at least some professors who may push you. Take responsibility for managing your time so that you complete the work required in your courses, and for handing assignments in on time. Some professors are willing to consider extensions and make-up exams while others will reduce your grade for anything handed in late. It's wisest to get into the habit of planning your work so you finish it on time and *not* to assume that you can always work things out with an understanding professor.

Academic honesty is expected from all college students. Most schools have an academic honor code and a procedure to be followed if students violate it by plagiarism or cheating. The consequences for academic dishonesty can range from a warning to failing grades to academic probation to dismissal. If you don't fully understand the academic honor code or are unsure of anything related to academic dishonesty, ask for help. An upperclass student, academic advisor, or professor would certainly be willing to respond.

You will also be responsible for doing the paperwork and meeting the deadlines for all academic procedures such as preregistration and adding or dropping courses. If you follow directions, you'll avoid stressful and time-consuming consequences such as not getting courses you need, not being able to drop a class after the deadline, or having to petition a dean or board to make an exception for your situation.

You should also know about the implications of the United States Educational Rights and Privacy Act of 1974, often referred to as the Buckley amendment. Once you are eighteen, or have entered a postsecondary institution, you are entitled to certain rights under this law. These rights apply to your educational records and who may have access to them. You have the legal right to see information recorded on your official student record. If you believe there is something incorrect in that record, you can challenge to have it changed.[2]

The way individual colleges interpret the Buckley amendment also affects the access your own parents can have to your educational records including your semester grade reports. If you are not claimed as a dependent on their income taxes, your parents can't have access to your records without your consent. If you are a dependent, your college's policy will determine what rights you and your parents have. Some colleges assume you are a dependent and allow parents access to educational records and grade reports unless you document your status as an independent. Other colleges assume you are independent and don't provide information to parents unless they request it and can document your status as a dependent. Still other colleges release grade-report information to parents without your consent only if there is a change in your academic status—for example, if you go on academic probation. Colleges are required to provide information, often in the college handbook or catalog, about college policies on access to and privacy of student records.[3]

Residential and Social Life

· · ·

"I was an R.A. for a freshman women's hall and while they were eager to take advantage of all the new opportunities available to them at the college, they were easily overwhelmed by it all—not one had come to school with the benefit of good self-direction skills. Some freshmen arrive at school and have no trouble adjusting; others, particularly women, appear to have real difficulty making the transition between living at home and the responsibilities of living in a residence hall."

—S. L., class of '93

· · ·

Your peer group is a powerful influence on your development in college. Take advantage of opportunities to get to know a wide variety of people. I remember one woman I met in college. We weren't friends, but I ran into her late one night in the basement of our residence hall. I was getting a soda from the soda machine, and she was getting cigarettes from the machine next to it. We started to talk. On the surface we had little in common, and we traveled in very different circles on campus, but we had a wonderful conversation. Actually, we talked all night. We probably never would have spoken more than a dozen words to one another if we hadn't been in the same place at the same time, and open to something new.

Many of your assumptions and values may be challenged by living with so many new people. You may find yourself rethinking some of your beliefs and developing new ones, or understanding your previously held values in a new way, or recommitting yourself to what you've always believed. Appreciate that there are other ways to look at the world; that doesn't mean you necessarily have to devalue the way you presently look at it.

■ ■ ■

"College students may pressure you because your values are conservative, but if you strongly believe in them, then hold onto those values. At the same time, listen to other people and respect them no matter how hard it may be to do so."

—Student, class of '91

■ ■ ■

First-year students tend to be more successful at college when they have a peer support system.[4] Such support might come from peers with similar interests, such as sports or theater, or similar identities, such as a shared religion or cultural background. Having a network in which you can feel readily understood and accepted is an important source of comfort during stressful times.

Take your time building your network of friends. Get to know them, what each can offer you, and what each needs from you. A friend of mine used to talk about "fifty-fifty relationships"—the kind where each person both gives and gets. Women often put others' needs above their own, so it's important to make sure that you, too, get things you need from your friends.

Decisions about how and with whom you spend your time will be up to you. The pressure many women feel to do everything and be totally successful can draw some of you into trying to do too much too quickly. It can be tempting to get involved in many exciting activities, sometimes at the expense of academics or sleep. You may be able to successfully juggle many different responsibilities at once. On the other hand, trying to do too much can make it hard to do any one or two activities really well, or can leave you feeling overextended or burned out. The section on time management in chapter 4 provides useful advice.

. . .

"My philosophy as a beginning college student was: Start small and then grow larger. I spent September checking out a bunch of organizations, but I didn't commit myself to do a lot of work in all of them right away. There were many years to do that. Once I felt I was comfortable with my schoolwork and with a few clubs, I decided to swim on the team in November. I didn't commit myself beforehand. When people asked 'Are you going to swim?' I said that I would have to see. I increased my extracurricular schedule only after I knew I was doing fine with academics. In the following years, I changed some of my activities. I had a motto: Every semester, do at least one new and fun thing."

—G. E., class of '91

. . .

If you live on campus, there will be policies and procedures you'll need to know and follow—signing housing contracts, completing room-damage inventories, abiding by room-change procedures, etc. Red tape may be a pain in the neck, but it's a necessary pain. You have a better chance of getting what you want when you follow established policies and deadlines.

All students have responsibilities in a group living situation. You will, for example, be expected to contribute to the safety and security of your living unit. You will also have some responsibility for the behavior of your guests. Your college may have a social honor code that describes behavioral expectations of you as a member of the college community. Understand those expectations, follow them, and recognize that you should be able to expect the same from everyone else.

What is illegal off campus is also illegal on campus. Violating college policies and laws about theft or the use and distribution of drugs, for example, can lead to college disciplinary procedures and also possible legal action. This includes state laws about the use and distribution of alcohol. Most colleges are struggling to design their policies in such a way as to encourage responsible choices regarding the use of alcohol. Know your college policies and the expectations of students, living groups, and organizations.

If you are not already taking responsibility for your personal finances, now is a good time to start. You'll need to keep accurate records of bank accounts and to be responsible about paying your bills. If you're working your way through school and have difficulty paying all your bills on time, try to work out payment plans with your creditors. If you are on financial aid or applying for it, fill out all forms by deadlines, and sign loan papers promptly. This will help you receive the money you need to pay your bills on time and cover your day-to-day expenses.

You may decide to share the cost of an item such as a refrigerator or long-distance telephone service with other students. Be aware that the person whose name is on the contract or order is the person responsible for the bill. If you take on that responsibility, you need to pay the *entire* bill. The phone company won't split the bill or force your friends to pay; you will need to get the money from them. If the bill is not paid in full and your name is on the account, you will be the one whose credit can be affected in the future. If you're going to share a phone or other financial responsibility, know the people you will be sharing with before you agree to be the person whose name is on the contract. It may also help to talk with them beforehand to work out an arrangement that is least likely to leave one person responsible for more than her share.

For Commuting Students

Some of you may be living off campus or at home and commuting to school. You won't have all the same natural opportunities to develop a peer network as those living in a residence hall, so you will need to make an even greater effort to develop your support system. One way to meet other commuters is to take advantage of any lounge or meeting space specifically set aside for commuting students. Some schools also have programs through which a commuter can affiliate with, or be "adopted" by, a residence hall and participate in that hall's activities. Check with the office in charge of residential life to see if such an opportunity exists on your campus. When you meet residential students in your classes, they may invite you back to the hall to study or have dinner. Take advantage of those opportunities. There are times when you can reciprocate; campus residents often welcome the chance to get off campus. Participate in clubs or organizations, if you have the time. If you're able to stay on campus rather than always heading home right after classes, you may be able to create some opportunities for meeting more students.

Have a cup of coffee in the student center, work out at the gym, or study in the library. Some colleges have offices of commuter affairs that handle the special needs of off-campus students.

WHERE TO LOOK FOR HELP

. . .

"I found that coming to college during the summer prior to the first day of classes was very helpful. I talked to current students and administrators and found this extremely beneficial to my transition to college."

—B. L., class of '94

. . .

Ask questions. Start with orientation, which consists of several days on campus, either during the summer or just prior to the opening of school. Most college orientation programs include meetings, workshops, discussions, and activities to help you make the transition into college. Use this time to find the offices and resources that provide support and structure. It can be harder to seek help when you're feeling confused and self-conscious. Check out the possibilities before you actually need them.

Academic Life

Start with your faculty advisor. If you find your particular advisor less helpful than you need, you can usually request a change, either through the chair of the department or through the dean or office in charge of new student advising. Don't be too quick to change, however. The advisor who challenges you to make your own decisions and encourages you to take some risks may be frustrating at times but may help you get more out of your academic opportunities.

You can also approach faculty members other than your specific advisor, especially if you feel comfortable with them or if you are interested in their area of specialization. Faculty members have scheduled office hours each week, or you can catch them just before or after class. Some professors will be around and available for many hours; others are limited by their research and writing demands or family commitments. If you have difficulty reaching an instructor, the Registrar's Office or academic department secretary should have his or her full schedule.

Some colleges use students as academic peer advisors. They answer basic academic questions, assist faculty advisors, and help you with your registration and course selection decisions. Often upperclass students are informal sources of information. Keep in mind, however, that their opinions are based on their own experiences and preferences. You need to decide what's best for you.

Academic development services offer assistance such as tutoring or consultation with a writing counselor to help with papers. These offices may run workshops on effective study techniques, time management, test preparation, and other academic skills. Also learn how to use the library and audiovisual services. No matter how well you did in high school, college work is different. Learn the ropes at the start to avoid stress later on.

Residential and Social Life

Student peer counselors in the residence halls have titles like Resident Assistant, Resident Counselor, or Head Resident. Since the term Resident Assistant, or R.A., is most common, I'll use that term throughout this book to refer to those student staff members who are generally the first people for you to approach with any questions or concerns. R.A.s are trained to be good listeners and to deal with issues such as homesickness, roommate conflicts, and personal problems. They can give you information about how the campus works, the policies you need to know, and what services are available for you. R.A.s are not there to solve your problems for you but to help you learn how to solve them for yourself.

R.A.s are often the first to pick up on, and respond to, crises on the hall. They may also plan and run educational programs and activities. As student staff members, R.A.s may have administrative and disciplinary responsibilities. While they're on your hall to help you, remember that they're not supposed to encourage or ignore situations that are dangerous or in violation of the law or college policy. One of the most important roles that R.A.s play is to help all residents understand what it means to live respectfully and responsibly as part of a group.

From the start, get to know your R.A. as a person rather than as someone who is only there in case of a crisis. It's often easier to talk to someone about a problem if you feel comfortable with that person first. Since R.A.s are also full-time students, there are limits to the help they can provide. They may refer you to other offices or help you identify additional on-campus resources to use.

You may not feel comfortable talking about some concerns with your R.A. If there are several R.A.s in a building, you can approach one of the others. If you want to talk with someone you won't see every day, someone a bit more removed from your life, the professional hall staff is the appropriate resource. Many college residence halls have a hall director or resident director. This person may live in an apartment in the hall, have an office there, or be located in a more central campus location. If your campus does not have individual live-in hall directors, there should be central office staff to contact.

Professional residence hall staff have been moving away from the old "house mother" model. You're more likely to find adults who have training in student development, educational programming, counseling, and administration. These individuals are professional educators with a genuine interest in college-aged students—they should, if they live in a residence hall!

Most residence hall staff fall under the direction of offices of residential life or offices of student affairs. Questions about housing and community living should be referred to these offices if they can't be resolved by the hall staff. Policies are generally set at this level.

Offices of student activities oversee campus organizations, social activities, student government, and leadership development programs. Other student services—financial aid, career development, minority affairs, international student affairs, the chapel, and contacts for students with disabilities, returning adult students, gay/lesbian/bisexual students, etc.—are described in later chapters.

Physical and Emotional Life

Most colleges provide some form of health services, with staff who may include physicians, nurse practitioners, physician's assistants, and health educators. If your college does not have an on-campus clinic or infirmary, it probably has a working arrangement with a local hospital or other community services. Know what your medical insurance will and won't cover. Some colleges offer their own health insurance policy and require that students either subscribe to it or submit proof that they have other coverage. The advantage to purchasing the college's policy is that usually it's been developed to offer the best possible coverage based on what the campus health services do and don't provide. If you're covered by your family's health plan, any claims you file will probably be known to your parents; that might be something you want to consider. In any case, be sure to have accurate insurance information with you, and know how to file a claim.

Colleges generally provide either on-campus counseling or information about community resources and referrals. Some counseling services have hours during which you can be seen on a "walk-in" basis. This means that you don't have to schedule an appointment and will be seen as soon as a staff member is available. Most services, however, work on a scheduled-appointment model, requiring you to call ahead to arrange a time to meet with a counselor or therapist. If you have strong feelings about seeing a female counselor or someone with a particular area of interest such as eating disorders or sexual abuse, you can say so when you call for an appointment. It's not always possible, however, for the Counseling Service to meet all specific requests.

Your first appointment with a counselor will probably be something called an "intake interview." The counselor will try to learn why you're there, what you want to work on in counseling, and any other pertinent information. It's very important that you be honest with the person who talks with you. (The counselor doing the intake may or may not be the therapist you eventually see on a regular basis.)

Perhaps you'll be scheduled to meet with someone weekly, or more often at first. You may also be asked if you would consider a counseling group instead of, or in addition to, individual counseling. If the Counseling Service is exceptionally busy, you may not be scheduled on a regular basis right away. You could be put on a waiting list. If you don't want to wait, consider asking for a referral off campus.

Some counseling services see students in long-term therapy for a semester, a year, or longer. Most college counseling services provide more short-term therapy. This means that they will see students only for a specified number of sessions. If you want more extended treatment, you'll probably be referred to off-campus counselors or agencies. Many college counseling services will see students for no extra charge (other than medication) if they have paid their regular health fees; others charge a nominal amount after a specified number of counseling sessions. Therapists in private practice can be expensive, but some of them, including community agencies, have sliding scales based on your ability to pay.

The foundation of a counseling relationship comes from building a sense of trust with a therapist. This can take time. It also takes honesty. If you find yourself having strong feelings about your sessions with your counselor, it's important that you talk about those reactions together. This is part of building the relationship.

Therapy can be difficult, since it means talking about painful parts of yourself. It's natural to get frustrated and even, at times, to feel angry toward your therapist. If, however, you find that you really aren't able to develop a trusting relationship with your counselor, say something. This should either improve your relationship or allow you to consider other alternatives. Don't worry that your counselor will be insulted or hurt. You have a right to change counselors if you feel it's best for you.

Not every counselor/client relationship clicks; that's no one's fault. A number of people find their most beneficial counseling relationships the second or third time they try. Just as different people like different teachers, and some people become your close friends because you instinctively feel comfortable with them, so the same is true for counseling relationships. It can be a tremendous relief to talk about difficult and confusing things with someone else—someone who is there to listen to you, to challenge you to look at things in new ways, and to provide a stable and supportive anchor as you do so.

A good therapeutic relationship has always reminded me of a walk in the woods with a strong guide. The woods belong to you, but you're never quite sure what you'll find. There are probably some beautiful treasures, but there may be unexpected and dangerous obstacles to get through to find them. At times it's scary to make the trip by yourself. A good guide gives you someone with whom to test out your questions and fears. A good guide helps you feel less alone and vulnerable as you confront some of the potential dangers. Sometimes just knowing that the guide is there gives you the strength to take some risks. You may discover that the problems were not as insurmountable as you thought, or that the hurt and the pain don't last forever or destroy you.

If you go to your college's counseling service, that doesn't mean there's something "wrong" with you or that you're weak. Many people have been in counseling at some point in their lives. College can be wonderful and exciting. It can also be confusing and stressful. If old coping skills don't work, develop new ones. Take the initiative to seek out help if you need to; rarely will you find it more available than on a college campus.

. . .

"Everyone has problems. It's just that ultimately the people who seek good advice and help when they have concerns are the ones who generally end up healthiest and happiest."

—G. E., class of '91

. . .

EDUCATING YOURSELF

If you haven't already been on your own, try to put yourself in some independent-living situations before you actually go to college. This will give you a better idea of how you actually deal with freedom and responsibility. For example, consider a residential summer program at a college away from home or a job as a counselor at a sleep-away camp.

Try to visit the college you're planning to attend sometime during the year before you start. If possible, *don't* plan to do this only during specific times set aside for visits from large groups of prospective students. Try to get as accurate a picture as you can of what it would really be like to live there. Stay over with someone in the residence halls. Wander around the campus and talk to as many different people as you can. Find out what their experiences have been like, bearing in mind that yours will not necessarily be the same. If you talk to alumni of your college, remember that their experiences occurred at least several years ago and that life at colleges changes all the time.

Books: Nonfiction, Anthologies, Biographies, Poetry, Plays

Conway, Jill Kerr, ed. *Written by Herself: Autobiographies of American Women: An Anthology.* New York: Vintage, 1992.

Gilligan, Carol. *In a Different Voice: Psychological Theory and Women's Development.* Cambridge, MA: Harvard University Press, 1982.

Gilligan, Carol, Nona P. Lyons, and Trudy J. Hanmer, eds. *Making Connections: The Relational Worlds of Adolescent Girls at Emma Willard School.* Cambridge, MA: Harvard University Press, 1990.

Josselson, Ruthellen. *Finding Herself: Pathways to Identity Development in Women.* San Francisco: Jossey-Bass, 1990.

Miller, Jean Baker. *Toward a New Psychology of Women.* 2d ed. Boston: Beacon, 1986.

Films, Videos, TV Shows, Plays

"A Different World." Explores student life at a historically black college. TV series.

My Brilliant Career. A young woman defies social expectations in Australia at the turn of the century.

On the Verge or the Geography of Yearning. Three Victorian women explore the future by traveling through time into the unknown. Play by Eric Overmyer.

The Sure Thing. Two first-year college students develop a love-hate relationship.

Uncommon Women and Others. A group of women reminisce about their senior year at Mount Holyoke College. Play by Wendy Wasserstein.

TWO

Family Ties

. . .

"My parents had a hard time accepting that I was gone. I was the oldest of four and when I left, I know it was a new experience for them."

—K. C., class of '91

. . .

Students come to college from all kinds of different family backgrounds. Some are from two-parent households while others were raised by single parents or two sets of divorced and remarried parents; by grandparents, aunts and uncles, or older brothers or sisters; or by adoptive or foster parents. Some new students have lived on their own before starting school, and others are coming directly from residential boarding schools. For all of you, however, there are changes involved in this important move. Although this chapter is meant for students from all kinds of families, for convenience' sake, "parents" in the plural will be used to refer to parental figures.

For most students, college presents the first real opportunity to establish identity and independence. Entering college is a significant step toward adulthood, as you leave your family and become a member of a new community. A new location can be exciting, and some of you may look forward to creating a life that's totally new and different.

Homesickness is also a common reaction for many students. The familiarity of family, friends, neighbors, routines, furniture, food, etc., all contribute to your feeling "at home" someplace. You may want some items around you at school that provide familiar comfort—a particular poster, photograph, hat, pillow, etc.

Until a new environment starts to feel more like home, you may try to hold onto what you left behind. Perhaps you'll want to call home all the time, will always think about what your family and friends might be doing, or will even go home many weekends. A constructive way to deal with homesickness is to become involved in activities, get to know new people, and create a new home on campus. After a time of adjustment, many students actually find themselves beginning to refer to school and their residence hall room as "home."

. . .

"My mom made the comment on the phone the other day that all I do when I come home for a weekend is sleep, eat, and do my laundry!"

—F. L., class of '92

. . .

Developing a sense of personal identity means becoming your own person, figuring out what you believe, value, and want from life, and taking steps to reach your own goals. Being at college exposes you to ideas and lifestyles you may never have fully considered before and provides opportunities for you to explore and try new things on for size.

I like to think of this process as your coming to college with a particular "wardrobe" of values, attitudes, and ideas. Some items were given to you by your parents, and some you selected for yourself in high school. On campus, you'll meet people with their own unique wardrobes. Some will be similar to yours and others will be different. You may see new items you'd like to try on. Perhaps you'll borrow them for a while and then return them. Or you may find some items so comfortable that you decide to buy them for yourself, either replacing items in your current wardrobe or adding to them. You could also find that some or much of your original wardrobe is really your favorite after all.

Your parents aren't there to approve or disapprove of your choices, although they may react as they become aware of them. Values, beliefs, and career and relationship decisions all follow this kind of process. Sometimes parents are afraid that you'll grow away from them and the values you grew up with. At other times they're secure that they've provided you with the skills to make your own choices, and they encourage your exploration.

. . .

"It wasn't until my sophomore year that my parents realized how independent I actually was. When this did happen, I received a really sweet card in the mail from my parents saying how proud they are of me and they support me 100 percent. This also included decisions and the changes I may have made in my values."

—F. L., class of '92

. . .

ENCOUNTERING AND RESPONDING TO THIS ISSUE

Relationships with Parents

As you spend time at college, your parents won't be as actively involved in your life as they were before. Most likely, they won't see you every day, and they'll need to trust you and the decisions you make. Communicating with your parents as you're going through the process of becoming your own person can help them understand who you are and the road you're traveling.

Sometimes parents try to influence you from a distance in subtle or not-so-subtle ways. We learn many spoken and unspoken beliefs and rules—things we should and shouldn't do—from our parents. The spoken rules are generally easier to recognize because they're clear.[1] The unspoken rules are more subtle. They're often communicated through mixed messages. Your parents may, for instance, say that your decisions are your own but then show disappointment when you quit the newspaper or change your major or cut your hair. Many of you internalize your parents' attitudes and values. You hear their voices and messages as if they were your own beliefs: "be the best in the class," "do what the people in authority say." Others of you see leaving for college as a chance to do the very opposite of what your parents say. You may try, for example, to purposely *not* be the best in the class, or to challenge authority and break rules. In both of these situations, your parents' wishes are still controlling your choices.

Parental expectations can affect students in a variety of ways. Some parents provide support and constructive challenges; others push you in directions you really don't want to go. They may comment about how much they've sacrificed to send you to college, or you may attend a certain school or major in a particular subject primarily because your mother or father really wanted you to do it. One 1991 graduate described how her father always wanted her to be a lawyer, and how he got very upset knowing that she didn't feel the same way. "I was always living," she said, "with my father's dream in my mind and not my own dreams." It's important to decide what *you* really want.

Your expectations of your parents can also contribute to problems and stresses. Be patient and try to understand your parents and how their backgrounds and experiences can affect their attitudes and the way they relate to you. Don't hold past incidents against them, and realize that they too may be going through changes.

Both parents and children often struggle to loosen the ties that bind them as parent and child, examine those ties, and retie them in more appropriate ways as both grow and change. The concept of a "secure base" is often used to describe a parent/child attachment that encourages exploration and experimentation.[2] The image this evokes for me is of an astronaut venturing out of a space capsule. You always remain connected to the capsule by a lifeline, but you can venture further and further away from the capsule to explore larger spaces.

Parents may consciously or unconsciously remain connected to you in ways that perpetuate parental control. Financial connections sometimes have extra strings attached.

- "As long as I'm paying for your education, you'll study economics or business."
- "Either you stop seeing your boyfriend/girlfriend or you won't get another cent from me."

You may need to decide whether you're willing to risk losing financial support in order to stand up for something you really want for yourself. Some students find ways to compromise with their parents and work things through with them. Others take their chances and make plans to support themselves rather than agree to their parents' conditions. At other times financial ties are simply the habitual way some parents relate to, and take care of, their children. While the intent may not be manipulative, the result continues to reflect a dependent relationship. Find ways to become at least somewhat financially self-supporting.

If your college has an orientation program or sessions for parents, encourage them to attend. These programs can help your parents prepare for what to expect and understand ways you may change. Most schools have moved away from the concept of in loco parentis—the idea that the school serves as an extension of your parents. Colleges today are less likely directly to supervise and monitor student life.[3] While some schools do exercise more authority, others prefer to help students learn to make their own intelligent choices and decisions. If your parents can hear college officials explain their philosophy and the reasons behind it, perhaps they'll be more accepting of your growing independence.

If you give your parents a copy of the college handbook, they can see what rules do and don't exist, and this may help them understand how you're getting used to being treated. Parents who didn't go to college may feel particularly alienated from your new experiences. Sending home copies of the school newspaper can help them get to know your new world better. This may also provide some common ground for discussion when you talk with them. Give your parents an opportunity to see you in action—on the athletic field, in a play, debating, in print, or on exhibit—to help them know you better and recognize your unique and developing talents.

Both parents and children experience major changes when a child begins to assert her independence. Some parents accept and encourage these changes. Others know that it's the healthy thing to happen but still have trouble letting go. While people need to learn from their mistakes, many parents wish they could spare their children unnecessary pain. Your parents may try to protect you from choices they think will hurt you. They may try to control your life, even after you're capable of handling your own decisions. On the other hand, some of you may continue to let your parents take care of you to the extent that you never really learn how to take care of yourself.

If you're unhappy or upset, it's a natural tendency to want to call your parents. It can be very hard for them to be far away from you when they think you're in pain or unhappy. If you do call or write, be clear with them that you're going to handle the situation but just need to let off steam or bounce some ideas around with them. Some parents want to pick up the phone and call someone to fix everything right away, but that approach only perpetuates your dependent role. Most colleges will want to talk directly to you rather than to your parents about problems you're having. My most constructive conversations with parents have been those in which we've talked together about how the student can best help herself, whom she can talk with, and what role each of us can play in making that happen.

There are bound to be times when you need your parents in ways you needed them as a child. I recall one situation when the school where I worked was hit by a virus epidemic. As I walked into my residence hall office one morning, I was greeted by several students who told me how sick everyone was. I wandered through the building and sure enough, there were dozens of people sleeping in hallways in order to be close to the bathrooms. They had blankets and pillows with them as they lay on the floor in pain and discomfort. Everywhere I went there were bodies— it looked like a postbattle scene from *Gone with the Wind!* "Do you want anything?" I asked them. One student just looked up at me and said weakly, "What I really want is my mother." A pitiful-sounding chorus of "me too" could be heard up and down the hall.

Working toward an Adult/Adult Relationship

■ ■ ■

"I have never doubted my mother's generosity of spirit. I have never doubted that, to the best of her ability, with all her heart and soul, she loves my sisters and me. But it is sometimes difficult for her to understand us on our own terms."
— Wendy Wasserstein, "My Mother, Then and Now"[4]

■ ■ ■

Achieving an adult/adult relationship with your parents requires *each* of you to let go of your expectations and see one another as you actually are.[5] This is difficult if you worry about disappointing one another or not being accepted for who you are. Disagreements need to be discussed and worked through, and each person may need time, information, and support to really understand and consider the other's point of view. This requires mutual respect and honest communication, which unfortunately is not the norm in every family.

As difficult as it sometimes is for parents to see their children as adults, students often fall back into more lazy, childlike, "take care of me" habits when at home, expecting someone else to prepare meals, do the dishes, and take care of the laundry. Perhaps taking on more responsibility at home will help your parents see you in a more adult light. Developing adult/adult relationships with your parents has to be worked at from both sides. It doesn't happen overnight or even during your first year or two at college; it's an ongoing process.

Some students are hesitant to assert themselves with their parents, especially if it means disagreeing with them. This is particularly true for women who are socialized not to express anger and for those who come from cultural backgrounds where deference to parents is expected. At times it's important for you to honestly tell your parents about something they do that hurts you. Learn to tell them in a caring and calm way what that is, how it has made you feel in the past, how it affects you now, and what you need from them.[6] For some parents, clearly hearing what you have to say may be enough to help them adjust their behavior. Realize too that your parents could also need to talk to you about ways you hurt them. This honest communication is sometimes painful, but it can take your relationship with one another to much more adult levels. Some discussions lead to negotiating new terms for how you deal with one another. These guidelines forge new connections in healthier ways. For example, you may agree to call home, but only once a week and when it's convenient for you.

When you go home on vacation breaks, changes are likely to be more obvious, and they often create the need for renegotiating rules at home. For instance, your parents may still expect you to be in by a certain time, while you've become used to coming and going as you please at college. Recognize the kinds of comments and situations that trigger defensive or childish responses from you. While you can't control your parents' reactions, you can control your own and perhaps begin to break some old patterns.

As you talk about your activities, friends, relationships, and academic experiences, you may find yourself challenging your parents. For instance, if you talk excitedly about some controversial ideas your political science professor discussed, this could cause some discomfort or anger in your parents. Or perhaps you recognize attitudes at home that now strike you as limited or prejudiced. It can be difficult to confront or question jokes or comments from your family that you would more readily confront from your peers in the residence hall or classroom. The unspoken rules in your family may become more obvious to you, but it can be tricky to challenge them, especially if one rule is that the parents make all the rules! Bear in mind that it may take your parents some time to get used to the changes in you; be patient with them. You could eventually have more adult and stimulating discussions with your parents and come to appreciate the knowledge, values, and experience they possess.

· · ·

"My father was the stupidest person in the world when I was eighteen, but when I was twenty-three I was amazed at how much he had learned in five years."

—Mark Twain

· · ·

If you're an older student returning to college, you can experience the effects of family ties in both directions—with your own parents and also with your own children, if you have them. In many families mom tends to be the person everyone depends on, and often moms see it as their role to put others' needs first. Give your own needs as high a priority as everyone else's needs. You deserve it.

The loudest cheers I've heard at graduation have often come from the families of older students. Proud cries of "Way to go, mom!" fill the air as women walk across the stage and accept their diplomas.

For Commuting Students

Those of you who continue to live at home with your family during your college years will have a different experience establishing your independence and identity. Your parents may see more directly what and how you're doing, which may help them understand and support your changes. Some, however, may find it difficult to see you as an increasingly independent person, especially if your living arrangements feel exactly like they did when you were in high school. Consider changing your patterns in some ways to emphasize the difference. Perhaps if you participate in some new activities or get to know new people, this will help your parents recognize that this is a new stage in your life. Consider staying on campus some nights, or purchasing a partial meal plan in the dining hall.

Your parents may freely acknowledge that your situation is different as a college student. If you have reason to believe they won't, try sitting down to talk with them *before* the first semester starts. Perhaps if you show them a copy of the residence hall housing contract, you can agree on similar freedoms and responsibilities, if you don't already have them, as you continue living at home.

Other Family Relationships

Your relationships with other family members, especially brothers and sisters, will be different once you leave for college. Family dynamics change as the roles you once played at home are no longer played or are filled by others. If, for example, you were the person who took care of younger brothers and sisters, the next oldest may now take on that task. Your return home on vacation may lead to some confusion or conflict once those new roles are defined. Expectations that you continue to fulfill outgrown roles, such as being "the baby of the family," can also be a source of tension.

Several years' age difference may feel large when you're younger, but as brothers and sisters grow up there's greater potential for more equal relationships to develop. I'm the eldest of four children, and three of us are within six years of one another. Visiting my grown sister and seeing her teach her fifth-grade class made me realize that she's no longer the little kid I used to torment with flying slippers during the night. She's now my friend as well as my sister.

. . .

"These many differences in our lives have come between my brother and me. We travel in orbits that rarely intersect, and in some ways we've become enigmas to each other. . . . And happily, to our mutual surprise, we learned in time for my brother's fortieth birthday that we could again—still—be great friends."
—Wendy Wasserstein, "Big Brother"[7]
. . .

If your home is one of the many described as dysfunctional, for example, with an alcoholic parent or abusive relationships, the impact of your going to college can be even more complex for both you and your family. Later chapters on alcohol and drugs, codependency, and sexual abuse provide suggestions and resources for you.

It's been estimated that half of all marriages end in divorce.[8] A high percentage of students entering college in the 1990s grew up in homes where their parents were separated, divorced, and/or remarried.[9] The impact of divorce on a child can be determined by a number of factors— your age at the time, how expected or unexpected the divorce was, your relationship with each parent, the degree of loss felt with the departure of one parent, relocation, ongoing communication between parents, ongoing contact with each parent, and financial repercussions.[10]

If your parents divorced when you were much younger, you may already have worked through many of your reactions by the time you enter college. Leaving for college, however, can revive old issues for both you and your parents. Questions about independence, personal identity, and intimate relationships may trigger feelings about the past, about both parents, and about yourself and the future.

Depending on the relationship between your divorced parents, and between you and each of your parents, family-oriented college events can sometimes create problems. There may be conflicts over who takes you to college, who attends Parents' Weekend, who comes to graduation, etc. Sometimes you'll feel caught in the middle, trying to balance your obligations to both parents. Some families put aside tensions for a weekend to celebrate college events, and others genuinely work together all the time to provide consistent support.

Every Parents' Weekend and graduation I'm introduced to more and more postdivorce families: "This is my mother and stepfather, my father and his wife, my brother, my half-sister, and my three grandmothers." If you feel like you're doing a juggling act when everyone is together, it may help to clearly define ground rules beforehand. For example, decide on dinner plans, who will attend an event if there are limited tickets, and what topics, if any, are off limits during the visit. It's helpful to establish understandings earlier rather than having to publicly debate them on the spot.

Parental separation and divorce are more common once children leave home. While this timing may seem to be less disruptive, it can still have a major impact on you. You may wonder if your parents would still be together if you hadn't left. You could feel abandoned or unsure of how your own future relationships will develop.[11] It can be hard to be away if your family is breaking up. Perhaps you're distracted by events at home, particularly if you're worried about one or both of your parents. Mature brothers or sisters, or objective relatives, family friends, or clergy at home can provide helpful information and reassurance. Your first responsibility is to take care of yourself; seek out support on campus.

A variety of other family crises—a parent's illness, hospitalization, death, or loss of a job—can upset and disrupt your life at college. Serious problems of brothers and sisters—drugs, breakdowns, accidents, or suicide attempts—can also cause great distress. Some students debate whether to take a semester off and go home or whether to stay at school because there's *really* nothing they can do at home. Guilt is often a prominent issue in these kinds of situations, both for students who stay at school and for parents who have to tell them bad news or need them at home.

Although it's not possible for all students, sometimes a brief visit home can help connect you with the reality of what's going on. This way you can make your own decisions. You can also set up future communication. Talk with your professors, academic advisor, or class dean about what's going on so that if you need to miss some classes, or if your school work begins to suffer, they're aware that there's a reason why and can work with you to manage the situation. Some students remain at school knowing that they might, at any time, need to go home quickly. It helps to have some friends who know your situation, as well as support from a counselor, residence hall staff person, chaplain, or other adult.

In situations where a family member dies, the return to school can be a way to get back to a familiar routine and stay busy. The grieving process takes a while, however, and certain times of the year can be difficult, such as the anniversary of a death, holidays, or Parents' Weekend. Regardless of the relationship you had with a person who dies, the loss can continue to affect you.

Some students, especially returning adults, find themselves in the role of caretaker to aging or ill parents. Decisions about ongoing care are difficult, particularly in light of other responsibilities. Some students take a smaller course load; others organize themselves to do their academic work and also take time for their family situation. For some students, finishing the degree is the most constructive thing they can do for their parents and for themselves.

WHERE TO LOOK FOR HELP

Financing a college education can be a major undertaking. It can be further complicated by problems between parents. Financial matters can have a great impact on you, particularly since federal financial aid rules don't provide great flexibility. Students are sometimes stuck in the middle, and vulnerable, when a parent contests settlements or child support payments, remarries, or doesn't follow through with financial commitments. If you're worried about bills and payments, ask the controller or bursar to communicate to you directly if s/he encounters any problems. Talk with your financial aid office about all the channels open to you to seek assistance and review of your situation, if necessary.

It may sound oversimplified, but the most obvious place to turn in order to deal with family issues is to your family. Deal directly with one another to untie and retie the relationship knots: it's the most basic way to do it. It can also be the most difficult. An objective third party who is acceptable to, and trusted by, both you and your parents may ease the communication among you. If they know both you and your parents, they can help you recognize old behavioral patterns and learn more constructive ones.

Working with a counselor or therapist and building an adult/adult relationship with him/her should help you to recognize that potential in yourself. As you experience and practice new ways to relate to a safer adult, you can learn skills to help you relate more as an adult with your own parents. Your counselor can also be a good source of support as you deal with parental responses to your growing independence, and s/he may be willing to meet with you all together to help resolve difficulties.

Parents can sometimes hear things from other people's children that they can't hear from their own. If your parents attend programs or discussions with other college students, they may better understand student issues and perspectives. Perhaps there are neighbors or some of your current friends to whom they'll listen. If your parents enjoy reading, movies, or plays, recommend specific ones for them. By exploring more on their own, they may be able to think about ideas in general before having to consider them in relation to you. These resources can also provide a focus for you to begin to discuss the issues with them.

Parents talking to other parents is another important source of information and insight. I've spoken many times, on panels, to groups of parents. Every once in a while a parent expresses unreasonable expectations, such as demanding that the college not encourage her child's independence and not treat her as a developing adult. It's always been interesting for me to hear other parents' reactions to these statements. Many more parents express confidence in their child's ability to deal responsibly with her own life. If you know others' parents who feel this way, they may be able to talk to your parents and begin to explain these ideas.

In the same way, children sometimes hear other people's parents better than their own. You can gain some valuable insights from older adult students, through volunteer work with others of your parents' generation, or through getting to know other adults like them, such as faculty, staff, and friends' parents.

The bottom line is that parents and children need to recognize one another as human beings with strengths and weaknesses. While you may not be everything the other wants you to be, you may each be much more than you appear to be.

EDUCATING YOURSELF

Books: Nonfiction, Anthologies, Biographies, Poetry, Plays

Berman, Claire. *Adult Children of Divorce Speak Out: About Growing Up With—and Moving Beyond—Parental Divorce.* New York: Simon and Schuster, 1991.

Bloom, Michael V. *Adolescent-Parental Separation.* New York: Gardner, 1980.

Bloomfield, Harold, and Leonard Felder. *Making Peace with Your Parents.* New York: Ballantine, 1983.

Coburn, Karen Levin, and Madge Lawrence Treeger. *Letting Go: A Parents' Guide to Today's College Experience.* Bethesda, MD: Adler and Adler, 1988.

Fassel, Diane. *Growing Up Divorced: A Road to Healing for Adult Children of Divorce.* New York: Pocket Books, 1991.

Fisher, Roger, and William Ury. *Getting to Yes: Negotiating Agreement without Giving In.* Rev. ed. New York: Penguin, 1991.

Forward, Susan, with Craig Buck. *Toxic Parents: Overcoming Their Hurtful Legacy and Reclaiming Your Life.* New York: Bantam, 1989.

Friday, Nancy. *My Mother, Myself.* New York: Dell, 1987.

Halpern, Howard. *Cutting Loose: An Adult Guide to Coming to Terms with Your Parents.* New York: Fireside, 1990.

James, Muriel. *Breaking Free: Self-Parenting for a New Life.* Reading, MA: Addison-Wesley, 1981.

Kubler-Ross, Elizabeth. *On Death and Dying.* New York: Collier, 1970.

Lenz, Elinor. *Once My Child . . . Now My Friend.* New York: Warner, 1981.

Silverstone, Barbara, and Helen Kandel Hyman. *You and Your Aging Parent: The Modern Family's Guide to Emotional, Physical, and Financial Problems.* New York: Pantheon, 1982.

Wallerstein, Judith, and Sandra Blakeslee. *Second Chances: Men, Women, and Children a Decade after Divorce.* New York: Ticknor and Fields, 1990.

Films, Videos, TV Shows, Plays

Class Action. Father and daughter lawyers, who are at odds personally, battle on opposite sides in court.

"The Cosby Show." Family TV series.

Dad. A businessman revitalizes his relationship with his aging father. Based on the novel by William Wharton.

Do You Remember Love? A female college professor develops Alzheimer's disease. Made-for-TV movie.

"Family Ties." Family TV series.

I Never Sang for My Father. A middle-aged son struggles to be seen as the adult he is by his aging father. From the play by Robert Anderson.

The Joy Luck Club. Tells the stories of four Chinese mothers and their American-born daughters. From Amy Tan's novel.

Nothing in Common. A young advertising executive is strongly affected by the impending divorce of his parents after over thirty years of marriage.

On Golden Pond. A woman tries to resolve unfinished business with her aging parents. From the play by Ernest Thompson.

Once Around. A woman's marriage to a very strong man upsets the balance in her close Boston family.

Only the Lonely. A middle-aged son manages to extricate himself from a possessive mother.

Ordinary People. A family is changed forever as each is confronted with truths about themselves and their relationships. From Judith Guest's novel.

Postcards from the Edge. Explores the complicated relationship between a show business star and her daughter, who is also an actress. From the book by Carrie Fisher.

"Sisters." Four grown sisters share complex family relationships. TV series.

Terms of Endearment. Follows an intense mother-daughter relationship from childhood through adulthood. From the book by Larry McMurtry.

Twice in a Lifetime. A working-class family is affected by a marriage coming apart.

THREE

Assertiveness and Conflict Resolution

When I did training of student residence staff, I liked to include one session on saying no. We started by sitting in a circle. Each person would then directly ask someone else in the group for something unreasonable.

- "Would you pierce my ears for me?"
- "Could you keep my pet ferret this weekend?"
- "Can my mom stay in your room when she visits me?"

The person asked would have to say no in the rudest way she could.

- "No way!"
- "Yeah, right."
- "In your dreams."

As a second step, requests became more realistic.

- "Could you lend me your psych notes?"
- "Can I borrow your car to take my brother to the airport?"
- "I sprained my ankle. Could you bring me up a sandwich from lunch?"

This time the responses were to be made in a clear and respectful way. It was harder for a lot of people to do. I could see them struggle, really digging for an excuse, feeling that only something monumental could possibly justify refusing a reasonable request.

- "Sorry, I went to chemistry after psych and put my notebook down on some radioactive material."
- "I can't, I'll be using my car that day . . . all day. I'm supposed to be at the World Series to sing the national anthem."
- "Sorry, I'm . . . uh . . . I'm accepting the Nobel Prize and I'll be in Sweden for lunch."

Some people said no, but in a wishy-washy way that communicated that they didn't really mean it and hated themselves for saying it. Others had the word stick in their throats until they finally pushed it out. We practiced this exercise for a while, and gradually people became more comfortable saying no.

- "Sorry, I'll be using my notes to study. Why don't you ask Rosa? She took the course last semester."
- "Sorry, I don't like to lend out my car, but I've got the number of the airport transportation service if you want it."
- "I'm not coming back to the hall after lunch, but I've got some fruit and cereal in the room if you want it."

This struggle reflects many of the messages women grow up learning—that we shouldn't ask for things, that our needs are less important than others' needs, that we should take care of people, and that it's not polite to refuse to do someone a favor. In our society women are often rewarded for being nonassertive, while men are rewarded for assertive, even aggressive types of behavior.[1] In later chapters on alcohol and drugs, codependency, sexual harassment, and sexuality, the importance of being able to be assertive will be explored in more specific contexts. Developing assertive skills can help you meet your needs and achieve your goals.

. . .

"Saying no had always been tough for me and I remember how enlightened I was after doing the staff training. It made me realize that after years of saying 'well, maybe . . . ' and 'well, uh . . . I guess' saying NO! was something I not only needed to relearn but to practice. It seemed easier to start on dogs rather than people— I'd be jogging, a barking dog would start chasing me, I'd stop in my tracks and yell 'NO!' The dog would stop, look at me, perplexed, then turn around and walk away. If you were brought up, like me, to make other people pleased, this was an exhilarating feeling. Assertive behavior comes easier to some than others, and if you're in the 'others' category practicing with barking dogs (or, if this seems too inhumane, pictures of an ex-) will lead to declining that extra project or telling a date that they're going too fast."

—O. L., class of '89

. . .

Terminology and Background Information

Behaviors are generally described as being on a continuum ranging from aggressive at one end to nonassertive at the other. Assertive behavior falls somewhere in the middle.

Nonassertive Behavior

When I started college, I wanted other people to like me, so I went out of my way to do what I thought they wanted. When we ordered pizza, I'd say anything was fine with me, even though I really didn't like sausage. I wouldn't have dreamed of asking if anyone else liked anchovies! When a woman on my hall asked to copy my sociology notes every time she cut class, I always loaned them to her, even though it annoyed me after a while to get up at 7 A.M. every morning to be in class while she slept in and then used my notes to study. When my roommate invited friends into the room and I had a quiz the next day, I went somewhere else to study. I didn't tell her that I'd prefer to stay in the room to do my work. These are examples of nonassertive behaviors.

Nonassertive behavior is failing to stand up for your own rights by not expressing your honest thoughts and feelings, or by speaking up but doing it so ineffectually that others still violate your rights. The character Charlotte, the older of two sisters living next door to the Conners on the TV show "Roseanne," displays a lot of nonassertive behavior. She's anxious to be well liked and overly accommodating to everyone, rarely asking directly for what *she* wants or needs—even when she's locked out of her own house in the pouring rain.

The goal of nonassertive behavior is to please people and avoid conflict. The implicit message that nonassertive behavior sends out is that what you think and feel doesn't matter, and that *you* don't matter. This can be communicated by what you say: "I don't care, whatever you want to do is fine with me" or "I know this sounds stupid, but . . . " How you say something also communicates that what you're saying doesn't matter. When you speak in a hesitant, inaudible voice, look at the floor, and end statements with question marks, you are sending nonassertive nonverbal messages.

Nonassertive behavior is often indirect. For example, making excuses rather than saying that you'd rather not go to the frat party is indirect nonassertive behavior. By being nonassertive, you may wind up doing things you don't want to do, and this may build up resentment over time. That resentment can be expressed indirectly—by withdrawing from people or by looking irritated without saying anything. Sometimes nonassertive people who let their anger build up eventually explode and act aggressively, seemingly out of the blue.

If you're sending out the message that your needs aren't important enough for you to express directly, it's unlikely that others will take them seriously. Other people may feel superior to you if you're consistently nonassertive because they find they can dominate you. Or they may feel guilty because they always get their own way when what they'd really prefer is to know how you feel. Others who care about you may get annoyed, eventually, if they never know what you think or want.

Aggressive Behavior

Aggressive behavior is standing up for your own rights, but doing it in a way that violates the rights of others. The characters of J. R. Ewing on "Dallas" and Erica Kane on "All My Children" often display aggressive behavior. The goal of aggressive behavior is to get what you want by dominating other people, often by humiliating them or putting them down. The implicit message is that the other person doesn't matter. Aggressive behavior is direct to an extreme and can come across as righteous and superior. If you act aggressively, you may have some guilt feelings later. Other people tend to be hurt and humiliated when they're dominated by aggressive behavior. They may be left feeling angry and even vengeful toward you. Aggressive behavior may get you what you want, but there can be some cost to relationships in the end.

My aggressive moments have usually come after a buildup of frustrating nonassertive responses. One year, on the day before the campus where I worked was to open for new students, several dozen families arrived early, expecting to move in. I explained that we weren't ready and that the halls didn't open until the next day. These parents demanded to move in anyway. As I continued to refuse, one of the mothers snuck away and found an open back door to the building. She entered the residence hall, parked herself in the lobby, and proclaimed loudly that she was liberating the building and that everyone could come in. They all did. One of the security officers told me she'd be glad to throw them all out, and I just screamed at her. Of course I apologized to the officer almost immediately, but I felt terrible, and things were uncomfortable between us for several days. I had aggressively yelled at her instead of at the people whom I really wanted to confront.

Assertive Behavior

Assertive behavior is defined as standing up for your own rights in ways that don't violate someone else's basic rights. It involves a direct, honest, and appropriate expression of your feelings and opinions. The character of Roxanne Melman, the legal secretary on "L.A. Law," has changed quite a bit over the years. She started out timid and soft spoken, doing whatever her boss, Arnie Becker, asked her to do, no matter how unreasonable the request. Over the years Roxanne has become much more assertive. In many ways this is a result of her growing respect for herself, and her behavior with others reflects this growth.

The goal of assertive behavior is to achieve fair, equal, and respectful results. The implicit message in assertive behavior is that both parties matter. Being assertive means telling someone what you think, feel, or want without attaching any demands. When you're discussing what to do over the weekend, you may say, for example, that you'd like to see the new Jodie Foster movie or hear the comedy act at the Student Center but are open to other suggestions. Assertive behavior doesn't demand that everyone do what you want to do. Assertive behavior is direct and to the point and communicates confidence and self-respect. Others know what you think and feel and that you're open to hearing what they think and feel.

To act more assertively on your own behalf, you need to believe that you have the right to

1. be treated with respect.
2. have and express your own feelings and opinions.
3. be listened to and taken seriously.
4. set your own priorities.
5. say no without feeling guilty.
6. ask for what you want.
7. ask for what you pay for.

8. ask for information from professionals, such as doctors and auto mechanics.
9. make mistakes.
10. change your mind.
11. offer no reasons or excuses to justify your behavior.
12. say "I don't understand."
13. say "I don't know."
14. be illogical in making decisions.
15. choose not to assert yourself.[2]

If you believe that you have these rights, you're more likely to act on them without apologizing or being susceptible to others' criticisms. Just because someone else—even someone you respect or want to like you—says she thinks you should or shouldn't do something, that doesn't mean you have to do it.

- "You don't really want to join that sorority, do you?"
- "Come on, only nerds stay in to study Friday night."

You have the power to choose to be different and not to think less of yourself for making that choice. There are plenty of people out there who want to dominate others; you don't have to help them out by relinquishing control over your own life choices. There are certainly times when you may choose not to assert yourself, but the important point is that it's your choice rather than a habit or someone else's choice for you.

If you choose to be more assertive, incorporate assertive skills into your natural style of relating to people. Continue to sound like you rather than like a list of textbook responses. If family and friends are used to you being nonassertive, they may be surprised as you become more willing and able to speak for yourself and ask for what you need. Some will like the change; others will need some time to get used to it. Still others who are, perhaps, more invested in being able to dominate you, may react negatively. Developing an assertive belief system may pose more conflicts if you come from an ethnic, cultural, or religious background that values putting individual needs after those of your family or community. In these cases you may choose to be more assertive in some situations, for example at school, but not at home.

Feedback

Feedback is one particular form of assertiveness. Constructive feedback, both positive and negative, is meant to be helpful and to let others know how their behavior comes across. Feedback tells people how they're affecting others. It is offered without the demand that they change, although you may let someone know the possible consequences if particular behaviors continue—for example, telling someone that if s/he continues to get drunk and out of control every time you go out together, you won't continue to go out with that person.

To help you understand what constitutes constructive feedback, here are some specific characteristics.[3] First, constructive criticism is descriptive rather than evaluative. You simply describe your reaction to some form of behavior, leaving the other person free to consider what you've said and to use it if she chooses to. By not judging or evaluating the other person, you are less likely to get defensive reactions. Second, good feedback is specific rather than general. It's more helpful to identify specific behaviors than to make general statements. For example, rather than saying "You always put me down," it's more specific to say, "Remember this morning, in the dining hall, when you said that I looked like I slept in my clothes? Everyone laughed and I was really embarrassed."

Third, feedback should take into account both your needs and the other person's needs. Don't give someone feedback just to get it off your chest and make yourself feel better. Communicate it in ways that take into account that you're equally concerned about helping her. Fourth, direct your feedback toward behavior that the other person can do something about. It's frustrating and unproductive to give someone feedback about something she has no ability to change. Fifth, generally feedback is most helpful when it's provided as soon as possible after the behavior occurs, when it's fresher in everyone's mind. Also consider, however, the person's readiness to hear your feedback and the availability of support if necessary. Giving someone feedback just before she goes off to take a big exam or when she's upset about a fight with her boyfriend/girlfriend isn't very considerate.

Finally, check to make sure the person has heard your feedback accurately. Keep in mind that people may misinterpret or make additional assumptions about what you've said. It shows real caring and concern to ask the other person to tell you what she heard so you can be sure it fits with what you intended.

If you've received feedback from someone, it's helpful to see whether that reaction is shared by others or whether it is specific to that one person. For example, teasing is interpreted by some as a sign of affection but can be uncomfortable for others. It's best, therefore, not to automatically tease everyone, to become more aware of people's reactions to playful teasing, and to avoid it if people appear to be made uncomfortable. Feedback comes in many forms. Sometimes it is direct and verbal, but at other times it comes in less obvious forms, for example through body language. Watch for it. React to it.

When I was an R.A., a student who lived on my floor came in one day to talk. She said she felt that people on the hall were uncomfortable with her and tried to avoid her but no one would tell her why. She asked if I would. Well, I was floored for a few minutes. My usual nonassertive response would have been to say that I didn't know, or that nothing was wrong and she shouldn't worry about it. But the truth was that people *were* somewhat uncomfortable with her, including me. She was a nice woman but was sometimes so eager to please others and be part of the crowd that she could be very dependent and follow others around like a shadow. I finally decided that since she really seemed to want to know, I'd try to be honest with her and tell her what I really thought. I did, and she listened. She didn't get defensive and she didn't get angry. She shed a few tears, but that seemed OK. She thanked me and left. Throughout the rest of the year, this student tried to work on the behaviors that tended to put other people off. She told me often how valuable our conversation and my honesty had been to her. I don't think she realized how valuable it was for me, too.

Sources of Misunderstanding

Women often learn irrational beliefs that get in the way of acting assertively. Look closely at the beliefs described below. Perhaps doing so will take away some of the power they could have to limit your ability to assert yourself.[4]

"If I assert myself, others will get angry with me and that will be devastating." Some people may get angry with you, but others may like you better, and more healthy relationships could develop. If you're standing up for legitimate rights, chances are you'll have more positive than negative results. If you assert yourself when it's appropriate, you don't need to feel responsible for others' anger; it's their problem, not

yours. If they become angry, you can choose whether to let that devastate you or not.

"I'm afraid that if I'm open with others and say no, I'll hurt them." You can't control whether or not people will be hurt by what you say. You might minimize that possibility by saying no in ways that communicate caring and respect. However, if they decide to be hurt because you said what you honestly felt, that's their choice. It's likely that most people will prefer to be treated honestly, and disappointment need not last forever.

"I need to avoid saying things or asking questions that make me look stupid." It's perfectly human not to know something or to make a mistake. Some people are more understanding than others, but learning from your mistakes is important. I can recall sitting in classes where the professor would ask if everyone understood what s/he had just spent twenty minutes explaining. By the looks on our faces, it was obvious that we were all pretty lost, but no one would acknowledge it. Finally, if a brave soul said, "Could you go over it again?" there would be a collective sigh of relief from the rest of us. There's a lot of strength in saying, "I don't know."

"It's wrong to turn down reasonable requests." It's acceptable to consider your own needs even if, at times, it means putting them before others'. You can't please everyone all of the time.

"Assertive women are cold, castrating bitches and people won't like me if I'm assertive." Aggressive behavior is designed to dominate and humiliate others. Assertive behavior is direct and honest and shows a genuine concern for others' rights and feelings as well as for your own.

Sometimes people do react the way you fear they will, but more often the results you imagine are more devastating than the actual experience. By not asserting yourself in order to avoid these imagined reactions, you may cause yourself more pain than you'd be willing to cause anyone else.

ENCOUNTERING AND RESPONDING TO THIS ISSUE

Academic Life

Classroom situations require the ability to be assertive. The longer you attend a class without saying anything, the harder it can be to speak up later on. Try to participate at least once, early in the semester. Smaller classes are obviously less intimidating, and it also helps to get to know people in the class rather than feel like you're surrounded by a sea of strangers.

In order to feel comfortable asking or answering questions and asserting yourself, particularly in coed schools, you may have to act counter to some of the sex-role expectations and messages with which you grew up. The chapter on sexual harassment discusses classroom climate in more detail.

A related situation involves asserting yourself with faculty members. Going to see them during office hours, asking for information about a test grade, discussing term paper topics, and finding out about internship possibilities are all situations in which it helps to be able to ask clearly for what you need.

Your life on campus also involves dealing, at times, with administrative offices. If you find it difficult to assert yourself with someone in authority, dealings with faculty and administrators may have you falling back into less assertive behavior patterns.

As an administrator, I most appreciated it when students approached me assertively. With nonassertive students it was sometimes hard to be sure what they were feeling and what they needed, and I had to draw the words out of them. I certainly didn't mind doing that, but the situation was often more uncomfortable for both of us than it had to be.

With aggressive students, whose goal was to get what they wanted regardless of how fair it was, I often had to work harder to be open and receptive and to avoid getting defensive. The demanding attitude of "you owe me" and "do it now" is generally not one that gets the desired results.

Assertive students asked me to take action, requested policy changes, or disagreed with me in ways that helped me hear them, consider what they had to say, and at times do something about it. What made the difference was that they were reasonable, communicated genuinely and clearly, and were willing to work with me to resolve the situation. I can't guarantee that every administrator or office will respond positively to your assertive approach. Being assertive should, however, at least leave you feeling better about yourself for having expressed your concerns or questions in an appropriate way at an appropriate place.

Residential and Social Life

. . .

"I was never very good in large groups: parties were unbearable without at least one familiar face (I'd *never* go alone!)."

—O. L., class of '89

. . .

Being able to introduce yourself to new people and interact in social situations also requires the ability to assert yourself. This isn't easy for everyone. Some students find that having a task to do, such as serving refreshments or checking IDs, gives them a good way to begin to interact. I eventually found that doing the photography at social events helped me to mingle, take pictures, and chat fairly comfortably with a variety of people. For those of you who attend a women's college and want to meet men, there's a need to be more assertive and take the initiative to create those opportunities.

If you attend a coed school, asserting yourself in extracurricular activities is important. Run for elected positions and serve in leadership roles; these are ways to establish yourself, make good use of your skills, and get valuable experience. Women's colleges often provide more leadership opportunities.

Conflict is an inevitable part of life and relationships, on college campuses and off. It's a real challenge to live with many people, all of whom have different ideas, needs, and ways of expressing themselves. As you grew up, you may have learned that for one person to get what she wants, someone else can't. Perhaps you also heard that conflict involves a power struggle, with one person winning and the other losing. Consider the definition of assertiveness and how its goal—fair and equal treatment—is inconsistent with this win-lose view of conflict resolution. An assertive approach suggests that conflict can best be dealt with when people are clear about their own needs, are willing to hear others' needs, and are able to consider a variety of solutions in which each gets some things and gives some things. This is more of a win-win situation.

As a resident, it's important to be able to express your opinions on decisions that affect you—establishing hall quiet hours, guest policies, use of hall funds, etc. In these types of decisions, upperclass students and those with the loudest voices may have unreasonable influence unless others stand up to be heard.

College handbooks, housing contracts, or residence hall living agreements describe specific rules governing all residents. If others' behavior in the hall is affecting you, it's expected that you'll take the first step and say something. It's important, for example, to know how to approach someone living next door and ask her, in a reasonable way, if she can turn down the stereo. You may be willing to discuss some compromises, like your studying elsewhere until a particular time or on certain nights, or her using headphones after a certain hour. The assertive attitude of "here's what I need, what do you need, and can we work something out" seems a most reasonable first approach.

One policy that often leads to conflict is the implementation of rules for overnight guests. Some students feel uncomfortable with male guests who impose on other residents. If such a guest is infringing on your rights, let him, or the person whose guest he is, know about it so he can change his behavior. Often that's all that's needed. If the behavior continues, talk to your R.A. to find out what the next steps are. When students start by going immediately to the R.A. or hall director rather than by talking directly with the guest or other resident, more tension and animosity are often created. It's more productive when students approach one another directly and discuss the situation and possible solutions. You can express the hope that the matter will be settled between you so it won't be necessary for you to go any further or involve anyone else. That way, the other person knows what the consequences will be if the behavior continues, and perhaps you'll feel less like you're "telling on" that person if you eventually have to involve the R.A. or hall director.

Gossip and taking sides in personal disagreements are destructive behaviors in residence halls. Some students justify talking about others by saying that they're only trying to help, that they care about their friends, or that they're just curious. In practice, gossip leads to feelings of distrust and betrayal. It can also be manipulative, as stories and facts become slanted and distorted by repeated tellings and biases.

The best thing that students can do to weaken the power of gossip is to refuse to listen to it. Although it's not easy, you could say that you'd prefer not to talk about other people, just as you'd prefer that others not talk about you. People continue to talk as long as others listen. If more people refuse to listen to gossip, perhaps fewer people will be hurt, and conflicts will remain in the hands of the people who are directly involved and who need to resolve them.

Roommates

Assertiveness and conflict management skills are most valuable in room-mate relationships. Roommates bring different living styles and habits with them. Sometimes they clash from day one; at other times they avoid doing anything to create disagreement or conflict. Even roommates who get along well may find there are some ways they get on one another's nerves.

Roommates differ in a number of ways, and the chapters on living in a diverse environment address some of these. Basic lifestyle differences cross over many of these lines, however, and often come to light in the close quarters of a roommate relationship. Habits and preferences about smoking, neatness, study habits, overnight guests, room temperature, playing music in the room, sleeping hours, and sharing are all potential sources of conflict. Successful roommates need not be best friends or alike in every way. It's more important that you be open to learning from one another and willing to communicate and compromise.

Most colleges ask incoming students to fill out questionnaires about their living habits to help the Housing Office put roommate pairs together. It's important to be honest as you fill out these questionnaires, but don't expect that doing so will result in your being assigned a roommate who's a perfect match. If you receive your roommate assignment during the summer and are able to communicate, make an effort to approach one another assertively. Talk about yourself and listen to what your roommate has to say. Set the tone for a mutually respectful relationship. For example, ask "How do you feel about overnight guests?" rather than demand, "There will be no overnight guests in our room."

Often, during orientation programs your R.A. or orientation advisor will structure time for roommates to talk about living together. There may be written exercises or guided discussions to help you talk about where you're from; your personal preferences about privacy, study habits, drinking, overnight guests, and use of the room; and how you express your feelings and like to be treated. These are opportunities to begin to develop an understanding of how you'll communicate with one another and work to resolve any differences that arise.

Orientation can be a hectic time, and it's tempting, especially if you're getting along well with your roommate, to gloss over this process. Believe me, some time and energy put into setting a foundation for the future can be very helpful. Some residence halls organize activities such as the Roommate Game, based on TV's "The Newlywed Game." This can serve as an often hilarious opportunity for roommates to learn more about one another and their reactions to living together.

Colleges differ greatly with respect to opportunities and policies for changing rooms. Running away from one roommate situation doesn't mean that the next one will necessarily be better. Learn to deal with conflict; it's crucial to future success. You may actually find that if you try, you can work out a good living arrangement with your roommate. If you can't, you can still consider other options later. Many colleges won't consider requests for room changes unless you've first made an effort to resolve your differences.

When room changes do occur, win-lose attitudes can lead to conflicts about who will move. Some students expect that the college will simply move their roommate out and let them stay in the room. That doesn't happen. Generally the person initiating the request is the one to move. When conflicts are discussed with a roommate, however, there may be greater opportunity to look together at all potential moves for each of you. When the situation is approached as a shared problem, rather than as one person being right and the other wrong, there are more possible solutions.

Conflict Resolution

• • •

"Approaching the conflict is often *very* difficult. Talking to an R.A. to help counsel on how to approach the other person, letting the person bounce ideas off the R.A., and practicing with her can be *really helpful.*"

—L. J., class of '91

• • •

Most conflicts result when both people have rights in a situation and those rights are incompatible: one roommate wants to study with the lights on at the same time the other wants to sleep with the lights off, hall residents debate about smoking and nonsmoking areas in the building, etc. It's important to be open to others and willing to negotiate and compromise when appropriate. As the Rolling Stones once sang, "You can't always get what you want but if you try sometimes, you might find you get what you need."

Sometimes the individuals involved can discuss and negotiate a resolution to a conflict. Often, however, it's helpful to have one or two objective parties mediate the process. Mediation is based on the assumption that those involved know best how to resolve their conflicts. Mediators try to structure the discussion so you each have a chance to speak without being interrupted. They facilitate communication when it gets muddled, and they try to help you arrive at some agreement. Mediators don't take sides or make decisions. The focus of mediation isn't on determining who was right or wrong in past situations, but on developing a way of living together in the future. Both individuals need to be willing to participate in a mediation in order to make it work, and both should feel comfortable with the mediators.

Whether you try to work a conflict out on your own or with mediators, try to figure out what the problem is from your perspective *before* you actually sit down to deal with it. Bear in mind that the other person may have a different perspective and that you need to be open to hearing that, too. There are probably as many versions of any situation as there are people involved—plus one. That is, if there are two people involved, there are probably three versions of the situation—one from each participant plus what actually *did* happen! You should also prepare by thinking about what you need in the way of a resolution and what aspects of the situation you'd be willing to compromise on.

Agree on a specific time and place to get together to work on the problem. The time should be convenient for all of you. While you shouldn't feel rushed by other commitments, you should have a time limit set so that you won't be going all night. Find a private place to do this that's also neutral for all involved—not in one participant's room or on one person's "turf."

Begin the session by making sure that the process and ground rules are clear and acceptable to everyone. Each of you should have the opportunity to summarize and define the conflict as you perceive it without being interrupted. Try to focus on specifics and facts rather than generalities or accusations. It helps, when talking about feelings, to describe what you feel rather than what the other person did, using the word "I" rather than "you." "I'm really frustrated about how messy the room is" is more effective than saying, "You're a slob to live with."

As you begin to respond to one another, attacks or miscommunications should be stopped and redirected or clarified. If things get too emotional for clear communication, you may take a short time out to calm down.

Each of you should have the opportunity to state clearly and simply what you'd like to see happen by way of resolution. When you're in conflict about a lot of issues, try to narrow the focus or agree on which specific behaviors might be most easily resolved in this discussion. It's also helpful to understand why particular behaviors are acceptable or unacceptable to one another, what types of events and actions tend to trigger the conflict, and how to avoid these behaviors or catch the problem earlier in the future.

After getting all this information out, you should then begin to generate possible solutions. Discuss them together and weigh the pros and cons of each and how acceptable they are to both of you. Your willingness to compromise on some points may make the other person willing to compromise on others. Each of you should be getting some things and giving others. Be assertive, however, and don't agree on something that you feel is unfair simply to get things over with. You have to live with the result.

If you reach a resolution, be sure you both understand exactly what you've agreed on and what steps should be taken if either of you breaks the agreement. Will you sit down again to renegotiate? Will you take the situation to a judicial board? It may be helpful to put the agreement in writing. Reevaluate the agreement in a couple of weeks to see how it's working out and whether any revisions are necessary. If you can't agree on a resolution, that needs to be acknowledged. Other available alternatives should be clarified and a door left open for future discussion.

I once mediated a situation involving six people. Nothing got resolved, and half the people wound up walking out in the middle, in tears. In the hours that followed, however, different combinations of those six talked together, some for the first time. On their own, they negotiated an agreement by which they lived together for the rest of the semester. As you begin to learn, and feel comfortable with, the process of negotiation and mediation, you may be able to apply those skills to future situations without always needing to involve a mediator.

. . .

"Conflicts with friends were 99 percent of the time due to miscommunications. Even though my friend Jennifer and I were as close as two friends could be (you know, wearing the same shirts to breakfast without prior warning, or knowing who the call was from before answering the phone), there were times when we'd take this link for granted and start making assumptions about the other's behavior. So when we fought, it was big—we've since learned how to communicate more directly, especially with seven hundred miles between us, but in the beginning we found our R.A. most helpful. In one particular instance, where a third friend was involved, we talked to our R.A. individually at first and then came together. We were able to express our hurt and confusion in a safe environment and after some tough discussion, many tears, and even the realization that we'd always have some areas of disagreement, we really knew that our friendship was worth the effort."

—O. L., class of '89

. . .

WHERE TO LOOK FOR HELP

Assertiveness-training programs are offered through various offices—counseling services, offices of student affairs, student activities and leadership development, women's centers, etc. In addition, other types of educational programs, such as groups on sexual communication or codependency, often incorporate principles and techniques of assertiveness training. Counselors can work with you on assertive ways to approach people and situations that are difficult for you. It's also helpful to practice, with friends or R.A.s, ways to respond assertively.

Try to get a copy of your college's organizational chart in order to understand the reporting/supervisory lines. This will help you identify the appropriate person to contact if your concerns are not resolved at the most immediate levels.

On most campuses, R.A.s and professional residence life staff do most of the mediation of roommate and residence-hall conflicts. Problems within clubs or organizations are probably handled through the Student Activities Office and/or student government. Conflicts with faculty and staff are resolved through offices of affirmative action, the ombudsperson, department heads, the Dean's Office, or the Personnel Office. In addition, some campuses specifically train individual students, faculty, and staff to perform mediation services for a variety of situations.

Familiarize yourself with the processes and structures on your campus for handling conflicts and infringements of rights. Some behaviors are clear violations of policy, some situations can't be mediated, and mediated agreements are sometimes broken. Know where and how to pursue a complaint and whether you have both administrative and peer judicial-board alternatives. Your college handbook should provide this information, and some campuses have staff members in charge of judicial affairs. Ask questions and understand what a judicial process will involve and what the possible outcomes could be. If you talk about using a judicial or disciplinary channel, that doesn't necessarily commit you to filing a complaint. Being informed about these processes may, however, give you some ideas for approaching the situation and can also help you sift through the alternatives available to you.

EDUCATING YOURSELF

Books: Nonfiction, Anthologies, Biographies, Poetry, Plays

Alberti, Robert, and M. L. Emmons. *Your Perfect Right: A Guide to Assertive Behavior.* 5th ed. San Luis Obispo, CA: Impact, 1986.

Bach, George, and Peter Wyden. *The Intimate Enemy: How to Fight Fair in Love and Marriage.* New York: Avon, 1976.

Baruch, Grace, Rosalind Barnett, and Caryl Rivers. *Lifeprints: New Patterns of Love and Work for Today's Women.* New York: Signet, 1983.

Bloom, Lynn, Karen Coburn, and Joan Pearlman. *The New Assertive Woman.* New York: Dell, 1975.
Faludi, Susan. *Backlash: The Undeclared War against American Women.* New York: Crown, 1991.
Fisher, Roger, and William Ury. *Getting to Yes: Negotiating Agreement without Giving In.* Rev. ed. New York: Penguin, 1991.
Friedan, Betty. *The Feminine Mystique.* New York: Dell, 1984.
Harragan, Betty. *Games Mother Never Taught You: Corporate Gamesmanship for Women.* New York: Warner, 1989.
Lange, Arthur J., and Patricia Jakubowski. *Responsible Assertive Behavior: Cognitive/Behavioral Procedures for Trainers.* Champaign, IL: Research Press, 1976.
Phelps, Stanlee, and Nancy Austin. *The Assertive Woman: A New Look.* 2d ed. San Luis Obispo, CA: Impact, 1987.
Schaef, Anne Wilson. *Women's Reality.* New York: HarperPerennial, 1991.
Smith, Manuel. *When I Say No, I Feel Guilty.* New York: Bantam, 1975.

Articles, Pamphlets, and Papers

Hall, Roberta M., and Bernice R. Sandler. "The Classroom Climate: A Chilly One for Women?" Washington, DC: Association of American Colleges, Project on the Status and Education of Women, 1983.

Films, Videos, TV Shows, Plays

Alice Doesn't Live Here Anymore. A recently widowed woman makes a life for herself and her son.
Fried Green Tomatoes. Through her conversations with a nursing home resident, a woman is encouraged to become more assertive. From the book by Fannie Flagg.
Marie. A woman fights to expose government corruption in Tennessee. Based on a true story.
Shirley Valentine. A housewife takes steps to explore more of life on her own. From the play by Willy Russell.
Twelve Angry Men. Conflict surfaces as a jury tries to reach a unanimous verdict in a murder trial. From the play by Reginald Rose.
An Unmarried Woman. A woman becomes independent and self-sufficient after her husband leaves her.
Willmar Eight. Eight women bank employees in Minnesota fight to try to get wages equal to those of their male counterparts. Documentary.
The Women's Room. A woman grows from submissive wife and mother to returning college student and assertive woman. Made-for-TV movie based on Marilyn French's novel.
Working Girl. A working-class secretary advances her own career.

FOUR

Taking Care of Yourself

If you really want to see an extreme example of people *not* taking care of themselves, try a college campus during final exam week. A good night's sleep is just a fond memory. Sugar and junk food replace three square meals a day. The most exercise some students get is running to the drugstore to buy aspirin or across campus to turn in a take-home exam by the deadline. This sort of stress can turn even the nicest people into sleep-deprived, strung-out strangers.

"Take care." We say it to each other all the time. Many women say it more than they do it themselves. Women are generally socialized to take care of others, so it's no wonder that many of us have trouble taking care of ourselves. The word "selfish" has generally had a negative connotation. This may discourage you from doing what you need to do at times—put yourself first. The qualifier "at times" is important here. Being selfish doesn't mean that you always put your needs ahead of others'; it does mean that you consider yourself as one of the people you need to take care of. You deserve it as much as anyone else.

The concept of wellness focuses on establishing a lifestyle that will promote long-term health and well-being. Health is defined not as being free of disease but as functioning at the highest level you can. Wellness is an approach that stresses activities intended to keep you well and make you less susceptible to illness and injury. The current wellness movement began in the 1950s and has grown substantially since the

1970s.[1] A number of colleges have wellness programs and classes, and still others have staff who infuse a wellness philosophy into their regular services and programs.

Wellness integrates the whole person—mind, body, emotions, and spirit—and is conceived along six dimensions:[2]

1. Emotional development.
2. Intellectual development.
3. Physical development.
4. Social development.
5. Occupational development.
6. Spiritual development.

Wellness includes fitness, diet, and stress management. All of these components are important for college students, but in the hectic pace of college life, it takes a commitment to pay attention to them. The irony is that what you dismiss today as not being important, such as eating right or exercising, may boomerang back and take more of your time later if you get sick or too stressed to function.

ENCOUNTERING AND RESPONDING TO THIS ISSUE

Fitness

. . .

"Always use a dial phone. Touchtone doesn't exercise the fingers and promote circulation like a good old-fashioned dial phone."
—Wendy Wasserstein, "The Body Minimal"[3]

. . .

Feeling physically fit can give you more energy to devote to your work, activities, and relationships. Exercise is also a good way to release stress. Try to exercise for twenty minutes to an hour at least three times a week, preferably five or six times a week.[4] This may sound like a lot of time, but the type of exercise can vary and can fit into your regular schedule. Some examples:

· Taking an active gym class twice a week.
· Bicycling on the weekend.
· Walking to and from your off-campus job.
· Going out dancing.

Start any exercise program in moderation, set reasonable and realistic goals, and slowly increase the time and difficulty of your program.[5] Don't do too much too quickly. Consult a doctor if you have any preexisting medical problems. Aerobic exercise, which involves continuous work at a comfortable intensity, tends to be more beneficial.[6] Among the advantages of aerobic exercise are

1. improved weight control.
2. stronger and healthier bones.
3. reduced risk of serious heart disease.
4. improved stress management.
5. increased productivity.[7]

Swimming, rowing, bicycling, basketball, running, and brisk walking are all examples of aerobic exercise. Anaerobic exercise, on the other hand, is of high intensity and is performed for more intermittent periods of time. Lifting weights and sprinting are examples of anaerobic exercise.[8]

Exercising with friends can be an enjoyable way to socialize. Informal frisbee games abound during nice weather, and joggers can be seen almost any time of day. Single-sex and coed intramural sports like volleyball, softball, or flag football provide an opportunity to play on a team with friends and also to get to know new people as you play against teams from other residence halls and social groups. Students often relax over sodas after games and argue good-naturedly the next day about bad calls and lucky shots.

· · ·

"My staff found a way to exercise together. We got up at 6:30 every morning and did aerobics. Unfortunately, around exam and final paper time, we began to slack off! I found a way to exercise for myself, though. I simply climb the stairs in my building. It's close and I can do it anytime."

—Y. T., class of '93

· · ·

Nutrition

(See also chapters 5 and 17.)

Diet plays a crucial role in your physical and emotional well-being. Some students become almost obsessed with their weight and physical condition; others understand little about nutrition. Sugar, for example, is assumed by many to be a good source of quick energy. That quick burst, however, is generally followed by an equally fast drop in energy.

Nutrients are substances obtained from food to help the body meet its physiological needs. They fall into several groups. Proteins build and repair muscle tissue. Carbohydrates and fats provide energy the body can use, with carbohydrates being the chief source of energy. Carbohydrates in their most natural form—breads, grains, beans, pasta, etc.— are most beneficial. Vitamins and minerals help the body release energy and regulate its functions. Water provides the medium for all those processes.[9]

Calories are the units used to measure energy and reflect the degree to which a food's energy can be stored in body fat.[10] Calories come in three different forms, and a balanced diet contains the following percentages of daily calorie intake: [11]

- Protein   10–15%
- Carbohydrate   60–70%
- Fat   20–30%

The number of calories you need per day is affected by your body size and weight and by your level of activity and exercise. Daily calorie requirements range between one and two thousand and are primarily genetically determined by the energy needed to maintain your body functions at the level of physical activity you do. This is called your basic metabolic rate. Vigorous exercise done regularly, over an extended period of time, can raise your basic metabolic rate.[12] The more active you are, the more calories are burned: light activity burns less than two hundred calories an hour; moderate activity, between two and three hundred; and strenuous activity, over 350.[13]

The experience of living and eating on campus can wreak havoc with even the best of dietary intentions. Meals are generally served at set times. You'll need to attend them to take advantage of menus with a variety of options planned to provide a healthy balance. Most campus food services issue menus ahead of time so you can anticipate what will be served and plan your calorie intake. Some food services provide nutritional information about dishes and/or offer low-calorie options.

You may sometimes miss meals or look for some variety—after all, how many different ways can the Food Service cook chicken?! If you go to a snack bar or off-campus restaurant or order in food, try to enjoy this freedom without overloading your choices with high-fat items.

Lots of students look for snacks as they study, watch TV, or stay up till all hours talking. "Who wants pizza?" is a common cry late at night, and packages of food from home often taste best in the early morning hours. Students wander the halls in search of munchies to go with their coffee and check out the lounges looking for both cookies and company. Vending machines that used to stock primarily candy, chocolate, and soda now include fruit and juice. Many residence halls have kitchenettes in the building, and some students rent their own refrigerators. If you keep snacks handy, try to stock some healthy items you enjoy. Provide a variety of refreshments at parties and events. Balance chips and dip with fruit, vegetables, cheese, and crackers.

Time Management

. . .

"In managing my time, I buy a daily planner organized by hour, and I block out specific sections of time. As an R.A., I can some-what control other-imposed time with my residents by posting my weekly schedule on my door."

—Y. T., class of '93

. . .

The overwhelming number of tasks and opportunities at college creates both excitement and frustration. There will be many things you want to do and only so many hours in the day (and night) to do them. Learn how to manage your time and use it effectively; this is a skill that will serve you well all your life. If you rebel at the thought of too much structure and organization, however, you may have to swallow hard, accept the need for *some* structure, and devise techniques that don't feel overly restrictive.

Consider three categories of time: [14]

1. Predictable time: things you have to do and need to do at particular times, for example, classes, meals, team practice, meetings, etc.
2. Discretionary time: recreational and social activities, hobbies, etc.
3. Other-imposed activities: unpredictable events such as emergencies, phone calls, or favors asked by friends and family.

Try to maximize your discretionary time—the time that's most yours to determine and control—by minimizing your predictable and other-imposed time commitments. Start by blocking out your schedule. Usually it's helpful to sketch out a long-term schedule for the full semester, and also to make a specific schedule for each individual week as you approach it.

Much of your predictable time is a given. For example, you need to plan on going to your classes. There may, however, be ways you can trim other commitments, either permanently or during some weeks when you're pressed for time. If you usually spend an hour at each meal, perhaps you can save time during midterms by spending only twenty minutes at breakfast, a half-hour at lunch, and forty-five minutes at dinner. Or, if you arrive at the very start or very end of the meal time, you may find that you can get in and out more quickly. While it's important not to cut away *all* the time you spend socializing or relaxing, this approach may allow you to make the best use of your time during stressful periods.

If you find that some of your extracurricular activities, clubs, organizations, or teams are taking up much of your predictable time, consider dropping one or more. There may also be some things that you *think* you have to do that aren't really necessary. You may assume that as the president of your club you have to handle everything, yet there are probably some tasks others would and should do. On the other hand, keep in mind that some activities that take a lot of time also offer many benefits. Playing on a team may be time consuming but can also provide stress release, physical activity, camaraderie, trips off campus, a social network, and positive attention.

Minimizing unpredictable other-imposed time is important if you want to maintain more control over your schedule. To cut down on unnecessary interruptions, you might get an answering machine or perhaps take your phone off the hook sometimes. A sign on your door stating clearly and nicely that you're studying until a particular time and would prefer not to be disturbed could also cut down on unnecessary interruptions. You may find, however, that it's impossible to avoid being interrupted or distracted by residence hall activity. Discover which times tend to be quiet in the hall and try to study then, or do your studying elsewhere.

When I was in college I found that I made the best use of my study time by going to dinner early and then going straight to the library rather than back to the hall, where there was always something going on. I would work at the library until about ten and then go back and feel comfortable hanging out and relaxing. You each have your own patterns of times during the day and night when you work most effectively. Try to schedule your classes and devise your study schedule so you're working at your most difficult tasks when you have the most energy.

As you make your schedule and define your long-term and short-term goals, keep in mind these ways to make your tasks more manageable: [15]

1. Prioritize your commitments. Try labeling as "A" those tasks that are most important and must be started immediately and finished as soon as possible. "B" tasks are less important, and "C" tasks are those that can be put off or even not done if necessary. Devise your schedule so you're spending about 80 percent of your time on "A" tasks.
2. Set concrete goals for yourself. Tell yourself that you'll do all the reading for your history course rather than "doing well" in history.
3. Break down larger tasks, such as writing a paper, into smaller more manageable ones, such as reading two books for the paper or drafting an outline.
4. Write a "to do" list for each week and even for each day. Cross off items as you complete them.
5. Reward yourself in some way for accomplishing tasks. For example, treat yourself to a night at the movies, a call to a friend, or a couple of your favorite jelly donuts.
6. Take breaks to exercise, relax, and socialize.
7. Take on harder jobs first so you can get them behind you.
8. Balance both academic and personal tasks.
9. Consider how smaller tasks can be fit into leftover time. Proofread a paper while doing your laundry. Take reading assignments with you on car trips. Exercise while watching TV.

It may take a while for you to develop a schedule and approach that works for you. Don't criticize yourself if, at first, you find that you're not managing your time as effectively as you had planned. Look at *why* you're not achieving what you'd hoped, and see if that knowledge can help you adjust the next time.

Stress Management

Students new to college experience an accumulation of potentially stressful situations all at once. Among the possible sources of stress are

1. a lack of time.
2. academic demands, increasing competition, and concern over grades.
3. expectations—your own and others'.
4. social acceptance.
5. interpersonal relationships.
6. group living.
7. separation from home.
8. budgeting and finances.
9. career anxiety.
10. sexuality.
11. discrimination based on gender, ethnicity, sexual orientation, etc.[16]

Even positive experiences, such as getting a solo in a dance concert or making the math team, can create stress. Not all stress is necessarily bad. What's important is how you cope with it. Moderate amounts of stress actually lead to better performance. Some situations that are overly stressful for one person stimulate and challenge another. How you *perceive* a situation determines whether it's a threat or a challenge for you.[17] When you feel that the situation requires more coping resources and skills than you possess, *then* the situation will cause you negative stress.

Acute stress is generally brought on by a specific event or cause, such as a big test, and it lasts for a more limited amount of time. Chronic stress has a more gradual buildup and lasts longer. It also includes more widespread world conditions and ongoing personal problems, for example, the national economy, unemployed parents, or the time demands of work-study jobs.[18]

The first step in dealing with stress is to recognize it and determine when it's affecting you in negative ways. Some of you may be used to functioning with stress, regardless of its physical and emotional toll. Physical and emotional indications of an unhealthy stress level include always being in a rush and never being able to take the time to do everything or to do things well; being unable to slow down and relax, even when you're taking a break or on vacation; and being irritable, moody, angry, or sad without an obvious reason. You may find it hard to concentrate, forget to follow through on things you don't usually forget, constantly think about things you have to do rather than focusing on present tasks, and have difficulty sleeping.[19] Recognizing your own signals may help you deal with stress before it becomes too overwhelming.

. . .

"Grant me serenity to accept the things I cannot change, courage to change the things I can, and wisdom to know the difference."
—Reinhold Niebuhr

. . .

The relationship between control and responsibility is an important one to understand. You're responsible for the things you can control, such as how long you study or whether you drink or not. When you feel responsible for things you *can't* control, such as a club accepting you for membership, your friends being happy, or your parents being proud of you, you're setting yourself up for frustration and stress.

Not being responsible for something doesn't mean that you don't care; it means that you recognize that there are limits to how much you can affect that situation. Confronting a friend with a drinking problem is a prime example. You can express your concern, try to get her to seek help, talk with a staff member yourself, and even get your friend to see a professional. In the end, however, your friend has control of her situation, and you aren't responsible for the choices she makes.

Coping with Stress

Coping with or managing stress is an important skill. Know yourself and your resources and potential support. Talk to someone about your feelings. That's one way to release some stress. It's important, however, that the other person not feel responsible for solving your problems.

The internal messages you give yourself can also help you control stress. If you tell yourself that you're "a jerk" and will never understand calculus because you did poorly on a test, you'll most likely feel badly about yourself. You may also experience more stress as the next calculus test approaches. Try instead to figure out why you did poorly on the test so you can deal with the next one differently. Talk to your professor, ask friends in the class for help, or find a tutor. Reassure yourself that doing poorly on one test, or even in the course, doesn't mean that you're not a good and smart person.

If you feel good about yourself, you'll probably be able to forgive yourself for mistakes without getting overwhelmed by them. Don't play over and over in your head situations where you weren't satisfied with your response or performance. Once you have learned whatever lessons there are to learn from the situation, make the extra effort not to think about it any longer.

Concrete action can help you let go of things and move on. Try writing down on a piece of paper what you want to put behind you in order to move on with positive feelings. Then rip up the paper, toss it in the trash, or burn it (outside the residence hall!). Physically taking that step can be a powerful release.

There are some specific ways you can work toward accepting and feeling positive about yourself. First, don't personalize criticism. See it as criticism of your behavior rather than of you as a person. Avoid or leave situations where you consistently feel inadequate or inferior. Take time to be alone with yourself, perhaps to read, meditate, take a walk, relax, exercise, or enjoy nature. Try to look at yourself through the eyes of people who value and respect you. Keep cards and letters from people who make you feel good about yourself; looking through them when you're feeling shaky can be a real boost. Learn from others how to change things about yourself that *you* want to change.[20]

Another way to manage stress is to avoid becoming overcommitted by taking on too many responsibilities. One student described herself as having a "helium hand . . . you know . . . every time someone asks for a volunteer, my hand just goes up like a balloon." If you have a helium hand, try sitting on it or counting to ten before volunteering for something while you decide if you really can take it on. It's important to be able to say no (see chapter 3), and it's also important to ask for time to think about something before committing yourself to do it. Make volunteer work a choice rather than a reflex.

■ ■ ■

"I wind up volunteering very often. I have been told I need to take time for myself because I do everything for everyone. Let me tell you, it is starting to wear me out—mainly because I keep giving and no one is giving back. I love helping people but I think I need to start setting some limits and taking care of myself."

—E. J., class of '92

. . .

The ability to relax may take some effort, contradictory as that may sound. In many group living situations, stress is contagious at some times of the year, such as during midterms and finals. It's helpful to have some place where you can escape and relax, or at least keep your stress to a manageable level. Some people study in private places or where there's a window with a peaceful view. Other students know people off campus they can visit, and still others take breaks to do totally unrelated things such as go bowling. You may also begin to recognize which people are relaxing for you to be around and arrange to spend more time with them when you need to unwind.

There are a variety of relaxation techniques that can provide release. Some are done on your own, using images and music. Others, like meditation and yoga, are learned in classes and workshops and practiced on your own. Still others, like biofeedback, are developed by working with a practitioner. Take some time out of your schedule now to learn these skills, as they may help you manage your busy schedule in more efficient and healthy ways in the future.

Humor is a good way to release tension when you're feeling stressed. Laugh in ways that don't put yourself or others down. One college senior who felt really stressed about her upcoming graduation and the fact that she didn't yet have a job got frustrated with people asking her over and over, "What are you doing after graduation?" She finally came up with a great response: "Going out to dinner with my parents."

Humor can help you let go of anxiety, anger, and fear, enabling you to "clear the system," in a way.[21] This in turn can allow you to deal more effectively with not very funny issues and situations. I recall one night when I was scheduled to go into a residence hall as part of an active investigation of harassing notes received in that hall. Prior to doing this, I attended a play on campus. I went into the theater feeling really tense and preoccupied. The play, *The Colored Museum*, by George C. Wolfe, was composed of a number of vignettes and several were funny . . . very funny. They were so funny, and I laughed so hard, that I could almost feel my head, my stomach, and my heart start to relax. I laughed until I cried and it was wonderful to cry over something funny for a change. When the play was over I went to the hall to conduct the meeting. Although I still felt *some* stress, I realized how important my time at the play had been. It was as if water had been applied to dry and parched soil. Without that soaking of humor, I think I would have just cracked and fallen apart.

Dealing with Anger

Women are often uncomfortable with anger. Many of us avoid expressing anger because we've been taught that "good" people don't get angry. Perhaps we're afraid that our anger will hurt or destroy the other person, or that we'll lose control and never be able to stop being angry.[22] It's very stressful to keep anger inside. Repressing anger is usually more destructive than expressing it; often others know that we're angry even when we think we're doing a great job of hiding it. You may more effectively manage your anger by

1. giving yourself permission to be angry without getting down on yourself for feeling that way.
2. not using anger to reinforce a negative self-image.
3. externalizing the feeling—pounding pillows, ripping paper, etc.
4. increasing your physical activity.
5. using your anger as a source of energy to reassess your situation, define your limits and boundaries, and free yourself from old patterns.[23]

Being on the receiving end of someone else's anger can be a more stressful experience than it needs to be if you're uncomfortable with that emotion. When I was in graduate school, one of my professors got very angry with me. Because he didn't yell or scream, I found it hard to believe that he was actually angry. This made him more angry. After he left, others in the class said they had never seen him that angry before, and I suddenly got very scared. I assumed that he must really hate me now. The next day I gathered up my courage to go in to see him. Would he throw me out of his office? Would he tell me to drop the class? I was amazed when he greeted me warmly. I apologized. He accepted my apology. We talked about what had taken place the previous day. We went on to work together that year, not as if nothing had happened, but as if something had happened that we had resolved. Learning that someone I liked and respected could get angry at me and not hate me was a very important lesson.

Depression

Stress, sadness, discouragement, and loneliness are common to most people at some point in their lives. When your regular coping mechanisms don't work and lead to a loss of self-esteem and feelings of worthlessness and helplessness, depression can result. Self-esteem is generally lowered when a large gap exists between your goals and what you actually accomplish, or between who and how you want to be and who and how you are. Depression can also result from a loss, such as the death of someone close; the end of a relationship; feelings of failure; or the loss of an important part of your life. Depression and grieving are normal processes for people to go through when they experience a loss. But when feelings of worthlessness or guilt prevail, and the gap between how things are and how you want them to be can't be closed, depression can become debilitating.[24]

There are some steps you can take to work your way out of a mild depression. Recognize that the feelings are temporary and often within your control. Identify what you can change in order to feel less negative, such as the messages you're telling yourself. Try to do things that make you feel good about yourself and be with people who treat you well. Isolating yourself when you feel depressed may only keep you in a depressive vacuum. Make an effort to stay in touch with friends and continue with activities that help you feel good. Take care of yourself physically, exercise, and keep up your physical appearance.[25]

A clinical depression is one in which the symptoms persist for more than two weeks.[26] If you're feeling depressed for that long, talk to an R.A., residence hall staff member, counselor, or chaplain. It's nothing to be ashamed of. It's actually a sign of strength to know when you need help and to ask for it. Get some objective assistance to sort through your feelings and consider new solutions. There are, at times, physical causes for depression, so also consult a physician.

Suicidal Thoughts and Feelings

If you find yourself thinking about suicide as an option, talk with someone immediately. Many depressed people have suicidal thoughts without ever acting on those thoughts, but the fact that you're considering it is an indication that you need some help. The Counseling Service is the most appropriate professional resource for you to use. If you're hesitant to talk with a therapist, you may talk to someone else first, but talk to someone.

Some students are hesitant to ask for help, fearing that if they tell someone how depressed they are, the college will ask them to leave. It's more likely that your taking the initiative to seek out a professional will be seen as a sign that you're taking steps to help yourself. You and your counselor may at some point discuss what you need in order to function successfully at school, and whether it's possible for you to get that ongoing support, but that's quite a different process. The Counseling Service is bound by principles of confidentiality, unless there's a question of immediate danger. Your dealings with a counselor are generally between the two of you, and having a knowledgeable and caring person to work with can be an incredible relief.

In group-living situations, each individual's behavior invariably affects others. If your behavior has been disruptive in the residence hall, you may be asked, by hall staff, to agree to seek help and to take more control of your behavior.

For Those Concerned about a Friend Who May Be Suicidal

If you're worried that a friend or roommate might be of harm to herself, let her know that you're concerned. Listen to her and try to evaluate the seriousness of the situation. Asking her if she's thinking of hurting herself won't put the idea into her head if she hasn't already thought about it. She may actually feel relieved to be able to talk about it. If she has a plan by which she'll act on her feelings, there's more risk. The more specific and realistic the plan, the greater the risk. Does she have in her possession the means to hurt herself, or are those means easily accessible to her? There's also greater risk if she's attempted suicide in the past, or if family members or close friends have committed suicide.[27]

A depressed person considering suicide sees limited options. If you can talk and explore additional alternatives, it might be helpful. If you find yourself feeling hopeless and helpless as you talk with your friend, or if she seems to dismiss all other alternatives with "yes, but . . . " or by giving reasons why they wouldn't work, those are signs that she needs more professional help.[28]

If your friend can identify or focus on the causes of the problem, perhaps you can help her decide what she wants to change or see differently, what resources she might use, and how she has coped successfully in the past. If she can begin to identify constructive first steps, or if she indicates some investment in the future—if she says, "I can't go to counseling tomorrow because I have to study for my two o'clock exam" or "I have a volleyball game Friday"—those can be positive signs. Sometimes making an agreement that your friend will call you if she feels like she's going to hurt herself, or that you'll get together in the morning to decide on next steps, may get you through the night. *Only do this if you feel comfortable with your friend's commitment and believe her. In any event, be sure that someone else knows of your concern.* Your R.A. is the most immediate person to contact, even if it's the middle of the night. That's what R.A.s are there for.

You're really not qualified to assess whether someone who is thinking about suicide is a danger to herself. While you can listen and support a friend, it's important that you not assume responsibility for her well-being. It's best to get your friend to agree to talk to a professional while reassuring her that you're still there as her friend. Tell her that you care enough to want to make sure that she's getting the best possible help.

If your friend is hesitant to talk to a professional, ask about her fears. Don't promise her that you'll never tell anyone else. It's important that you be able to seek help if you need it. If your friend is unwilling to talk directly to a counselor, an intermediary step may be to tell her that *you* need to get some help for yourself in order to help her. If you can then communicate back to her the kinds of things a counselor said, or your impressions of the counselor's receptivity, this may make her more willing to take that step herself.

If you're seriously concerned about your friend's immediate safety, trust your judgment—even if she tries to talk you out of it or tells you she's fine. Contact your R.A. If s/he isn't home, try another R.A. in the building or a residence director. On most college campuses there's someone available twenty-four hours a day, usually the Security Office. Security can also contact other staff members on call for emergencies. Know the emergency numbers and call them if you need to.

If your roommate or friend does try to commit suicide, the health and counseling services will generally work with her to assess her situation. They'll determine whether she can develop the necessary support to work on her problems while remaining on campus. Some students really want or need to leave school. For others a suicide attempt is the point at which they hit bottom, recognize that some things need to change, and begin to work with a counselor at changing them.

If you have a roommate or friend who is returning to the residence hall after a suicide attempt, you may have a variety of feelings that you need to deal with.

- I'm scared. How do I know she won't do it again?
- I'm angry. I didn't come to college to watch someone else all the time.
- I feel guilty. I should have seen it coming.
- I feel uncomfortable. Do I talk to her about it when she comes back or do I pretend that nothing happened?

It may be helpful for you to talk to someone, perhaps your R.A. or professional residence hall staff, about your feelings. You can also talk with a counselor, but s/he won't be able to talk to you about your friend; the focus will need to be on *you,* or on providing general information about suicide attempts. The counselor can also clarify the difference between a suicide attempt and a gesture, which is usually more a cry for help than a life-threatening act.

The process I usually followed before a student returned to her residence hall worked well. I met with friends and roommates in the hall who knew what had happened. We talked about how they felt about their friend coming back to live with them. I asked whether there were things that they wanted to talk about with their friend before she came back and how they would prefer to do that.

I also talked with the student who had attempted suicide about her feelings going back to the residence hall and what she needed and didn't need from her friends. Often everyone involved really wanted to talk before getting back together in the hall. When this happened, it usually made the return more comfortable. It allowed students to talk about their fears and to see their friend in a much more calm, rational, and genuine way than they had last seen her. This was often very reassuring.

Some friends feel that they have to "watch" someone who returns to the hall after a suicide attempt or gesture. That often feels stifling to the returning student, who may be quite secure in the fact that she's not a danger to herself. Your friend wouldn't be released back to the residence hall if counselors felt that she was of risk to herself or others. That doesn't mean that you'll immediately feel totally comfortable. You can indicate to your friend that if she wants to talk, you're willing to, but don't force her. Allow her to talk if and when she chooses to. She may prefer to deal with her problems with her counselor and get back to relating to you as a friend.

WHERE TO LOOK FOR HELP

Self-help activities, workshops, and programs may be conducted through your counseling service, offices of residence life, student affairs, career development, and minority affairs, the chaplains, and the women's center, among other places. Many of these offices make use of peer counselors and facilitators in this work. Serving in this type of helping or educational role and receiving some professional training and supervision can be a great opportunity.

There may be courses on wellness, and a number of colleges also have special seminars, classes, and programs to orient new students to college life. These programs generally deal with skills, information, and issues that help you learn more about yourself, others, and succeeding at college. If these courses are optional, consider taking one. Some colleges also have special-interest housing options designated for students interested in wellness.

Resources for exercise and fitness will be found through physical education and athletics. While there are likely to be more formalized activities such as varsity sports and intramural tournaments, there are also times when facilities such as pools, weight rooms, and gyms are open for all students to use. This information will help you schedule informal exercise times. For a change of pace, consider community resources, such as the pool at the Y or local high school track.

Approach your physical well-being in a preventative way. Find a health-care provider with whom you feel comfortable at the Health Service. Have regular checkups and follow any advice you receive. For diet and nutrition issues, staff at the Health Service and Food Service are good resources. Local hospitals or health-care facilities may also offer informational or educational programs.

Help with managing your time and study habits can be found through a variety of channels. Centers for academic development often have workshops, and computing services have staff to assist you in mastering the use of word processing and computing equipment. The college library provides assistance to help you learn what resources are available there and how to make the most effective use of them.

Deal with stress before it interferes with your performance as a student. If you can identify the cause of your stress, you can look toward particular sources of help. For example, if your financial situation is constantly on your mind, talk with someone in the Financial Aid Office to help you gather information you need. Stress related to academics can be discussed with an advisor or class dean, particularly if you're thinking about options for dropping a course, changing a major, or taking time off. If your stress relates to future career plans or jobs, the Career Development Office would be an appropriate resource.

If stress turns to depression, seek help. In addition to the resources previously mentioned, some colleges and off-campus communities have hotlines to call if you or a friend is in crisis.

EDUCATING YOURSELF

Books: Nonfiction, Anthologies, Biographies, Poetry, Plays

Ardell, Donald. *High-Level Wellness: An Alternative to Doctors, Drugs, and Disease*. Emmaus, PA: Rodale, 1977.

Braiker, Harriet B. *Getting Up When You're Feeling Down: A Woman's Guide to Overcoming and Preventing Depression*. New York: Putnam's, 1988.

Brallier, Lynn. *Successfully Managing Stress*. Los Altos, CA: National Nursing Review, 1982.

Brody, Jane E. *Jane Brody's "The New York Times" Guide to Personal Health*. New York: Times Books, 1982.

———. *Jane Brody's Nutrition Book*. New York: Bantam, 1982.

Cousins, Norman. *Celebration of a Life*. Rev. ed. New York: Bantam, 1991.

Davis, Martha, et al. *The Relaxation and Stress-Reduction Workbook*. Oakland, CA: New Harbinger, 1982.

Doress, Paula Brown, Diana Laskin Siegal, and the Midlife and Older Women Book Project in Cooperation with the Boston Women's Health Book Collective. *Ourselves, Growing Older: Women Aging with Knowledge and Power*. New York: Simon and Schuster, 1987.

Dunn, Halbert. *High-Level Wellness*. Arlington, VA: Beatty, 1972.

Edlin, Gordon, and Eric Golanty. *Health and Wellness*. 3d ed. Boston: Jones and Bartlett, 1988.

Gershoff, Stanley, with Catherine Whitney and the Editorial Advisory Board of the Tufts University Diet and Nutrition Letter. *The Tufts University Guide to Total Nutrition*. New York: HarperCollins, 1991.

Keirsey, David, and Marilyn Bates. *Please Understand Me: Character and Temperament Types*. Del Mar, CA: Prometheus Nemesis, 1978.

Kroeger, Otto, and Janet Thuesen. *Type Talk: Or How to Determine Your Personality Type and Change Your Life*. New York: Delacorte, 1988.

Lakein, Alan. *How to Get Control of Your Time and Your Life*. New York: McKay, 1973.

Levy, Marvin, Mark Dignan, and Janet Shirreffs. *Life and Health*. 5th ed. New York: Random House, 1987.

MacLean, Helene, ed. *EveryWoman's Health*. 5th ed. New York: Fireside, 1980.

Ogle, Jane. *Age-Proofing.* New York: New American Library, 1984.

Otis, Carol L., and Roger Goldingay. *Campus Health Guide: The College Student's Handbook for Healthy Living.* New York: College Board, 1989.

Rice, Phillip L. *Stress and Health: Principles and Practice for Coping and Wellness.* Monterey, CA: Brooks/Cole, 1987.

Rowh, Mark. *Coping with Stress in College: Everything Students Need to Know to Manage the Pressures of College Life.* New York: College Board, 1989.

Sanford, Linda T., and Mary Ellen Donovan. *Women and Self-Esteem: Understanding and Improving the Way We Think and Feel about Ourselves.* New York: Penguin, 1985.

Shanghold, Mona, and Gabe Mirkin. *The Complete Sports Medicine Book for Women.* New York: Fireside, 1985.

Smith, Sandra, and Christopher Smith. *The College Student's Health Guide.* Los Altos, CA: Westchester, 1988.

Steinem, Gloria. *Revolution from Within: A Book of Self-Esteem.* Boston: Little, Brown, 1992.

Tubesing, Donald A. *Kicking Your Stress Habits: A Do-It-Yourself-Guide for Coping with Stress.* Duluth, MN: Whole Person Press, 1981.

Turow, Scott. *One L.* New York: Warner, 1988.

Vickery, Donald. *Take Care of Yourself: The Consumers Guide to Medical Care.* Reading, MA: Addison-Wesley, 1986.

White, Evelyn C., ed. *The Black Women's Health Book: Speaking for Ourselves.* Seattle: Seal, 1990.

Articles, Pamphlets, and Papers

American College Health Association. "Depression: What It Is, How to Help." Rockville, MD: American College Health Association.

Gurin, Carol Duchow. "Depression." *Ms.,* December 1987.

Films, Videos, TV Shows, Plays

Broadcast News. A variety of people in a TV newsroom try to deal with the stresses of their hectic lives.

'Night Mother. A mother tries to persuade her daughter not to commit suicide. From the play by Marsha Norman.

Ordinary People. A high school student fights the depression and family problems that led to his suicide attempt. From the novel by Judith Guest.

The Paper Chase. First-year law students struggle with the stresses of law school.

Permanent Record. A high school student's suicide has a profound effect on his friends.

FIVE

Eating Disorders

I looked at the seven women at the front of the room and couldn't help smiling. I recognized some from times when they weren't doing so well, and the times had certainly changed for them. Students listened closely as these women, also students, told their stories. They described their struggles with food, weight, self-esteem, and eating disorders. They talked openly and honestly about their lives and how they had turned them around. One or two had spent time in the hospital or an in-patient program. Some had taken time away from campus to get treatment; others had remained at school while working with counselors. All were in recovery from eating disorders and were now offering help to others. As members of the Eating Disorders Task Force, these students were speaking out to other women on their campus. They provided inspiration and hope for those in the room who had eating disorders, and also for those worried about friends.

Terminology

Eating disorders aren't simply about food and weight. They involve the use of food and weight management as a means of trying to solve other emotional conflicts.[1] Struggles with food and weight are really symptoms of these deeper emotional conflicts.

Anorexia nervosa, an extreme fear of gaining weight and becoming fat, leads to deliberate self-starvation. Anorexia is a progressive disorder in which the fear doesn't lessen as weight is lost, and the individual becomes increasingly addicted to dieting.[2] Anorexics refuse to maintain a minimal normal body weight. Anorexia is clinically defined as a weight loss leaving the individual approximately 15 percent below the weight expected for her age and height, or as failing to gain weight from normal growth, leading to a body weight 15 percent below what would be expected. Amenorrhea (loss of menstrual periods) for at least three consecutive cycles is another diagnostic criterion.[3] Obsessiveness with food is reflected in constant talk about it, preparation of meals for others, and rituals and compulsions in relation to food.[4] An anorexic, obsessed with becoming thin, develops a distorted perception of her own physical appearance. She may actually be quite thin but will see only a heavy person when she looks in the mirror. Anorexics try to burn calories quickly, and compulsive exercise is used as another way to lose weight.[5]

Bulimia also involves an overconcern with body shape and weight. Bulimics deal with this concern by recurrent and secretive binge eating. A binge is self-defined. One woman might consider one candy bar to be a binge, while for others it might be large amounts of food, usually junk food, consumed quickly and then purged by self-induced vomiting or use of laxatives or diuretics. Compulsive exercising is another form of purging. During binges bulimics fear that they won't be able to stop eating.[6]

Bulimics are harder to recognize than anorexics, as they often maintain normal or near-normal body weight. Binging and purging are used as a way to escape depressed feelings and anxiety. The secrecy and planning that go into the binging and purging cycle begin to dominate the bulimic's life.[7]

Anorexia and bulimia are both complex social, physical, and emotional disorders. They are potentially dangerous and can prove fatal. The medical effects of eating disorders include menstrual irregularities (even the cessation of menstrual periods), lethargy, dehydration, and intestinal and stomach problems. Vomiting can become spontaneous, and excessive vomiting may cause tearing and bleeding of the esophagus and can permanently erode tooth enamel. The most serious physical effect of eating disorders is an electrolyte imbalance that may lead to heart irregularities and potentially to cardiac arrest.[8] Singer Karen

Carpenter's death at the age of thirty-two was attributed to cardiac arrest related to an eating disorder.

Background Information
(See also chapter 17.)

. . .

"Body-image is directly related to low self-esteem, and in this society the media does a terrific job at keeping it low."

—O. L., class of '89

. . .

Approximately 90 percent of those with eating disorders are women.[9] This isn't particularly surprising, as women in our society grow up learning that who they are is often defined by how they look. This is learned from parents, friends, magazines, advertisements, television, and the movies. Many women accept the standards set by others—standards of size, thinness, and glamour that few of us can reasonably meet. How many women do you know who look like Cindy Crawford, Naomi Campbell, Kristi Yamaguchi, Rosie Perez, or the models in the *Sports Illustrated* swimsuit issue? The pressure to be thin is a pervasive message in American culture. If you judge yourself by others' ideals and try to be what you think they want you to be, you may continue to think you're never good enough when you're really just fine. If you believe you have to look a certain way to attract the people you want to attract, you might treat your body in unhealthy ways that are simply not necessary to achieve the approval you seek. Developing an eating disorder is one of those ways.

Research on eating disorders—predisposing factors, family histories, etc.—is ongoing. The information offered here will most likely continue to be revised and refined in the future. At present studies suggest that the most common ages for developing an eating disorder are between fifteen and eighteen, ages that often coincide with transitions into high school and college. The stresses and many choices encountered by adolescents can create great anxiety. Some professionals view anorexia in particular as a way for a woman to react to these stresses by attempting to maintain at least the physical appearance of a child as part of an attempt to avoid more adult roles and responsibilities.[10] Although the incidence of eating disorders occurs across gender, ethnic, and socioeconomic class lines, it is thus far higher among white middle-class and upper-class families, where concerns about wealth, status, and achievement are most frequently stressed.[11] Traits describing those most susceptible to developing an eating disorder—intelligence, sensitivity, success orientation, wanting to be a "superwoman"—are common to many college women.[12] Though often excelling academically and in extracurricular activities, women vulnerable to developing eating disorders also set unreasonably high goals for themselves and try to be perfect at everything.[13]

Eating disorders are more common in families where physical appearance and slimness are stressed and weight control is emphasized. Food tends to be a central issue in these families—a sign of affection, source of nurturance, center of socializing and activity. It can also be a symbol of power as parents attempt to regulate food choice and eating habits. The struggle over food reflects the power struggle in the family around independence and individuality.[14]

• • •

"The idea of being able to control one aspect of my life is how my eating disorder began. The ability of controlling what I put in my mouth or more accurately what I didn't gave me control of my life, or so I thought. This control which I was so pleased I had, soon became a distorted set of fears. It was a fear of being fat, a fear of not being good enough, and many others which somewhere along the way took control of me."

—E. V., class of '90

• • •

Parenting styles and dynamics play a role in the development of a child's eating disorder. Overinvolvement and overprotectiveness by one (most often the mother) or both parents contribute to the struggle over independence. Underinvolvement and distancing by one (most often the father) or both parents lead a young woman to seek approval from that absent or more distant parent. She wants to be valued for who she is rather than how she looks. If she doesn't receive this sense of being valued, her self-esteem suffers. This lowered self-image leaves her more susceptible to pressures to be thin and to look a certain way, or to be supersuccessful at everything she does.[15]

Eating disorders are more common in families with a history of them, or of other kinds of substance abuse.[16] Rules tend to be rigid in these families, and conflict is avoided. Family members try, on the surface, to please one another. Hostility, though felt, is rarely openly expressed.[17]

Successful treatment of eating disorders is often complicated by resistance. Women with eating disorders deny that they have a problem or need outside help to solve it. Various types of treatment have been used, and often two or more social, medical, and psychological approaches are combined—individual psychotherapy, group therapy, family therapy, nutritional counseling, behavior modification, cognitive restructuring, support groups, and/or medication. The immediate goal of treatment is to change eating patterns, but the ultimate goal is to enable a woman to develop more effective ways of dealing with life's problems. Successful treatment will result in a woman achieving separation from her family and becoming an autonomous adult. She replaces self-defeating thinking patterns and develops healthier interpersonal skills.[18] Among the overall goals of therapy are for a woman to

1. accept and appreciate her body in its "natural" state.
2. learn to like herself and develop an identity based on something other than how she looks, or how much she does or doesn't eat or exercise.
3. relinquish childhood for womanhood.
4. take risks.
5. make decisions and accept responsibility.
6. learn to trust.
7. learn new ways of thinking.
8. realign relationships.
9. live in the present.
10. accept that the difficulty, and the solution, is within herself.[19]

ENCOUNTERING AND RESPONDING TO THIS ISSUE

▪ ▪ ▪

"I was a perfectionist . . . and did everything I could to maintain control in my life. Going to college broke up any previously set patterns, however, and 'controlling' food seemed the easiest way to regain predictability."

—O. L., class of '89

▪ ▪ ▪

More and more students every year identify themselves or others as having eating disorders or being in recovery from them. Various studies indicate that as many as 20–30 percent of college women engage in bulimic behavior.[20] The pressure to succeed—get good grades, be well liked, excel in activities—is intensified in a college setting. There's more independence and greater competition, while new sources of support still need to be developed.

Residence hall living brings students together in very close quarters. Hall showers and bathrooms are used by entire floors of students. It takes effort to find or create a feeling of privacy. In a group-living situation, each person's behavior can influence the day-to-day lives of other residents. As residents get to know and care about one another, they're likely to be aware of changes in mood and behavior. It's hard to hide eating habits and patterns when you eat together in college dining halls. Today's college women know more about eating disorders, and they're often able to recognize signs of bulimia and anorexia. If students are worried about a friend, they're likely to say or do something about it.

Some group-living situations, however, may actually encourage anorexic or bulimic behaviors. When students focus their conversations on physical attractiveness, weight, diets, and food, the atmosphere can induce unhealthy eating patterns.

. . .

"When I was a first-year student in college, my friends and I would either eat or drink too much and vomit and/or fast *together*. Many sorority women *encourage* this."

—C. J., class of '91

. . .

Take time to look at the group-living environment in your residence hall—the conversation, posters, activities. Do they emphasize physical appearance? Are food and refreshments a prime focus? Do you feel overly self-conscious about how you look and what you do? You can play an active role in shifting the atmosphere to benefit others as well as yourself. Try changing the topic of conversation if it becomes too weight oriented. Avoid being drawn into obsessions with food or talking about others' eating habits. Some students get so caught up in trying to figure out whether someone has an eating disorder, or in trying to help someone who does, that they can think of little else. Other students recognize that their living situations are unhealthy for them and request a housing move. These decisions are not always easy to make, but the changes can make all the difference in the world.

The following suggestions may help you avoid the thought patterns and eating habits that tend to lead to eating disorders:[21]

1. Avoid fad diets.
2. Avoid frequent weigh-ins.
3. Emphasize health, not weight.
4. Avoid excessive hunger.
5. Avoid comparisons.
6. Don't set a weight goal.
7. Try to develop positive feelings about your own body.
8. Try to eat regularly during the day.
9. Treat yourself to favorite foods occasionally.

For Those with an Eating Disorder

. . .

"Unfortunately, your roommate, who can also become your closest friend and confidante, is prone to accept you as you are and disregard your 'crazy dieting habits.' Others' acceptance of an eating disorder can be the most harmful factor of all."

—D. K., class of '94

. . .

Living in a residence hall with anywhere from a dozen to several hundred to a thousand other students can create a range of difficulties if you have an eating disorder. Students often invest much time and energy into trying to hide their eating habits and bulimic behavior, often without great success. Starting college can be hard enough without the added stress of carrying around such a secret. I would encourage you to confide in someone who can support you. While a first instinct may be to simply tell your roommate, I'd urge you also to talk to a staff member with whom you feel comfortable. Once you confide in a staff member, you're not alone. You have a potential advocate. Talk about *how* she can help you. You may check in regularly to talk about how you're doing in general. You could ask her to help you identify some ways to deal with situations that are difficult for you, especially in relation to food. Perhaps she can suggest additional support and professional resources on and off campus.

The very idea of talking to someone else may feel uncomfortable to you. However, being alone with your secret could prove even more uncomfortable. Others' efforts to identify people with eating disorders can lead to speculation and gossip, which will only contribute to your feelings of shame, guilt, and isolation.

Staff in your residence hall have been trained in basic listening skills. If you're uneasy talking directly about your own eating disorder, try easing into the conversation by talking first about eating disorders in general. Or try interacting with the staff member in ways that have nothing whatsoever to do with food and eating. Playing an intramural sport, watching a video, or listening to music together, for example, can help you get to know one another. If you build a comfortable rapport, it can be easier to start talking more personally with someone in a position to help you.

It's hard for roommates and friends to meet your needs if they don't know what those needs are. For example, it may be helpful for you if socializing doesn't always focus around food and alcohol, or if your friends don't spend two hours hanging out over dessert in the dining hall where you're surrounded by food. Once you tell your friends, they may suggest alternatives, and perhaps you can then socialize in ways that are more healthy for you. If you're unable to avoid get-togethers over food and drink, the mere presence of friends who are aware of your discomfort can still be helpful. They can be respectful of your needs.

. . .

"I also experienced difficulties with the fact that meal times were often the only social times. As a result, I looked forward to and remained focused on meals because that was when I would see my friends. I found it important to try to schedule/arrange for other times for us to get together so that I didn't feel like meals shared equaled relationship sustenance. Going for a walk together or getting coffee are two nice alternatives."

—H. J., class of '93

. . .

Perhaps some people you tell *won't* understand. Or you may encounter students who understand but aren't willing to make the effort to help. Use this information to make decisions about whom you spend time with. Others may want to help but may inadvertently do so in ways that do more harm than good, such as by being overprotective. If this happens, *tell* the person what you do and don't need from her. By talking to others you may find that you're not alone. Many students have probably had their own experiences with eating disorders, either personally or through family and friends.

Friends and peers can't take the place of professional help. They can't be friends and therapists at the same time, and they're infinitely more qualified to be friends. No matter how much they may want to, others can't change your behavior and mindset; ultimately, only you can do that. Get involved and put your energy into activities you enjoy. Remember that there is much more to you than just your eating disorder.

For Friends of Those with Eating Disorders

. . .

"The last thing I wanted to do was talk to someone, especially someone that I hardly knew. In retrospect, I think that keeping 'the secret' was very empowering. To tell would have been to risk losing control to someone else. I think for some, an eating disorder may be the stereotypical 'call for help.' For me, and others I'm sure, it was more a challenge to myself to gain some kind of control and keep it. The 'help' of others was exactly what I was running from."

—Student, class of '91

. . .

There are a number of ways you may discover that someone you live with or care about has an eating disorder. The most obvious indications are marked changes in weight, compulsive exercising, fasting, vomiting, or excessive laxative use. It's also possible that a friend will confide in you that she has an eating disorder. She may be asking for help, or she may be seeking your support for her behavior or even suggesting that you join her.

If you're aware that someone is having active problems with an eating disorder, it's important that you not deal with it alone. First, find out as much as you can about these disorders. Don't assume that someone who displays anorexic or bulimic behaviors is necessarily suffering from an eating disorder. There can be other medical reasons for these actions, and not all exceptionally thin women are anorexic.

How to respond to a friend or hallmate with an eating disorder is a complex question. I learned a great deal about this several years ago, during a period when one residence hall of about sixty women was having problems. Someone was vomiting in the bathrooms and not cleaning up fully. We took the usual first steps of talking to people in the hall about resources available and encouraging them to see someone from the Health or Counseling Service. The bulimic behavior continued. Different bathrooms and hall trash bins were eventually used, and frustration grew. People began to watch one another and listen for anything suspicious. Concern was turning to anger.

After an incident that took place when only a small number of people were in the hall, I decided to try a different approach. I spoke individually with the residents who had been there at the time, asking each to help me figure out how to reach the person responsible for the bulimic behavior. I asked each person to put herself in the position of that person and to tell me what I could say or do that might have some effect.

I heard very different advice from those who were familiar with these types of behaviors than from those who were not. Several of those who felt they didn't know much about eating disorders thought we should take a hard line. They suggested we tell everyone that this behavior could not be tolerated in a group-living situation and that if we found the person responsible we would remove her from the residence. This would, of course, be combined with urging her to get professional help as we had been doing all along.

Those I spoke with who understood more about eating disorders had a different slant. Several of them looked me very directly in the eye, acknowledged that they had their own difficulties, but said they were not responsible for this current situation. *They* felt we should avoid adding to feelings of shame and guilt. Several suggested we provide hall members with very clear information about the impact the behavior was having on other people, such as the housekeeper who cleaned up and the custodian who emptied the trash bins. They thought this would give whomever was responsible the opportunity to hear and understand *why* she needed to look at her behavior, and hopefully do something about the situation. We provided this information, brochures about the physical dangers of bulimia, and the names of counselors on and off campus, to each resident. Eventually the vomiting stopped. The most important lesson I learned from this experience was the value of putting as much information as possible in the hands of the only person who can really change the behavior.

The following concrete suggestions may help those of you who have roommates or friends who are bulimic:

1. Remove binge-type foods (high-calorie junk food) from the room, or if that's not possible, put the food out of sight.
2. Allow your friend to set her own eating habits. Don't look over her shoulder or act like her parent.
3. Be available to listen to your friend, and don't trivialize her pain. At the same time, don't let yourself get pulled into giving more time or energy than you're able to give.
4. If your friend repeatedly asks you about her weight or how she looks, suggest that it's more important how she feels about herself than what you think.
5. If your friend binges and purges, she will also probably be moody at times. While she has a right to be irritable, you don't always have to be the person on whom she takes it out. You have a right to remove yourself from her when her moods affect you.
6. If your friend eats your food and then vomits, that's stealing. Confront her and ask for compensation.
7. If your friend uses a shared bathroom to vomit in, let her know it bothers you.[22]

Confronting a friend about her behavior—whether it's binging and purging or starving herself—is one way to try to help her. For many of us women, however, who are often brought up not to express anger or create conflict, the idea of confrontation is terrifying. Perhaps we assume that if we confront someone, terrible things will happen—she'll fall apart and it will be our fault, she'll get angry at us, or she'll get really upset and cry. Confronting someone doesn't have to fit the ugly image you may have of it. It can be done gently; it can be done with care. If the person is someone you're close to, she may not even be surprised when you finally do confront her. Sometimes caring about someone *means* expressing anger and dealing with it. If I'm confronting someone, I sometimes say that I care enough about them to risk their getting angry at me for saying what I need to say.

Anger isn't always pleasant, but it's also rarely the disaster you fear. It's much healthier to get feelings out than to keep them bottled up. You may say what you need to say and find that your friend doesn't get angry. If she does, she might still appreciate your effort. Even if she stays angry for a while, you may have saved her life.

. . .

"I also felt more love and concern than I had in a long time when confronted. I felt enormously relieved. I knew that I had lost control of my eating habits but I was too proud to ask anyone for help. A close, emotionally supportive yet highly observant and realistic friend gave me an ultimatum. She told me that I had to either (1) attend a meeting for people suffering from eating disorders or (2) inform my parents, R.A., or an on-campus counselor. This was the most frightening yet alleviating thing anyone ever told me. Through that one evening of self-realization I faced the facts. I agreed to attend one of a local hospital's eating disorder group sessions. I only went once but I felt like I had finally woken up. I could have died before I really gave life a fair chance."

—D. K., class of '94

. . .

The most important factor in confronting someone is that you care and can genuinely say you're concerned about her. If you *don't* care, then someone else ought to do the confronting. Talk with your friend about how you honestly feel; don't just try to say words that sound right. It helps if you think about what you feel in relation to her and speak from those feelings, using the word "I." For example, saying "I'm worried about you" is more effective than saying "You need help." While people can disagree with what you say about them, they can't really disagree with what you feel. Include specific examples of why you're worried. It's also more constructive to comment on how your friend appears emotionally—sad or anxious—rather than how she appears physically—skinny or healthy.[23]

Confrontation doesn't always mean talking directly to a friend about your concerns. Be tuned in to things she says during regular conversations. Your friend may mention that she's sick and tired of the way people in the hall gossip about one another, that she's not enjoying college as she had expected she would, or that she's angry at her roommate. You can respond to those feelings and see where the conversation goes. Some of what she's feeling may be related to the eating disorder or to the feelings underlying it. This can give you the opportunity to talk, and perhaps to suggest professional counseling. If she's hesitant, offer to help her make the appointment or even to walk over with her for the first session.

Sometimes a friend *will* get angry with you for bringing up what she's been trying to hide. Usually, however, the reason you know about it is that she hasn't been able to hide it as well as she thought. Perhaps she'll tell you to mind your own business or deny that there's a problem. Then again, she may hear you but not be comfortable acknowledging her problem. It could take several confrontations, coming from different people and adding up over time, to get your friend to finally recognize her problem. If you're one of the first people to say something, don't expect immediate results. What you have said, however, may become one piece of a puzzle. When enough pieces get added to the puzzle, it becomes harder for your friend to keep denying the problem, and perhaps she'll finally do something about it. The process of healing and recovery takes time. Your support and acceptance can be very important. It's also important to know when to "back off." Becoming overinvolved in your friend's situation can perpetuate struggles over independence that underlie many eating disorders.

You aren't a professional counselor or therapist. Recognize your limits—how much of your time, caring, and energy you can give to your friend. If you're finding that your efforts to help her are getting in the way of you living your life and doing your school work, then you are allowing her needs to come before your own. Even though women are often taught to value this quality, it's not always healthy. Set limits on what you give; that's not the same thing as rejecting someone, just as confronting someone doesn't mean you hate her. Both can be done with care and respect.

WHERE TO LOOK FOR HELP

· · ·

"Going away to college was especially hard for me because in my recovery from anorexia I was trying to learn to eat spontaneously again—this wasn't possible. I had a one-hour time slot in which I could eat, hungry or not. Other times of the day I would get starved. I had to decide whether I would stuff myself (which never felt comfortable) in order to insure that I could make it until the next meal or eat whatever amount felt best for me at the time and then carry around trail mix or fruit for later. I found the latter to work really well. I felt comfortable at meals and also had munchies for when I got hungry in between meals."

—H. J., class of '93

. . .

There are a variety of strategies, like the one developed by H. J., that you might use to become more comfortable with your situation at college. Your food services staff can also be of help to you. Perhaps they'll provide nutritional information about food served at each meal so you can make more healthy choices and decisions. If you're an athlete or a dancer, some members of the physical education faculty or staff could work with you on diet, exercise, and physical conditioning. Athletic trainers in particular are good contacts.

It's important to consider the physical effects an eating disorder can have, and health service staff are valuable resources in this regard, even if you're not yet ready to talk directly or are more worried about someone else than about yourself. The Health Service may have staff with expertise in nutrition and diet. Some health services also offer educational programs about eating disorders. Attending these programs can be a good way to identify particular staff members interested in the issue.

If you visit your campus health service or any physician for other matters, it's important for you to be completely honest. Some prescribed medications can be dangerous to take if you're also binging and purging.[24]

Since eating disorders involve both physical and emotional factors, counseling resources are also important. You may be able to manage your treatment on campus by working with both health and counseling services. If more extensive treatment is necessary, consider programs offering specific treatment for eating disorders. Some hospitals have out-patient programs and also designated in-patient units for those with eating disorders. There are also a number of specialized residential treatment facilities around the country.

As discussed earlier, family relationships play a key role in the development of eating disorders. Therefore it's equally important that family relationships be addressed as part of the treatment. A counselor may work with you to help you understand and deal more constructively with your family situation. Perhaps family therapy is available to you all at home, or your parents and siblings could seek their own professional assistance there while you're doing the same at college. Therapy groups and support groups for those with eating disorders and other groups for their family and friends can be valuable sources of help.

Another resource to look for on campus is a peer support network or group. These provide an opportunity to talk with others who have "been there." There may be formal or informal networks of students who are in recovery. Sometimes peer support groups offer educational programs or have a hotline or phone number that can be called for information or support. Check bulletin boards and the campus newspaper, or contact your residence hall staff, women's center, or health and counseling services.

■ ■ ■

"As I looked back, I realized how often I had overlooked my own needs—once I started addressing them, my life began to change. My interest in holistic health blossomed, and I saw myself as a whole person rather than just as a body. I still catch myself on occasion complaining about my thighs or eating more when under stress, and I know that the obsessive-compulsive behavior may always be part of me (though that part gets smaller and smaller). But I now have (and began to have when the Task Force was formed) a clearer perspective, and I allow myself to be human."

—O. L., class of '89

■ ■ ■

EDUCATING YOURSELF

Books: Nonfiction, Anthologies, Biographies, Poetry, Plays

Boskind-White, Madeline, and William C. White. *Bulimarexia: The Binge/Purge Cycle*. 2d ed. New York: Norton, 1987.

Bruch, Hilde. *The Golden Cage: The Enigma of Anorexia Nervosa*. New York: Vintage, 1979.

Brumberg, Joan Jacobs. *Fasting Girls: The Surprising History of Anorexia Nervosa*. New York: Plume, 1989.

Chernin, Kim. *The Obsession: Reflections on the Tyranny of Slenderness*. New York: HarperPerennial, 1982.

———. *The Hungry Self: Women, Eating, and Identity*. New York: HarperPerennial, 1986.

Hall, Lindsey, and Leigh Cohn. *Bulimia: A Guide to Recovery: Understanding and Overcoming the Binge-Purge Syndrome.* Carlsbad, CA: Gurze, 1986.

Kano, Susan. *Making Peace with Food: Freeing Yourself from the Diet-Weight Obsession.* Rev. ed. New York: HarperPerennial, 1989.

Kinoy, Barbara, and Estelle B. Miller, eds. *When Will We Laugh Again? Living and Dealing with Anorexia Nervosa and Bulimia.* New York: Columbia University Press, 1984.

McFarland, Barbara, and Tyeis Baker-Baumann. *Shame and Body Image: Culture and the Compulsive Eater.* Deerfield Beach, FL: Health Communications, 1990.

Miller, Caroline. *My Name is Caroline.* Carlsbad, CA: Gurze, 1991.

O'Neill, Cherry. *Starving for Attention.* New York: Dell, 1983.

Orbach, Susie. *Fat Is a Feminist Issue: A Self-Help Guide for Compulsive Eaters.* New York: Berkley Publishing Group, 1982.

———. *Fat Is a Feminist Issue, II: The Anti-Diet Guide to Permanent Weight Loss.* New York: Berkley Publishing Group, 1987.

Robertson, Matra. *Starving in the Silences: An Explanation of Anorexia Nervosa.* New York: New York University Press, 1992.

Roth, Geneen. *Feeding the Hungry Heart: The Experience of Compulsive Eating.* New York: Signet, 1989.

Sherman, Roberta Trattner, and Ron A. Thompson. *Bulimia: A Guide for Family and Friends.* Lexington, MA: Lexington Books, 1990.

Siegel, Michele, Judith Brisman, and Margot Weinshel. *Surviving an Eating Disorder: New Perspectives and Strategies for Family and Friends.* New York: HarperPerennial, 1988.

Stein, Patricia M., and Barbara C. Unell. *Anorexia Nervosa: Finding the Lifeline.* Minneapolis: CompCare, 1986.

Novels

Levenkron, Steven. *The Best Little Girl in the World.* New York: Warner, 1991.

Organizations for Information and Assistance

American Anorexia/Bulimia Association
    418 East 76th St.
    New York, NY 10021
    212-734-1114

Anorexia Nervosa and Related Eating Disorders
    P.O. Box 5102
    Eugene, OR 97405
    503-344-1144

National Association of Anorexia Nervosa and Associated Eating Disorders
    Box 7
    Highland Park, IL 60035
    708-831-3438

Overeaters Anonymous
   P.O. Box 92870
   Los Angeles, CA 90009
   213-618-8835
   (See also local chapters in the phone book.)

Hotlines

Food Addiction Hotline: 1-800-872-0088

Films, Videos, TV Shows, Plays

Foodfright. Video of musical cabaret-style stage performance that toured the
   country.
Karen Carpenter Story. Chronicles the life and death of pop singer Karen Carpenter. Made-for-TV movie.
(See also listings in chapter 17.)

■ SIX ■

Alcohol and Drugs

It's the first week of classes. New student orientation is an exciting and exhausting memory. Two seniors down the hall welcome all the first-years to the floor by sharing a couple of six packs of beer. You have a great time and stay up talking until 2 A.M. The seniors tell you there'll always be a cold six pack available in their refrigerator.

T.G.I.F.—thank God it's Friday—and everyone seems to be celebrating. You've got a lab report due on Monday and three hundred pages to read in a history book as thick as the Manhattan Yellow Pages. You're feeling a little anxious about all the work you've been assigned so far. There's a keg in the second floor bathtub, and people are walking around the halls with cups of beer, stopping into open rooms to say hi. One group is playing quarters and doing shots of tequila. What sounds like an earthquake downstairs is only a hot and heavy game of indoor hockey. The shrieks from the lounge come from a group playing *Pictionary*, but the people watching TV and eating popcorn seem oblivious to the noise. What do you feel like doing?

You and your roommate go to a fraternity party Saturday night. It's loud and crowded. Your roommate seems to be having a good time, but you're not feeling too comfortable. Do you take a deep breath and go over to talk to a guy you recognize from Spanish class? Do you take a cup of the spiked punch and hope it relaxes you a bit? Are you wondering what else is going on around campus tonight? If you decide to leave, what about your roommate? You'd agreed to keep an eye on one another at the party. You check with her and she says a couple of other women from the hall are also there and she'll be fine if you leave. What do you do?

You're missing some of your friends from home when a few sophomores upstairs invite you in to watch videos. Someone starts to pass around a joint. Do you take a toke? Do you just pass it along? Or do you say goodnight, head back to your room, and maybe call a friend from home?

Looking around the dining hall at Sunday brunch, you see all kinds of people. Your next-door neighbor mentions that her boyfriend knows people who know people who can get some really good coke if anyone wants it. One or two people are interested, others say "no thanks." One woman wonders what the big deal is; besides, she prefers Pepsi. You see some students who were drinking and having fun last night now on their way to the library to study. There's one woman who keeps asking if she had a good time at the party—she can't remember.

Alcohol use is illegal for those under the age of twenty-one, and college campuses are not above the laws governing underage drinking and use of illegal drugs. To some students, however, the idea of going to college includes images of partying all night, easy access to drugs, and free-flowing alcohol. That's what you see in films like *Animal House*; it's what you sometimes hear from more experienced students. Drinking is often glamorized and assumed to be part of the road to popularity. Some students can't drink safely, and others prefer not to drink at all. At college, you'll have many choices to make about when, where, how, why, and especially whether to drink or use other drugs. Know the facts and the possible risks, and understand yourself as you make these choices.

. . .

"If you are going to drink, then be a responsible drinker. Know your limits, and also take care of yourself and friends. It can be scary to find yourself lying somewhere unfamiliar and you don't know how you got there."

—Student, class of '91

. . .

Terminology

Drugs include prescription medication, over-the-counter drugs, caffeine, cigarettes, alcohol, and illegal substances. *Stimulants,* including amphetamines, cocaine, and nicotine, speed up bodily functions such as heart rate and respiration and can cause heart damage. Stimulants are sometimes used by students to stay up studying, and amphetamines are occasionally prescribed as part of weight-loss programs. *Hallucinogenic drugs,* such as LSD and mescaline, alter perceptions and can result in recurring psychological effects. *Depressants* slow down the work of the central nervous system. In addition to alcohol, which is considered to be the drug of choice on college campuses today, other depressants include barbiturates, tranquilizers, and pain killers. These drugs are sometimes legally prescribed. *Narcotics* such as heroin, morphine, opium, and codeine are strong pain killers and also have depressant effects on the body. They create dependencies quickly.[1]

It's helpful to distinguish between more responsible drinking patterns and those that can lead to problems. Some students drink at parties or when they're out with friends or hoping to meet people. *Social drinkers* are able to drink more than one or two drinks without becoming drunk. Responsible drinkers, they can go for long periods of time without drinking at all. Other individuals may drink as much, or less, but will drink to the point of intoxication. They lose control, pass out, or act irresponsibly or even dangerously.[2]

Heavy drinkers drink regularly, even daily, and alcohol is an important part of their lives. What makes heavy drinkers different from alcoholics is that they don't develop a tolerance for alcohol, don't feel withdrawal symptoms when they stop, and can remain at the same level of consumption for many years. Heavy drinkers can decide to stop for a period without severe discomfort. For the heavy drinker, drinking is a pleasure rather than a necessity.[3]

When use of alcohol, or any other drug, interferes with life activities—physical condition, social relationships, emotional health, academic performance—then use has become abuse.[4] Of the students who use alcohol or drugs at college, a significant number develop serious abuse and dependency problems.[5] Those who are dependent on a substance are afraid to be without it. If confronted, they may deny that they're using it, downplay the seriousness of their dependence and refuse to quit, or be unable to quit even if they try. As *alcoholism* or a *chemical dependency* develops, the individual needs to use more and more of the substance to feel good or to achieve the same results.[6] She'll continue to use the substance even though bad things happen as a result.

■ ■ ■

"I think that in the 'addicted' stage of drug abuse, the emotional and psychological dependency on the drug far outweighs the physical dependency. It is not only necessary to abstain from taking that drug, it's also necessary to change the behavior pattern and lifestyle—perhaps resolve issues that might incite you to take the drug."

—M. L., class of '92

■ ■ ■

Background Information

Although the use of illegal drugs has declined somewhat over the last ten years, substance use and abuse, especially of alcohol, remains a problem on college campuses. Over 40 percent of college students surveyed in 1991 said they had tried marijuana, almost 10 percent had tried LSD, and a similar percentage had tried cocaine. Approximately 4 percent of those surveyed drank daily. Heavy drinking—five or more drinks in a row—has remained at the same level as it was ten years ago.[7] Another recent finding is that college students who drink alcohol today are more likely to "binge"—drink to get drunk—than college students ten to fifteen years ago.[8] A 1993 story on the television program "20/20" reported on this phenomenon, described by partying college students as "drink till you puke." What this attitude fails to recognize is that too much alcohol consumed too quickly can lead to alcohol poisoning when the liver cannot process it out fast enough, and breathing becomes dangerously depressed. Every year approximately a dozen college students die this way.[9]

Any situation where you drink more alcohol than your body can metabolize is considered alcohol abuse.[10] How much you weigh, how quickly you drink, what you drink, and how you're feeling in general all contribute to the effect alcohol can have on you. When there's a low level of alcohol in your bloodstream, you may feel stimulated, confident, less inhibited, and more sociable. As you drink more, however, the depressant effects slow down activity and can impair your ability to think, make judgments, and perform motor functions such as driving a car. Some individuals are more susceptible to alcohol addiction based on hereditary or physical or genetic factors.[11]

The physiological effects of other drugs are often complicated by the fact that their strength and purity vary greatly. Often someone smoking pot, for instance, can't be sure exactly what she's smoking and what the effects will be.[12]

Alcohol generally has a stronger physiological effect on women than on men because women seem to metabolize alcohol more slowly. Women have a lower percentage of total body water, and body water serves to dilute alcohol. So a woman of the same weight as a man, who drinks the same amount of alcohol, will have a higher concentration of alcohol in her bloodstream. Women develop liver disease more quickly and with less alcohol consumption than men. There is also a correlation between alcohol abuse and rates of ob/gyn problems, including fetal alcohol syndrome and other birth defects.[13]

Consider that

- between one-third and one-half of the alcoholics in the United States are women.[14]
- the number of young female drinkers is increasing faster than the number of young male drinkers.[15]
- the incidence of alcoholism among divorced women is much greater than in the general population.[16]
- one in four lesbians is an alcoholic.[17]
- women more frequently abuse prescription drugs, such as tranquilizers, which physicians more often prescribe for them than for men with similar symptoms.[18]

When substance use turns to abuse, women and men are often judged by a double standard. Aggressive, out-of-control, uninhibited behavior in a male may be accepted or even seen as funny. The same behavior in a woman can lead to gossip, embarrassment, and isolation. Women are often pushed, in this way, into more private and isolated drinking habits.[19]

. . .

"In my position as a student health educator on alcohol, I see women who have experienced many problems because of alcohol yet nobody ever confronted them. They needed to hit bottom and ask for help themselves. The behavior of a chemically dependent male is generally more visible and noticeable than a woman's behavior."

—L. M., class of '93

. . .

While substance abuse is a major problem for women, they are less likely to seek help and treatment for themselves.[20] Part of this reluctance is attributable to society's expectations that women should take care of others first. Also, most treatment programs are still designed for, and dominated by, men. Women need programs that focus on their specific needs.[21]

The use of alcohol or drugs affects the ability to think clearly and make good judgments. This can leave women especially vulnerable in sexual situations. Alcohol and drug use may dull some of your important internal warning signals. You may be less careful, for example, in situations where someone gives you more alcohol after you've said no, or keeps touching you more intimately than you'd like. It's often not easy to discuss your needs directly in a sexual situation. Alcohol can make this process even more difficult and may affect your decision-making abilities. This could lead to unprotected and unsafe sex.

Alcohol abuse can also result in unwanted sex. One partner may not be able to clearly communicate no; the other may not be able to hear or understand that no. The abuse of alcohol contributes to the incidence of acquaintance rape.[22] Imagine being somewhere, drinking, and not remembering anything until you wake up in a place you don't know, with a person you don't want to be with, doing something you don't want to do.

ENCOUNTERING AND RESPONDING TO THIS ISSUE

The majority of students on most college campuses are below the legal drinking age of twenty-one. Living and drinking on a college campus does *not* mean that you're protected from the law. At some schools staff "write up" students for violating college, state, and federal alcohol policies and laws. In addition to an educational response such as referral to counseling or to an alcohol awareness program, there may be a disciplinary response from the school as well. Furthermore, staff and student leaders can be held accountable for students' violations of the law. In 1988, for example, two student officers at one of Princeton University's eating clubs were held legally responsible for not intervening at a party during which forty-five students, many of them underage, suffered alcohol-induced medical problems. The club officers, one male student and one female student, were sentenced to thirty days in jail and fined five hundred dollars each.[23]

When colleges prefer that students learn to make their own intelligent choices and decisions, their policies stress alcohol and drug education and student responsibility. These schools are less likely to see themselves as agents of law enforcement but will act when necessary. They'll respect your right to make your own decisions but will intervene if there are signs of substance abuse, blatant illegal use, distribution, or danger to yourself or others.

In any case, you are responsible for your decisions about drinking. You may choose not to drink at all or perhaps to drink in moderation. You are also responsible for your behavior. Being drunk, high, or under the influence is not an excuse for your actions. Most often, the choices you make in the privacy of your own residence hall room will be your own business. Sometimes your private business becomes more public. You may be drinking in your room with friends and making noise that disturbs others, your behavior may cause damage or complaints, or you may be depressed and regularly sleep through your classes.

If you choose to drink, the following suggestions may help you drink responsibly:[24]

1. Know your general limit. Be aware that the effects of alcohol may vary at different times, so listen to your own body's signals to tell you when you've had enough.

2. If you're going somewhere where you have to pay for drinks, take a limited amount of money.
3. Drink only when you really want to, not simply to get drunk.
4. Eat something before or while you drink. High-protein foods are especially good.
5. Be careful about unfamiliar drinks.
6. Use mixers with alcohol. Juice or water are better than carbonated beverages such as soda.
7. Don't play drinking games and don't encourage others to do so.
8. Try to pace your drinks slowly.

Nearly one-third of all college students experience some difficulty as a result of drinking during the academic year.[25] Some of these difficulties cause personal pain—loss of friends and problems getting along with others, problems with concentration or memory, academic difficulties, unwanted sexual activity, suicide gestures or attempts. Others can lead to behavior requiring legal or disciplinary action—driving under the influence, vandalism, personal accidents or injuries, fights, assaults, violence toward others.[26]

How do you know when to be concerned? What are some of the signs that you have a substance-abuse problem? Alcohol and substance abuse is progressive. It won't just go away; it will get worse. The following questions, asked about yourself or others, may help you recognize when substance use may be moving toward abuse:[27]

1. Has the drinking or drug use become more solitary than social?
2. Has it become more regular?
3. Does it take place during academically important times such as scheduled classes and exams?
4. Is it done to relieve a problem, to feel "normal," or to do better at something, such as academics or sports?
5. Is just one drink/joint/hit never enough?
6. Is too much money being spent on drugs or alcohol?
7. Is it rare for days or weeks to go by with no use of alcohol or drugs, and no thoughts of them?
8. Are there blackouts—not remembering what happened during a period under the influence?
9. Have there been alcohol- or drug-related accidents, arrests, fights, sicknesses?

Relationships are also affected by substance abuse, particularly if one person in a relationship recognizes a problem and the other doesn't. A variety of feelings may surface and create pain between family members, roommates, close friends, and boyfriends/girlfriends. Anger at the disease can mix with the love that exists. One person may be ashamed of the other's behavior and her own inability to do anything about it. Behavior under the influence is often unpredictable, and it can be scary to wonder what will happen next. If one person wants desperately to help the other and can't, she may feel powerless and guilty. If important relationships are being affected because of alcohol or drugs, that's another sign that there's a problem.

If you are concerned about your own drinking or drug-related behavior, take some steps to look at your situation. One particular self-monitoring technique has been used by Ann Schmidt, a substance-abuse counselor at Yale University.[28] This process can help you define your substance-use patterns and determine how much control you have over them. Keep a written record of where, what, and how much you drink; whether there were any consequences associated with the drinking; and how you felt each time. If you have questions about your own alcohol or drug use, work with an R.A., residence staff member, health educator, or counselor to consider some changes. If necessary, set limits on your future drinking and make decisions about reasonable and safe drinking practices for yourself. Students who are dependent on alcohol tend to have trouble keeping to set limits. If this is the case, consider not drinking at all.

For Those with Substance-Abuse Problems

. . .

"I found that marijuana and drugs like acid (LSD) and mushrooms (but especially pot) are as socially acceptable as alcohol at my college. While some may argue that pot is not addictive, I found an overwhelming number of people who are extremely dependent on pot. By this I mean that they are either constantly high or in search of getting high."

—M. L., class of '92

. . .

Approximately half of the students with substance-abuse problems at college arrive on campus with them.[29] If you are one of these students, you may already be in recovery, having begun to take steps to help yourself before going to college. Others of you may not yet be aware that you have a problem. If you have an alcoholic parent, you're up to four times more likely to develop a drinking problem.[30] The friends with whom you spent time before coming to college were also a source of influence on your style of substance use, abuse, or abstinence. You're entering an environment where there's a higher incidence of alcohol use than in the general population.[31] This move may expose you to temptation; it will also, however, provide an opportunity for you to change some old habits.

You need to feel unpressured and relatively comfortable in your living situation. The Housing Office can tell you if any residence halls or floors are designated as substance free; there seem to be more of these options being created every year. Certainly other students with whom you live need to be understanding if you want to limit substance use in your room. There may be a place on your original housing form to request a nondrinking roommate. I've seen these kinds of requests increase over the years and urge you to ask for what will be best for you.

If you find yourself in a living situation where the alcohol or drug use is not healthy for you, say something to your roommate or hallmates. They may be more than willing to adapt. If a reasonable compromise can't be worked out, talk with the professional housing staff. Find out if there are other living options available for you, and be honest about the kind of environment you need.

Try also to spend time with people who participate in activities that are enjoyable without being centered around alcohol. Some parties and activities may be clearly advertised as substance free. Organizations or events publicized with alcohol-related slogans or posters are obviously not the best choices. While hazing is not officially sanctioned on college campuses, some informal initiation traditions still involve alcohol. You may choose to avoid some of these situations and to attend others knowing what to expect and being prepared to take care of your needs. Overall, it can be fun to attend *any* event in the company of people who are not focused on alcohol and will respect your right to set limits on your drinking or to abstain.

■ ■ ■

"First year and rookie athletes do participate in heavy drinking initiations. None of this drinking is forced, and everybody has the right to refuse (and some do), but I am so concerned about those students who are not sure if they want to drink, but do because of lack of self-esteem, confidence, and their need to fit in. These are the ones that are subtly forced to drink."

—L. M., class of '93

. . .

For Friends of Those with Substance-Abuse Problems

. . .

"People assume I can't handle anything to do with alcohol and so they don't invite me to parties. They shut up if they're talking about alcohol and I come into the room. They assume I don't have fun because I don't drink and that's *very* far from the truth."

—Student, class of '90

. . .

If you live closely with other students, you may find some who have already identified themselves as alcoholics or substance abusers and are in recovery. You can support them in their efforts and help to shape the environment around them. The assumption on many college campuses is that everyone drinks, and drinking is fun for everyone. That's not necessarily true. This assumption creates uncomfortable situations for people who want or need *not* to drink. You can help by challenging this assumption, serving nonalcoholic beverages as well as alcohol, and organizing ways to have fun that don't focus on alcohol. Some terrific parties have great music and no alcohol. Questioning traditions that are alcohol-centered may be difficult for you, but others will appreciate those questions being raised. If you're present when *anyone* is being pressured to drink or teased for not drinking, support that person's right to say no.

The more you learn about substance abuse and the recovery process, the better you can understand what friends may need from you. While you can support and encourage your friends in their recovery, you are not responsible for them. *Ask* how you can help rather than totally taking charge of the situation. Even the same person may prefer different treatment at different times.

. . .

"I need patience from others in my recovery. Sometimes it's OK for me to be with people who are drinking and other times it's not. My recovery process isn't static."

—G. S., class of '93

. . .

Women are generally socialized to care about others and keep them from being hurt. With substance abusers, however, this kind of help often has the opposite effect. You *enable* substance abusers when you wittingly or unwittingly act in ways that protect them from the consequences of their behavior.[32] If a person never feels the negative results of what she does, she'll have little reason to change. Some common ways students enable friends to continue abusing alcohol or drugs include

1. waking them so they don't miss classes.
2. making excuses for them when they're absent or late to class, sports practice, rehearsal, etc.
3. giving them notes for classes they miss due to the effects of alcohol or drug use.
4. taking care of them, putting them to bed, and cleaning up after them when they're sick as a result of alcohol or drugs.
5. making excuses for them with hallmates who may be annoyed with their behavior.
6. substituting for them at work when they're too drunk or hungover to go.
7. supporting their excuses for why they drink or use drugs excessively.
8. lying to protect them when college security or the administration responds to incidents where alcohol was involved.

It's not easy to stop doing these things for someone you care about, but you're not really helping by protecting her. In these situations, tell your friend what you're no longer willing to do for her *and why.* Explaining could help you feel better about saying things that are hard to say. Sometimes the person will hear it, and other times she won't. In the long run it's the best action you can take for both of you, even though it may hurt you both at the time.

. . .

"Most of my friends are heavy pot smokers, and when they are stoned, it is almost impossible to motivate them to do anything or to relate to their experiences. This is frustrating for you and it can infringe on your time, academics, social life, etc. I've had friends who were too stoned to deal with whatever the situation called for. It's hard to intervene in this situation. I think the only way really is to express those concerns to your friends, and force them to modify their behavior around you or important events or refuse to deal with them in their state. They are really the only ones that can change their behavior."

—M. L., class of '92

. . .

There may be times when you're so concerned about someone that you want to *do something*. First, ask yourself what you want to accomplish. Perhaps you simply want to be heard by your friend. She may be more likely to listen if you don't ask her to actually change anything right away. Try passing along your concerns about what she seems to be doing and what may happen as a result. Whether or not your friend chooses to look at or change her behavior is up to her.

Intervening

You may, however, want to go a step further and interrupt a friend's pattern to get her to stop using alcohol or drugs. This process is called an intervention. It should be well planned and carefully organized, and you should consult with a professional before attempting a formal intervention in order to practice what you want to say and how to say it. Remember too that changes don't happen overnight. The basic principles of intervention are adapted in the paragraphs that follow for less formal efforts to help a friend.[33]

Don't talk to your friend until you feel ready to. Also, before confronting your friend, learn as much as you can about alcohol and chemical dependency and identify specific resources available for your friend. If you're presently trying to change her behavior by either punishing her or protecting her, stop.

Plan to confront your friend with at least one other person who is close to her and who has also directly seen her behavior when she has been under the influence. It's harder for several people to be ignored. Prepare clear and specific information about incidents related to her substance abuse that have been of concern to you. Focus on situations you have each directly observed.

Meet with your friend in a private place and at a time when she has not been drinking. It's important that your approach be based on genuine caring for your friend and that you express that caring often. Avoid expressing anger, frustration, and criticism. Describe the incidents and how her behavior makes you feel. Present your information calmly, clearly, and objectively. You may want to talk about the consequences you feel further drinking will have for her health, life, and relationship with you. Expect some denial, anger, and tears. Think beforehand about how these emotions from this friend are likely to affect you and consider the most effective ways you can respond.

Offer a variety of on-campus and community resources for her to consult. Suggest she make a commitment to seek out one or more of the resources. If she is unwilling to do so, try to get her to agree that she will if there is another incidence of abusive drinking behavior. Recognize your limits. Regardless of the results, know that you have done the best you can do. Leave the door open for further talk; some people need time to think about what has been said before being able to consider it seriously.

Take time afterward to talk again with a staff member or counselor about how *you* are doing. Continue to use support resources for yourself as needed. In the days that follow, talk with your friend about a variety of other things; there's much more to her than just a substance-abuse problem.

WHERE TO LOOK FOR HELP

Understand your college's alcohol and drug policy and how it's implemented. If the focus is on help and education, an R.A. who lives on the hall can be a particularly good source of information, referrals, and support. Knowledge of illegal behavior may put some R.A.s in the position of having to respond as a staff member. If you don't want that to take place yet, try talking to them hypothetically (e.g., "What if . . . "). You may be able to get information, suggestions, and advice without compromising the R.A.'s responsibilities. If there are professional residence hall directors, they can bring additional experience and expertise to the situation. Don't assume that residence staff are to be feared; most often they're there to help.

Distributing or selling drugs is illegal and dangerous. Becoming known as a source of good drugs can be a dubious and risky title to hold. That reputation can quickly make its way through the campus. It may also be heard by those in the administration and security, or law enforcement officers from off campus. Dealers can generate negative attention that extends to minor users and those living in the same room or around them.

If you're involved in drug distribution, stop. If your friend or roommate is, you can be in a difficult position. One first step is to talk honestly with your roommate. Tell her how you feel and why you're uncomfortable with what's going on. She may not be aware of all the risks or of the fact that her activity is as widely known as it is. She may agree to make some changes. If not, decide what you can do to protect yourself. Consider moving to another room or residence hall; think about whether to talk to someone on the staff. Your R.A. or hall director could help you handle the situation or may be able to respond to it without directly involving you.

Once they are aware of drug dealing on campus, college staff need to respond. If there's sufficient evidence, disciplinary responses could include a warning, college judicial action, forced removal from the residence halls, suspension, or even expulsion. When there are rumors rather than hard facts, or when the students who know what's going on are unwilling to make an official statement, staff may respond in other ways.

Counselors and physicians are bound by an expectation of confidentiality. This allows them to hear information without having to act in a disciplinary way for the college. Perhaps you can talk more freely in these situations. If you're particularly worried about a friend's physical well-being, encourage her to see someone at the Health Service. If you're concerned about yourself, try to find a medical practitioner you can trust. The more honest you are with medical personnel, the more help they can be to you.

Health educators and substance-abuse counselors are particularly helpful if you're looking for resources or are preparing to confront a friend. They may also know of peer counseling groups or networks of students in recovery who reach out to others with abuse problems.

Many colleges sponsor educational programs, lectures, and films about issues of alcohol and drug abuse. There may be an alcohol/drug awareness day or week scheduled during the academic year. Perhaps your campus has a chapter of BACCHUS, a national program for alcohol awareness and education. These programs offer one way to expand your knowledge. If you attend with friends, this can break the ice and provide an opportunity for you all to talk about the issue.

Groups such as Alcoholics Anonymous (A.A.), Narcotics Anonymous (N.A.), Cocaine Anonymous (C.A.), and Al-Anon (for family and friends) provide positive role models, practical advice, and a social network of people who understand. If meetings are held on your campus, that information will probably be listed in your school newspaper and will be available through your R.A. and the health and counseling services. Off-campus meetings are usually listed in local newspapers, or you can check the phone book and call to request information about meetings in your area.

Some students resist the "higher power" concept central to these twelve-step programs, feeling it's too religious. Be aware that "higher power" doesn't necessarily have to be God. It can be anything outside of you, such as a parent, boyfriend/girlfriend, team, tradition, or symbol.[34]

Attending a meeting for the first time can be scary, especially if you tend to feel uncomfortable in groups. Talk to someone who already attends so you'll know what to expect. This person may offer to take you to a meeting. If a group is not designated as "closed," a friend who is not an alcoholic can accompany you. Some meetings are also specifically designated as beginners' meetings, for women only, or for gay men and lesbians. Twelve-step programs are effective for some individuals and not for others, but they provide one definite alternative to consider.

■ ■ ■

"There is no cure . . . it's like my medicine. I keep going to meetings; it's part of my life."

—Student, class of '90

■ ■ ■

EDUCATING YOURSELF

Books: Nonfiction, Anthologies, Biographies, Poetry, Plays

Allen, Chaney. *I'm Black and I'm Sober.* Minneapolis: CompCare, 1978.

Cocores, James. *The 800-Cocaine Book of Drug and Alcohol Recovery.* New York: Villard, 1990.

Ford, Betty, with Chris Chase. *Betty: A Glad Awakening.* New York: Jove, 1988.

Gordon, Barbara. *I'm Dancing as Fast as I Can.* New York: HarperPerennial, 1989.

Hafner, Sarah. *Nice Girls Don't Drink: Stories of Recovery.* New York: Bergin and Garvey, 1992.
Johnson, Vernon E. *Intervention: How to Help Someone Who Doesn't Want Help.* Minneapolis: Johnson Institute, 1986.
Marshall, Shelly, ed. *Young, Sober, and Free.* New York: Hazeldon Educational Materials, 1987.
Mooney, Al J., Arlene Eisenberg, and Howard Eisenberg. *The Recovery Book.* New York: Workman, 1992.
Peluso, Emanuel, and Lucy Silvay Peluso. *Women and Drugs: Getting Hooked, Getting Clean.* Minneapolis: CompCare, 1988.
Swallow, Jean. *Out from Under: Sober Dykes and Our Friends.* San Francisco: Spinsters/Aunt Lute Books, 1983.
Wholey, Dennis. *The Courage to Change.* New York: Warner, 1988.
Yoder, Barbara. *The Recovery Resource Book.* New York: Fireside, 1990.

Novels

Anonymous. *Go Ask Alice.* New York: Simon and Schuster, 1971.

Articles, Pamphlets, and Papers

American College Health Association. "How to Help a Friend with a Drinking Problem." Rockville, MD: American College Health Association, 1984.
Matthews, Anne. "The Campus Crime Wave." *New York Times Magazine,* March 7, 1993.
Steele, Donald W. "Managing Alcohol in Your Life." Mansfield, PA: Steele Publishing, 1986.

Organizations for Information and Assistance

Al-Anon
1-800-344-2666
Alcoholics Anonymous World Services
475 Riverside Dr.
New York, NY 10015
212-870-3400
(or consult your local telephone book)
American Council for Drug Education
204 Monroe St.
Suite 110
Rockville, MD 20850
301-294-0600
Cocaine Anonymous
3740 Overland Ave.
Suite G

Los Angeles, CA 90034
1-800-347-8998
Narcotics Anonymous
1-800-662-4357
National Black Alcoholism Council
1629 K St. NW, Suite 802
Washington, DC 20006
202-296-2696
National Clearinghouse for Drug and Alcohol Information
1-800-729-6686
National Council on Alcoholism and Drug Dependence
12 West 21st St.
New York, NY 10010
1-800-NCA-CALL
Women for Sobriety
Box 618
Quakertown, PA 18951
215-536-8026

Hotlines

Alcohol 24-Hour Hotline   1-800-821-HELP
Cocaine 24-Hour Hotline   1-800-COCAINE
Drug 24-Hour Hotline   1-800-821-HELP

Films, Videos, TV Shows, Plays

The Broken Cord. A college professor adopts a child with fetal alcohol syndrome. Made-for-TV movie based on the book by Michael Dorris.

"Cagney and Lacey." Various episodes of TV series show Chris Cagney's alcohol addiction and recovery process.

Clean and Sober. A substance abuser is pushed to finally confront the problem. Depicts both institutionalized treatment and a twelve-step program.

Days of Wine and Roses. Alcoholism has a shattering impact on the lives of a couple. From the play by J. P. Miller.

"The John Larroquette Show." The night manager of a bus station struggles to maintain his new sobriety. TV series.

M.A.D.D.: Mothers against Drunk Driving. After her daughter is killed by a drunk driver, Candy Lightner creates a national organization to fight the problem. Made-for-TV movie based on a true story.

The Morning After. A chronically dependent woman is caught up in a murder.

"Murphy Brown." Comedy about a TV news reporter who is also in recovery. TV series.

Passion Fish. A woman in recovery from a drug problem pushes her employer to deal with her own alcohol dependency.

Sarah T.: Portrait of a Teenaged Alcoholic. A teenager battles a drinking problem. Made-for-TV movie.

SEVEN

Codependency

Heather is the president of the Debate Society. She has an elected executive board of five other students but still feels more comfortable doing all the work herself rather than trusting others to do any of it. Delayne is writing an honors thesis. She's also the captain of the swimming team, works ten hours a week in the dining hall, volunteers at a rape crisis hotline, and is determined to do a perfect job at everything. Mei-Lin is an R.A. She's convinced that she should be able to solve all the problems of all the students on her floor. Her R.A. job is becoming her life. Jeannie considers herself a wonderful friend. She's always trying to help her roommate and spends hours listening to her problems and trying to help her, even if it means Jeannie doesn't get her own work done or has to change her own social plans. "After all," Jeannie says, "my friends are the most important part of my life."

Do you know any of these people? *Are* you any of these people? Could you become one? Heather, Delayne, Mei-Lin, and Jeannie are demonstrating some of the traits that have been called codependent. The term "codependency" has perhaps been overused in the popular media and has sometimes become a target of jokes and parody. Regardless of what they're called, however, these behaviors and attitudes have a significant impact on people's lives.

Terminology

. . .

Q: What happens when a codependent dies?
A: Someone else's life flashes before their eyes.[1]

. . .

Most people show at least some codependent traits, and many codependent behaviors and beliefs can exist without disrupting lives and relationships in an obvious way. If codependent beliefs and behaviors become reflex ways of interacting rather than conscious choices, however, they can interfere in people's lives. *Codependency* is perhaps best defined by describing specific behaviors that characterize it. The questions that follow can help you identify the characteristics of a codependent lifestyle or pattern of relating to others.[2]

Are you so preoccupied with others that you neglect your own needs and feelings? Are you more concerned with their problems and social life than with your own? Do you always do what they want to do and go where they want to go? Do you live in someone else's shadow and get your identity from that person—are you Pat's girlfriend, Yvonne's roommate?[3]

Is your self-worth determined by how others see you? Do you try to be perfect and please others, regardless of what you want? Do you join a club, run for office, play a sport, or major in a subject when you don't really want to because it meets others' expectations? Do you question your own perceptions unless others confirm them? For example, will you wait to say that a party is boring until others say it first?[4]

Do you often become depressed or ill because of trying to control what can't be controlled, such as someone else's drinking or what other people think of you? Do you try almost too hard to help others? Have you been told you overdo the caring and kindness? Do you feel others' pain when they're hurt? Do you need to be involved in everything they do? Do you do things for them that they can, and should, do for themselves?[5]

. . .

Q: How many codependents does it take to screw in a lightbulb?
A: Never mind. I'll do it.[6]

. . .

The concept of codependence originated in the field of chemical dependency and the study of the families of alcoholics. More and more students seem to be identifying themselves as *adult children of alcoholics*.[7] In an alcoholic family, alcohol and alcohol-related behavior are the dominant issues to which family members react. Children of alcoholics often feel responsible for stopping their parents' behavior and protecting the family secret. Adult children of alcoholics usually have developed their codependent behaviors as a means of coping with, and surviving in, their family structure. Different roles may be assumed by children in an alcoholic family, and some of the roles can be combined and overlap at times. The *hero* is usually the oldest child. She takes over parental responsibilities, makes sure the house functions, and provides stability for younger siblings. In high school, these are the students who get high grades, are team captains, and chair committees. They feel responsible for everything, need to control, and can't relax or have fun. As adults, they often "burn out." The *scapegoat* is the problem child or angry troublemaker. She takes the blame for the family problems and thus diverts the focus from the real problem. She receives negative attention for her behavior. The *lost child* never causes any trouble and tends to almost disappear. She may do well academically but have few friends and be sad and alone most of the time. The *mascot* or *clown* acts as a tension reliever, distraction, and center of attention. She may find it hard to be taken seriously, and family members may not see how she really feels and who she really is.[8]

While the concept of codependence originated in the field of chemical dependency and treatment, the view of codependency has broadened considerably. These terms can apply to members of families that are dysfunctional for other reasons besides alcoholism.

Background Information

Codependency starts at home. It can develop in families in which one or more parents have any of a variety of addictive or compulsive behaviors involving alcohol, drugs, gambling, food, sex, power, work, spending money, etc.[9]

Ways that families relate and communicate also contribute to the development of codependent behaviors. In most families there's some foundation for the development of codependent behaviors. Did your family keep secrets and not talk about problems or painful experiences— your sister's expulsion from college, your mother's breast cancer, your brother's arrest for drunk driving, your father's losing his job? [10]

Were feelings not openly discussed in your family? Were you put down or made to feel ashamed for expressing anger, grief, fear, etc.? Was communication in your family indirect, including one person acting as a go-between or messenger for two others. For example, was it your mother who always told you that your father was proud of you, or was your brother the one to let you know that your sister was angry with you? [11]

Were you expected to be perfect in school and at everything you did? Were there strong expectations about the roles family members should play: mom is always right; women shouldn't be assertive; I'm the oldest, I'm supposed to be a lawyer like dad? [12]

Did your parents teach you to be helpless? Do they still take on responsibilities that you can handle for yourself, preventing you from developing your own skills—always doing your laundry for you, giving you unlimited money rather than enabling you to learn to budget or earn money on your own, or calling the college to complain and fight your battles for you? [13]

Any of these family tendencies may develop codependency. Furthermore, our society and institutions—the schools, churches, etc.—perpetuate many of the characteristics of codependency by teaching that they're desirable traits to have.[14] These characteristics resemble many of the ideals women are brought up to value—taking care of others, being unselfish, and deferring to others' needs and expectations.

ENCOUNTERING AND RESPONDING TO THIS ISSUE

When codependent behaviors become habits, they can limit the opportunities college offers. Codependent habits can keep you from developing healthy relationships, enjoying life, and feeling satisfied with yourself as a human being. Codependent habits are like bricks in your pockets as you try to fly. If you've become used to carrying these bricks, you may not even realize you have them. So check your pockets, *all* your pockets. Unloading the bricks at a comfortable rate can free you up to fly, if and when you're ready. Once you put aside the bricks, you'll have more choices than you've ever had before. And the choices will be yours to make.

Entering a college environment, particularly if you're going to be living on campus, will place you in a group situation that can feel like a new family. Each of you brings your own pattern of relating to others. What was a necessary way to relate at home can be less effective in this new environment.

For Adult Children of Alcoholics

. . .

"The recovery process really began for me in college. One of the things that I began to understand was that my parents' addictions were THE dominant forces in my life. I wish more people could understand that. People were forever asking me why I 'obsessed' about it so much. It wasn't that I was obsessing about it; it was just that I was beginning to see how key a role their addictions had played in my life and how who I was had been informed by it."

—H. F., class of '91

. . .

The move to college poses two general possibilities for the adult child of an alcoholic (ACOA). ACOAs may recreate their family patterns each time they go into new situations.[15] On the other hand, college can present an opportunity for ACOAs to recognize the survival skills they have learned and to change those that are no longer healthy.[16]

Changing habitual patterns of behavior is a complex task. Start by learning as much as you can about ACOAs and the impact of your own family situation on your present behavior. Don't be embarrassed to talk to a professional; it could be one of the most important steps you can take to create a better life for yourself.

Much of the work to be done is work you do within yourself. Keep your own written journal. Writing about the past may help you discover some codependent patterns in your relationships. Exercises such as identifying your own needs and listing feelings you do and don't express are other ways to generate information about yourself. If you feel uncomfortable talking to others, the written material from your journal can help you break the ice and share your feelings with a professional or peer support group. Some of the steps in the recovery process involve developing or relearning skills such as assertiveness, self-disclosure, and setting limits. Seek out training and workshop opportunities to develop these skills, preferably as they relate to codependent relationships.

Think about your choices of academic courses and extracurricular activities and avoid continuing codependent behaviors. The self-defeating need to be perfect may lead you to select an academic program in which you can "prove yourself." You may take extra credits, work excessively hard, and never feel like you've done well enough. Talk with your academic advisor about taking a reasonable and varied course load each semester, including at least one course that you expect to really enjoy. Many schools offer the option of taking some classes pass/fail or pass/no credit. This is one way to take some grading pressure off yourself. Also, avoid comparing yourself and your grades to others. This only perpetuates unrealistic expectations and feelings of "I should do better."

As you consider various extracurricular activities, take the time to look at their potential for drawing out your codependent behaviors. Some programs involve caretaking, such as volunteering at a local hospital, peer counseling, or tutoring. Other activities are major responsibilities such as stage managing a play or being president of a club. It may be best to postpone these kinds of activities until you're sure you can do the job while also taking good care of yourself.

One recent graduate talked about how lack of trust and fear of being abandoned are big issues for her as an adult child of an alcoholic. She described herself as having been abandoned by those most important to her (her parents) even when they *were* present, because "an alcoholic is never really there for anyone—they cannot be." If you, too, are a child of an alcoholic, these feelings can continue to interfere, throughout your life, with your ability to develop trusting intimate relationships. Perhaps the most important area for you to begin to reconstruct, then, is your pattern of relationships with others. Even though they may have been unhealthy and painful, your interaction patterns and your role in your family were familiar to you. When you move on to college, where most students find themselves without already established relationships, you might fill the void in some detrimental ways. You might continue your codependency by staying closely tied to your family and going home often. You might also develop friendships with people who have strong needs to be taken care of and thus evoke familiar codependent reactions from you.

Think about the opportunity you'll have to fill the void with more healthy relationships. It may initially feel awkward interacting in new ways, but make the effort. There are questions you can ask yourself to consider whether relationships with new acquaintances are likely to continue or change your codependent patterns. Go back to page 109 earlier in this chapter. Look at your new relationships in light of the questions listed there. If being with your new friends makes you feel like you did at home, keep looking for other friends.

. . .

"One pattern I see when I look back on my college friendships is that I developed a lot of close friendships with *very* 'stable' people. I think this served two connected purposes for me. It freed me from relationships where I was so distracted by 'saving/rescuing' the other that I didn't focus on myself so that I *could* begin to be my own caregiver. I was involved in 'healthy' relationships involving *give and take*. I actually leaned on these friends quite a bit—a whole new, almost foreign experience for me—and wonderful, both because of the wonderful sense of having people that could and would help me take care of me and because the quality of what I could give in return was so much improved, richer, *better*."

—H. F., class of '91

. . .

Your family situation will change in some ways as a result of your being away at college, but it can still affect you. You may be concerned about your parents and brothers and sisters at home. That could drain some of the energy you need to establish the necessary separation and adjustment to college.[17] The process of detaching yourself from your codependent relationship with your parents can be painful for all involved, but necessary for your survival. As you recognize that you can't assume responsibility for them, resetting your boundaries will change the delicate family balance. This can create some disruption and unhappiness at home. Remember that refusing to take responsibility for your parents any longer doesn't mean that you stop caring about them or are rejecting them. What it does mean is that you're no longer willing to enable them to continue with a self-destructive addiction. You can do this while still caring about them and taking steps to help them help themselves.

There will probably be some difficult times in the school year for you. Parents' Weekend or other visits by your family to campus can be a source of anxiety. There's the potential for an alcoholic parent to drink too much when your new friends are around. Not knowing what to expect can be stressful. Adult children of alcoholics may also feel anxiety about returning home for school vacations and holidays. Particularly if you're changing your patterns of responding, you may fear being pulled back into old habits. It can also be more difficult to work at detaching yourself when you're back living with your parents.

Some students make a variety of vacation plans that can limit the amount of time they return home if they don't feel ready to handle a long visit. Others prepare for the trip with a therapist, support group, or other friends. They may role play, talk through their concerns, and perhaps exchange telephone numbers for a call if the situation becomes too difficult.

For Others with Codependent Characteristics

The issues of caretaking and responsibility are especially relevant for you. First, be aware of how you handle any jobs or extracurricular activities that involve responsibility. If you find yourself wanting to do everything yourself, needing everything to be perfect, or being unwilling to delegate tasks to others, that's a signal that you're repeating some codependent patterns. Think about how you could respond differently.

Helping roles tend to attract codependent types. You could be drawn to college positions such as R.A., crisis hotline volunteer, or academic tutor. The good you can do for others in these positions feeds your self-esteem. Be aware of the fine line, though—the point when everyone else's needs start to become more important than your own. Many potentially codependent traits make you a wonderful helper and peer counselor. It's important, however, to take care of yourself before taking on any significant helping role. Once you're in the role, it's crucial to have a strong support and supervision network.

Codependent students often struggle when they're worried about a friend with, say, an eating disorder or an alcohol problem. Many become so caught up in the other person's problem that they ignore their own needs. These friendships resemble a hurricane. The person with the problem behavior is at the eye of the hurricane, in many ways the calmest player in the scenario. She may be unaware of how much she's affecting others. Even if she is aware, she has the control: only she knows how seriously self-destructive she is. She's the only one who can decide whether to get help or not and whether to make use of that help if she gets it. In the meantime, the friends surrounding the eye of the hurricane are often forcibly battered by the strong winds.

As a concerned friend, talk to someone outside of the hurricane who can provide you with safe shelter. Recognize the limits of what you can and can't do for your friend. When you find yourself preoccupied with your friend's safety and well-being, that should signal you that something more than your involvement is needed. Some students protect one another from staff on campus who are there specifically to help because they are fearful of what that help would entail, or that their friend will be angry with them for "telling." In sheltering a friend, however, you sometimes wind up hurting yourself by failing an exam, not sleeping, or focusing all your conversations with one another on what the friend said and did. Share your concern with a professional who can help your friend and also remind you that you're not responsible for her happiness and recovery.

Helping someone without hurting yourself is a tricky balance. Visualize a big heap in the middle of the floor—a heap of pain or confusion that someone has brought to you and dumped there. Sometimes they dump it and say, "What are you going to do?" You may want to pick up the whole heap and take care of it right away, no matter what it takes. Maybe you'll drop everything else and spend tremendous amounts of time and energy to make it all better. When you do all the work on someone else's heap, however, you prevent her from learning how to fix it herself. In a way, you're also taking something away from her—the belief that she has the capacity to do it herself. A more healthy approach is for you to look at the heap together. You can talk about what needs to be taken care of and on which pieces each of you will work. You're still helping her, but without taking over. Encourage her to assume part of the responsibility for her own heap. Perhaps that helps her even more.

. . .

>After a while you learn
>the subtle difference between
>holding a hand
>and chaining a soul
>and you learn
>that love doesn't mean
>leaning
>and company doesn't always
>mean

security.
And you begin to learn
that kisses aren't contracts and
presents aren't promises
and you begin to
accept your defeats
with your head up and your eyes ahead
with the grace of a woman
not the grief of a child
and you learn
to build your roads on today
because tomorrow's ground is
too uncertain for plans
and futures have a way of falling down
in mid-flight.
After a while you learn
that even sunshine burns
if you ask too much
so you plant your own garden
and decorate your own soul
instead of waiting
for someone to bring you flowers.
And you learn
that you really can endure
that you really are strong
and you really do have worth
and you learn
and you learn
with every good-bye
you learn . . .
—Veronica A. Shoffstall, *After a While*[18]

• • •

For Friends of Adult Children of Alcoholics and Others with Codependent Characteristics

Reading about and understanding codependency is an important first step. Avoid getting pulled into the codependent dynamic. Your friend will need to unlearn her patterns of relationships. If you respond to

her differently than she is used to, it can help her learn healthier behaviors.

Encourage free expression of feelings, understanding that this may be
difficult for your friend. It's important she realize that she can express
frustration and even anger without your hating or abandoning her.
Communicate with your friend directly and clearly and make your actions consistent with your words. Don't use a middle person or messenger and refuse to serve in that role for her—"Gabriella wants to know if
you're angry at her." Avoid gossiping about others with or around her
or even listening to any gossip.

If your friend tries to rescue you or take responsibility for you, gently
but firmly take back the responsibility that's yours. Let her know that
you'd prefer that she not help you in that way even though you understand her wanting to. Be clear about your boundaries. If you feel yourself
being smothered by your friend, explain your need for time away from
her and for relationships with other people. Redefining boundaries
doesn't mean you stop being friends. If you find yourself needing to say
or do things your friend may interpret as letting her down or abandoning
her, try to explain what you're doing. Ask for what you need, and take
care of yourself. These are behaviors it's important for your friend to
learn; perhaps your modeling them will help. Encourage your friend to
assert herself and ask for what she needs from you. You may not always
be able to give it to her, but it's important she learn that it's OK to ask.

If your friend is overly hard on herself for not being perfect or not
doing something well enough, confront those unrealistic expectations.
Genuinely praise her actual strengths and accomplishments. Help your
friend identify and take part in activities that she can enjoy. Have fun
with her, but recognize that people have fun in different ways. Social
situations involving drinking may be difficult for her if she's an ACOA.

Realize that your friend may not want to invite you home or have
you meet her family. She may also feel uncomfortable and unsure of
how to act with *your* family. Understand that your friend may sometimes respond to you in confusing ways. Perhaps something you say or
do will remind her of someone in her family and she may react to that
memory. You may gently question where her response came from and
reassure her that your relationship with her is different.

. . .

"The *slightest* things often felt like major rejections to me."

—H. F., class of '91

. . .

WHERE TO LOOK FOR HELP

Some helpers know more about codependency than others do, but start with the helper with whom you feel most comfortable. Individual therapy with a counselor, on or off campus, can be a valuable way to develop new relationship patterns. You can learn more by reading and attending campus and community programs, films, workshops, and awareness sessions on adult children of alcoholics and codependency. Some academic courses, perhaps in health, psychology, or sociology, may also explore these topics.

Al-Anon and Alateen twelve-step groups are designed for families and friends of alcoholics. Meetings may be offered on campus and in the community. Check the local telephone book and newspaper for information. ACOA groups are another type of twelve-step program more recently developed. CoDA twelve-step groups are patterned after A.A. and the only requirement for attending is a desire to have healthy relationships. Participants generally share information about how their codependency developed, how it has affected their lives, and what they're learning in recovery.[19] CoDA groups would be most appropriate for those who are not actually adult children of alcoholics but have codependent concerns. Some adult children of alcoholics choose to attend both ACOA and CoDA meetings. You may want to try several different meetings in order to find those with which you're most comfortable.

Some college counseling services run therapy groups that are more structured than twelve-step programs and are led by one or two therapists knowledgeable about codependency issues. If your college doesn't offer such groups, some may be available through community agencies or private therapists. Besides looking in the local newspaper, call hospitals and social-service agencies for information.

EDUCATING YOURSELF

Books: Nonfiction, Anthologies, Biographies, Poetry, Plays

Anderson, Louie. *Dear Dad: Letters from an Adult Child.* New York: Viking Penguin, 1989.

Beattie, Melody. *Codependent No More: How to Stop Controlling Others and Start Caring for Yourself.* New York: HarperPerennial, 1987.
Black, Claudia. *It Will Never Happen to Me.* New York: Ballantine, 1987.
———. *Double Duty.* New York: Ballantine, 1990.
Burnett, Carol. *One More Time.* New York: Avon, 1987.
Lerner, Harriet Goldhor. *The Dance of Anger.* New York: HarperCollins, 1987.
Schaef, Anne Wilson. *Co-Dependence: Misunderstood—Mistreated.* New York: HarperPerennial, 1986.
Subby, Robert. *Lost in the Shuffle: The Co-Dependent Reality.* Pompano Beach, FL: Health Communications, 1987.
Wegscheider-Cruse, Sharon. *Another Chance: Hope and Health for the Alcoholic Family.* Palo Alto, CA: Science and Behavior Books, 1981.
———. *Choicemaking for Co-Dependents, Adult Children, and Spirituality Seekers.* Pompano Beach, FL: Health Communications, 1985.
Weinhold, Barry, and Janae Weinhold. *Breaking Free of the Co-Dependency Trap.* Walpole, NH: Stillpoint, 1989.
Woititz, Janet Geringer. *Adult Children of Alcoholics.* Pompano Beach, FL: Health Communications, 1983.
———. *Struggle for Intimacy.* Pompano Beach, FL: Health Communications, 1985.

Organizations for Information and Assistance

Adult Children of Alcoholics
   2522 W. Sepulveda Blvd.
   Suite 200
   Torrance, CA 90505
   310-534-1815
Adult Children of Alcoholics, Al-Anon, and Alateen
   1-800-344-2666 (for group meetings throughout the U.S.)
Children of Alcoholics Foundation, Inc.
   P.O. Box 4185
   Grand Central Station
   New York, NY 10163-4185
   212-754-0656
Co-Dependents Anonymous
   P.O. Box 33577
   Phoenix, AZ 85067-3577
   602-277-7991
Families Anonymous, Inc.
   P.O. Box 528
   Van Nuys, CA 91408
   818-989-7841
Gamblers Anonymous
   3255 Wilshire Blvd.

No. 610
Los Angeles, CA 90010
213-386-8789
Nar-Anon Family World Service Office
P.O. Box 2562
Palos Verdes, CA 90274
213-547-5800
National Association for Children of Alcoholics
31582 Coast Hwy.
Suite B
South Laguna, CA 92677
714-499-3889
O-Anon General Service Office (for families and friends of compulsive overeaters)
P.O. Box 4305
San Pedro, CA 90731
213-547-1570

Films, Videos, TV Shows, Plays

The End of Innocence. A woman struggles from birth through adulthood trying to be perfect and please others.

The Great Santini. Two teenagers struggle growing up in a dysfunctional family headed by their Marine father. From the novel by Pat Conroy.

Ordinary People. A dysfunctional family finally confronts its problems. From Judith Guest's book.

The Prince of Tides. The secrets kept in a dysfunctional family affect the children as adults. From Pat Conroy's novel.

Shattered Spirits. A family is affected by their alcoholic father. Made-for-TV movie.

▪ EIGHT ▪

Sexuality

❦

The year was 1957. Dick Clark looked about the same as he does today. "Wake Up Little Susie," sung by the Everly Brothers, was a hit. In that song, Susie and her date fall asleep at the movies and wake up at 4 A.M. terrified that their "reputations were shot." "Wake Up Little Susie" was banned by some radio stations for its "suggestive" lyrics.[1] The changing lyrics of popular songs over the years since then reflect many of the changing attitudes about sexuality—heterosexuality in particular.

In the early sixties the Beatles asked to hold our hands, and the Doors took it a step further, suggesting we light their fire. In the seventies Rod Stewart tried to convince us that tonight was the night, and in the eighties Marvin Gaye sang about the powers of sexual healing. Women also became more assertive. In the seventies Roberta Flack said she felt like makin' love, Patti LaBelle asked "voulez-vous couchez avec moi, ce soir?" and Gloria Gaynor declared that she would survive. In the eighties Tennille asked the Captain to do that to her one more time, and even Olivia Newton-John wanted to get physical. In the nineties Color Me Badd declared that they wanted to sex us up.

The beat of campus life has often played at an even faster speed than society's sexual song. College is considered a place of great personal freedom and experimentation, including sexual activity. If you're planning to live in a college residence hall, sorority house, or an off-campus apartment, you may already have heard about what a great time you

Doonesbury copyright G. B. Trudeau. Reprinted with permission of *Universal Press Syndicate*. All rights reserved.

can have now that you're on your own. No curfew, coed halls, lots of parties, condom machines in the Student Center, no parents around to know when you come in—or don't. Some students deal well with this freedom. They are able to set their own limits, say yes when they want to and no when they want to, and have a wonderful time. Others arrive at college and do what they think they're expected to do—whether they really want to or not. Living at a pace set by others can be exhausting after a while. Keep sight of what *you* really want and need.

There used to be much more strict rules in college residence halls, such as curfews and limited hours for coed visitation. My favorites were the ones dictating that when we had a male guest (only during scheduled visitation hours), we had to keep the door open at least six inches, and there had to be three feet on the floor at all times. As strange as rules like these sound today, they did sometimes give women something to fall back on when they didn't want to become involved but were uncomfortable saying so. The responsibility now falls more directly on you to take care of yourself and clearly say yes or no.

Today, sexual choices, decisions, and consequences are far more complex than ever before. The spread of sexually transmitted diseases (STDs), particularly AIDS, has created the need for more thoughtful and careful sexual choices and protection.

There's a funny and powerful scene in an AIDS awareness program that filmmaker Robert Townsend made for cable TV. It shows a man and a woman about to go to bed together for the first time. They hear a voice: "When you make love with someone, you're also making love to everyone they've ever slept with." At that moment, the bed is suddenly filled with other people. Lots of other people. The couple is surprised at first, and then they take a good look at all these past lovers. Passion turns to caution as some important questions begin to get asked.

The need for greater responsibility, assertiveness, and communication can have a positive impact on all your relationships and sexual experiences. Taking time, taking care, and taking care of yourself as you make these decisions can lead to more satisfying relationships overall.

Background Information

Your sexual responses to people can involve sexual thoughts, fantasies, dreams, or emotional feelings about them. You may or may not choose to act on those thoughts or feelings. You may also be surprised by some of your reactions, crushes, and attractions, and you may even be confused about your sexuality at times.

The scale below was developed by Dr. Alfred Kinsey. The range from zero to six describes the degree of sexual responsiveness people have to members of the same and other sex. While some people appear to be exclusively homosexual or heterosexual in their actions, thoughts, and feelings, many others fall at varying points along the continuum. Kinsey found that homosexual thoughts and feelings often occur in many individuals who define themselves as heterosexual, and heterosexual thoughts and feelings occur in many who identify themselves as homosexual.[2]

0. Exclusively heterosexual.
1. Predominantly heterosexual, incidentally homosexual.
2. Predominantly heterosexual, but more than incidentally homosexual.
3. Equally heterosexual and homosexual.
4. Predominantly homosexual, but more than incidentally heterosexual.
5. Predominantly homosexual, incidentally heterosexual.
6. Exclusively homosexual.

. . .

"I have a heterosexual friend who had a history of unsuccessful relationships with men. I never liked any of the guys she dated because of their destructive and disrespectful behavior. This definitely put a strain on our friendship. After one particularly manipulative relationship and a nasty breakup, she took a vacation from dating to recuperate. She started hanging out a lot with two of her friends who happened to be a lesbian couple. After spending some time with this couple she commented to me one day about how much she had learned about loving, mutuality, and respect from observing her friends' relationship. Apparently she did learn something because after that her boyfriends were pretty cool, and her whole approach to relationships had much more self-respect involved."

—S. L., class of '90

. . .

Women's sexual lives have often been defined from a male perspective, and it's important for women to explore their sexuality from a female point of view. Some goals to work toward in creating healthy emotional and sexual relationships include

1. shared responsibility and power.
2. voluntary, nonexploitive activity.
3. emotional pleasure and caring integrated with, or instead of, intercourse.
4. emphasis on process rather than on performance.
5. shared contraceptive and/or health protection.
6. mutual respect, fun, and romance.[3]

Both men and women have been taught to play particular roles in their relationships with one another. The process of learning new and more equal roles is underway as men and women work together to understand new ways to look at sexual relationships.

ENCOUNTERING AND RESPONDING TO THIS ISSUE

. . .

"College is a time to experiment and some of us even rebel, but we've got to be fully aware of the consequences and overcome our hangups around our sexuality. But if mistakes are made—and they will be made—we can know what we learned from them, get rid of the guilt, and get on with our lives."

—O. L., class of '89

. . .

Relationships

Some of you may already have had, or may currently be in, a healthy intimate relationship. Others of you may not have had a serious relationship yet. Still others may not have been satisfied by the relationships you've had. The issue of abusive relationships is an important one and will be discussed in chapter 10.

Many of the messages you receive as women growing up could lead you to seek relationships based on traditional sex roles.[4] Women are often taught that being part of a traditional couple is the norm and that they need to be in a relationship to feel fulfilled, worthwhile, and popular. Women are often expected to put their energy into maintaining a relationship and supporting their partner, particularly if that partner is a male. That relationship is expected to take priority over personal achievement. This focus can make you dependent on a male partner, as opposed to developing your ability to "make it" on your own if the relationship ends or you choose to leave it. It's important, within a relationship, for you to continue to develop your own self-reliance, assertiveness, self-confidence, and independence.[5]

Lesbians also feel pressure to be part of a couple.[6] Since social opportunities for lesbians and bisexuals are usually harder to find than heterosexual-centered social activities on campus, having a partner can also relieve the stress of trying to find ways to meet people. Bisexuals and lesbians who are not "out" may find it especially hard to meet others with similar orientations.

If you believe that it's crucial to be part of a couple—heterosexual or homosexual—you may become involved in relationships before you're ready, or you may stay in unhealthy relationships because you don't like being alone, or single. A strong feeling of self-esteem is an important part of choosing to be single. Finding people with whom to build intimate relationships is a complicated process, and not being involved in a relationship should not translate into negative feelings about yourself.

While single status can be lonely, it can also offer you the freedom to make your own choices and decisions based on what's best for you.[7] The kinds of messages you believe can affect how you feel about yourself. Thinking "If I go to the party alone I can meet a lot of people and leave when I want to" is more positive than thinking "If I go to the party alone everyone will think I can't get a date and that I'm a real loser." Sometimes if you let go of the pressure or expectation to be part of a couple, you'll be able to relate in a more relaxed way with others, and perhaps relationships will develop more naturally.

. . .

"When I let go of one old relationship, I was amazed at how my friendships blossomed. My personal meditative time increased as well and I made faster headway on that self-esteem process which I know is lifelong! It's not that I became antirelationship alto- gether—it's just that when I asked myself 'do I enjoy my own company? what makes me interesting?' and didn't know the an- swers, I knew it was time to blaze the trail alone. And it wasn't so bad. When I did enter into a long-term partnership, I knew more clearly what my needs were and didn't have to sacrifice my friends or my private time."

—O. L., class of '89

. . .

Intimacy is necessary for a lasting relationship, but it can be difficult to achieve. Intimacy involves both people in a relationship allowing themselves to be really known by the other. Since many of us often struggle with knowing *ourselves,* this mutual process can be tricky. It means sharing secrets and showing your vulnerabilities and insecurities to one another. That can be scary to do, especially if you have trouble accepting your own secrets and insecurities. There's always the fear that if your partner sees these "weak" or "bad" parts, s/he may reject you and want to end the relationship.

Yet if you share secrets or show your vulnerability, other people may come to care about you—maybe even more than before. They may also feel safer showing you some of their insecurities. Trust takes a long time to build, and people approach it differently. Don't assume that because you've trusted your partner with something, s/he'll automatically do the same. People's past experiences can affect them for a long time, and some particular topics or issues may trigger fear or distrust for one or both of you. Accept that each of you might, at times, need to move at a slower pace. You can't *make* someone trust you, but you can work to develop a relationship in which you both feel more and more safe to trust each other. Remember that you can't change other people. You can't make them more thoughtful or more spontaneous, for example, unless they want to be.

Some people fear that committing to an intimate relationship means losing their own identity to that of their partner.[8] They worry that instead of being known for who they are and what they accomplish, they'll always be, say, "Chris's girlfriend." Others worry that they'll have to give up their own priorities in favor of their partner's. In some couples, one partner always decides what the weekend plans are, or speaks for both, and the other allows and even encourages that. Retaining your individuality in a relationship is partly a result of being clear about what you want and your partner being willing to listen and respect your needs.

- "I need at least one night a week to stay in and hang out with my roommates."
- "When we go out, if I really want to dance and you don't, I need to feel it's OK for me to dance with other people."
- "I need you to understand that there are some things I deal with in therapy that I'm not ready to talk about with you yet."

• • •

"Oftentimes when you're in 'bliss' it's hard to extricate yourself from your significant other, especially when you have work to do. I am living with my boyfriend in a college apartment and we've come to the understanding that school takes precedence over other things at the moment. What also helps is that we've tried to respect the other person's decisions when it comes to deciding between work and leisure. This way, we cannot blame each other for not getting work done because it was our own decision to play instead of work."

—M. J., class of '93

• • •

Even if you learn to ask for what you need, that doesn't mean that the other person can or will always give it to you, but at least s/he knows what you want. It's the other person's choice whether to respond, and then it's your choice what you do next. For example, you may decide that it's OK that s/he can't give you what you ask for and that you will stay in the relationship anyway. Or you may decide to look outside of the relationship to fulfill that particular need while continuing to work at the relationship. Or you may begin to question whether staying in the relationship is best for you. Relationships have their ups and downs, and they require effort from both partners to keep them growing. Sometimes you have to decide whether it's best for you to keep working at a relationship or to end it. In making this decision, consider the following questions.[9]

1. Do you constantly give in to the other person's needs to avoid fights; does it feel hopeless to even try to work things out?
2. Does it feel like there's no room for the relationship, or for you, to change and grow?
3. Does it seem that life is no better for you in the relationship than it would be out of it?
4. Is your partner abusive to you, physically or emotionally?

Lesbians and bisexual women often have to explore their relationships in an environment where everyone is assumed to be heterosexual. While TV and film images of loving heterosexual relationships abound, there are few such models for lesbians and bisexual women. This makes it harder for lesbians and bisexual women to appreciate the potential scope and depth of their relationships, and it also makes heterosexual women less likely to understand the love between two women.

There are a number of areas that are important to work at if any relationship—heterosexual or homosexual—is to develop and grow. Take time to nurture the relationship rather than taking it, or the other person, for granted. This could entail taking time out from daily routines to plan a special treat or send a caring note. Share the power around decisions and long-term planning. Allow conflicts to surface, and work together to solve them creatively so there's no consistent pattern of one person winning all the time and the other person losing all the time. Because women have often been socialized to put others' needs first, this may take some extra effort for many of you.[10]

Each partner should have personal time for a hobby, interest, etc. Recognize that there are limits to closeness and that you don't need to be with one another constantly. Enjoy some separateness and time apart. Have other friends rather than being one another's sole source of emotional support.[11] This point may be particularly applicable to lesbians, who, partly because they share the same gender, may at times feel even closer than heterosexual couples.[12]

Decisions about Sexual Activity

· · ·

"By the end of the seventies, feminism had brought more under-standing that real liberation meant the power to make a choice; that sexuality, for women or men, should be neither forbidden nor forced."

—Gloria Steinem, "Words and Change" [13]

· · ·

On many college campuses, especially among close groups of friends, one person's business quickly becomes everyone's business. There's often curiosity about when someone comes home, who's seeing whom, and who's sleeping with whom. Sometimes there's pressure from friends to move faster in a relationship than you want to, or perhaps there's pressure to end a relationship with someone your friends don't like. Decisions about whom you see and whether or not to be sexually active are yours to make for yourself. A decision to have a sexual relationship should *not* be determined by

1. someone else.
2. alcohol or drugs.
3. loneliness or depression.
4. peer pressure.
5. an ultimatum (the threat from a partner that unless you have sex the relationship may be over).
6. fear of rejection (being afraid that if you don't have sex, the relationship will be over).[14]

Sex should be about pleasure and connection for both partners. In order to take responsibility for your own sexual life, it's important to learn about, and understand, your own sexuality. Women have often been taught to be ashamed of, or embarrassed by, their sexual feelings, and as a result they may deny these feelings or feel guilty about having them.[15] Learn about and accept your own body and sexual response patterns; this is one way to discover what's sexually fulfilling for you if or when you choose to become involved in a sexual relationship.

· · ·

"If you feel like you really need to have sex and you can't wait until you're in love, learn to masturbate. It can be the greatest skill a woman can learn. You no longer *need* a partner to satisfy your body. You have yourself."

—S. A., class of '93

. . .

Some women choose to remain virgins and abstain from certain sexual activities until they're married or in a committed relationship. Some people choose to be celibate for periods of time in their lives. They may be seeking a break, wanting to use their energy in other ways, or looking for new and different ways to express their loving feelings.[16] Celibacy leads some women to a feeling of greater personal freedom and power as they experience more control of their own energies and lives.[17] Not engaging in sexual activity also lessens fears of pregnancy and sexually transmitted diseases, including AIDS.

The choice to become sexually active ought to involve honest and direct communication about what you feel and what you and your partner need from one another. This is an important way to develop a sexual relationship that is satisfying for both of you. Honest communication is also crucial in discussing concerns such as birth control and STDs, including AIDS. You may feel uncomfortable talking about sexual issues, but it's vitally important to do so. Perhaps you're worried that what you say will be threatening to your partner or will be perceived as criticism. You may be embarrassed by talking candidly and saying particular words. Telling a partner that you enjoy being touched in a particular place or that something they're doing makes you uncomfortable is, however, an important way to help yourself experience more enjoyable sexual relationships. The fantasy of having a partner who is so wonderful that s/he knows exactly what you want and when you want it is just that—a fantasy.

Contraception

Over 20 percent of college women become pregnant.[18] While contraception ideally ought to be a shared responsibility, most college men still expect their female partners to assume responsibility for birth control.[19] Being careful isn't good enough. Heterosexual contact in which semen is deposited near the vagina can be enough to cause pregnancy in some cases.[20]

Since you'll carry the consequences of an unwanted pregnancy, you need to take time to think about the different methods of birth control before you become heterosexually active. Find out about your options and consider each in light of several criteria. First, how safe is it? Are there side effects or risks of illness or future infertility? How effective is it in preventing unwanted pregnancy if used consistently and correctly? What is your health status? Some birth control methods pose a risk if you're being treated for certain medical conditions or have a family history of some conditions. What is the pattern of your sex life? Some methods are better if you have sexual relations regularly and are less advisable if you have them only occasionally or if you aren't involved in an ongoing relationship. Finally, consider your feelings, fears, and instincts. Are you, for instance, uncomfortable with a method like the diaphragm, which requires you to insert and remove it each time you have intercourse? [21]

Some contraceptive methods, such as birth control pills or a diaphragm, require a prescription or fitting by a doctor or other clinician. Others, like condoms and spermicidal foam, are available over the counter in the drug store. A number of colleges have begun to install condom machines on campus. Many college health services provide birth control counseling, information, and sometimes prescriptions. If you're thinking about becoming sexually active with a man, see a gynecologist or other trained clinician to consider your options and make an informed choice.

Many experts suggest using more than one birth control method to provide increased protection and backup. Abstinence and sterilization aside, the most effective birth control methods, if used consistently and correctly, are the birth control pill or a combination of a latex condom and spermicide with nonoxynyl-9.[22] The condom and spermicide, in addition to serving as a birth control method, are also helpful in protecting against the spread of STDs, including AIDS.

The "morning-after" pill can be helpful for one-time unprotected sexual intercourse but should not really be considered a contraceptive method. This type of pill is often given to rape survivors. If taken by a woman as soon as possible within seventy-two hours after intercourse, it can prevent the survival of a fertilized egg. Some risks are associated with the morning-after pill, and you should fully discuss with your doctor the advisability of using it.[23]

Talk with your partner about contraception *before* you become sexually involved. You may feel uncomfortable talking about birth control, perhaps because of the way sexuality was dealt with in your family, religion, or culture. You may feel that talking about it is unromantic or spoils the mood.[24] The consequences of not talking about it, however, could spoil much more.

Pregnancy

If you miss a period after having had sex, it's important to determine as soon as possible whether or not you're pregnant. Home pregnancy tests are one option, but they ought to be confirmed by a doctor. Your college health service may offer tests. Check with them to find out how soon an accurate test may be taken.

Local clinics, medical practitioners, family planning organizations, and women's health centers are other alternatives. Early detection will provide you with the greatest number of options, either for a safer abortion or for the best possible prenatal care for you and your baby.

Abortions are safest within the first three months; those performed later are more expensive and run greater risks of complications.[25] Your decision may be a difficult one, but the sooner you make it, the better. Consider talking with others—perhaps your partner, close friends, a clinician, a counselor, a clergyperson, or family members. The following procedures are generally used, depending upon the number of weeks that have elapsed since your last menstrual period began: [26]

8–12 weeks	D and C (dilation and curettage)
7–13 weeks	vacuum aspiration
13–16 weeks	D and E (dilation and evacuation, which is a combination of a D and C and vacuum aspiration)
16–24 weeks	saline abortion

When I was in graduate school in 1969, I remember hearing a classmate talk about her decision to get an abortion when she was an undergraduate. Her decision had been made with her boyfriend and was well thought out and deeply felt. This was before *Roe v. Wade,* however, and the choices for women back then were far more limited than the options available today. As a college student in 1969, to have the procedure done by a real doctor, my friend had to leave the country, fly down to Mexico, and look for a man at the airport wearing a pink carnation in his lapel. This man took her to the doctor, another perfect stranger, who performed the abortion.

In the post–*Roe v. Wade* era, your campus health service may offer some abortion procedures themselves, or they may help you identify appropriate facilities off campus. Check your health insurance to see what coverage you have. Many of the health insurance policies offered through colleges cover part or all of the cost of the procedure. It's a good idea to have someone such as your partner, a friend, a family member, or your R.A. accompany you to the procedure and be there for you later.

Regardless of whether you wanted to terminate the pregnancy or not, you're likely to experience a variety of intense emotions later. You may feel relief, but also some sadness and a sense of loss. Some women feel this especially around the time when they would have given birth. You may also, however, feel a sense of personal strength from having made and followed through on a difficult and important decision. There could be some guilt or fear about not being able to have a child at some later time.[27] If your religion takes a stand against abortion, this can raise additional conflicts for you. A counselor, clergyperson, or participation in a postabortion support group could give you a chance to work through some of your feelings.

Should you choose to carry the pregnancy to term and have the baby, you'll need to make some other decisions. Will you be able to stay in school? How long will you be able to remain in residence on campus if you live in a hall now? How will you balance continuing your education with your responsibilities as a mother? Will you raise the child yourself and/or with the help of your partner or family? Will you put the baby up for adoption or consider placing the child in foster care?

A number of women choose to have abortions and complete their education. Some eventually marry their partners, some don't. Other women leave school to have their babies; some of them return later to complete their education, and others don't. I knew one student who chose to have her child, which was due shortly before she was scheduled to graduate. She planned ahead, and with the help of her family and college staff from a variety of offices, arranged to live on campus until the baby was born. She received the necessary prenatal care through the Health Service and then lived off campus with a relative until she finished her academic work. I'll always remember seeing her at the reception for graduating seniors and being introduced to her beautiful two-month-old son.

Sexually Transmitted Diseases (STDs)

. . .

"I know that up until I got an STD myself, I was only really concerned about becoming pregnant."

—Student, class of '93

. . .

Next to colds, sexually transmitted diseases are the most common infections among young adults.[28] Every year more than ten million Americans get STDs.[29] One in six teenagers contracts an STD.[30] There are more than twenty types of STDs, and those listed below are among the most common.

Chlamydia, the fastest-spreading STD in the United States, especially among 15–25-year-olds, is a bacterial infection in the urinary and reproductive organs. There are often no early symptoms, so you can have the disease without knowing it. Untreated, chlamydia is a common cause of pelvic inflammatory disease (PID) and can cause infertility. It can be passed to an infant by an infected mother during birth. Chlamydia can be cured by antibiotics.[31]

An estimated 10–20 percent of sexually active college students are infected with the *human papilloma virus* (HPV).[32] HPV causes *genital warts,* which generally appear one to three months after sexual contact. There may be no symptoms until the warts appear. Genital warts raise the risk of cervical cancer, and you should have regular pap smears to detect any problems early. HPV can affect children born to infected mothers. The warts can be treated, and if they return, repeated treatment is necessary. *Don't* use drugstore medication for other kinds of warts on genital warts; see your doctor.[33]

Herpes simplex II, or genital herpes, is very common, with five hundred thousand to one million new cases appearing each year. It's a virus that results in painful blisters on and in the genital area and sometimes around the mouth. There is thought to be a link between herpes and cervical cancer, and it's recommended that pap smears be done twice a year. While there's no cure for herpes, it can be treated. Recurring attacks tend to take place under stress and are usually less painful and heal faster than the original infection.[34]

There are one to two million new cases of *gonorrhea* each year. Most occur in those under twenty-five years of age. Gonorrhea is a bacterial infection that is hard to detect because there may be no symptoms. Gonorrhea can be treated with antibiotics, but if left untreated it can cause PID and possibly lead to infertility. Pregnant women can infect their unborn babies.[35]

The infection rate of *syphilis* is at its highest level in forty years. A bacterial infection, syphilis enters the bloodstream and can infect vital organs. Syphilis can be cured with penicillin, but if left untreated can eventually cause death. Pregnant mothers can pass the infection on to their unborn child. The open sores of syphilis make it easier for HIV to invade the body.[36]

What's common to all STDs is that they're spread through unprotected sexual contact with an infected person. This only reinforces the need for partners to talk to one another about past history. Volunteering information about your own history and experience may encourage your partner to share his or hers. Keep in mind, however, that some partners won't tell you the truth or may not even know that they've been exposed to an STD. If you're uncomfortable with *anything* you see or hear, think long and hard before you decide to have sexual relations with that person.

There are several ways to reduce your risk of contracting an STD:[37]

1. Limit the number of sex partners you have.
2. Observe your partner's body for anything unusual before having sexual relations.
3. Wash with soap and water before and immediately after sexual contact.
4. Use a latex condom and nonoxynyl-9 spermicide properly during heterosexual relations. If the condom is put on before any contact and properly removed afterwards, this is a good preventative measure. Latex dental dams are good barriers for oral sex with women.
5. Urinate immediately after sexual contact. This can flush out some germs, but more so for men than for women.
6. If you're sexually active, ask your physician for specific tests for STDs as part of your regular checkup.

If you let it, having an STD can affect how you feel about yourself and your sexuality. It's important not to blame yourself or to see the STD as punishment. Seek out information, get treatment if needed, and don't risk passing it along during any time you may be infectious.

AIDS

AIDS is the most lethal sexually transmitted disease. The National Centers for Disease Control predict that AIDS will soon become the number one killer on college campuses.[38] College is a time when many students are developing their patterns of sexual relationships and experimenting with various partners and behaviors.[39] This can increase vulnerability, although college students tend to feel a sense of invulnerability—that AIDS won't happen to them. AIDS can happen to anyone.

This myth, that "it can't happen to me," is reinforced by the potentially long lapse—anywhere from two to eight years—between contracting the virus and developing symptoms.[40] There are many students on campuses now who are capable of spreading AIDS but are unaware that they have it. Some estimate that from thirty to eighty thousand students on U.S. college campuses carry the HIV virus but don't show symptoms.[41]

Acquired immune deficiency syndrome (AIDS) is a condition in which the body's defense system for fighting infections breaks down. This makes the individual more susceptible to diseases she would otherwise be able to fight. There's no cure for AIDS, and those who have it eventually die from the infections they develop.

AIDS is caused by a virus called human immunodeficiency virus; those who have the virus in their system are said to be HIV positive. The virus can produce milder illnesses called AIDS-related complex (ARC). There's no way to predict for sure when HIV will develop into ARC or into "full-blown" AIDS.

Currently the rate of spread of HIV is slowing in the gay male community and rising in the heterosexual population.[42] This increase among heterosexuals is largely a result of more women becoming infected.[43] While some groups, such as gay men and intravenous drug users, have been described as high-risk groups, others prefer to talk in terms of all individuals being at risk if they participate in high-risk behaviors. There are five ways in which a person can get infected with HIV:[44]

1. Having sex with someone who is infected with HIV (through blood, semen, vaginal secretions, urine, or feces).
2. Sharing intravenous (IV) needles with someone who is infected with the virus.
3. Receiving blood transfusions or blood products from someone infected with HIV (in 1985 the blood banks adopted guidelines for screening out blood with HIV).
4. Using sperm from an infected donor for artificial insemination.
5. Being born to a woman infected with HIV.

AIDS is transmitted by intimate sexual contact and exposure to contaminated blood. This means that the exchange of bodily fluid, such as semen or blood, can pass HIV through any open areas on the skin. Among the more risky sexual activities are anal intercourse and unprotected vaginal intercourse between men and women. Fellatio on a man not using a condom is a higher risk than previously thought.[45] Oral sex on a female, either by a male or by another woman, is risky during menstruation. Researchers believe that HIV is more easily transmitted from men to women than vice versa because there is more of the virus in semen than in vaginal secretions.[46] HIV is less easily spread through sex between two women, but it can happen, and lesbians also need to follow safe sexual practices.[47]

A woman with HIV is likely to transmit the virus to her child. It's also possible that becoming pregnant may speed up the development of ARC or AIDS in a woman who carries the virus. Women are susceptible to different infections than men, and they may also tend to wait longer to seek diagnosis and treatment.[48]

HIV is *not* transmitted through casual contact. You can't get it from living in the same residence hall or even in the same room with someone who has the virus. You can't get it from taking care of someone with HIV, from eating food they've handled or prepared, from having them cough or sneeze near you, from swimming in the same pool, or from casual kissing.[49] Although HIV is present in the saliva of those infected with the virus, thus far there don't appear to be cases in which the disease has been transmitted by kissing. Risk could arise, however, from prolonged deep or rough kissing if it damages the tissues around the mouth.[50] The kinds of items to avoid sharing are toothbrushes, razors, and tweezers because of the possibility of blood being passed through their shared use. Students with HIV don't pose any risks to you by living, working, and attending class with you unless you engage in high-risk sexual behavior with them.

There has been much discussion and confusion about HIV testing. The blood test currently available tests for the presence of antibody to HIV; it does not test for AIDS or ARC. A positive test tells whether a person has been exposed to HIV but it can't determine when they will develop AIDS.[51]

Decisions about testing should be made very carefully, and a test should not be taken just to check yourself out. Consult first with a trained HIV counselor or health-care professional. This person can help you determine whether you have participated in activity that may have put you at risk. It's important to find out whether the testing would be confidential, meaning that the information would be in your confidential file, or anonymous. Although confidential testing *is* confidential, there is still the possibility that some individuals—even trustworthy ones—could have access to that information. Anonymous testing, on the other hand, uses only numbers. Protecting your anonymity can be important, since not just those with positive tests, but even those who simply take the test, may become subject to unreasonable fears and discrimination affecting areas such as employment, housing, and insurance coverage.

If you test positive for HIV, you may not develop symptoms, although you can still be infectious. Therefore take steps to protect others, learn new ways to be safely intimate with loved ones, work to maintain your own physical health, and get assistance from a counselor. Learning to live with HIV, to stay optimistic and productive, and to maintain a sense of humor has become a focus for many who have the virus.

■ ■ ■

"Sometimes I wonder how I'd feel if they found a cure tomorrow. The irony is that I think I'd be depressed. I've tried so hard to be realistic about this change of fortune, that it's become a part of who I am and if that part were taken away I know there'd be something missing. . . . I'd get over it though!"
—Peter Adair, Janet Cole, and Veronica Selver,
Absolutely Positive[52]

■ ■ ■

At some point, you may learn that family members or friends have HIV. There are some ways you can be of particular help:[53]

1. Be available to them.
2. Encourage them to make their own decisions about their treatment, their lives, etc.
3. Offer help but don't force help on them.
4. Encourage them to take ongoing care of their health.
5. Encourage them to avoid using alcohol and drugs.
6. Offer to accompany them to medical appointments, if they wish.
7. Continue to be supportive of them even if others are not.
8. Take care of *yourself*. Find someone you can talk to about your feelings.

WHERE TO LOOK FOR HELP

Developing trusting and loving relationships is an important source of strength throughout your life, but intimate relationships are always complex. Past experiences with partners and with your family can certainly affect your ability to develop successful and fulfilling relationships. Sometimes it can help to examine the "baggage" you carry with you and develop more effective ways of relating. Some counselors will also work with couples, both heterosexual and lesbian, on relationship issues.

Your campus health service is one of the most important resources for issues of sexuality. Get to know the nursing and medical practitioners and find a health-care provider with whom you feel comfortable discussing sexual questions. This is particularly important if you're making decisions about sexual activity. Many health services offer health-education programs and workshops about contraception, sexuality, sexual orientation, AIDS, other STDs, pregnancy, etc. There may be awareness days and weeks on your campus, and educational materials provide more information. On some campuses, "safe-sex" kits are available and condom machines may be centrally located in order to encourage less risky sexual practices.

Often student peer educators play active roles in teaching other students about sexuality and sexual issues. Support groups may also be offered, for example, for students with STDs and for women who have been unable to achieve orgasm.

Other groups and offices on campus—the Women's Center, gay/lesbian/bisexual student groups, student affairs and student activities offices, and the physical education department—may sponsor programs on sexual issues. Sexuality is generally an important part of wellness courses, as is assertiveness, communication, negotiation, and decision making. All of these skills play a key role in developing safe and healthy relationships.

If you've tested positively for HIV, I would encourage you to meet confidentially with the director of your campus health service. If the Health Service is aware of your condition, they can inform you of any outbreak of communicable disease that could pose a risk for you and help to minimize that risk. Fears of being treated differently because you're HIV positive are certainly understandable, but health services are confidential. Also check to see if your college has written guidelines for protecting the rights of members of the campus community with HIV.

There are often off-campus clinics and agencies that can meet your needs. Clinics with a focus on women's issues provide a number of health-care and educational opportunities. If you're seeking birth control methods or are considering an abortion, you might explore community options if your campus health service doesn't offer what you need, or if you would prefer to deal with these questions off campus. If you're seeking an abortion off campus, explore your options in some detail. Some facilities may only perform first-trimester abortions, so find out which procedures are offered, how much they cost, whether you have health insurance that will cover it, the atmosphere at the facility, the attitude of the staff toward women, and the availability of counseling.[54] Your age and the state laws regarding parental consent or notification should also be considered.

If you feel that you're at risk for HIV and wish to look into testing possibilities, there are telephone numbers listed in the resources section of this chapter to help you find anonymous testing sites near you.

Another potential place to turn is your family. Discussing sexual issues may be easier in some families than in others, but family members are one source of help to consider.

If you're a lesbian or bisexual, the climate on your campus can affect how free you feel to deal with sexual questions and issues. Your health and counseling services need to be receptive to students of all sexual orientations. It can be hard enough to see a doctor or therapist without also wondering whether you'll have to come out to that person and what her/his reaction will be.

You may begin to get a sense of openness from the questions asked on intake forms or at your first session. You may feel uncomfortable if your physician or counselor automatically assumes that you're heterosexual and that being sexually active just means being active with men. As one student asked, "How do you tell them without bopping them in the nose?" There's no easy answer. If you feel comfortable doing so, you could say something directly, or you might avoid using male pronouns and hope the doctor or counselor picks up on it. If you don't feel you can continue with a particular doctor, you certainly can look for another. The Health Center, Women's Center, or lesbian/bisexual organization may also have some referrals if you prefer to see a lesbian or bisexual doctor or counselor off campus.

EDUCATING YOURSELF

Books: Nonfiction, Anthologies, Biographies, Poetry, Plays

Ashe, Arthur, and Arnold Rampersad. *Days of Grace: A Memoir*. New York: Knopf, 1993.

Bell, Ruth, et al. *Changing Bodies, Changing Lives: A Book for Teens on Sex and Relationships*. Rev. ed. New York: Random House, 1988.

Boston Women's Health Book Collective. *The New Our Bodies, Ourselves*. Updated ed. New York: Simon and Schuster, 1992.

Brown, Melanie. *The New Celibacy*. Rev. ed. New York: McGraw-Hill, 1989.

Chalker, Rebecca, and Carol Downer. *A Woman's Book of Choices: Abortion, Menstrual Extraction, RU-486*. New York: Four Walls Eight Windows, 1992.

Cook, Stephani, and Richard Lumiere. *Healthy Sex . . . and Keeping It That Way: A Complete Guide to Sexual Infections*. New York: Simon and Schuster, 1983.

Corea, Gena. *The Invisible Epidemic: The Story of Women and AIDS*. New York: HarperCollins, 1992.

Faderman, Lillian. *Odd Girls and Twilight Lovers: A History of Lesbian Life in Twentieth-Century America*. New York: Columbia University Press, 1991.

Frumkin, Lyn, and John Leonard. *Questions and Answers on AIDS*. New York: Avon, 1987.

Glaser, Elizabeth, and Laura Palmer. *In the Absence of Angels: A Hollywood Family's Courageous Story*. New York: Putnam's, 1991.

Green, G. Dorsey, and Merilee D. Clunis. *Lesbian Couples*. Seattle: Seal, 1988.

Hite, Shere. *The Hite Report: A Nationwide Study of Female Sexuality*. New York: Dell, 1987.

Janus, Samuel, and Cynthia L. Janus. *The Janus Report*. New York: Wiley, 1993.

Johnson, Karen, and Tom Ferguson. *Trusting Ourselves: The Sourcebook of Psychology for Women*. New York: Atlantic Monthly Press, 1990.

Kubler-Ross, Elizabeth. *AIDS*. New York: Collier, 1989.

Otis, Carol L., and Roger Goldingay. *Campus Health Guide: The College Student's Handbook for Healthy Living*. New York: College Board, 1989.

Oyler, Chris. *Go Towards the Light*. New York: Signet, 1990.

Rubin, Lillian B. *Intimate Strangers: Men and Women Together*. New York: HarperPerennial, 1984.

Shilts, Randy. *And the Band Played On*. New York: Penguin, 1988.

Tannen, Deborah. *You Just Don't Understand: Women and Men in Conversation*. New York: Ballantine, 1991.

Articles, Pamphlets, and Papers

American College Health Association Task Force on AIDS. "AIDS: What Everyone Should Know." Rockville, MD: American College Health Association, 1987.

American Council for Healthful Living. "Common Sexually Transmitted Diseases." Orange, NJ: American Council for Healthful Living, 1988.

Charlottesville AIDS Resource Network. "Safe Sex." Rockville, MD: American College Health Association, 1986.

Clark, Kay. "Talking with Your Partner about Herpes." Santa Cruz, CA: Network Publications, 1984.

Hiatt, Jane, and ETR Associates. "Birth Control Facts." Santa Cruz, CA: Network Publications, 1986.

Nelson, Mary. "Chlamydia." Santa Cruz, CA: Network Publications, 1984.

Sloane, Beverlie Conant. "Partners in Health." Columbus, OH: Merrill, 1986.

Washington Center for Cognitive-Behavioral Therapy. "Coping with Herpes: The Emotional Problems." Washington, DC: Washington Center for Cognitive-Behavioral Therapy.

Waters, Christina. "Talking with Your Partner about Birth Control." Santa Cruz, CA: Network Publications, 1984.

Women's AIDS Network. "Lesbians and AIDS: What's the Connection?" San Francisco: San Francisco AIDS Foundation, 1986.

———. "Women and AIDS." 3d ed. San Francisco: San Francisco AIDS Foundation, 1987.

Organizations for Information and Assistance

American College Health Association
P.O. Box 28937
Baltimore, MD 21240-8937
410-859-1500

American Council for Healthful Living
c/o Jane Westlake
Elite Graphics
285 Changebridge Rd.
Pine Brook, NJ 07058
201-882-9769

Boston Women's Health Book Collective
   240 A Elm St.
   Somerville, MA 02144
   617-625-0271
National AIDS Clearinghouse
   P.O. Box 6003
   Rockville, MD 20849-6003
   1-800-458-5231
National Women's Health Network
   1325 G St. NW
   Washington, DC 20005
   202-347-1140
Planned Parenthood or Family Planning
   check in local phone book

Hotlines

National Abortion Federation Hotline
   1-800-772-9100
National AIDS Hotline
   1-800-342-AIDS
   1-800-344-7432 (Spanish)
   1-800-243-7889 (TTD)
National Sexually Transmitted Diseases Hotline
   1-800-227-8922

Films, Videos, TV Shows, Plays

André's Mother. A mother struggles to deal with her son's death from AIDS, and with his lover. PBS movie from a play by Terrence McNally.

Angels in America, Part 1: Millennium Approaches and *Part 2: Perestroika.* Explores sexual, political, and religious issues. Two related plays by Tony Kushner.

As Is. Explores the impact of AIDS on one man, his ex-lover, and his family and friends. Play by William Hoffman.

The Big Chill. A group of college friends get back together years after graduation.

Cloud Nine. Sex roles and sexual identities are explored in this play by Caryl Churchill.

Common Threads: Stories from the Quilt. Follows the creation of the AIDS memorial quilt. Made-for-cable documentary.

Destiny of Me. Tells the story of an early AIDS activist. Play by Larry Kramer.

Everybody's All American. A football hero has trouble leaving his glory days behind and moving on, while his college sweetheart/wife changes and grows. From the novel by Frank Deford.

Falsettos. Celebrates relationships of all kinds and the importance of family. A musical play by William Finn and James Lapine.

In the Shadow of Love. A high school woman learns the hard way that AIDS can happen to anyone. Made-for-TV movie.

Kramer vs. Kramer. A troubled marriage breaks up. From the book by Avery Corman.

Lianna. A woman leaves her marriage and explores relationships with several women as she recognizes her lesbian identity.

"Life Goes On." One story line explores the life of a teenager who is living with AIDS. TV series.

Long-Time Companion. A group of gay men find their lives changed forever by the AIDS crisis.

Lovers and Other Strangers. Two young people marry and their wedding brings together many couples struggling with their own relationships. From the play by Renee Taylor and Joe Bologna.

The Normal Heart. Chronicles the fight against AIDS and the politics that get in the way. Play by Larry Kramer.

Rambling Rose. A sexually active young woman moves in with an upper-middle-class family during the Depression.

Roe v. Wade. A landmark case challenges the illegality of abortion. Made-for-TV movie.

The Ryan White Story. A teenager with AIDS, and his mother, fight courageously against the discrimination he encounters in his hometown and school. Made-for-TV movie from his autobiography.

The Sterile Cuckoo. A romance develops between two new college students. From the book by John Nichols.

Summer of '42. Teenage boys on vacation during World War II obsess about sex, while one learns what it's really all about.

The Sure Thing. A male college student learns about relationships and sex.

Tally's Folly. A romantic relationship begins between two very different people. Play by Lanford Wilson.

Tootsie. A man passes as a woman in order to get an acting job.

When Harry Met Sally. Irritation turns to friendship, then to love during this postcollege relationship.

▪ NINE ▪

Sexual Harassment

❦

I was in graduate school at the time. I didn't have the knowledge to label what I was experiencing, but my reaction back then tells me that I knew something wasn't right. The course was on nontraditional counseling methods, and as a final exam we each had to meet with the professor in his office to demonstrate our ability to use various techniques we had studied.

I remember going in to take my final. I did what I was supposed to do, and then the professor said he wanted to show me another technique. He had me close my eyes and visualize a beach in detail. He then told me to see myself on that beach. He asked what I was wearing. A bathing suit? I was starting to feel uncomfortable. "No," I said, "jeans and a turtleneck." "A suit of armor" was what I really wanted to say. There was a silence. Then he asked if I could see him on the beach. I was feeling pretty vulnerable, sitting there in his small office with my eyes closed while he tried to control what I saw. I took the control back. "Nope . . . just me . . . no one else," I said quickly, opening my eyes. I left as soon as I possibly could. Luckily, this wasn't a professor I was dependent on in any way. He wasn't my dissertation advisor, and he wasn't in my major department. I wonder sometimes how this incident might have affected my reactions and my future differently if he had been more important in my graduate program.

Twenty to thirty percent of female undergraduates are sexually harassed by at least one professor.[1] Only about 5 percent of these women, however, report the harassment or file a grievance.[2] Sexual harassment is a problem. It happens all the time even though it's not always recognized as harassment.

- A professor comments that women rarely do well in his physics class.
- A fraternity sponsors a wet t-shirt contest.
- Men on campus rate new female students by holding up scorecards as they walk past.

Terminology

Sexual harassment is discriminatory, illegal, and damaging to the academic community. In 1980 the Equal Employment Opportunity Commission (EEOC) amended Title VII of the 1964 Civil Rights Act to include sexual harassment as a form of sexual discrimination in the workplace. Sexual harassment is also covered as sex discrimination in education under Title IX of the education amendments of 1972. On the basis of these laws, *sexual harassment* in an academic setting can be defined as

unwelcome sexual advances, request for favors, innuendos and other verbal or physical conduct of a sexual nature when (1) submission to such conduct may be explicitly or implicitly a term or condition of a student's academic success, or (2) submission to or rejection of such conduct may be used as the basis for academic or other decisions affecting the student and his or her total educational experience, or (3) such conduct has the purpose or effect of substantially interfering with a student's academic performance or creating an intimidating, hostile, or offensive educational environment.[3]

While it's possible for women to harass men, it's much less likely.[4] Instances of female professors harassing male students and some same-sex harassment have been reported, but such incidents are far more isolated.[5] By far, most sexual harassment is directed by males toward females.

There are two general types of sexual harassment. The first type, called *hostile environment,* creates just that—an environment that is unwelcoming and intimidating for women. Gender harassment contributes to a hostile environment when generalized sexist remarks and behavior are directed at women because they're somehow seen as "inferior." While not necessarily intended to gain sexual cooperation, this behavior does communicate degrading attitudes toward women. Women can be affected even when the comments aren't directed specifically to them. Although gender harassment may not always be intentional and is often ingrained into the American culture, it's still harassing. Seductive behavior—for example, a professor asking unwanted questions about your personal sex life—is inappropriate and offensive and can also make the learning environment uncomfortable.[6]

Bargain situations constitute another type of sexual harassment. They occur when requests for sexual activity are directly linked to favored treatment by someone in a position of power. Sexual bribery occurs when sexual activity or other sex-related behavior is solicited by the promise of a reward, for example, when a professor suggests that you'll get a better grade or that he'll hire you as his research assistant if you cooperate. Sexual coercion is the opposite bargaining approach: soliciting sexual activity by implying or threatening some punishment or negative consequence if you refuse. For example, a professor might suggest that your grade will suffer or that you'll never get a graduate school recommendation from him if you don't cooperate. Sexual imposition can include kissing you against your will, sexual assault, and other sexual crimes, including rape.[7]

Background Information

. . .

"My art studio professor used to feel up all the female students by slipping his hands under our arms to 'help us out.' He got away with it because when we complained, the faculty committee said that we were being uptight about it; he was 'just that kind of guy.' "

—S. A., class of '93

. . .

The socialization process in the United States encourages some of the attitudes and beliefs that allow sexual harassment to occur and not be recognized. In 1991, when the U.S. Senate was voting to confirm Clarence Thomas's nomination to the Supreme Court, the question of whether the predominantly male Senate really understood the issue of sexual harassment was often asked. "They just don't get it" was the phrase used by a number of women at that time to describe the reactions of many senators after Professor Anita Hill alleged that Judge Thomas had harassed her. They couldn't understand, for example, why a woman would continue to work for someone who had harassed her or why she would continue to stay in touch with him for years afterward. Many women, however, understood only too well that sexual harassment is widespread and that sometimes you don't blow the whistle if you want to protect your longer-term career goals.

The debate generated by the Thomas-Hill hearings has led to much discussion and to greater awareness among some members of both sexes. Senator Barbara Mikulski and then Senator Al Gore followed up the hearings by organizing a series of presentations for senators and their partners in order to generate more discussion about gender differences. In the 1992 elections, the increased number of female candidates reflected a move by women to claim their place in the political power structure. Emily's List, a political fundraising group, has become a more and more powerful force endorsing and supporting female candidates for public office.

The denial of sexual harassment as a problem is really an extension of stereotypical male/female roles that suggest that it's natural for men to pursue women. This kind of thinking fails to recognize the power differential between males in positions of authority and females in positions of less authority. The fact that many women are socialized to be less assertive and to defer to more dominant male wishes also leaves women vulnerable to sexual harassment. Those who challenge sexual harassment are sometimes seen as "breaking the rules," even by other women. Attitudes about power and the privilege it offers to "superiors" can send the message that some people have a right to expect others to do what they ask. This expectation can extend to sexual favors.[8]

Women are socialized to accept many unwanted, even offensive sexual interactions as a fact of life without labeling them as harassment. This may be particularly true of the more subtle gender harassment situations. For example, many women passively smile at jokes and winks as sexual comments are made in a classroom. Some also grin and bear it when they're bothered by the display of sexist pictures and/or centerfolds on residence hall doors and windows.

ENCOUNTERING AND RESPONDING TO THIS ISSUE

The Academic Setting

• • •

"I had a close encounter, unsolicited, with a respected male professor during my junior year. To me, his proposition was shocking and disturbing. Being a junior, and presumably enlightened in some vague, feminist way, I thought my response should be mature, thoughtful, casual—in other words, highly sophisticated. Even then I was sure he counted on that, that I wouldn't tell anybody, that I wouldn't react in a childish way, and tattle. For weeks I see-sawed between 'It's no big deal, don't blow it out of proportion,' and 'Oh my God, what should I do?'

"Judging by the anger I now feel, what I should have done was slap him in the face. What, I had to wonder, had I done to encourage him? Was I too enthusiastic, too apt in my work for him? Was I too obviously excited by the insights and knowledge I was acquiring in his class? I was forced to question every grade he had given me, every conversation we had held. And worst of all, I decided not to continue my rewarding studies in his department, out of shame and embarrassment, and the risk of running into him again.

"I now realize my feelings are similar to those of rape victims. Even now, I feel anger, helplessness, and indignation over this abuse of the professor/student relationship. How dared he?"

—A. J., class of '83

• • •

First-year women in college tend to have less confidence in their intellectual capabilities than first-year men.[9] Professors have a great deal of power, although that power may be more subtle in college than in the workplace. Faculty members can't hire and fire you, but they can have a significant influence over your academic performance, intellectual development, and career potential. Besides controlling grades and letters of reference, faculty members also influence academic and career counseling and often provide access to graduate schools, professional networks, research opportunities, and internships. Faculty members have sometimes been called "career gatekeepers."[10]

Some groups of students are more likely targets of sexual harassment by male teachers. Graduate students' research and careers are often affected by their association with certain faculty members. Undergraduates hoping to go on to graduate study will need support and recommendations from influential faculty members for grad school admission and fellowships, especially if they hope to enter fields in which women are in the minority. Students on financial aid may be more dependent on their jobs and assistantships to stay in school. Women who are vulnerable in other ways—experiencing a death in the family, being on academic probation—may also be susceptible to those in positions of power.[11] False cultural stereotypes that characterize some ethnic groups as being unlikely to assert themselves by resisting and others as being very sexual may contribute to the vulnerability of some women of color.[12]

Hostile environments can develop as a result of a variety of behaviors by professors: [13]

1. Addressing the class as if there were no women present.
2. Always using the term "he" to refer to students.
3. Listening intently to male students but not to female students.
4. Interrupting women more than men.
5. Treating women who ask extensive questions as troublemakers (this often happens to returning adult students).
6. Calling female students "girls" and male students "men."
7. Using sexually offensive or degrading pictures or reading materials inappropriate to the tone or purpose of the course.
8. Telling jokes that are derogatory toward women.
9. Making suggestive comments about women's physical appearance.
10. Making derogatory remarks about gays, lesbians, returning adult students, etc.
11. Encouraging or allowing these actions to continue in a classroom when others exhibit them.

A hostile academic environment can undermine enthusiasm for learning. Some women try to limit the impact of a hostile environment by keeping a low profile and not participating as actively as they might in class. They may not show up for class, may drop the course, or may even change majors or career directions.[14] Hostile environments tend to occur more often than overt instances of individual sexual harassment, but they are more difficult to identify.

Professors who harass come from all age groups, academic ranks, academic disciplines, and family situations.[15] One-on-one instances of sexual harassment occur in varying degrees and include

1. uninvited pressure for dates or sexual activity.
2. repeated requests for dates or contacts, after you've said no.
3. inappropriate questions about your personal life.
4. unwanted touching, pinching, or other physical contact.
5. demands or requests for sexual favors, accompanied by threats concerning grades or promises of preferential treatment.
6. unwanted pressure to intensify sexual relationships that began as mutually consensual.[16]

The question of consensual relationships is the subject of much debate on campuses. Some universities prohibit even consensual relationships between students and faculty, noting the inescapable factor of the power differential. Others view these rules as interference with the rights of individuals. This remains a difficult issue, and you ought to think seriously about all the possible complications if you're considering a romantic relationship with a professor.

Sometimes a professor's interest can be flattering, particularly if you interpret it as being related to your academic abilities and future opportunities.[17] You may be inclined to give the professor the benefit of the doubt and trust that his intentions are good. Or perhaps you're caught in the bind of needing a professor because he is, for example, your major advisor, the only person teaching several required courses, or well known in his field and a valuable graduate school reference. Try to avoid becoming overly dependent on any one professor in this way.[18]

Some women remain in sexually harassing situations because they want to achieve certain professional goals. They struggle to find some way to "hang in" academically while taking great pains to protect themselves. Others compromise their professional goals in order to avoid private or prolonged contact with the professor. Still others risk forfeiting their goals by confronting the harasser or by leaving the situation. None of these alternatives is a fair burden for a woman to carry as she seeks the best possible education for herself.

There are five typical approaches taken by faculty members who sexually harass students.[19]

1. *The counselor-helper* encourages you to confide in him. He learns about your vulnerabilities and then uses these vulnerabilities to draw you into a more sexual relationship.
2. *The confidant* treats you as a friend and equal by sharing personal information about himself and then asks for the same from you. The emotional intimacy that develops is generally more than you want.
3. *The intellectual seducer* flaunts his knowledge and elicits personal information under the pretext of course-related material or experiences.
4. *The opportunist* uses circumstances to take advantage of you, such as physical contact in an art or physical education class or on trips off campus.
5. *The power broker* uses rewards or punishment to get sexual favors.

It should be stressed that while these approaches can be a prelude to sexual harassment from *some* individuals, other faculty members may simply be friendly and may offer assistance out of a genuine concern and desire to help. One way to tell the difference is to gauge how comfortable or uncomfortable you feel in the situation, and how willing the faculty member is to stop once you've told him it makes you uncomfortable.

Sexual harassment is likely to take place as a series of escalating incidents. If the harasser is someone you've respected and trusted, you may, in the early stages, wonder whether he's joking or whether you're just misinterpreting his behavior. This experience is confusing and disruptive. You may struggle to figure out what's going on, and you may be fearful of what could happen if you challenge the behavior. Many women cope by trying to ignore the situation and hoping it will just go away.[20]

A student who is sexually harassed by a faculty or staff member may feel vague dissatisfaction with college, her major, or specific courses. Loss of academic self-confidence and self-esteem may follow, and grades can decline. She may feel violated and degraded, often by someone she had respected, and this may result in feelings of powerlessness, vulnerability, and self-blame. General depression can result, often surfacing in changes in eating and sleeping patterns and physical illnesses. A woman being harassed may feel isolated from other students, may change her attitudes or behaviors regarding sexual relationships, may be irritable with family and friends, and may find it hard to concentrate.[21]

The approaches, patterns, and effects described above also apply to actions of members of the college staff, especially those who are in positions of power over you, such as coaches, work/study supervisors, tutors, R.A.s, or those with responsibility for hiring or appointing students to particular positions.

Dealing with Sexual Harassment

Women have been socialized not to make waves, and this may deter you from asserting yourself in situations where another person has power over you. If you're unsure, trust your feelings. Remember too that if the professor's behavior makes you uncomfortable, you have a right to say something. It doesn't matter if other students aren't bothered by the same behavior. Different people have different reactions.

In instances of sexual harassment, a first step is to be sure the individual knows that you don't welcome the behavior and that you want it to stop. Citing specific behaviors may initially make the professor less defensive than if you come right out and call him a harasser. If the behavior persists, however, after you've told the professor you don't welcome it, clearly say that his behavior is harassing to you. Say the word. That should leave little doubt about whether he's been told how you feel.

When you talk to the professor, be clear. Don't soften the message by smiling or looking away, and don't let him divert you with personal questions. The format of the three-part letter described below may help you plan what you want to say. You also might feel more comfortable practicing beforehand with a friend or R.A. Arrange to meet the professor in a place that feels safe to you, and perhaps bring a friend along if that would make you more comfortable.

If you'd prefer to communicate without having to interact personally with the harasser, consider sending a letter containing three parts. Start by stating exactly what happened, for example, "You stroked my arm" or "You asked me to dinner twice last week." This should be done in an objective way. In the second part of the letter, express how what happened has made you feel, then and now. In the third part of the letter, clearly state what you want to happen, for example, "I don't want you to make any physical contact with me or ask me out again. I want this to be the end of the matter and I don't want to talk about it." Send the letter through the off-campus mail system to make sure that the date is officially postmarked. If you send it return receipt requested, there can be no question of it having been received. Be sure to keep a copy of the letter for yourself.[22]

You can also help yourself by keeping a written diary or journal documenting incidents and conversations you have with the harasser. Record dates, places, what happened, and who else, if anyone, was there. Also record how you're being affected, for example, that you went to the Health Center with stomach problems or missed two days of classes. Such records can be valuable if you file a complaint later.

It's helpful to compile evidence of your performance in the course, particularly if you anticipate filing charges. Retain tests, papers, and evaluation materials to protect yourself later. That will make it harder for your professor to say that a poor grade in the course was a result of your actual performance rather than retaliation for your unwillingness to become sexually involved.

See if other students have experienced similar behavior, as there is often a pattern.[23] When I worked at some colleges for more than a couple of years, it was amazing how some of the same names kept being mentioned by students. If you discover that others have had the same kinds of experiences, this can keep you from unfairly blaming yourself.

Tell someone else about what's happening. When Anita Hill alleged that Clarence Thomas had harassed her, Professor Hill's corroborating witnesses were people to whom she had confided at the time of the alleged harassment. A logical person to turn to, initially, is the harasser's supervisor or department chair, or perhaps the academic dean of your college. If you're unsure how receptive these people may be, seek out another faculty or staff person for advice.

Finally, many colleges have students do written evaluations of their courses each semester. You can use this opportunity to provide feedback about the professor and about the climate in the classroom. If professors' comments and actions create a hostile environment for women, they should know it. Some professors genuinely welcome the feedback and will try to adjust their behavior. If these evaluations are read by department chairs or used in tenure and promotion decisions, the professor may need to do some thinking and perhaps answer some pointed questions. At the least, you've made others aware of potential harassment in a classroom.

KAL, Cartoonists and Writers Syndicate.

Reporting Sexual Harassment

When Anita Hill came forward with allegations of sexual harassment, skepticism and aggression were directed toward her. If this woman, a tenured professor and graduate of one of the country's top law schools, received such a response, it's understandable that college students would be hesitant to report sexual harassment. Many are. They fear reprisal because they're generally in a powerless position in relation to the harasser. Some women don't tell about their experiences because of unfair traditional views that victims are "losers," that the victim must have provoked the action or willingly participated, and that she deserved whatever happened.[24] Many people attack the character of the victim and blame her.

Reporting harassment, however, is one way to document patterns and to hold habitual harassers accountable for their actions. Multiple complaints against the same individual create a stronger case. If your campus has an affirmative action office, that's the most appropriate place to take your concern. By doing so you're also putting the institution on notice that a situation exists, and it has a legal obligation to respond. The response does not necessarily have to involve you. It can, for example, include more general educational efforts within the particular department where the harasser works.

There are both formal and informal channels for handling sexual-harassment complaints. Informal complaints may be written or not, are not formally investigated, and don't result in formal disciplinary action. The intent of an informal process is more educational and is designed to resolve the situation to the satisfaction of both parties.[25] If your campus has an ombudsperson, this individual may be the appropriate person to contact. On campuses without such a staff member, the Affirmative Action Office or some individual will be designated to handle the informal resolution of complaints.

When lodging an informal complaint, talk with the ombudsperson or designated staff member to help you plan a course of action. Perhaps you'll decide initially to handle the situation yourself. If so, the staff member will probably ask you to check back to let him/her know how it was resolved. Talk to the ombudsperson *before* you speak with the harasser. This is helpful if you fear retaliation because it documents your concern early.

Another approach is for the ombudsperson to talk to the faculty member. S/he would describe to the professor the behavioral concern that you have brought to her/him. Ninety percent of the time, there's agreement that the behavior took place, although not necessarily about what the behavior meant. Depending on the severity of the behavior, resolution may include an end to the behavior, an apology, a demotion, or voluntary resignation without formal disciplinary procedures.[26]

If an agreeable resolution can't be reached, the ombudsperson may meet with the faculty member and/or dean or department chair. The ombudsperson will try to mediate and negotiate a resolution that will prevent further incidents and ensure a less hostile academic or work environment. Accommodations such as permitting you to switch sections or having another faculty member read and grade your coursework may be part of the agreement. Other faculty members in a department can be helpful in negotiating informal resolutions.

Formal complaints need to be written by you as the complaining student or by someone else with your confirmation. Complaints are filed with the Affirmative Action Office or with another office designated to handle formal complaints. An investigation is required and can result in formal disciplinary action. If you file a formal complaint, you should expect confidentiality, an impartial investigation, protection from retaliation, and assurance of an administrative solution if the charges are proven.[27] Get a copy of your college's sexual harassment and grievance procedures to help you understand your rights and responsibilities in the process. There are often deadlines for certain steps to be taken, and it's important for you to be aware of anything that could affect your ability to fully pursue your complaint.

You don't need surprises. Ask questions of the affirmative action officer in order to understand what steps you need to take and what to expect from the process. The formal process may involve a hearing in front of one or two people or perhaps before a somewhat larger board. Ask about the composition of the hearing body. Are faculty, staff, and students involved? Do you have any options if you feel that someone hearing the case is biased? What role/power does the hearing person or group have? Do they make the final decision or do they make recommendations to someone else?

Those doing the investigating won't take your side. That doesn't mean they don't believe you; their role requires impartiality. Find out what your rights are regarding advocacy and support. Don't go through a formal process alone. Find a calm, knowledgeable person you trust to accompany and advise you. Consider someone from the faculty or staff rather than another student because the power dynamics will be different if you rely solely on student support in a complaint against a faculty or staff member.

If you are unwilling to file a complaint in the case of a serious problem, ask if the college will initiate the investigation. You might still need to serve as a witness or file a statement, but in some situations the institution may be willing to bring the complaint. It may also decide to take that step if yours is one of several charges against the same person.

You also have the right to bypass your college's internal procedures and go through the regular court system. Title IX of the 1972 education amendments prohibits sex discrimination in educational institutions. This is the federal law under which a student can seek to hold an educational institution liable if she experiences sexual harassment there. Traditionally, the result of a successful lawsuit has been withdrawal of federal funds from the institution.[28] In 1992, however, the U.S. Supreme Court unanimously ruled that a student who has been sexually harassed may seek financial damages from the school where the harassment occurred.[29] State tort laws provide another avenue through which students may seek to claim monetary damages for emotional suffering and distress related to sexual harassment.[30] Instances of assault or rape can be pursued under regular criminal statutes.

Peer Harassment

. . .

"The guys who lived in my dormitory used to come into the women's bathroom and whip open the shower curtains, all in the name of fun. It was pretty funny until it happened to me."
—S. A., class of '93

. . .

While harassment by male students of female students doesn't involve the same power component as sexual harassment by a professor or supervisor, it still affects the atmosphere on campus for women. Peer harassment, often founded on the power of "male privilege" or physical strength, runs the gamut from sexual teasing to sexist bullying to emotional and psychological harassment to sexual harassment to sexual aggression. Studies at individual campuses have shown 70–92 percent of the women experience some unwanted sexual attention or insult. Often this behavior is shrugged off or accepted with "that's what it's like at college" or "boys will be boys."[31]

Sexual harassment that contributes to the creation of a hostile climate on campus for women includes public displays of sexist posters and pictures; sexist graffiti, bumper stickers, and advertising for events and parties; and social activities focusing on women's sexuality. More personal harassment includes extreme sexual bantering and jokes, lewd comments about a woman's body and sexual activities, giving women pornographic materials, and unwanted touching or kissing. Sexual attention that persists after you have given a clear message that you aren't interested is one sign that the behavior has crossed the line from expressing sexual interest to imposing it. Also, comments and questions that may be appropriate as part of an ongoing relationship are less appropriate, and even harassing, from a stranger or someone you have just met.[32]

Some men will act in groups in ways that they wouldn't act individually, and more serious incidents of peer harassment take place in groups of men. Fraternities are often involved in peer harassment, perhaps as part of pledging and hazing rituals. Examples of group harassment include publicly rating the attractiveness of women; yelling, whistling, and shouting; exhibitionism such as "mooning"; and physical intimidation.[33]

Some women aren't offended by these behaviors. Some consider it flattering. Still others are uncomfortable speaking out about "feminist" issues and potentially being labeled radical. The desire to be seen as a good sport and one of the gang induces some women to go along with such activities. When a little harassment is ignored, tolerated, or encouraged, however, it tends to escalate or increase. As more people in a crowd accept that this behavior is OK, more participate, and it becomes harder for someone to stop it. Women who have supported this behavior up until then or have been silent about it may find themselves in situations that become more and more extreme, perhaps resulting in sexual assault or even gang rape.[34]

Anger against women is one underlying motive for peer harassment. Others may have to do with power, control, and the need to feel superior to another group. Some women are singled out more often as targets of peer harassment, including Jewish women, large-sized women, lesbians, women in traditional male fields of study, women of color, and women who are politically active in women's issues.[35]

Peer harassment can have negative effects on both men and women. Women receive the message that they aren't taken seriously. Their aspirations may be undermined, and self-doubt may be created or reinforced. For men, the implication that women don't deserve equal respect can interfere with their ability to develop healthy male/female relationships. Men who don't take women seriously in college may be poorly prepared for a working world in which women could be their colleagues or supervisors.[36]

If you're harassed by male students, several of the steps described in the previous section also apply here. Stating clearly that certain attentions and behaviors are unwelcome, sending a three-part letter, and documenting your experiences are all approaches to consider.

You may be hesitant to report incidents of peer harassment because you don't want to be seen as blowing the whistle on behavior that's supposedly accepted among students. However, there are probably more students than you think who find it unacceptable but are afraid to speak out. There can be strength in numbers, so consider asking others who have been offended to join you.

If the peer who harasses you has power over you—for example, your supervisor at a work/study job, a teaching assistant, or your R.A.—you may have recourse through the college's grievance procedure. Check with your affirmative action office.

WHERE TO LOOK FOR HELP

If you're subjected to peer harassment, informal mediation/negotiation could take place through student, staff, or faculty assistance, depending on the situation. Your college's student conduct code ought to describe behavior expected of all students, and it should have provisions for student complaints against other students. You may have several options in addressing these concerns, such as the dean of students, dean for Greek affairs, Affirmative Action Office, or Student Judicial Board. When you discuss your options, find out what's involved in each. What's required of you? What is the scope of possible results? What protection exists for you? If you're assaulted or threatened, you should definitely contact your campus security office.

Learn as much as you can about sexual harassment and your rights. Read policies and materials put out on your campus and know which individuals are designated to deal with complaints. If educational programs are offered, attend them. They could help you identify sources of information and support. By the questions other students ask you may even be able to discover others who are having experiences similar to yours.

Academic courses in areas such as psychology, sociology, and women's studies may also provide information. Seek out female role models and mentors on the faculty. They can help you explore your field and career from the perspective of a woman who has succeeded.

I encourage you to use the ombudsperson and Affirmative Action Office for reporting instances of sexual harassment. When there's a centralized location for documenting concerns, there's greater likelihood that repeaters will eventually be identified. You don't have to press charges if you report, but the Affirmative Action Office needs to have statements on file. You could wind up being one of several women whose complaints could combine to form a stronger case against the same person.

Some campuses have student counselors or advocates trained to assist in instances of sexual harassment. If you're hesitant to approach the administration, consult with a peer group. In such groups peers can talk to you about your options, and they too may know if others have expressed concerns about the same person. If you want to talk about informal resolutions, generally the dean of the faculty or vice-president for academic affairs is the person to go to with complaints about faculty; the dean of students, for complaints about other students; and the director of personnel, for complaints about staff and administrators. If you want to resolve a problem by dropping a class or switching sections, or through any other means that involve academic policies and procedures, explain your situation to your advisor or academic dean. S/he may be able to offer exceptions to rules and deadlines.

The stress around sexual harassment and related decisions can affect you in a variety of ways. Friends, counselors, hotlines, peer support, your R.A., residence staff, and chaplains are all potential sources of help.

EDUCATING YOURSELF

Books: Nonfiction, Anthologies, Biographies, Poetry, Plays

Dziech, Billie Wright, and Linda Weiner. *The Lecherous Professor: Sexual Harassment on Campus*. Boston: Beacon, 1984.

Gomez-Preston, Cheryl, with Randi Reisfeld. *When No Means No: A Guide to Sexual Harassment*. New York: Birch Lane, 1993.

Henley, Nancy M. *Body Politics: Power, Sex, and Nonverbal Communication*. New York: Touchstone, 1986.

Katz, Montana, and Veronica Vieland. *Get Smart! A Woman's Guide to Equality on Campus*. New York: Feminist Press, 1988.

Langelan Martha J. *Back Off! How to Confront and STOP Sexual Harassment*. New York: Fireside, 1993.

MacKinnon, Catharine A. *Sexual Harassment of Working Women: A Case of Sex Discrimination*. New Haven, CT: Yale University Press, 1979.

Miramontes, David. *How to Deal with Sexual Harassment*. San Diego, CA: Network Communications, 1982.

Sumrall, Amber Coverdale, and Dena Taylor. *Sexual Harassment: Women Speak Out*. Freedom, CA: Crossing Press, 1992.

Tong, R. *Women, Sex, and the Law*. Totowa, NJ: Rowman and Allanheld, 1984.

Articles, Pamphlets, and Papers

Gite, Lloyd. "Workplace Problems: Sexual Harassment and Racial Discrimination." *Black Collegian,* April–May 1982.

Hall, Roberta M., and Bernice R. Sandler. "The Classroom Climate: A Chilly One for Women?" Washington, DC: Association of American Colleges, Project on the Status and Education of Women, 1982.

Hughes, Jean, and Bernice Sandler. "In Case of Sexual Harassment: A Guide for Women Students." Washington, DC: Association of American Colleges, Project on the Status and Education of Women, 1986.

Moses, Y. T. "Black Women in Academe: Issues and Strategies." Washington, DC: Association of American Colleges, Project on the Status and Education of Women, 1989.

Project on the Status and Education of Women. "Sexual Harassment: A Hidden Issue." Washington, DC: Association of American Colleges, 1978.

———. "Peer Harassment: Hassles for Women on Campus." Washington, DC: Association of American Colleges, 1988.

Sandler, Bernice. "Writing a Letter to the Sexual Harasser: Another Way of Dealing with the Problem." Washington, DC: Association of American Colleges, Project on the Status and Education of Women, 1983.

Till, F. "Sexual Harassment: A Report on the Sexual Harassment of Students." Washington, DC: National Advisory Council on Women's Educational Programs, 1980.

Organizations for Information and Assistance

Equal Employment Opportunity Commission
    1801 L St. NW
    Washington, DC 20507
    202-663-4264
    1-800-669-4000
National Association for Women in Education
    Suite 210
    1325 18th St. NW
    Washington, DC 20036-6511
    202-659-9330
Project on the Status and Education of Women
    Association of American Colleges
    1818 R St. NW
    Washington, DC 20009
    202-387-3760

Films, Videos, TV Shows, Plays

Oleanna. A college student and her professor struggle over the question of sexual harassment. Play by David Mamet.

Prime Suspect. A female detective inspector solves a murder case despite the sexism she encounters among her colleagues. PBS miniseries.

Silence of the Lambs. A serial killer tries to intimidate a female FBI trainee through mental power and extreme manipulation games. From the book by Thomas Harris.

Thelma and Louise. Two women assert themselves, and after resisting violence with violence, they experience life on the run.

Working Girl. A young woman rises from the ranks to become a success at business.

TEN

Sexual Abuse, Rape, and Personal Safety

"Cruelty might be very human, and it might be very cultural, but it's not acceptable."
— Jodie Foster, Academy Award acceptance speech
for her role in *The Accused*[1]

Several years ago, the college where I worked offered a panel about personal safety as a regular part of new-student orientation. I was joined on the panel by the director of security, a self-defense instructor, and four students. Several of these students were rape awareness educators who ran workshops during the school year. One student spoke candidly about her own experience as a survivor of an acquaintance rape during her first year at the college.

After every one of our presentations, new students came up to thank the presenters. There were always several who identified themselves as survivors of rape, incest, or violent homes. Our open discussion of the issue seemed especially important to them. As survivors speak out about their experiences, they are said to be "breaking the silence." Hopefully, as that silence lifts, the undeserved shame that thrives in silence and isolation will also begin to fade.

The transition from home to college raises issues of sexual abuse in several ways. You may begin to recognize that you've been victimized in the past, and you may experience the effects of that violence as you interact with others on campus. Or you could have a roommate, friend, or girlfriend/boyfriend who is a survivor, and s/he may need your understanding and support. You also never know when you, or someone you know, will be a potential victim.

Some of this chapter may bring up painful memories for those of you who are survivors. Others of you might prefer just not to think about it. Not thinking about it, however, creates a false sense of security and can make you careless. You make yourself vulnerable if you believe the myth that college campuses are totally safe places insulated from the "real world." You need to be as aware of your safety on a college campus as you would be anywhere else. Most violence on campus is actually student-to-student violence.[2]

The traditional-aged college population is vulnerable to violence for several reasons. As you enter college, you enter a new environment with many different kinds of stress. You've lost day-to-day contact with your parents—both their restrictions and their support—and you're also more distant from high school friends. There's often heavy peer pressure in college to socialize and experiment. The availability of drugs, especially alcohol, also contributes to the vulnerability.

Terminology

An *abusive relationship* is one in which one partner deliberately acts to hurt the other by what s/he says or does. Actions that are verbally or emotionally abusive include public humiliation, continuous criticism and name calling, threats of harm to you or someone or something close to you, or manipulation with lies. Physical abuse involves one partner attempting to hurt the other through physical force. This may mean frequent pushing, shoving, slapping, hitting, or punching. It can also include objects being thrown, abandonment in dangerous places, refusal to help a sick partner, or threats with a weapon. The abuse becomes sexual abuse when, for instance, a partner insists on more sexual attire than the other wants, minimizes the other's feelings about sex, subjects the other to unwanted touching, or forces sex or unwanted sexual acts.[3] Quite simply, abuse is an act of mistreatment and disrespect, with one partner misusing the power s/he has in the relationship.[4]

Child sexual abuse is defined as a sexual act imposed on a child or adolescent by force or manipulation, where there is an imbalance in age, size, power, or knowledge. While such abuse was initially labeled as *incest* only when the abuser was a parent or other family member, the definition of incest has been expanded to include anyone the child depends on and trusts—a teacher, clergyperson, coach, babysitter, etc.[5] Sexual activity can include fondling, exhibition, or sexual intercourse.[6] Regardless of what the specific act was or how often it occurred, if the experience was a violation for a child, then that child was sexually abused.[7]

In most states, *rape* involves a sexual assault, usually vaginal penetration, against the victim's will, by force or threat of force, or when the victim is physically or emotionally unable to give her consent. Some states include anal and oral sex in their definition of rape.[8]

The difference between the terms "victim" and "survivor" is an important one to understand. A *victim* is someone who is currently suffering abuse, and a *survivor* is one who is no longer being subjected to the act.[9] Using the term "victim" is a more passive way of describing someone who has previously experienced sexual abuse. If a woman sees herself passively, she may be more likely to believe that she has little strength and power, and her self-concept can suffer. This may even make her more vulnerable to additional victimization. The concept of "survivor," a more active and powerful term, indicates that someone has experienced abuse and has been strong enough to survive it. With the encouragement and support of others, a survivor can learn to appreciate her strengths and use them to take more control of her life. The process of moving from victim to survivor is a long and painful one, but it's a way to take back some of what's been taken away.

Background Information

■ ■ ■

"Years ago, during a wave of crimes against women in Israel, a council of men asked Golda Meir to put a nighttime curfew on females. Meir said no. If men were the problem, she answered, let the council enforce a curfew against men."
—Ellen Goodman, "The Double Standard"[10]

■ ■ ■

Sexual abuse isn't really about sex—it's about power and aggression. The way our culture socializes men and women to behave with one another is a large part of the problem. Men are often socialized not to express emotions but to keep them inside. When a man feels emotional pain and has no socially acceptable way to express it, anger and violence directed toward others can result.[11] Men are generally socialized to be sexually aggressive and sexually active, to think primarily of their own sexual needs, and not to view women as equal partners. Many men have learned that it's their role to initiate sexual activity and to try to get what they want by persistence, persuasion, and force if necessary. A man may also believe that when a woman says no, she really means maybe or yes, for he believes that she's been socialized not to yield too easily to sexual involvement. These beliefs and pressures can lead some men to persist in situations where the woman is not a willing partner.

- 25 percent of college men say that they would be willing to use force to get sex.[12]
- Among college women, 83 percent report having suffered some attempt at forced sexual contact in a dating situation.[13]

Women, on the other hand, have been socialized to defer to men, especially if the man is seen as attractive, bright, from a "good" family, or belonging to the best fraternity. While men are taught to persist in sexual situations, women are taught not to be too aggressive in expressing their wishes. Rather than being firm and clear, women often try to get out of unwanted sexual situations without hurting or embarrassing the man, or without being seen as a bitch. Unclear messages can further confuse the man. This may mean, for example, that a woman has to repeat her point and even raise her voice, express annoyance, or physically remove a man's hand from her body to emphasize what she means.

Men and women also interpret communication differently. Coming in for a cup of coffee may mean coming in for a cup of coffee to a woman but may be interpreted by some men as an interest in a sexual relationship. Women need to be clear about what they want and don't want, and men need to hear them and not discount or reinterpret what women say.

One 1992 episode of the TV show "L.A. Law" effectively demonstrated the different interpretations of communication. In that show, a famous young male baseball player was accused of rape by a woman he had met at a bar and taken to a party. The woman's story was believable, but the man also passed a polygraph test supporting his plea of innocence. The baseball player told his lawyer what the woman said during their time together, what he knew she *really* wanted, and what he physically did. When the athlete finished talking, still believing that his story clearly showed his innocence, his lawyer said to him softly, "What you just described is rape." The athlete looked shocked and confused. It clearly wasn't rape to him; that's why he'd passed the polygraph.

The culture that fosters sexual aggressiveness in men also creates fear for many women—fear that can cheat them out of opportunities. Even women who have never been assaulted may try to protect themselves by avoiding situations they see as potentially dangerous. This can extend to missing out on educational, cultural, or social activities in the evening, or not feeling safe to go for a relaxing walk by themselves at night. Some women take this to an extreme and avoid doing anything. Others are reasonably careful rather than overly scared. Still others, however, convince themselves that nothing can ever happen to them and thus fail even to take realistic precautions.

Abusive Relationships

Approximately 20 percent of college students experience violent behavior in dating relationships.[14] It's likely that many college students grew up in homes where there were abusive relationships between their parents, for spouse violence occurs in at least one in ten families in any given year.[15] Children in these households learn violence as a model for dealing with conflict in intimate relationships. Some students come to college with this expectation as they enter into relationships with their peers. While certainly not all students from abusive family backgrounds perpetuate abusive behavior, this behavior is more likely from those who have experienced it personally or seen it at home.[16]

Abusive relationships and battering occur primarily in heterosexual relationships; however, there are also instances of abusive relationships between lesbians. There has tended to be even greater silence surrounding lesbian battering, partly to avoid additional homophobic reactions from society. This silence and denial can make the situation even more isolating for the lesbian survivor, whose support system is often also her partner's.[17]

• • •

"I didn't realize that my girlfriend was abusing me until after we broke up for other reasons. But looking back and seeing the patterns of abuse helped me to become a survivor rather than remain a victim; once I recognized what was going on, I could take action. Because it was a lesbian relationship, I felt like I had to keep a perfect face for the world."

—S. A., class of '93

. . .

The cycle of violence, for all abusive relationships, follows a pattern. Tension builds with increasing stress, frustration, and communication problems. The victim tries to pacify the aggressor. Violence or battering occurs, after which there is a cooling-off period, and perhaps the partners are separated in some way. The batterer then returns and promises to stop the abusive behavior. The victim takes him/her back and there is a "honeymoon" period during which things seem to be better. Tensions begin to build again, however, and violence or battering repeats. With each repeated cycle, the violence tends to become more severe and the cooling-off, promise, and honeymoon periods become shorter.[18]

The patterns of relationship violence on campus and in the residence halls are similar to those in society. Incidents of courtship violence and battering are often not reported. Sometimes women don't identify what happened to them as criminal, sometimes they think that nothing will be done if they report it, and sometimes they fear that they won't be taken seriously if they do. They may also be afraid that their peers will ostracize them if they speak out, especially about someone who is popular and well liked.[19]

Incest

It's been estimated that one out of three girls and one out of seven boys are sexually abused before they're eighteen years old.[20] Though boys are often abused when they're younger, as they grow older they may be able to physically resist their abuser. For women, the abuse tends to continue as they reach sexual maturity.

More and more people are identifying themselves as survivors of incest. The effects of incest on the survivor include

1. lowered self-esteem.
2. a general feeling of danger and lack of safety.
3. difficulty in trusting others.
4. self-blame, guilt, and shame.

5. inability to rely on instinctive feelings about people and situations.
6. feelings of having their boundaries, body, and privacy violated and having lost the right to control over their life.
7. isolation from others.
8. development of inaccurate perceptions of sexuality and what sexual relationships are all about.
9. difficulty in developing healthy intimate and sexual relationships.
10. inability to find, from family, the trust and support needed to help in the transition to college.[21]

Many of the coping mechanisms women develop to survive involve minimizing or denying the abusive behavior. Some pretend that it wasn't that bad or that it didn't happen. A woman may "split" herself, in a sense, and begin to feel like more than one person. For example, she may split the person who is abused at night from the happy little girl who does well in school. This may help her cope in the short run, yet it will contribute, in the long run, to her feeling less than whole. Those who totally block out the memories may experience pain as an adult without understanding its cause.[22]

In several states, the statute of limitations for filing a suit has been extended in cases where individuals have realized that they had repressed their memories of being sexually abused as a child. While legal action can be a difficult process, for some women it is therapeutic to speak out and to stand up to someone against whom they had been so powerless.[23]

Emotionally, survivors of incest may experience problems with depression, anxiety, substance abuse, eating behavior, vulnerability to additional victimization, and other self-destructive behaviors.[24] Despite this list of devastating effects, one very important fact must be remembered: women who have survived incest must possess great strength and courage to have come through such an ordeal.

Rape
The risk of rape is four times higher for women between the ages of sixteen and twenty-four than for any other age group, and approximately half of the men arrested for rape are twenty-four or younger.[25] According to a nationwide survey on over thirty college campuses, one in four females responding had had an experience that met the legal definition of rape or attempted rape.[26]

When I was growing up in the fifties and sixties, the word "rape" brought to mind the image of a scary stranger jumping out of the bushes late at night. That's what I was taught. Some students *are* attacked by strangers, but far more—approximately 84 percent—are attacked by people they know.[27] This has become known as acquaintance rape. For many years, women were hesitant to call these incidents rape because they didn't fit the image or definition they had been taught. Much of what we've learned about rape is inaccurate, and we're just beginning to relearn the facts: [28]

1. *No one* deserves to be raped—not even if she asked the man out, let him buy her an expensive dinner, wore a tight dress, went back to his apartment, or drank or did drugs. *No one asks to be raped.*
2. It's rape whether the man uses a weapon or not, or whether the woman fights back or not. Verbal threats, alcohol, physical or emotional weakness, or isolation are all tactics that can overwhelm a woman.
3. It's rape even if the woman has willingly had sex with the man before.
4. Everyone has the right to say no and have that respected, regardless of the sexual activity up until that moment. Women have a right to change their minds.
5. Men *can* stop. Men don't need to physically have sex with an unwilling partner after becoming aroused. They can still control themselves.
6. In 93.2 percent of rape cases, both the man and the woman are of the same race.[29]
7. Women rarely falsely accuse others of rape. Only 2 percent of all rape charges are unfounded.[30] This rate of false reporting is the same general rate as for other violent crimes.

ENCOUNTERING AND RESPONDING TO THIS ISSUE

. . .

"I am a survivor of date/acquaintance rape. It happened the summer before my freshman year of college one day when my parents weren't home. A few months short of my two-year anniversary with my boyfriend, he came over and decided it was time. He carried me upstairs to my room, told me he knew I wanted it, held my wrists together and slapped me when I protested. I thought I owed him after dating him for so long. He had been in college that whole year before and said all his fraternity brothers had sex with their girlfriends. He needed us to do this to prove he still loved me and vice versa. We discussed it (making love) many times before this happened, and he knew I wanted to wait. I told him NO. I protested, but at the same time thought I owed him that. I realize now he was wrong, he had no right to do what he did and I did all I could do. It took talking to someone to make me realize that what happened was not my fault. It still hurts, and feelings come back when rapes occur on campus. But I have support now, and I'm making it through even though it still sometimes hurts."

—E. J., class of '92

. . .

The way men and women treat one another on your campus will help to define what behaviors are acceptable and unacceptable. Those definitions need to come from both women and men. The term "rape culture" is often used to describe the effects of socialization that were presented earlier in this chapter. A campus on which there's an emphasis on men "scoring" contributes to some men feeling they're expected to be sexually aggressive with women even if they resist. Fraternities, athletic teams, and other groups of men have sometimes reinforced these attitudes and have protected members from the consequences of their actions. In the movie *The Accused,* for example, this kind of protection takes place until one man speaks out with the truth.

Women can also contribute to a campus culture that accepts, or at least doesn't challenge, questionable behavior. At one school where I worked, a residence hall used to hold an annual party with a Hawaiian theme. The party was advertised as a "Get Leid" party. Some women felt that this was just a name for the event and that the party itself was no different from most other parties on campus. Other women thought the advertising sent out an implied message to men who attended—a message that these women weren't comfortable supporting.

On some campuses, sexually aggressive and abusive behavior is ignored or condoned by silence. Other colleges have begun to incorporate statements into their codes of student conduct about the unacceptability of this kind of behavior. Peer pressure is a powerful force. As both men and women understand the need for relationships and sexual activity to be mutually respectful and consensual, perhaps the climate on campuses will become safer and healthier for everyone.

For Those in an Abusive Relationship

If you're concerned about whether you may be in an abusive relationship, do some thinking about past relationships—those modeled in your family and also your own past dating patterns. Some of the early warning signs of an abusive partner include

1. jealousy and possessiveness.
2. isolating you from friends and family.
3. trying to control you, for example, by giving orders or being bossy.
4. violent behavior, a history of fighting, bragging about mistreating others, and losing his/her temper quickly.
5. pressure for sex or withholding it to get his/her way.
6. blaming you when s/he mistreats you, for example, saying that you made him/her do it.
7. a history of bad relationships and blaming the other person for all the problems.[31]

Pay attention when others who care about you express sincere concern about your partner and how you're being treated. Friends can often see patterns that are hard for you to recognize from within a relationship.

Don't blame yourself for being in an abusive relationship or for being attracted to someone who treats you that way. What's important is recognizing what's unhealthy for you and getting out safely. It's not necessarily easy to leave. Sometimes being in any relationship feels more fulfilling than being alone. There may be some things about your partner that you really love and don't want to lose. Some women stay because they fear worse harm if they try to leave or because they're emotionally or economically dependent on their partner. Often women stay because they've lost their confidence in themselves and feel they have no power to change the situation.[32] Take steps to build your self-confidence and independence so that you feel you have choices and don't have to stay in unhealthy situations.

Although abusive partners may promise that they'll change, very few actually do. The most encouraging signs of change are seen when abusers accept full responsibility for their actions, examine all the ways in which they try to control and dominate, commit themselves to a program for batterers or counseling, and remain violence free for one year.[33]

For Friends of Those in an Abusive Relationship

If you're concerned about a roommate or friend who appears to be involved in an abusive relationship, do *not* confront the abuser. This could be dangerous for you and could intensify the abuse for your friend. If you feel comfortable doing so, gently approach the abused person about how you see the situation. You don't have to confront her but can make yourself available to talk or ask questions to help her explore her feelings. Try to be nonjudgmental and supportive. If you try to force her to recognize that she's in an abusive relationship, or if you take control of her situation for her, it may do more harm than good. Don't expect your friend's behavior to change overnight. Leaving an abuser can take a long time and may involve several returns before she is ready to leave for good. Try to be patient with your friend as she builds up her self-esteem. What may feel easy for you may be much more difficult for her. Remember that you can't make your friend's decisions for her. Do whatever you can to communicate your concern, but don't forget to take care of your own needs and safety.[34]

For Incest Survivors

If you're aware that you're an incest survivor, leaving home to go away to college can create feelings of safety and independence and a sense of having finally escaped from the abusive situation.[35] If you haven't talked to anyone yet about your abuse, you could feel some stress about maintaining the secret.

Many children cope with their abuse by forgetting or repressing it. Memories can be triggered by a variety of events in college—a particular touch from a date, attempts to engage you in a sexual relationship, a certain gesture, or even a specific song playing on the radio. It's thus possible that you may find yourself identifying as a survivor for the first time after you're away from home. If this happens, talk with someone at your college counseling service as soon as you can. You may also experience some physical or emotional aftereffects, such as fear of being alone in the dark or compulsive behaviors, without knowing the reasons why.

E. Sue Blume's book, *Secret Survivors: Uncovering Incest and Its After-effects in Women,* describes these effects in more detail.

Incest survivors often experience problems with intimacy, relationships, and sexuality. As a survivor, you may have difficulty enjoying sexual relationships, or you may have reactions to particular sexual acts that bring back memories of the abuse. Having experienced a sense of powerlessness around sexuality and betrayal in a trusted relationship, you may find it difficult to develop healthy intimate relationships. Some survivors protect themselves by avoiding intimate relationships altogether. Some survivors take the other extreme and continue to submit to any sexual overtures because they have come to devalue their own bodies or have never learned that they have the right to set limits.[36]

It's important to realize that you have more resources now than you did as a child. The healing process, once you're ready to begin it, is one that you shouldn't attempt alone. Have at least one other person to help you—perhaps another survivor, a counselor, a caring partner, or an understanding family member. Ellen Bass and Laura Davis have written a tremendously helpful book called *The Courage to Heal: A Guide for Women Survivors of Child Sexual Abuse.* In it they describe the stages of the healing process in detail. The book is an excellent resource for survivors and those who care about them. The goals of recovery from incest are to

1. express your feelings about the sexual abuse and the abuser.
2. understand sexual abuse in ways that are not destructive to your own self-image.
3. reduce any feelings you may have of responsibility and guilt.
4. recognize the negative impact the abuse has had on your feelings about yourself and on your relationships with others.
5. learn more assertive behaviors and communication skills in both sexual and nonsexual situations.
6. develop more appropriate ways of expressing and meeting your needs.
7. learn more healthy life skills such as decision making and setting limits.[37]

While you can never erase what happened, and while the healing process will be ongoing, remember to give yourself credit for each positive step you take. Do things you're proud of and that you want to do.

Take breaks in the process—it's hard work—to enjoy your self and gain energy. Be with people who value your strength and appreciate you.[38]

As a college student, you may find it difficult to have two priorities at once—concentrating on the healing process and functioning up to your potential as a student. Perhaps you'll have to make some choices. Some students try to focus on their academics and postpone dealing with the impact of their abuse. A few manage to do this, while others have difficulty. Some students take a semester or a year off from school. Perhaps they hold a less demanding job and work on their recovery with a therapist and/or support group and sometimes with their family. Many of these students return to finish their education when they come far enough through their healing process to be able to concentrate on their academics again.

For some students, going home to work on healing is impossible, especially if the abuser is still present. Some rent apartments in locations where they have the necessary support, and others consider treatment facilities that offer what they need.

If you remain in school as you heal, there may be some situations that are particularly stressful for you. Decisions about going home on vacation should be yours to make, and you may need to set some ground rules for your own safety. If your family perceives paying for your education as a way to maintain control over you, explore financial aid options and also the possibility of working part-time to begin to develop more independence.

If you're a survivor who is a returning adult student, say, a mother with children, you may encounter a whole different range of issues. Seek out a support system with at least some members who share your life experiences.

For Friends of Incest Survivors

If someone tells you that s/he is an incest survivor, s/he's shown great courage and trust in you. The more you know about child sexual abuse and the healing process, the less that friend will need to teach you. The following suggestions are offered to you as a friend: [39]

1. Believe the survivor and let your friend know that you're willing to hear whatever s/he has to tell you.
2. Validate the anger, pain, fear, and damage that's been done.

3. Stress that abuse is never the child's fault.
4. Don't sympathize with the abuser. For example, don't say "but he seemed so nice" if he's someone you've met.
5. Express your compassion and feelings without overwhelming the survivor's feelings.
6. Understand that healing is a long and slow process.
7. Encourage your friend to get support—perhaps counseling and/or a support group.
8. Accept that as the survivor heals, there may be changes in your relationship.

One particular behavior evokes great concern and confusion for roommates and friends. Some survivors tend to hurt themselves through acts such as burning their skin with cigarettes or scratching and cutting themselves with knives or razors. This is very scary for a roommate or friend who perceives it as a serious suicide attempt. For the survivor, this kind of self-mutilation may not actually be a suicide attempt; rather, it may be a continuation of the pattern of abuse to which she has become accustomed. It can provide a physical release for the pain she can't talk about.[40] Someone who self-mutilates needs to find a safe place to talk; helping her connect with a professional counselor is probably the best thing you can do. Your fear is understandable, but learning more about the issue and talking to a professional yourself may help to put it in perspective.

If you're intimately involved with an incest survivor in the process of healing, understand that this can have an impact on your relationship. You may experience the effects of your partner's difficulties with trust, intimacy, and sex. Those struggles, however, have less to do with you specifically than with her/his past experiences of betrayal and abuse. While s/he may tell you not to take it personally, it can still be hard for you.

For Rape Survivors

If you are a rape survivor, you may experience a variety of feelings as you make the transition into the college environment. There are some fears common to women who have been raped. Fear of being alone and of particular objects and places that remind you of the attack can surface in your new environment. You may feel uneasy in some situations and may need to create safety nets such as going places with friends or avoiding drinking. It can be helpful to trust a roommate, friend, or R.A. by telling her the truth. This way you can have at least one ally who understands that you may have strong reactions to some situations. If you find that your feelings and fears get in the way of your daily functioning—for example, that you're unable to concentrate on your schoolwork or are afraid to meet people—you should probably look for help.

Distrust and fear of men, or of some types of men, may also occur. This can affect whether you choose to attend certain events or go out with particular people. Decisions about living arrangements such as a coed or single-sex hall are also important to consider. You need to talk with your roommate about overnight guests if the ongoing or unexpected presence of a man in your room could feel intrusive and compromise your privacy and feelings of safety.

Peers sometimes make insensitive comments during residence hall discussions, such as, "She was drunk and she went up to his room, what did she expect?" Acquaintance rape, especially, tends to be a crime in which survivors are often treated poorly. It's important always to remember that if you were raped, it was not your fault. Other women may say things that blame the victim in order to distance and protect themselves. If they can blame something the other woman did and claim that they would never do it, perhaps they can make themselves feel less vulnerable. It can be frustrating for a rape survivor to hear these kinds of comments. You may choose, in some situations, to respond. At other times you may feel safer not saying anything.

While each person responds to a rape in her own way, there is a general process called the *rape trauma syndrome* that describes several stages survivors experience. Individual timetables differ, and the process may take place over several weeks or several years. If you were raped by someone you knew and trusted, as most women are, the process may take longer because you could be less likely to identify what happened as rape and to talk about it.[41] It's helpful to have a general idea of the kinds of feelings and reactions to expect.

The first stage, *impact,* generally lasts from a few days to a few weeks. Immediately following the rape, a woman generally feels anxiety, disbelief, and fear. Some women are visibly upset and cry while others seem very calm and in control. Some normal behaviors, such as sleeping and eating, may be disrupted. This is usually a time when decisions are made about reporting to the police and telling others.[42]

A period of *outward adjustment* follows. The survivor generally returns to normal life and appears to be adjusting. She denies that she's still upset and often suppresses her feelings. This reaction allows the woman to feel more in control, temporarily.[43]

Resolution occurs over time, perhaps weeks or months. The survivor realizes that her life has been changed by the rape. She may feel depressed and may spend time reliving the incident and feeling anger, guilt, fear, desire for revenge, and self-blame. At this stage she needs to talk about her feelings. The depression is a normal reaction to the trauma of rape.[44]

Integration is achieved when the survivor can talk about the incident with some degree of comfort and perspective. She can sort things out and integrate the experience, neither denying it nor being dominated by it. Women reaching this stage may emerge as stronger women with positive attitudes. Some address issues of prevention, help other survivors, or work on educational efforts.[45]

The stage in your recovery at which you enter college may affect how you respond to and deal with your new environment. The cycle of feelings may also repeat, to some degree, in new situations, so that even if you've integrated the experience before leaving for college, you could find yourself feeling some of the old fears and anxieties when you first arrive.

What to Do If You Are Raped

In a traumatic situation such as rape, it is extremely difficult to try to reduce the actions you should take to a clear-cut set of steps. Circumstances vary enormously, but the steps below may help you feel at least some control over what happens next.

First and foremost, believe in yourself and don't blame yourself for what happened. Get to a safe place. If possible do *not* shower, bathe, douche, brush your teeth, go to the bathroom, or change your clothes. Even though you may really want to clean up, doing so would destroy evidence. If you absolutely have to change your clothes, put them in a paper bag but don't allow anyone else to touch them; otherwise they can't be used for evidence. Tell someone you trust what happened—

contact a friend, roommate, R.A., or campus security as soon as possible. If there's a campus or local rape-crisis hotline, you can call. They may provide a counselor/advocate or emergency-room companion to support you. If you're a lesbian, you may request the support of a lesbian counselor, if one is available.[46]

Get medical help. You should be checked by a doctor as soon as possible. Your friend, support person, or counselor/advocate can accompany you to the hospital, Health Center, or doctor's office. Take a change of clothes with you, since what you're wearing will be kept as evidence if you make a report. You will be treated for any injuries and checked for the possibility of pregnancy or sexually transmitted diseases. If you agree to have evidence collected, the doctor will do so. Having the evidence collected doesn't commit you to pressing charges. However, if you *don't* have it taken at that time, you can't go back later and get it. You have the right to have someone of your choice with you in the examining room, and you can also ask any law enforcement officers who may be present to leave during the physical exam.[47]

Decide whether you want to report the rape to the police or other law enforcement authorities. In the case of acquaintance rape, your college may have specific reporting structures. Reporting will mean explaining what happened in detail. You have the right to request a female officer if you prefer. You can also report the crime but not file charges. This way, if there are past or future reports against the same individual, the police can build a stronger case. Take some time to recover in a place where you feel safe and supported.[48]

Your college may have a policy or process for communicating to the campus about incidents of rape. Rapes by strangers raise the question of the college's obligation to warn students of dangerous situations. The conflict between protecting the privacy of the survivor and communicating information to the rest of the campus community is a complicated one. Providing basic information to other students can often protect the survivor by cutting down on rumors and gossip and disseminating only the facts that need to be known. Survivors are generally willing to do this, often saying they don't want anyone else to go through what they have experienced. Whenever possible the survivor should be given the opportunity to read and approve the release before it is distributed to the campus. This can help her feel some control and prepare herself for the immediate attention that will be focused on the situation.

If the rape happened in your residence hall, you may want to consider how you can make your room feel safer for you. Some students change residence halls or rooms; others prefer to stay where they are but ask to have the lock changed. One woman I knew had difficulty sleeping because being in the room kept reminding her of the attempted rape. I suggested that she move her furniture around and change the posters on her walls so she could look around without seeing the exact same surroundings she associated with the attack. It seemed to help.

Your class dean or academic advisor may work with you to make accommodation for school work missed or affected by the incident. Some students choose to reduce their course load for the semester.

Families can be an important source of support, or they may add to the stress. Some students tell their parents as soon as they can. Others fear their parents' reactions and worry that they may blame them, pull them out of school, or be too upset or angry to handle it. Some never tell their parents. Others tell their parents only after they've had time to deal with the rape themselves.

One student who didn't want to upset her parents initially chose not to tell them. Within a few weeks, and with the help of a counselor, she decided to call them. In another situation, campus security called me in the middle of the night to tell me that a student had been raped. I went directly to the student's room. She was already on the phone long-distance to her parents, and by the time we had all returned from the hospital and police station her parents had arrived on campus. These parents were a primary source of support for their daughter from the beginning.

If your attacker was another student, you could find yourself running into him around campus or in the residence hall. If you're pursuing a disciplinary hearing or have filed charges, time will elapse before any resolution is reached. Speak with your dean of students to find out what options are available to help you feel safer on campus.

Victimization surveys estimate that only about one in ten rapes is reported.[49] Reporting a rape can often be a frightening experience. If you decide to press charges, there are three basic options to explore.

To file *criminal charges,* consult with someone at the district attorney's office. If s/he feels that there is sufficient evidence, your attacker will be arrested and prosecuted. The case would be brought by the state against the accused rapist, and you could be subpoenaed to testify as a witness.[50]

By filing a *civil lawsuit,* you are seeking monetary compensation for damages rather than a jail term for the rapist if he's found guilty. In a civil suit, you hire a lawyer and pay for any expenses; the lawyer generally works for a percentage of the financial settlement. There are some advantages of a civil suit over a criminal suit. In a civil suit the attacker can be forced to testify, and there is less burden of proof. Your lawyer must present a preponderance of evidence against your attacker rather than prove his guilt beyond a reasonable doubt. Also, the decision in a civil suit can be made by a less-than-unanimous jury. Civil cases can also be settled out of court. One disadvantage is that the attacker will not go to jail even if found guilty. Civil cases also take longer to get to court than criminal proceedings, and there can be some financial cost to the survivor.[51]

A third option, if your attacker was another student at your college, is to pursue a complaint through your *college judicial process*. College judicial systems are generally not bound by the same standards of guilt as the criminal courts. There may also be a variety of punishable offenses. The sanctions in college systems could include probation, suspension, or expulsion if the rapist is found guilty. Colleges, however, are sometimes caught in a bind as they seek to be fair to both of the students involved. The seriousness of a rape charge goes beyond what some college judicial structures are currently designed to handle. If you pursue this route, I would encourage you to make use of a supportive staff counselor/advocate throughout the process. Be aware that most colleges don't permit lawyers to participate in campus judicial proceedings.[52]

If your attacker was from another college, or if the incident occurred on another campus, explore your options there. You could ask your own dean of students to help you find out what process you need to follow at that other school if you want to pursue a complaint.

In the end, the decision about what to do or not do needs to be yours. Pressing charges can help you feel that you're taking some action on your own behalf. The process can also, however, leave you feeling further victimized.

For Friends of Rape Survivors

. . .

"When I give my presentations, I usually tell them that what I'm saying applies to *every single* person in the audience, male and

female alike—with one in four women experiencing rape or attempted rape, that means everyone at some point in their lives will
have to deal with a survivor, whether they know it or not at
the time."

—I. S., class of '92

. . .

Friends closest to rape survivors are often greatly affected. Some friends
start to feel responsible—"I should have gone with her when she wanted
to leave," "I never should have introduced her to that guy." Other
friends struggle with wanting to help but not being sure how and are left
feeling frustration, anger, and fear.

As you try to help a friend, neither ignore nor overconcentrate on
your own feelings. Keep track of them as you would monitor nearby
traffic through your rearview mirror if you were driving a car. You need
to check your mirror regularly so your feelings don't sneak up and
overtake you, but you can't drive *only* looking in the rearview mirror or
you'll drive off the road. Focus on your friend, but pay attention to your
own feelings. Know what you can and can't give, and get help and
support for yourself if you need it.

If you're the first person the survivor approaches after a rape, follow
the suggestions presented in the earlier section on what to do if you are
raped. You can emotionally help a friend who has been attacked by
believing her and listening to her. Let her tell her story at her own speed
and when she wants to. Specific questions and probing may feel intrusive. Let her control the conversation. Comfort her if she's agitated, but
try to calm her down without implying that she shouldn't feel what she
feels. You can offer her, say, a cup of tea or a hug, but don't force
anything on her or assume that you know what she wants or needs.
Reinforce that the rape wasn't her fault, and provide protection if she's
feeling unsafe. Help her organize her thoughts but let her make decisions
that need to be made. She needs to feel some control over her life.[53]

If you've been in an intimate relationship with the survivor, let her
decide when to resume sexual activity. Don't pressure her, and also
recognize that some particular acts or sensations may trigger unpleasant
memories.

If your friend was a virgin when she was raped, female support is
especially important. At some point it can help her to hear from a
woman she trusts about more positive sexual experiences and a woman's
right to decide when and with whom to have sex.[54]

There may also be times when your friend experiences flashbacks and needs some extra support. The "anniversary" of her rape or the occurrence of another rape on campus may be particularly difficult times for her. I knew one woman who was raped by a stranger during her first semester on campus. She did an incredible job achieving academically and as a student leader, but she also carried some of the pain and fear with her for several years afterward. Since I had been with her through that traumatic night, she was able to call me when things got bad without feeling like she had to explain why. There were some times when she was afraid to be alone and we went for long walks together. She needed to work things through at her own pace. It took a while, but she did.

Personal Safety Precautions

I prefer to use the word "precautions" rather than "prevention" because there's no sure way to prevent sexual violence, and if you believe that you can prevent anything, you may unreasonably blame yourself when you don't. The precautions listed below come from a variety of resources.[55]

In Your Residence Hall
1. Close your door and lock your room, especially when you're sleeping.
2. Keep your shades or blinds drawn at night.
3. Keep your keys in a safe place, not in the door, above the doorframe, or in an easily accessible hiding place.
4. Keep exterior doors to your residence hall closed and locked. If you see any propped open, unprop them.
5. Question unescorted nonresidents in your hall. Even if you recognize someone's boyfriend/girlfriend, you have no way of knowing whether they've broken up or whether the resident wants to see him/her.
6. Call security if you're afraid to approach someone.

Around Campus and in the Community
1. Don't hitchhike.
2. Walk with someone else if you have to walk at night.
3. Walk purposefully and be alert and aware. Don't wear a walkman.

4. If you have long hair, tuck it in, and avoid wearing dangling jewelry that someone could grab.
5. Walk closer to the curb than to buildings, trees, and shrubbery. If a car stops, even to ask directions, keep some distance from it.
6. Try to vary your routes and routines.
7. Walk in well-lit areas.
8. Know the locations of emergency phones on campus.
9. If you have to walk home alone, let friends know the route you'll be taking and when they can expect you. You might also arrange to call the friends you left to tell them you've arrived home safely, or let security know your route, calling them once you arrive.
10. If your campus has a shuttle bus and/or security or student escort services, use them.

If you have to risk making a fool of yourself to feel safe, it's a reasonable risk to take. I remember one woman who told the story of walking on another campus in her home city shortly after she had heard that there had been several sexual assaults on that campus. As she walked from her car to the library, she heard someone walking behind her. She walked faster. So did the person behind her. She stopped suddenly, turned around quickly, and with a wild look in her eyes she threw her books in the air, raised her arms to the sky, and screamed at the top of her lungs, "Lord, don't let me kill again!" Whoever was behind her took off in the opposite direction. She never saw who it was, and didn't really care.

In Your Car
1. Have your keys ready as you walk to your car.
2. Check the back seat of your car before getting in.
3. Keep your doors locked.
4. If you feel you're being followed as you drive on campus, head for the campus security office or a well-lit and well-populated area.

In General Social Situations
Plan beforehand how you'll get home. Be cautious about accepting rides from people you've just met, no matter how nice they seem. Have money for a cab or bus, bus schedules, and phone numbers of friends you can call in a pinch so you don't have to be dependent upon others for

transportation. If you're stranded on another campus, try to find another woman to stay with.

Be assertive and say no when you want to. If you drink alcohol, use it responsibly. About 75 percent of the men and at least 55 percent of the women involved in acquaintance rapes had been drinking or taking drugs just before the attack. Rape, however, is still rape, and people are responsible for their actions regardless of whether alcohol or drugs were involved.[56]

Friends can look out for one another. Prearrange a signal if you want others to rescue you from an uncomfortable situation. At one college where I worked, the women created something they called "the loser dance." If they were uncomfortable with the person they were with and needed some help, they would use a particular hand movement, making an L out of their thumb and index finger, and wave it around as they danced. Other students, seeing the L signal, would find some way to help their friend extricate herself from her unwanted and persistent dance partner. Even if you don't have this kind of prearranged signal, if a friend looks uneasy, give her an opportunity to get out of a situation. For example, tell her she has a phone call or that you need her help with something. She can always go back to be with the person if she wants to.

In Dating Situations

1. On a first date, plan ahead where you're going and avoid dark, secluded places, including your date's apartment.
2. Introduce your date, by name, to at least one friend and/or make sure at least one of your friends knows his name and what your general plans are.
3. If you go on a blind date, try to go with another couple.
4. Try to be assertive and say what you really mean. Set sexual limits and give clear, firm messages about what they are.
5. Be wary of errands or emergencies being invented where your date needs you to go with him to a private place or where other people are supposed to be present but aren't.
6. Remember, you don't have to do something that you don't want to do in order to avoid hurting his feelings or embarrassing him. Protest loudly or leave if you feel you need to.
7. Examine your attitude about money and power and consider whether having money spent on you makes you more hesitant to say no. If it does, you may want to pay all or part of your own way.

Behavioral Cues: Be Wary of Men Who . . .

1. Ignore your personal space boundaries—sit too close, touch you all the time, or become overly friendly very quickly.
2. Express anger or aggression toward women in general or as individuals.
3. Don't listen to you, ignore what you have to say, and make decisions regardless of what you want.
4. Try to make you feel guilty if you resist their sexual advances.
5. Act excessively jealous or possessive of you.
6. Drink heavily and/or try to get you to drink more than you want to.
7. Have shown previous sexually aggressive or violent behavior.
8. Are preoccupied with sexual behaviors and language.
9. Seem happiest when with their buddies, teammates, or frat brothers and rely heavily on their opinions.

Learning self-defense or martial arts techniques can be another preventative measure to take. Some of these courses focus as much on feelings and attitudes as they do on physical moves and can help you feel more confident and in control. Some of these new reactions will feel awkward if you're not used to them. Practice can make you feel more comfortable.

Finally, one of the most important things to remember is to trust your gut feelings or the "little voice" inside. If you feel uneasy with someone, his/her behavior, what s/he wants you to do, or the situation, listen to those feelings. You don't have to be nice all the time. Don't ignore or discount the little voice inside that tells you to say no, to walk out, or to yell. Trust that little voice and put your own needs first.[57]

WHERE TO LOOK FOR HELP

On Campus

The Security Office and dean of students will generally have information about safety issues. As a result of the 1990 Student Right to Know and Campus Security Act, colleges are now required to make their violent-crime statistics available. It's important to consider several points if you review such statistics. Rape, especially acquaintance rape, is a vastly underreported crime, so statistics may be misleading. However, also keep in mind that if rapes are being reported, that's also an indication that people feel they *can* report them—a positive sign. Colleges that say they have no problem with violence against women probably do but don't know, or don't want to know, that they do.

Ask questions. What steps are taken on campus to address issues of personal safety? Is there any sort of escort service? Are whistles distributed to all students? Are there emergency phones around campus? What programs are offered by security and other offices? How are problem areas, such as poor lighting or broken locks, identified and corrected?

Educational programs may be offered to educate students about issues of incest, rape, and personal safety. Often students play an active role in these programs. Going to lectures and workshops can give you the chance to talk with presenters afterward if you want additional information, resources, and referrals. Increasing numbers of institutions are offering programs during new student orientation—attend them. Other campuses have individual sessions or credit courses on self-defense or martial arts. Some academic courses, in psychology, sociology, and women's studies, may also deal with issues of violence against women.

At some colleges, male students are playing an important role in educating other men about communication and nonaggressive behavior. Active groups of men working against violence against women are a very positive force. Some women involved in rape-awareness education prefer to focus their energy on working with women rather than spending their time educating men, since women are more likely to be victimized by violence. Men talking to men fills an important gap and also provides a safe forum for men to explore their feelings, attitudes, and necessary changes.

The individual in charge of judicial affairs is the appropriate contact to help you understand how the process works if you ever need to initiate disciplinary proceedings. If there's a women's center on campus, issues of women's safety are often a prime concern for them. Women's centers and health or counseling services may provide support or therapy groups for survivors of incest and rape. Some campuses also have their own peer-counseling services for survivors, and perhaps hotlines that can be called.

If you feel unsafe or threatened on campus, talk to someone—your R.A., residence staff, the dean of students, campus security. It helps if someone in authority knows of your fear. Even if you don't want someone else to intervene just yet, these staff members can help you if you feel in immediate danger anytime in the future.

. . .

"In 1989, I was sexually assaulted in my college dorm. I was one of three women in my dorm who had been assaulted by the same man. Thanks to ourselves and our strengths, with the assistance of our R.A. the problem was for us satisfactorily resolved. He was banned from our hall by way of a residence government decision and several complaints were launched against him with our campus security."

—Student, class of '91

. . .

If you're in an abusive relationship with someone who is not a student at your college, you may have some different options providing you're willing to file a complaint. If you've been physically abused, talk with your security office about the possibility of having the person trespassed from the campus or of pursuing a restraining order through the courts.

If you're being harassed or are trying to avoid contact with someone who has abused you in the past—a parent, an ex-partner, a recent acquaintance—you should be able to block the release of any information, including your campus address and phone number. Start with your dean of students and the Registrar's Office to find out what procedure you need to follow.

Many campuses put out brochures on personal safety information for students, including precautions, emergency procedures, and numbers to call. Keep this information handy for yourself and to help others.

Informal student communication networks may surface when formal processes on campus are seen as less receptive. At Brown University in 1990, for example, some students persisted in writing the names of alleged acquaintance rapists on a bathroom wall. The debate that followed on campus led, among other things, to a reevaluation of how the campus handled sex-related complaints. The results have included the establishment of new policies, a sexual assault task force, and a mandatory meeting for first-year students.[58]

Off Campus

. . .

"I know that when I was facing all that court trial stuff, I was completely dependent upon and grateful to my advocate. She got angry for me when I was still in shock and the D.A. refused to prosecute because of lack of evidence."

—S. A., class of '93

. . .

Larger cities and some smaller communities have rape-crisis centers and/ or hotlines. Such centers provide counseling for survivors and counselor/ advocates for immediate emergency-room support and for assistance during a trial. Rape-crisis centers can also provide opportunities for students to work as volunteers, often receiving valuable training as part of the process. The victim-witness assistance program at the courts can advise and assist you through any legal proceedings.

Your community may have one or more shelters for battered women who are in abusive relationships. Shelters may not be an option for many students, however, since these facilities are generally designed for those who have nowhere else to go.

Colleges and/or communities sometimes sponsor events such as Take Back the Night marches, speakouts, and demonstrations against violence against women. Participation in these events often evokes a great sense of strength, sisterhood, and power reclaimed by women. These experiences can be an important part of the healing process for those women who have had that power taken away from them at some point in their lives.

Networking with other recovering survivors is often helpful. Some agencies and organizations are specifically designed to meet the needs of incest survivors. For example, Marilyn Van Derbur Atler, a former Miss America, has recently spoken out as an incest survivor. She also founded a facility called the Kemp Foundation for Adult Survivors. Survivors of Incest Anonymous is a twelve-step program for incest survivors; you may be able to find a group at your college or in the nearby community. Some of the resource organizations listed in the next section can suggest other ways to meet survivors.

EDUCATING YOURSELF

Books: Nonfiction, Anthologies, Biographies, Poetry, Plays

Armstrong, Louise. *Kiss Daddy Goodnight: A Speak-Out on Incest*. New York: Simon and Schuster, 1978.

Bart, Pauline, and Patricia O'Brien. *Stopping Rape: Successful Survival Strategies.* Elmsford, NY: Pergamon, 1985.

Bass, Ellen, and Laura Davis. *The Courage to Heal: A Guide for Women Survivors of Child Sexual Abuse.* New York: HarperCollins, 1988.

Bass, Ellen, and Louise Thornton, eds. *I Never Told Anyone: Writings by Women Survivors of Child Sexual Abuse.* New York: HarperPerennial, 1991.

Blume, E. Susan. *Secret Survivors: Uncovering Incest and Its Aftereffects in Women.* New York: Ballantine, 1991.

Brownmiller, Susan. *Against Our Will: Men, Women, and Rape.* Rev. ed. New York: Bantam, 1986.

Caignon, Denise, and Gail Groves, eds. *Her Wits about Her: Self-Defense Success Stories by Women.* New York: HarperPerennial, 1987.

Davis, Laura. *Allies in Healing: When the Person You Love Was Sexually Abused as a Child.* New York: HarperCollins, 1991.

Estrich, Susan. *Real Rape.* Cambridge, MA: Harvard University Press, 1987.

Forward, Susan, and Craig Buck. *Betrayal of Innocence: Incest and Its Devastation.* New York: Penguin, 1988.

Graber, Ken. *Ghosts in the Bedroom: A Guide for Partners of Incest Survivors.* Dearfield Beach, FL: Health Communications, 1991.

Herman, Judith. *Father-Daughter Incest.* Cambridge, MA: Harvard University Press, 1981.

Ledray, Linda. *Recovering from Rape.* New York: Holt, 1986.

Lobel, Kerry, ed. *Naming the Violence: Speaking Out about Lesbian Battering.* Seattle: Seal, 1986.

McNaron, Toni, and Yarrow Morgan, eds. *Voices in the Night: Women Speaking about Incest.* Pittsburgh: Cleis, 1982.

Madigan, Lee, and Nancy Gamble. *The Second Rape: Society's Continued Betrayal of the Victim.* New York: Lexington, 1991.

Maltz, Wendy, and Beverly Holman. *Incest and Sexuality: A Guide to Understanding and Healing.* Lexington, MA: Lexington, 1987.

Martin, Del. *Battered Wives.* Rev. ed. San Francisco: Volcano, 1981.

Miedzian, Myriam. *Boys Will Be Boys: Breaking the Link between Masculinity and Violence.* New York: Doubleday, 1991.

NiCarthy, Ginny. *Getting Free: You Can End the Abuse and Take Back Your Life.* 2d ed. Seattle: Seal, 1986.

Parrot, Andrea. *Coping with Date Rape and Acquaintance Rape.* New York: Rosen, 1988.

Poston, Carol, and Karen Lison. *Reclaiming Our Lives: Hope for Adult Survivors of Incest.* Boston: Little, Brown, 1989.

Rush, F. *The Best-Kept Secret: Sexual Abuse of Children.* New York: McGraw-Hill, 1981.

Russell, D. *The Secret Trauma: Incest in the Lives of Girls and Women.* New York: Basic, 1987.

Saldana, Teresa. *Beyond Survival.* New York: Bantam, 1987.

Sanday, Peggy Reeves. *Fraternity Gang Rape: Sex, Brotherhood, and Privilege on Campus.* New York: New York University Press, 1990.

Warshaw, Robin. *I Never Called It Rape: The "Ms." Report on Recognizing, Fighting, and Surviving Date Rape*. New York: HarperPerennial, 1988.
White, Evelyn. *Chain Chain Change: For Black Women Dealing with Physical and Emotional Abuse*. Seattle: Seal, 1985.
Wisechild, Louise, ed. *She Who Was Lost Is Remembered: Healing from Incest through Creativity*. Seattle: Seal, 1991.
Zambrano, Myrna M. *Mejor Sola Que Mal Acompanada: Para la Mujer Golpeada/For the Latina in an Abusive Relationship*. Seattle: Seal, 1985.
Ziegenmeyer, Nancy. *Taking Back My Life*. New York: Summit, 1992.

Novels

Corman, Avery. *Prized Possessions*. New York: Simon and Schuster, 1991.

Articles, Pamphlets, and Papers

Barrett, Karen. "Date Rape: A Campus Epidemic?" *Ms.*, September 1982.
Caruso, Beverly. "The Impact of Incest." Center City, MN: Hazeldon Educational Materials, 1987.
Gibbs, Nancy. "When Is It Rape?" *Time*, June 3, 1991.
Hughes, Jean O'Gorman, and Bernice R. Sandler. "Friends Raping Friends: Could It Happen to You?" Washington, DC: Project on the Status and Education of Women, Association of American Colleges, 1987.
Los Angeles Commission on Assaults against Women. "Surviving Sexual Assault." New York: Congdon and Weed, 1982. (Includes specific information for lesbians, older women, women with disabilities, and those who are not U.S. citizens.)
Matthews, Anne. "The Campus Crime Wave," *New York Times Magazine*, March 7, 1993.
Pritchard, Carol. "Avoiding Rape on and off Campus." Wenonah, NJ: State College Publishing, 1985.

Organizations for Information and Assistance

Incest Resources and Referrals
Women's Center
46 Pleasant St.
Cambridge, MA 02139
617-354-8807
Incest Survivors Anonymous
P.O. Box 5613
Long Beach, CA 90805-0613
310-428-5599
Incest Survivors Resource Network, International
P.O. Box 7375

Las Cruces, NM 88006-7375
505-521-4260
National Coalition against Domestic Violence
P.O. Box 34103
Washington, DC 20043-4103
202-638-6388
National Coalition against Sexual Assault
P.O. Box 21378
Washington, DC 20009
202-483-7165
Survivors of Incest Anonymous
P.O. Box 21817
Baltimore, MD 21222
410-282-3400
VOICES in Action, Inc.
P.O. Box 148309
Chicago, IL 60614
312-327-1500

Hotlines

Rape Crisis Hotlines
see your local phone book

Films, Videos, TV Shows, Plays

The Accused. A survivor experiences the emotional, legal, and moral issues surrounding her rape and how society and the judicial system treat her.

The Burning Bed. A battered wife finally kills her abusive husband. Made-for-TV movie from the book by Faith McNulty, based on a true story.

Extremities. A woman turns the tables on her attacker. Based on the play by William Mastrosimone.

It Still Hurts. Educational video produced by Auburn University.

Something about Amelia. A teenage daughter reveals her father's sexual abuse. Made-for-TV movie.

What's Love Got to Do with It? Singer Tina Turner escapes from an abusive relationship and succeeds as a rock star on her own. Based on a true story.

When He's Not a Stranger. A first-year college student is raped by a popular upperclass athlete and takes her case to the college discipline system and the courts. Made-for-TV movie.

■ ELEVEN ■

Living in a Diverse Environment

■ ■ ■

"Give people a chance. Nobody gets very far if they 'expect' someone to be a certain way—unless it's expecting them to be worth knowing."

—W. C., class of '93

■ ■ ■

We're alike in many basic human ways. We like to hear that we've done a good job and that someone appreciates us. We like to be treated with respect. We like to feel unthreatened and safe from danger. Sometimes we focus so much on our differences that we forget the ways we're similar. At other times we want so badly to see ourselves as the same that we overlook the differences—differences that are an important part of who we each are.

In recent years, the old "melting pot" image of everyone merging into a single group has been challenged by the concept of cultural pluralism. In a pluralistic community, members of distinct groups live side by side and are willing to acknowledge each other's dignity, to benefit from each other's experience, and to recognize each other's contributions. Pluralism encourages each group to maintain and celebrate its unique cultural identity.[1]

Some have described pluralism in terms of a salad bowl metaphor, in contrast to the melting pot image. In a salad, all the ingredients—

tomatoes, green peppers, lettuce, sprouts, mushrooms, etc.—are mixed together, but they maintain their own unique tastes and textures. Imagine the difference if all these ingredients were, instead, whipped up in a blender to make a "salad shake." What would be sacrificed?

Terminology

. . .

"One day I remember I asked my first roommate what kind of music she liked. And she said, 'Oh, I like you know, like your music, like Michael Jackson and Janet Jackson . . . you know, like black music.' She just assumed that I liked this kind of music, which I don't happen to like, because it's sung by black people and I'm a black person."

—Student, class of '90

. . .

An *assumption* is defined as "the supposition that something is true."[2] It's natural to make assumptions when confronted with people and situations unfamiliar to you. You make an assumption when you don't know much about an individual, and you expect certain things from him/her primarily on the basis of preconceptions you have about the group to which s/he belongs. For example, if you see someone from a particular background, you may falsely assume certain things about that person's family, academic performance, or reactions to particular situations.

A *stereotype* is a general viewpoint about a group of people that is not based on fact.[3] Take a moment to think honestly about groups of people who might be unfamiliar to you—southerners, New Yorkers, Arab Americans, very wealthy people, working-class people, etc. What images come to mind? Now think about where those images came from. It's likely that what family and friends told you and the way individuals from these groups were presented in the media contributed to impressions you have about them. This is a pretty indirect way to learn—kind of like the old telephone game, in which a story gets passed along from person to person and ends up sounding very different from the original story. Even positive stereotypes obscure the fact that within any group, individuals have very different experiences. The term "model minority," for example, is often applied to Asian Americans to emphasize their supposed success. This stereotypes all Asian Americans as hard-working, highly educated, and financially successful. This myth ignores the reality that 70 percent of all Asian American workers don't fall into the middle or upper class.[4]

Prejudice consists of conscious or unconscious beliefs and attitudes about members of a particular social group.[5] These are usually negative judgments or assumptions, often made without the benefit of much actual experience with that social group. These judgments are often based on stereotypes. Prejudices can be held by *everyone*. For example, middle-aged people can have prejudices about adolescents, adolescents about the middle aged, heterosexuals about homosexuals, homosexuals about heterosexuals, Latinas/Latinos about Irish Americans, and Irish Americans about Latinas/Latinos.

Probably the most frequent instances of prejudice and discrimination take place when people are unaware of the effect their actions have on others. Graffiti, jokes, insensitive use of language, or comments or actions based on stereotypes may not be intended to hurt others, but they still do. For example, even if every person in a residence hall of one hundred is well intentioned and voices only one insensitive comment or question each semester, that still means that something painful will be said almost every day.[6] Over time this can interfere with a student's ability to focus on being a student and perform up to her academic potential.

Open bigotry may be declining, but more subtle forms of prejudice in which people don't see themselves as biased remain. These biases are expressed less directly and in less negative forms, but they're still expressed.[7] One way we have learned to justify prejudice is by "blaming the victim."

· · ·

"There are, for instance, very few black professors at Harvard, where I taught for many years. Why? The prejudiced person attributes that fact to something about blacks rather than to something about Harvard or the means by which tenure decisions are made."
—Thomas Pettigrew[8]

· · ·

Discrimination is defined as treating people differently on the basis of a prejudice.[9] This can be seen, for example, in situations where weight limits are set for cheerleaders (discrimination based on size) or visiting

Peanuts reprinted by permission of *UFS, Inc.*

privileges in hospital intensive-care units are denied to same-sex partners. Discrimination implies that some people are "better" than others.

Social power involves access to resources and privileges within the dominant culture and its institutions.[10] You have social power when you can influence others and get what you want. Power includes what you have, what you can get, and who you know. This is a key concept to understand. Power gives those who have it the opportunity to act on or enforce their prejudices, if they choose to. On the other hand, power also allows those who have it to make or change the rules by challenging or changing those practices that continue to treat some groups unequally.

Oppression is defined as discrimination, conscious or unconscious, against a person or group on the basis of stereotypes and prejudices. Oppression is possible *only* when people have the power to act on their prejudices.[11]

$$Oppression = Prejudice + Power$$

Those being oppressed are deprived of some basic human rights or dignities and are, or feel, powerless to change the situation.[12] Oppression can be reinforced at several different levels—personal, cultural, and institutional.[13]

Internalized oppression occurs when members of an oppressed group accept or believe the prejudicial messages about themselves. For instance:

- I'm only seventeen. How could I possibly question what that dean says?
- I have a learning disability. There's no way I could possibly go to law school.

- I'm on full financial aid. Maybe I don't have as much of a right to be here.
- Women don't major in physics.

. . .

"My experience leads me to believe that contrary to what I thought, I had actually been contributing to my own stereotyping. Like the hero in Ralph Ellison's novel *The Invisible Man,* I had become invisible to white Americans, and it clung to me like a bad habit. Like most bad habits, this one crept up on me because I took it in minute doses like Mithradates' poison and my mind and body adapted so well to it I hardly noticed it was there."

—Mitsuye Yamada, "Invisibility Is an Unnatural Disaster: Reflections of an Asian American Woman"[14]

. . .

Background Information

As you enter college, you'll be sharing living and learning space with people who are likely to differ from you in a number of ways—ethnic background, religion, age, sexual orientation, socioeconomic class, etc. It's anticipated that diversity of all kinds will be increasingly reflected in future first-year classes.[15] Consider that

- in the late 1980s, 14 percent of all adults in the United States and 20 percent of the children under seventeen were members of ethnic minority groups.[16]
- by the year 2000, 33 percent of all school-aged children will be ethnic minorities.[17]
- in the last decade the number of students with disabilities attending colleges has tripled.[18]
- studies predict that increasing numbers of international students and returning adult students will be attending college.[19]

As the population changes, your college should prepare you to live, work, and play an active role in that changing world. Many schools, however, still reflect attitudes and biases that are not responsive to individuals from groups that have traditionally been underrepresented on their campuses. Some of you may not be fully aware of the historical and cultural context that members of different groups carry with them. Perhaps your classmates will include one or more of the following:

- A Japanese American student who was born in the United States and whose family had been confined to an internment camp here during World War II.
- A student who immigrated to the United States from Cambodia as a child.
- A student who is a lesbian from a small midwest town where she was only exposed to antihomosexual attitudes while growing up.
- A Jewish student whose grandparents fled from the Nazis in Europe.
- A Native American student who was born and raised on a reservation.
- A returning adult student who has raised a family of six.

It can be a valuable experience to get to know people as individuals and to appreciate where they come from, who they are, and what they have to offer. Broadening your individual world is a key to your future success.

．　．　．

"I learned lots of new viewpoints in my classes and by living with women whose lives didn't exactly parallel mine (and I *still* liked them!). I realized I had a lot of deprogramming to do. But 'coming into your own' is a very exciting process, and I tried to use the resistance from my family as a challenging source of strength."

—O. L., class of '89

．　．　．

Sources of Misunderstanding

Being open to new ideas is exciting, but it can also feel scary, particularly if those new ideas conflict with what you've always believed. Remember, though, that you can expand your world without having to devalue or abandon your own current experience. There's room for many ideas to exist together. At times you may revise or change beliefs, and at other times you may reaffirm and reinforce them.

Colleges these days continuously reevaluate themselves and their efforts to confront prejudice and discrimination. Diversity orientation programs, discussions about the inclusive or exclusive content of classroom assignments and lectures, and debates about free speech and potentially offensive terms are common on many campuses. The debate about language and terms is a volatile one. The term "political correctness" has become a lightning rod, often overshadowing the original intent of the efforts. Institutions are taking important steps to address past unfair practices, and many professors are finding new ways to expand the content of their courses. These efforts, however, tend to get less public attention than the more zealous opinions expressed on both sides of the issue. These extreme views have, unfortunately, dominated the debate.

Antiharassment speech codes have been discussed at a number of institutions, including Brown, Stanford, Penn State, and the universities of Michigan and Wisconsin. The implementation of these codes has, in several instances, been challenged in the courts on the basis of First Amendment freedom-of-speech rights.[20] Many colleges are struggling to find a balance between maintaining the right to free speech and academic freedom while still protecting individuals' rights to be free from discrimination and harassment on their campus.

As a new student, entering a diverse community in which such issues are hotly debated can feel unsettling and even intimidating, especially if you haven't had much experience living with different kinds of people. You may feel like you're trying to get on board a moving train. Some new students find themselves unintentionally insulting classmates. Others feel that they're "jumped on" by upperclass students who expect them to already know what they're trying to learn. Students sometimes say that they feel as though they have to "walk on eggshells"—that they're afraid to say or do anything that might be offensive to someone else. One student responded to this by saying, "That's great . . . it means that you're learning . . . that you're thinking about things in new ways and considering how others may feel."[21]

. . .

"I remember on the first day of school a student in my dorm who was from Africa was wearing a Nelson Mandela t-shirt with a political statement of his printed on it. I commented on the fact that I thought it was a really cool shirt. I asked where she got it and she replied that it was from home. I then asked 'Why is it in English?' assuming that if it was from her home, Africa, that it wouldn't be in English. She looked at me quizzically and replied, 'Because he said it in English' and went on her way, leaving me feeling pretty ignorant. I felt like a fool ('Hi, I'm your R.A., allow me to be the first to utter an ignorant remark'). It illustrated for me that you can never stop learning/educating yourself. A couple of weeks later I came out of my room early one Saturday morning to find a bunch of people watching a news program, 'News from South Africa.' I plopped down and watched. Although one would think that the TV is generally not the place to educate oneself, the news was well done, dealt with current events, and I could educate myself without asking any ignorant questions that could hurt others by my asking them."

—S. L., class of '90

. . .

The definitions, ideas, and suggestions offered in this chapter, and in the more specific chapters that follow, are designed to help you understand the direction in which the train is moving and get a running start so that you can successfully jump on board.

Some concepts and ideas, particularly those that have generated strong opposing views, are often misunderstood. One such concept is affirmative action. Affirmative action programs involve sets of policies, procedures, and programs designed to reverse the negative impact of past discriminatory actions against groups that have historically been oppressed. The legal premise for affirmative action programs is that in order to prevent discrimination, it is necessary to take positive steps to overcome its accumulated effects.[22]

Today's efforts need to be seen in their historical context and in light of what they are seeking to rectify. The analogy I like to use is of a sports game where one team has, for more than three quarters, had all the rules written in their favor, gotten to put twice as many players on the field, and enjoyed favored treatment by the referees. Then, with five minutes to go in the game, and the score 286–29, the referees decide to try to make the game more fair. They let the other team field more players than the winning team, change some of the rules to give the previously disadvantaged team some breaks, and call more disputes in their favor. The winning team suddenly gets angry about the changes and claims that the other team is being given unfair advantages and preferential treatment—even though they are still way behind in the score and are unlikely to catch up in the five minutes left of the game. If you're a member of the "winning team," but have just been put in the game for the first time, it makes sense that you would feel frustrated with the current situation. It's important to remember the full context.

Perhaps once the score is even and both teams have equal playing advantages, the rules can be the same for all teams and the game can be a fair match. The process of compensating for past imbalances takes a long time to accomplish and involves not preferential treatment but *differential* treatment. Groups that have been discriminated against in the past are treated differently from groups that have not been objects of discrimination. The practice of affirmative action *doesn't* mean that all members of minority groups are admitted to college through these policies. This kind of assumption can lead to dangerous attitudes that some people "deserve" to be at college more than others.

Another source of misunderstanding involves the use of the term "reverse discrimination." This term is sometimes used by members of dominant groups when they feel excluded from a particular club or event, or when they find themselves in the numerical minority in some situation and are challenged in some way. As mentioned earlier, prejudice can exist in all directions, but discrimination is *only* possible when one group has the social power to enforce its biases. Therefore the term "reverse discrimination" is not accurate when applied to individual situations in which a group that has less overall social power has more local power.

For example, have you ever been in a situation where, as a member of a traditional majority group, you felt uncomfortable being in the minority?

- A white woman at an African American event.
- A straight woman at a gay club.
- A Christian at a Jewish religious service.

Think about how you felt and why. Now consider the fact that you were there for a limited amount of time; that in most other group settings, you were probably in the majority; and that you were probably in this unfamiliar setting *by choice.* Students from minority groups on your campus generally have little choice about spending most of their time in situations where they're in the numerical minority—in classes, in their residence halls, in town.

This leads to the question of "safe spaces" on campus for minority students of all kinds. Special-interest housing areas and organizations such as Hillel for Jewish students, the Gay/Lesbian/Bisexual Alliance, Muslim Students' Organization, and Latino/Latina Students' Group are sometimes perceived as movements toward separatism or self-segregation. While there are some students who advocate strict separatism, for others these housing options, organizations, and their socializing space provide an opportunity for separateness that is needed at times. They offer the knowledge that there is somewhere to go where you can talk about what you're experiencing and feeling with others who identify and understand. While many students gravitate, when they need support, to those with whom they feel close, this tends to be more visible among some groups such as women of color, returning adult students, and international students.

Other misunderstandings arise when people repeat myths or ask questions based on misconceptions they've learned. Some of these comments may "trigger" frustrated or angry responses. Even though they're not intended to hurt or annoy others, they still can. Several of the trigger comments noted below sound like well-intentioned efforts to be supportive and understanding. Sometimes, however, what we think will be helpful really isn't.

"I'm not prejudiced." It's virtually impossible to grow up in the United States without developing some prejudices. The likelihood that you have no prejudice is generally hard for others to believe. It tends to sound like you're setting yourself up as a perfect person. Maybe you don't want to be prejudiced, which is great, but people are more likely to respond positively when you acknowledge your biases and work at changing them and the system.

"I know exactly how you feel." No two people are exactly the same. No one stands in another's identical place with the exact same personal experience and history.

"I'm not responsible for what happened in the past." You may not have done something, but it's important to recognize that you may have benefited from it. That's also part of your cultural heritage. For example, you may not have set a club's "whites only" policy, but as a white person that policy gave you an advantage if you wanted to join. You aren't responsible for the past but you are responsible for the present and future, and your actions will say far more than your words.

"You're being oversensitive." This is another version of blaming the victim rather than accepting someone's personal feelings in the situation. Often, too, others' reactions include the accumulated impact of many similar incidents and comments.

"We don't have any problems here with discrimination." Discrimination is imbedded in our culture and institutions and it's a problem

whether we see it or not. The perception may be that there is no problem "here" because people are afraid to speak up about it, or because some people have found "here" to be so oppressive that they simply stay away or move out. The fact that some people are not a visible part of "here" may, in itself, indicate that there is a problem.

"I don't see you as _____*; we're all just people."* This kind of statement denies the fact that different groups have different cultural contributions and have also had different experiences in the U.S. African Americans, for example, have experienced a legacy of slavery and discrimination, and Native Americans have a history of betrayal and mistreatment at the hands of the U.S. government. Ignoring these differences denies some realities.

· · ·

"Freshman year one of my newly made close friends told me 'It's easy for me to be friends with you because I can forget you're black and just remember you're you.' At the time I couldn't figure out exactly *why* that bothered me, but it sure did! Later I realized it bothered me because I couldn't see why she had to 'forget' I was black because I *am*. Further, what she didn't understand was that I had no desire to be seen as 'without color.' Being an African American is part of my identity and affects me greatly. Larger society identifies me as such. Further, so do I. I see no reason to transcend my African American identity. It is a key part of who I am and something I am *proud* of—not something I wish to be diminished."

—H. F., class of '91

· · ·

Misunderstandings also stem from using terms and expressions we were taught, growing up, without knowing where they came from and what they mean. For example, the song "Ten Little Indians," a staple in many elementary schools, was originally used to count dead Native bodies during the invasion of the West.[23] Negative stereotypes have also been perpetuated by their use in marketing products and events—the Sambo's restaurant chain, the Frito Bandito to sell chips, the use of the "tomahawk chop" and proliferation of Native American names for professional and college sports teams. Exposure to these stereotypes used in a widespread manner contributes to false messages we grow to accept without questioning.

ENCOUNTERING AND RESPONDING TO THIS ISSUE

Campus Climate

Only in bias-free climates can all students achieve their personal and academic potentials, enrich their lives, and learn the information and skills needed to relate effectively in the changing world. In such climates, people understand how and why they differ from one another, viewing differences as alternative world views rather than as deficiencies.[24] To achieve a bias-free campus environment, there must be total institutional commitment to that goal. As you consider institutions, try to look for that degree of commitment. Are there, for example, stated goals and policies? What is and isn't included in the college's nondiscrimination statement? Who voices the commitment to a bias-free campus? How strong and sincere is the commitment?

The first choice you make is the decision of which college to attend. The school you choose, the atmosphere there, the neighboring off-campus community, and the student population can affect how comfortable you feel once you arrive. Some colleges describe their campuses as "like home." While the buildings, facilities, furnishings, food, and traditions may feel like the home some students left behind, it may be nothing like the home other students are used to. This can create some discomfort and feelings about not fitting in or belonging there.

· · ·

"At home I share a room with two sisters. Upon reaching college my first year, I found that I had one roommate and that my room at school was larger than my room at home. It kind of annoyed me, throughout the year, when my roommate would sigh and say, 'It's just so hard to share a room with someone.' "

—Student, class of '94

· · ·

As you explore college climates, you may weigh the advantages and disadvantages of attending a college that has a religious affiliation. Some schools include a direct religious component, such as compulsory chapel services or social rules governed by the church's teachings. The consistency of a school's expectations and rules with your religious practices could affect how comfortable you feel living there. This can work in both directions—feeling uncomfortable in too strict an environment or feeling alienated in a too-permissive one.

African American students may explore the possibility of attending one of the historically black colleges. Black colleges offer an environment for learning without high levels of conflict and without some of the isolation often experienced by black students at predominantly white colleges.[25] While black colleges provide reduced racial tensions and more role models on the faculty and staff, they generally don't have as many resources and facilities as many of the larger, better-endowed, predominantly white institutions.[26] Decide what your priorities are. It is possible to have both experiences; some students at predominantly white colleges choose to spend a semester or year as a visiting or exchange student at a black college, and some students at historically black colleges do the same at a predominantly white college.

All students are affected by campus climate, but especially those who attend colleges where they are in the numerical minority. There are a number of ways you can research campus climate. First, you'll probably receive printed information from the colleges you're considering. Those materials may give you an indication of the college climate for different groups. Since these kinds of materials are designed to attract students, however, they don't always present a realistic picture of campus life. Look at the extracurricular offerings. Do they include a variety of options? What kinds of clubs and organizations are on campus and how are they supported by the institution or student government? Request general information about recent college events and speakers to help you see if there are activities relevant to you. If you visit campus, posters advertising events will also tell you something. Look over past copies of the campus newspaper to get a "feel" for the tone of the campus.

What kinds of services and programs exist on campus for you? Perhaps the college handbook or phone directory will have listings that tell you whether there is, for example, a particular staff liaison for students with disabilities; for lesbians, gays, and bisexuals; for minority affairs, returning adult students, international students, etc. Are there specific meeting spaces or resource libraries for various groups? If there are, and if you feel comfortable doing so, check these out if you visit campus and have some time on your own while there.

Review the course catalogue to see if academic classes include a variety of perspectives and contributions. The opportunity to take classes from, or work with, potential mentors—people whose work or writing you admire—and to have strong positive role models can be both exciting and valuable.

There are other questions to ask in order to learn about the climate on campus. How many students of your ethnic background, of your religion, with disabilities, etc., are on campus? What is your potential social network like? How isolated are you likely to be, especially in your living situation? What resources and opportunities are there at other nearby schools for interaction with peers from your group? What is the off-campus community like? How hostile or welcoming does it seem to be? What are the opportunities for finding a strong network beyond the campus?

Get a sense of how safe the climate on campus feels for your group and what experiences there have been with harassment or violence of any kind. The Affirmative Action Office, Campus Security Office, and Student Affairs Office should have information available about hate and bias incidents and how the campus handles them.

Talk with faculty and staff as well as students. Their perspective will be helpful. You can also identify potential mentors and sources of support.

．　．　．

" 'Many' is an important word. I am afraid that by talking to one or two people of color, you may be fooled by their own individual experiences, which may not be helpful on a more general level."

—K. C., class of '91

．　．　．

As you look at campus climate, remember that within any institution there are likely to be many different variations along every dimension. It's usually possible to find environments on any campus that will be comfortable for you, although it may take time and you may have to look for them.

While campus climate is influenced by a number of factors, there are some steps that you can take to shape your immediate environment. For example, sitting through endless discussions in which other students seem to know the same people, vacation in similar places, and shop at comparable stores can leave you feeling like an outsider. Constructively deal with the discomfort by recognizing your own unique strengths, finding friends and acquaintances who are more inclusive, and getting to know people beyond the surface. Some students have always been around those of similar background and choose to continue in that circle; others are quite open and eager to know a variety of people.

Everyone can play a role in affecting the overall campus climate. While campuses often reflect the biases of society, they offer more opportunities to work actively against discrimination. Once you learn how to do so, you can play a similar role in other settings and in the future.

• • •

"In Germany they first came for the Communists and I didn't speak up because I wasn't a Communist. Then they came for the Jews and I didn't speak up because I wasn't a Jew. Then they came for the trade unionists and I didn't speak up because I wasn't a trade unionist. Then they came for the Catholics and I didn't speak up because I was a Protestant. Then they came for me and no one was left to speak up."

—Martin Niemoller, "In Unity"[27]

• • •

A model developed by the Equity Institute is based on the view that all forms of oppression are interrelated. This model is presented as a wheel. The key to this image is the analogy of something powerful held together by spokes. As individual spokes are torn down, the entire wheel should begin to weaken.[28]

Earlier in this chapter the term "social power" was defined. Each spoke of the wheel described above involves a dominant group (e.g., men, uppersocioeconomic class, heterosexuals, white) which has social power, and a targeted group (e.g., women, lower and working class, homosexuals, people of color) without that power. Generally the dominant group has defined the norms such as standards of beauty and what holidays are celebrated and how. Each of you may, at some times, find yourself in a position of power over others, and at other times in a position where others have power over you. You each need to work at pulling down the spokes where you are members of the dominant group. For example, white people have a responsibility to work at dismantling racism, and men can play an important role in pulling down the sexism spoke.

Being an Ally
An ally is defined as a person whose attitudes and behaviors don't put others down, who is committed to increasing her own understanding of issues related to oppression, and is actively working toward eliminating oppression on a variety of levels.[29] Allies believe that oppression is

pervasive and that it hurts everyone, including those in the majority and in positions of social power. Allies may experience stress if they recognize a gap between what they believe and what they practice or don't speak out against.[30] For example, if you believe in equal opportunity but recognize instances of discrimination around you, you may have to ask yourself some hard questions. Are you going to do something about it? If not, can you really say you believe in equal opportunity? If you do something, are you prepared for the reactions you may get from others?

An ally can function at a personal level by, for example, educating herself or speaking up when someone tells an offensive joke or makes an inaccurate statement. For example, Montel Williams's audience-participation TV talk show dealt one day with the topic of gay and lesbian committed relationships. At one point a man in the audience said a number of inaccurate and prejudiced things about homosexuals. He sat back down and then Mr. Williams said, "Wait. . . . I can't let you get away with that and I'll tell you why." He proceeded to calmly and logically point out the fallacies in the other man's statements, without attacking the man. Instances like this happen often on college campuses.

. . .

"Some seem to think that just because they're telling a joke, it reflects an understanding of how unjustified the stereotype is. I find it a dangerous means through which negative attitudes and stereotypes can be perpetuated. People laugh at the jokes and tell others to 'lighten up.' Thus, any attempt to confront the joke is seen as being uptight. It can be difficult to confront the issue in front of a group. Therefore, it may be better to wait until you can talk to the person alone. However, addressing the issue right then may be more effective."

—K. E., class of '91

. . .

At a cultural level, an ally can write a letter to the campus newspaper about, for instance, a fraternity event that perpetuates negative stereotypes. At an institutional level, an ally can work toward changing policies and practices that are discriminatory.

The following are some other examples of people from dominant groups acting as allies:

1. A predominantly male residence hall government refuses to hire a band known to make hostile remarks about women.

Doonesbury

BY GARRY TRUDEAU

Doonesbury copyright G. B. Trudeau. Reprinted with permission of *Universal Press Syndicate*. All rights reserved.

2. A wealthy student in a leadership role questions whether the price of club dues should be reviewed so no student would be excluded from joining simply because of the cost.
3. A student consistently raises the question, whenever places for meetings and events are scheduled, of whether the location is accessible for people in wheelchairs.
4. A student group responsible for planning social events on Spring Weekend plans some activities appropriate for returning adult students and their families.

. . .

"One of the most disturbing situations in my college career was the rash of racist slurs graffitied on the sidewalk or sent to individual students via anonymous notes. Never before had I experienced so much hatred so close—and it wasn't even affecting me firsthand. But it was affecting me, it was affecting all of us and these messages of hate inspired a community of solidarity. Every member of my hall united to create a banner stating our support of the women directly targeted and soon the whole campus was covered with such banners. We went through the difficulty in confronting our own personal prejudices and the awkwardness of finding the right words to express our outrage. I didn't feel that I had to be black, or Jewish, or gay to be an ally. But again, I realized that change didn't happen overnight."

—O. L., class of '89

. . .

One basic goal of an ally is to help the targeted person feel less alone. It can be hard for someone to feel like she's constantly having to defend or explain herself in some way. The willingness of a member of the dominant group to speak out can be very important. Even if the person you question or respond to doesn't really hear you or understand, you've shown support for members of the targeted group. A second goal for an ally is stopping behavior that's hurtful to others. Silence, such as smiling at a sexist joke or staying quiet when someone is making fun of large-sized women, can be interpreted as saying that you agree with or support what's being said. A third goal of an ally is to help another person understand something new. That person might then begin to think about it, learn, and choose to change her behavior in the future.

It's sometimes easier to talk about being an ally than it is to act as one. There are fears that hold people back in some situations. You may worry that others won't like you if you speak up. That's certainly possible, but you may also find that some people will like you more. Consider which is more important—what others think of you, or standing up for what you think is fair.

. . .

"I can't stress enough how important it is to me as a lesbian to have straight allies, especially knowing that my allies are willing to be mistaken as lesbian or bisexual. In the beginning of my sophomore year the lesbian bisexual alliance, in which I was very active, held our first dance of the year. I knew I could count on my lesbian friends to be there, but imagine my surprise when five or six straight first-year students from my hall showed up! I knew they were running the risk of being labeled as lesbian or bisexual, and thus opening themselves up to possible harassment and gossip. It meant a lot to me that they came despite all this."

—R. C. S., class of '94

. . .

Another fear is that others will begin to target you. This is particularly an issue if the oppression you're trying to interrupt involves a more invisible difference such as sexual orientation. You may be tempted to use qualifiers such as "I'm not gay, but . . . " However, if you're trying to support a specific group, a simple "I don't like these jokes because they're putting people down" is more appropriate than qualifiers that make it sound like you're trying to distance yourself from that group.

Another fear is that you won't know exactly how to say what you want to say and will confuse things or make a fool of yourself. It can help to learn as much as you can about the issues. It takes time to internalize concepts well enough to explain them to others, especially if you're still in the process of learning yourself.

I found myself in this situation several years ago, during a training session for over two hundred student leaders. Questions were being asked and comments made that I knew needed to be challenged because they were perpetuating the myth that all prejudice was oppression. I tried to explain the point that it was the addition of power to the prejudice that created oppression, but I was unsure of how to follow up if questioned much further. Finally, I stopped and said that I felt really uncomfortable because I knew that I needed to respond but I wasn't sure I could put all the ideas together clearly enough to explain them. I felt annoyed at myself and upset that I hadn't known exactly what to say and how to say it.

When the group left at the end of the session, two students told me that they had really liked it when I had said I was uncomfortable and didn't know what to say. What I realized then was that it was all right to struggle, that I needed to keep struggling, and that being honest about how I was feeling was probably the most important thing. People may get impatient, but they usually know when you're genuinely trying, even if your words are slow in coming or not quite perfect. Remember, change is accomplished in small steps.

Terms, Language, and Free Speech

. . .

"Dean Kagan, distinguished faculty, parents, friends, graduating seniors, Secret Service agents, class agents, people of class, people of color, colorful people, people of height, the vertically constrained, people of hair, the differently coiffed, the optically challenged, the temporarily sighted, the insightful, the out of sight, the out-of-towners, the Eurocentrics, the Afrocentrics, the Afrocentrics with Eurailpasses, the eccentrically inclined, the sexually disinclined, people of sex, sexy people, sexist pigs, animal companions, friends of the earth, friends of the boss, the temporarily employed, the differently employed, the differently optioned, people with options, people with stock options, the divestiturists, the deconstruc-

tionists, the home constructionists, the homeboys, the homeless, the temporarily housed at home, and God save us, the permanently housed at home."
—Garry Trudeau, opening speech at Yale University's Class Day, May 1991

• • •

As mentioned earlier in this chapter, questions of language and free speech are being hotly debated and discussed on college campuses. These efforts to define terms in ways that don't perpetuate negative attitudes or stereotypes reflect the belief that people should have the right to name themselves. We've often used names for groups that have been imposed on them by others who have had the power to do so. Think for a minute about your own given name. For example, if you're named Katherine you may prefer to be called Katherine, Kathy, Kate, Katie, by your middle name, or by something else entirely. You should have the right to say "please call me Katherine" or "I prefer to be called Kate" even if someone else feels they would rather call you Kathy.

Consider also the connotations of names and where they began. For example, though the term "handicapped" is often used, it originated as a derogatory image of someone begging on the street "cap in hand." [31] The terms used for different groups will also vary over time, for as groups continue the process of self-examination, they may choose different names for themselves. Furthermore, there's not always agreement within groups about a single preferred term. For instance, Joanne might prefer to be called black, while Lakesia prefers to be called African American.

There are also ways you can use more inclusive language in your daily interactions. One way to show respect for those who are gay, lesbian, or bisexual is to use gender neutral terms rather than assuming everyone is heterosexual. This means asking, "Are you seeing someone?" rather than "Do you have a boyfriend?" If you have a friend you know is lesbian or bisexual, ask how her partner is, by name, in the same way you would ask a heterosexual friend about her partner.

Members of some groups have taken terms that had been considered derisive when used by others to insult them, and have adopted them within their own communities in an effort to diffuse their power as slurs.

The political action group Queer Nation is one example. This doesn't mean, however, that members of this group want heterosexuals to call them "queers."

Similarly, the English language symbolically associates white with good and dark with evil. Phrases such as the "black sheep of the family," a "blacklist," and "blackballing" someone from a club all have negative connotations. Excusing a "little white lie" or describing someone's past as "lily white," however, have more positive connotations. Hearing terms such as these as you were growing up subtly builds associations about the meaning of colors. These associations can contribute to the development of prejudices and stereotypes.

Residential and Social Life

. . .

"I heard myself from freshman year think, 'yeah, right. My faith is secure, I know where I stand.' But being around different people really challenged me. My faith was strong, but encountering so many people of different religions that I knew only a little about provoked many questions—who am I to think my beliefs are right? How can one religion be right? No matter how strong your faith is, I think college diversity inevitably will have some effect on your development."

—K. L., class of '93

. . .

Living in a college residence hall offers a wonderful opportunity to learn about others and challenge yourself at the same time. Your most immediate and sometimes your most intense relationship will be with your roommate. Living with a roommate can be complex under *any* circumstances. There are always compromises to be worked out, especially in situations where roommates also have to contend with feelings and stereotypes about their differences. You may fear saying the wrong thing or having a different lifestyle "forced on you." Get to know one another and talk honestly about your fears to get past them.

. . .

"Keep in mind that most likely, much of what you've always heard about homosexuals is not true, or is based on the exception, not the rule. Your lesbian roommate is not going to try to seduce you, or look at you when you undress. In fact, she may be more modest than you are! If you are gay or lesbian or bisexual, don't assume either. Maybe your roommate or the people living in your dorm don't know much about gay culture, but that doesn't mean they aren't willing to learn."

—W. C., class of '93

. . .

Some particular issues need to be discussed and negotiated by roommates if they are to live together respectfully. Your residence hall room is your home, and you should both be able to surround yourselves with items that make you feel at home. This includes expressing personal identity through music and posters and decorations on the door or walls. You can celebrate pride in who you are without minimizing or putting down your roommate or others on the floor. Discuss what rules you'll have about visitation, guests, and expressions of affection in the room. The same criteria should apply for both other- and same-sex guests.[32]

Some roommate situations are negotiated with the cooperation of both parties. This experience is a valuable one, and roommates should make every effort to achieve it. There are other situations, however, in which the living arrangement is simply unworkable and is too disruptive for one or both roommates. It's necessary, in those situations, to consider a change. Refer to chapter 3 for more information about resolving roommate conflicts.

Group living in residence halls has a powerful impact on students' overall experience of college life. Some call it a miserable experience and others the absolutely best time of their lives. Respect for one another is a crucial part of living together successfully. One way to indicate respect is to take the time and care to use someone's name correctly. Learn how to pronounce others' names accurately and don't assume a nickname or Anglicize a name to make it easier for you unless the other person initiates that. Often Latino/Latina names include two last names such as Maria Diaz-Hidalgo. One name is from the father's family and the other from the mother's. Use both. Often Vietnamese and Cambodian names are written with the family name first, so someone named Dith Pran, for example, would be called Pran.

Though college sometimes feels like "its own little world," campuses are not immune to world and national events. At times, students from particular backgrounds or lifestyles are more directly affected by current events, for example, the uprising in China, a plane crash in Pakistan, anti-Korean violence in New York, Arab-Israeli tensions in the Middle East, the 1992 riots in Los Angeles, or incidents of gay bashing. Be sensitive to the fact that intellectual talk about something may be painful for a person who is more directly and personally involved. For example, students who were from the Middle East and students with family and friends in the U.S. armed forces were all deeply affected by the Persian Gulf War.

It can be a challenge for women who are in the minority on a campus (e.g., returning adult students, lesbians and bisexuals, students with disabilities, women of color) to find fulfilling social activities. While you may certainly participate in, and enjoy, many campus activities, most will reflect the values and culture of the majority population. Some specialized organizations and groups develop activities in order to help you meet others with similar social interests and lifestyles. Groups sponsor parties, conferences, speakers, and informal get-togethers. These opportunities provide safer places to relax and be yourself. Positive interpersonal support—friends and mentors—are important to success at college. Preorientation programs, such as those run for students of color, international students, and returning adult students begin to build support networks of friends, faculty, and staff.

Participation in campus life, especially in leadership roles, complements and stimulates academic life. Some leadership roles put you in very visible positions, and at times leave you pulled in different directions by others' expectations—those of your group, the student body that elected you, the administration that appointed you. A strong and trusted personal support system can help you sort through these expectations and your reactions to them. You may concentrate on relationships with individuals of your own group, you may choose to seek support elsewhere, or you may look for a mixed network of resources.

Respect the rights of others to socialize in the ways they choose, and stand up for your right to do the same. Strict Muslims, for instance, are prohibited from drinking alcohol and dancing with members of the other sex. This means structuring different ways to socialize or attending events with alcohol and dancing while not participating in, or being pressured to participate in, activities that go against religious values.

Dating habits can be influenced by religious factors and cultural values. Religious teachings and your parents' feelings about issues such as intermarriage, homosexuality, premarital sex, divorce, and abortion can play a role in your social life and your feelings about the decisions you make.

WHERE TO LOOK FOR HELP

On Campus

The quality of life on campus is monitored by agencies such as the Student Affairs Office, the Office of the Dean of Students, and the Student Activities Office. The residence life and housing offices oversee campus living situations. If your living environment is uncomfortable or hostile, talk with your R.A. Concerns not resolved at this initial level can be directed up through your residence hall director and central housing and residence life offices.

The Career Development or Placement Office may have information about nondiscrimination policies and histories at the companies, agencies, institutions, and graduate schools you eventually consider. The office may also help you contact alumni from your group who can be both sources of information and mentors for you.

Offices and services exist for all students, and sometimes particular staff members are especially trained to respond to the needs of specific groups of students—returning adults, international students, etc. There may also be specific offices on campus to work with, and for, particular groups of students. Offices or liaisons for international students, minority affairs, gay/lesbian/bisexual students, returning adult students, and students with disabilities, for example, are often designed to help students work within the existing system and assist them if the regular channels are insufficient. These offices provide basic counseling and support and sometimes advocate for the needs of particular groups of students when policies and decisions are being made.

Individual clubs, organizations and groups sometimes have their own offices or "centers." The functions of these student organizations include social activities; political action; emotional support; services such as peer counseling, hotlines, referral networks, and resource libraries; educational programs such as speakers bureaus, workshops, films, lectures; leadership training; and opportunities to network with others outside the campus such as alumni and groups at other colleges and at regional conferences.[33]

• • •

"I have been cochair this year of a support group on campus and I'm now on the Special Needs Advisory Board. I also made contact with the local independent living center and I've done some volunteer work for them. All these things, I realize now, empowered me to feel I was a part of the process and I no longer felt as if things were being done to me."

—Student, class of '95

• • •

Some support groups or activities on campus are specified for certain people in order to provide comfortable sources of help. For example, some twelve-step groups for those in recovery (see chapter 6) are designated for lesbians, gays, and bisexuals or for African Americans. Some exercise classes are open only to large-sized women. Adult students may find groups on divorce, parenting, and making the transition back into school.

It's important to know what to do in the event that you experience or see someone else experience, discrimination, harassment, or bias-related violence. The University of Massachusetts suggests that you keep a detailed record of incidents and the dates and times at which they occurred. Include the names of those responsible, if you know, and any witnesses. Tell someone you trust about what's happening, and get help and information about further steps available to you from an appropriate office—affirmative action, security, dean of students, minority affairs, residential life, ombudsperson (if your campus has one). Review your college handbook and any policies and written brochures or material put out by your institution about grievance and judicial procedures. Know your resources before you have to use them.[34]

Off Campus

Many on-campus offices such as the health and counseling services and the Office of Services for Students with Disabilities will refer you to appropriate off-campus agencies and resources. Also make your own effort to get to know what's available in the off-campus community — churches, festivals, cultural organizations, political groups, volunteer opportunities, social services, etc. Local newspapers often have listings of events, activities, and meetings in the community. Many larger cities and some smaller towns with significant gay and ethnic populations have separate newspapers or newsletters that give much information about what's going on in town. Your community may also have one or more specialized bookstores, and they're good places to browse and meet people—other Christians, returning adult students, lesbians, gays, and bisexuals, people of color, etc. Often these stores have bulletin boards sharing information about services, entertainment, clubs and restaurants, social events, and resources.

EDUCATING YOURSELF

. . .

"I went to work on my racism actively and aggressively, which in large part meant scrutinizing cultural misunderstanding. I was going to get beyond my racism if it killed me . . . it *was* killing me. Racism was altering my ability to think clearly, it was affecting my creativity, it was determining my friendships, it was narrowing my vision, it was denying me full personhood. In time, I found two teachers: Jewish feminist Ricky Sherover Marcuse, who was one of the forces behind a practice called Unlearning Racism, and Black activist Jim Dunn, who worked with an organization in New Orleans called HUMAN. These fine teachers helped me to forgive myself for not having escaped that which burdens all children, the learning of prejudice. I went back over every encounter with other cultures I could remember: in music, in film, in jokes, in language, in real life. I celebrated that which I had instinctively valued and defended. I meticulously undid that behavior which uncharacteristically hurt me or anyone else, for it is not my nature to destroy intentionally. I learned to sit quiet, to not always know what to do. I began to notice what freedoms of expression and movement I took for granted, avenues that were not open to people of color. And I fought to rid myself of assumptions about how people think, what people want, and where people come from. It was like learning to walk again."

—Holly Near, *Fire in the Rain . . . Singer in the Storm*[35]

. . .

You learned what you were taught but you can also unlearn, change, and grow. It may feel awkward, at first, to change old habits, such as the language you use. However, the only way to really feel more comfortable with what's new is to use it—kind of like breaking in a new pair of shoes. When you consider how the population is projected to change in the future, it'll probably be helpful to have a variety of different kinds of shoes to wear. Think of breaking in new shoes as preparing to walk most effectively through that new territory.

The learning process is an ongoing one, and it's not always comfortable. Some people react to feeling uncomfortable by giving up, avoiding what's difficult to confront, and staying with what's familiar. Others choose to interrupt the cycle. If you opt for change, you will not find it easy. When you recognize assumptions, stereotypes, and prejudices, you may become stuck in the guilt you may feel. Perhaps you will look for members of the oppressed group to "forgive" you or tell you that they don't hate you. This only adds more stress for them. Sometimes you have to hear the frustration and anger felt by those who have experienced oppression—hear it without getting defensive or making excuses, even though defensiveness is a very natural response. You can't change or excuse the past. You *can* acknowledge it, let go of the guilt, and take responsibility for making a difference in the future.

∎ ∎ ∎

"For as long as any differences between us mean that one of us must be inferior, then the recognition of any difference must be fraught with guilt."

—Audre Lorde, *Sister Outsider*[36]

∎ ∎ ∎

Members of targeted groups should not always be expected to educate others. This doesn't mean that you can never ask anyone any questions. Having an ongoing friendship with someone often involves a natural give and take about all kinds of issues. This is quite different from asking questions of a new acquaintance with the sole purpose of being taught by her. Remember, too, that while every person's identity as a member of a particular group is a significant part of who she is, it's not *all* she is. Also be aware that one person from a group doesn't speak for, or represent, everyone from that group.

There are many ways to learn without putting the responsibility on others to educate you. You can take academic courses, participate in

WHERE I'M COMING FROM   BY BARBARA BRANDON

Where I'm Coming From copyright 1992 Barbara Brandon. Distributed by *Universal Press Syndicate*. Reprinted with permission. All rights reserved.

workshops, read books, and attend films, plays, lectures, and programs. Many schools offer various "awareness" days and weeks throughout the year when you can educate yourself about some of these issues. The suggestions at the end of each of the specific chapters that follow also provide you with direction. Remember, too, that doing volunteer work, reading a book, or attending a workshop may make you feel like you've learned some significant things, but it doesn't make you an expert or mean that your work is finished.

The process of educating yourself will also provide opportunities for you to meet many more people on your campus. Some people may challenge you or wonder why you're there, but if your intent is genuinely to learn and expand your circle of acquaintances, then hang in there. You'll learn a lot and meet some wonderful people. You're entering college at a particularly exciting time, when individuals and institutions are struggling to adapt to a changing world and to redress some past imbalances. It is a time that offers many challenges and many opportunities.

TWELVE

Ethnicity and Culture

College offers you a range of new worlds. You can enjoy meals cooked by international students from India, Japanese tea ceremonies, readings by Latina poets, and dance concerts featuring music and movement from a variety of different cultures.

The celebration of Kwanzaa is an interesting example. Observed from December 26 to January 1, Kwanzaa is a cultural celebration that reflects on black history and accomplishments; like many holidays, it is a time for joy and sharing. During Kwanzaa, people light candles and describe what the seven principles of Kwanzaa mean to them through songs, poems, dance, and personal statements. Kwanzaa celebrants express the principles of unity, self-determination, collective work and responsibility, cooperative economics, purpose, creativity, and faith.[1]

Terminology

The term *race* is a biological concept used to classify people with similar physical characteristics, such as skin color, facial features, hair, and physical stature. Classifying people on the basis of physical characteristics has led to some misunderstanding of what the term "race" means.[2] All of us combine different degrees of black and white in our skin color. The strength of the sun differs in various parts of the world, and our ancestors developed their skin tone in order to protect themselves from the rays of the sun. Those of us with darker skins are descended from people who lived in hotter climates.[3] People who believe that biological differences such as skin color make one group superior to another have given these biological distinctions social power. The suggestion that various races are not equal has been used, at times, to justify differential treatment and exploitation of some groups by other groups.[4]

■ ■ ■

"Living in India made me understand that a white minority in the world has spent centuries conning us into thinking a white skin makes people superior, even though the only thing it really does is make them more subject to ultraviolet rays and wrinkles."
—Gloria Steinem, "If Men Could Menstruate"[5]

■ ■ ■

Ethnicity is a sociological concept that describes a group of people who share a social and cultural heritage passed down from previous generations. This may include similar customs, religion, language, geographic origin, and history.[6]

There are many different definitions of *culture*. One definition describes culture as the beliefs, traits, and behaviors shared by members of a group and communicated to others.[7] Culture may also be described as what a stranger needs to know to behave appropriately in a new setting.[8] Terms such as "culturally deprived" or "culturally disadvantaged" offend the groups to which they refer because they imply that one culture is less legitimate than another.[9]

The term "minority" means "the smaller in number of two groups constituting a whole."[10] This is a quantitative term, but it has been applied in a qualitative way to groups who are treated unequally because they're different; a minority group is often inaccurately defined by the fact that they are oppressed rather than by any numerical criteria.[11] Minority classification has often meant more restricted options in education, jobs, housing, etc., and less access to power and upward mobility.[12] Consider that

- in the world, people of color are in the numerical majority, making up as much as 85 percent of the world population.[13]
- in the next century, people of color will become the numerical majority of the population in the United States.[14]

The term *people of color* was created by various ethnic groups who are distinguished by brown, red, yellow, and black skin hues; origins from all over the globe; and a common experience of conquest, control, or mistreatment by European nations.[15]

Background Information: Racial Identity Development

Much has been written in recent years about individual identity development during late adolescence and early adulthood, including the development of an individual's racial identity. The models of racial identity development are based on the premise that people go through a process of developing their racial consciousness by moving through several stages. In these models, the final stage is an acceptance of race as a positive aspect of themselves and of others.

For a number of reasons, the models presented below should be applied cautiously. First, keep in mind that there's nothing inherently good or bad about being at a particular stage of development. Secondly, be aware that real-life experience is rarely as clear cut as a model on paper. The phases of development do not occur in neatly demarcated stages that follow one another in a simple forward progression. Finally, it is important to note that some criticize these models as being too rigid, as classifying individuals in ways they shouldn't be classified, or as using labels to judge or patronize. These models may also, at times, appear to be "blaming the victim," or putting the bulk of the responsibility on the individual rather than acknowledging that majority institutions also need to change and develop. For all these reasons, consider these models as a source of information, not as rigid criteria for evaluating people. Perhaps they'll help you understand the growth process in yourself and others.

As individuals move through different stages in the development of their own racial identities, there may be times when they feel anger toward those in other groups. Friendships, both within racial groups and across them, can be affected as people go through changes at different paces. In such cases, friends should be patient with one another. People need to be able to feel and express anger without being told not to do so. Friends may find themselves able to come back together as stronger friends once they've both gone through those stages of anger and separation.

Majority Racial Identity Development

Psychologist Janet E. Helms has identified five general stages of the development of majority racial identity awareness.[16] At the *contact stage,* the individual doesn't see herself as a racial being and is largely unaware of the social and political implications of race. She may have a naive curiosity about people from different cultures, but by and large, she tends to ignore or downplay ethnic differences. For example, she's likely to say things such as "people are just people" or "I don't see you as black." College students from very homogeneous white communities may be at this stage because they've had very limited contact with those from other ethnic groups.

If an individual chooses to interact with minority group members, she is eventually forced to acknowledge that prejudice and discrimination exist and that she is part of the majority or dominant group. This is the *disintegration stage.* As the differences become more apparent, she may begin to feel guilty and seek to distance herself from her own majority group. She may feel that she's different from other white people, overidentify with the targeted group, or try to protect them from negative experiences. She may feel overwhelmed by the scope of the problem. None of these reactions is productive in the long run. The person in this stage is often caught between the norms of her own cultural group and her growing realization that these norms need to be challenged. Overidentification with minority culture, or overprotection of them, could lead to rejection by the majority group. Some at this stage choose to retreat into the dominant culture and limit their contacts with other groups.

An individual who tries to resolve her feelings of helplessness moves into the *reintegration stage.* Here the person's focus is on herself as a member of the majority group. There is a tendency to minimize similarities with other groups, to idealize her own majority group positively, and to evaluate others negatively. Others are stereotyped out of fear and anger. Some choose to distance themselves from minorities and perhaps to focus their energies on other issues, for example, world hunger. Others come to terms with the guilt they felt during the disintegration stage. Once they accept their feeling of responsibility as whites in a society where whites have the power, they may find their anger and fear lessening.

With this acceptance, the white individual moves into the *pseudo-independent stage,* characterized by a sincere intellectual acceptance of racial differences. The pseudo-independent person is interested in the similarities between groups and focuses her interactions on members of the other group whom she sees as similar to her. There's some emotional distance at this stage, and while the person's intellectual approach is sincere, her feelings have not yet reached the same level as her thoughts. This is the stage where people know the "right" things to say, but those ideas aren't yet connected to their hearts. As interactions increase with different members of the minority group, that connection is developed.

In the *autonomy stage* the person moves beyond the knowledge of racial similarities and differences to a genuine acceptance. Differences are not seen as better or worse. An autonomous person has internalized a positive white racial identity, and she values and seeks out cross-cultural experiences.

Minority Racial Identity Development

Four stages are generally experienced by minority group members as they develop a positive racial identity.[17] The *acceptance or pre-encounter stage* is characterized by a limited awareness of her own culture. Her attitudes and beliefs are internalized from the majority group's values, and she accepts stereotypes about herself. At this stage, the person tends to deny her own group and tries to be like the dominant group. She believes that assimilation, or fitting in, is the preferred method for problem solving.

At the *resistance or encounter stage,* this denial begins to break down. This can happen through a series of experiences that challenge the internalized majority group values and stereotypes. It can also result from a significant event such as a very negative experience with the majority group or a very positive experience with the minority group. This creates an openness to a new identity. As the search for that new identity begins, there is a new and deep recognition of the trauma of discrimination.

At the *immersion or redefinition stage,* there's a transition from the old identity to a new one. The individual totally rejects the old and glorifies the new. This can play out in feelings of anger and hostility toward anything associated with the dominant group and its institutions. There can also be hostility directed toward other minority groups. The person becomes totally involved in learning about her own culture and in political actions designed to confront the system and fight oppression.

At the *internalization stage,* the individual feels progressively more

WHERE I'M COMING FROM   BY BARBARA BRANDON

comfortable with her new identity. She becomes able to renegotiate with the majority from a different and stronger base than before. She feels confident about her racial identity and proud of her cultural heritage. She begins to question whether total rejection of the majority group is really necessary in order to connect with her own group's positive features. At this stage, the individual can also consider and evaluate the cultural values of the dominant group and of other minority groups. A commitment to work actively toward elimination of all types of oppression emerges.

Biracial Identity Development

The development of a positive racial identity in biracial individuals is naturally more complicated. This description of five stages offers some beginning thoughts.[18]

The *personal identity stage* generally occurs when the individual is young. Her sense of who she is tends to be independent of any particular ethnic background. Usually the biracial individual comes under pressure, often from society, to *choose a group categorization*. The choice may be to assume a multicultural identity or to select one of her ethnic identities as the dominant one. The choice may be between the majority or minority culture, for example white or Latina, or between one of two minority cultures, such as Asian American or Native American. The decision is influenced by status factors such as ethnicity of neighbors and parents' peers; social support factors such as parental style, familial acceptance, and cultural acceptance; and personal factors such as physical appearance. On campus this pressure could mean the student feels as though she has to choose between belonging to different groups.

If a choice is made, or imposed, the *enmeshment/denial stage* is characterized by confusion and guilt, as well as a feeling of some disloyalty toward the parent of the culture not chosen. In the *appreciation stage,* the individual learns more about her other ethnic culture while maintaining an identification with the one she had chosen. Learning about family history on both sides is important to establishing a positive sense of a dual cultural identity. At the *integration stage,* the person is able to recognize and value all of the ethnic groups that are part of her bi- or multiracial identity. She is able to integrate both parents' backgrounds into a cohesive whole for herself.

Background Information: Some Different Cultures

With so many different people living and learning together in a college community, everyone needs to respect and understand different values, backgrounds, and communication styles. Often the institution and its policies will reflect the values and expectations of the dominant culture. Therefore, to create a campus receptive to all, cultural differences need to be understood.

Any attempt to summarize characteristics of a group runs the risk of perpetuating generalizations and stereotypes. There are, however, several important factors that shape the development of a group and of specific individuals in it: [19]

1. Immigration experience—willing or forced, at what age, how many generations back.
2. Religious and spiritual influences.
3. Sex-role socialization.
4. Family influences.
5. Socioeconomic status.
6. Lifestyle.
7. Values.
8. Behavior.
9. Level of ethnic identity and acculturation.

Acculturation is the process of adopting the cultural traits of a society into which one has moved.[20] Acculturation is not always voluntary; sometimes it is expected; at other times it is forced. Within any group, and within any family, the balance between ethnic identity and acculturation for each generation and each individual is likely to evolve and vary.

African Americans

The term "African American" is one of several used to refer to U.S. citizens of African descent. This term may also refer to those from the West Indies, the Caribbean, and Central and South America who are of African descent.[21] The term "black" or "black American" is also used.

African Americans were first brought to the United States in 1619 as indentured servants and remained as slaves for over two hundred years. Slavery was legally sanctioned by the U.S. Constitution until 1865. When slavery was legal, laws, customs, attitudes, and beliefs all rationalized the institution of slavery and encouraged a sense of white superiority. A civil rights act was passed in 1875, only to be declared unconstitutional by the Supreme Court in 1883. From 1896 to 1954 African Americans received unapologetically inferior legal treatment in the United States. They were subjected to long-standing inequities in education, economic opportunities, housing, and social status. The civil rights acts passed by Congress between 1957 and 1965 were important legal steps, but progress has been slow and uneven.[22]

The church is often a focus of social and civic activities for many African American families. Religion influences views, and the family, including the extended family, is valued strongly. Hard work, education, and social mobility are valued, particularly by middle-class African Americans.[23] In general, the learning and communication styles of African Americans focus on people and activities rather than things, nonverbal communication, a keen sense of justice, and a preference for freedom and personal distinctiveness.[24]

Asian Americans

Asian Americans include Chinese Americans, Japanese Americans, Korean Americans, Pacific Islanders, Filipinos, and Vietnamese.[25] Each ethnic group has its own distinct subculture, values, and customs. Some Asian Americans were born in their countries of origin while others were born in the United States. While they share some cultural links, they can also be very different from one another.

The term "Oriental" has fallen out of use. It was coined by the English to describe those subject to British colonial rule in Asia and Northern Africa. The term originated as a comparison to the Western cultures, which were called "Occidental."[26] The term "Oriental" connotes stereotypes such as the silent and submissive woman, and, to modern ears, distorts the fact that a number of Asian Americans were born here and are U.S. citizens.[27] There are also differences within groups based on social class, geographic origin, and generation in the United States.[28]

There's often a false assumption that a person who is Asian will get along well with all other Asian Americans. Historical relationships between Asian American groups may vary greatly, however. For example, in the early 1900s Japan annexed Korea and made it a colony of the Japanese empire, taking away Korean land, culture, independence, and lives. This situation persisted until 1945 and has caused much hostility between these two Asian cultures.[29]

Probably the most important event to affect Japanese American families was their confinement to internment camps by the United States during World War II.[30] While no similar action was taken against German Americans, Japanese Americans were singled out. They were denied due process, and their rights were violated by a government that was supposed to protect them. After the war, society largely ignored this action and denied that it had ever happened. It was only in 1988 that an act of Congress acknowledged and addressed this crime perpetrated on Japanese Americans. The internment-camp experience, and a reluctance to talk about it, has created considerable trauma, internalized shame, and repressed anger among Japanese Americans.[31]

Asian Americans have been affected by racism, cultural value conflicts, and generational conflicts between parents and their children. As successive generations move into the American culture, traditional Asian values often begin to change. The family is most highly valued in Asian culture, and children are expected not to bring shame to the family name. Respect for parents is expected and generalizes to respect for other older authority figures. Hierarchical roles give men and elders more status and the right to make decisions. Women tend to have a more nurturing role. Academic achievement and success are valued.[32] The communication style valued by Asian Americans includes an emphasis on cooperation and collaboration rather than confrontation; an aversion to direct requests or statements; humility and discretion; and caution in expressing emotions, especially anger and hostility.[33] Those from Vietnamese backgrounds, in particular, may smile at times when it appears inappropriate to do so. Smiles are often a stoic response to adversity or cover hostile feelings.[34]

European Americans

As the dominant American culture, white European Americans rarely see themselves as having an ethnic identity. Yet Irish Americans, Italian Americans, Polish Americans, and others all have distinctive cultural backgrounds that can be explored and appreciated. Consider a white Eastern European American who had never really thought much about her ancestry or heritage. One day she watches a TV show, "Brooklyn Bridge," and everything she sees—the clothes, the apartment, the food, the values—feels familiar. Or think about an Italian American who watches the movie *Moonstruck* and feels as though she's seeing her own family on the screen.

European Americans—U.S. citizens of European descent—stress values of competition and individual achievement; independence and autonomy; rigidity and urgency with time, schedules, and deadlines; and linear thinking. Though varied, the communication patterns of European Americans are those often taken as the "norm" in the United States. These include eye contact and a firm handshake; assertiveness; written rather than oral communication; a willingness to discuss emotions, problems, and feelings; and a direct approach to conflict.[35]

International Students

International students in the United States come from many different ethnic and cultural backgrounds. They differ from the other cultural groups in this section in that they have not immigrated permanently to the United States. International students are not U.S. citizens. Their families remain in their home countries, and international students maintain their own national citizenship while attending college in the United States.

Many international students coming to the United States for the first time to attend college experience what has been called culture shock. They may be unsure of how to act in many situations. Certainly a major transition for anyone involves some degree of discomfort, but anxiety tends to increase the more the new environment differs from the old one. Those differences are apt to be far greater for those traveling long distances and adapting to a new language, customs, values, expectations, climate, and social system.

The different countries and cultures international students come from vary greatly and are likely to influence their ways of thinking, behavior, values, and attitudes. Some of the dimensions that may vary include the value of manual labor, what constitutes "success," and the importance of time and deadlines.[36]

Be careful about assuming too much before you actually get to know someone. All international students are not necessarily new to the United States. Some have attended boarding school in this country, and others have been here on exchange programs or extended visits. Some come from homes where one or both parents are American.

I recall opening day at one college where I worked. I was speaking with Mary, a new first-year student from Kansas, who was anxiously awaiting the arrival of her roommate Rita—from Portugal. Mary wondered if there'd be any language barriers and was excited about introducing Rita to life in the United States. Well, Rita finally arrived and Mary greeted her warmly, speaking slowly and clearly. Rita raised an eyebrow. Mary, thinking Rita couldn't understand her, spoke even more slowly, asking her if this was her first time in America. Rita just started to laugh hysterically. Finally she responded in an accent quite familiar to me, "We've only been in Portugal a couple of years, I'm from Brooklyn."

Latinas/Latinos

The term "Hispanic" was created by the federal government as a census category for U.S. citizens from over twenty-five Spanish-speaking nations whose countries of ethnic origin were colonized by Spain.[37] A number of Hispanics prefer to name themselves according to their own nationalities. "Latino/Latina" (male/female forms) is a self-definition created by those who speak Spanish and are of Spanish descent. This includes Cubans, Puerto Ricans, Mexicans, Mexican Americans, and people from the Spanish-speaking countries of Central and South America.[38] Those from Central and South America may prefer to be identified by their national origin—for example, as Colombians or Panamanians—but may also use the term "Latina/Latino."[39]

"Chicana/chicano" (female/male forms) is a term of self-definition for many Mexican Americans. It reflects a concern with preserving their cultural heritage and identity rather than assimilating into the dominant culture.[40] Puerto Ricans, one of the major Latino/Latina groups recognized in the United States, are U.S. citizens.

Traditional Latina/Latino values also vary from group to group and among different families. These values include strong family ties and reliance on an extended family system; a patriarchal nuclear family in which the father is expected to protect and provide and the mother to hold the family together; religion as a central influence; respect for the individual, for others, and for character over action and possessions; and community.[41]

With respect to traditional interpersonal and communication characteristics, Latinas/Latinos prefer physical expressions of greeting and have a gregarious and hospitable nature. They emphasize cooperation and respect for authority and consider it impolite to disagree. Assertive behaviors, especially toward elders, are seen as rude. On some occasions, eye contact is viewed as disrespectful, and direct confrontation is generally avoided.[42]

Native Americans

Native Americans are the descendents of the original inhabitants of the North American continent. There are a large number of different tribes with different languages, customs, and traditions. Individuals identify themselves first as members of a particular tribe such as Cherokee, Sioux, or Yahi, and then as Native American. Although the term "American Indian" is preferred by many tribes and the national organization, it's objectionable to others because it's based on Christopher Columbus's mistaken belief that he had reached India and that the people he found were Indians.[43]

Native Americans have a history of military defeat, ethnic demoralization, and forced displacement at the hands of the U.S. government.[44] Many government policies were designed to force Native Americans to give up their land and cultural heritage.[45]

Native Americans have extended family networks. Respect for individuality and noninterference in others' business, modesty and humility, and giving, sharing, and cooperating are all valued above materialistic possessions. Natural phenomena such as the full moon, location in space, and internal feelings determine the passage of time. Childhood and old age are valued, and religion is a strong force, emphasizing a deep reverence for nature and desire for harmony between the individual, the tribe, and the land.[46]

Native Americans often need to develop two identities if they move outside the Native American community. They seek to retain their own values while living within the dominant culture. While there are differences between tribes, there are some common communication patterns among Native Americans. Direct eye contact is considered disrespectful, especially with authority figures, as are firm handshakes and many kinds of physical touch. Personal questioning is perceived as rude, and discussion of oneself offensive. An oral tradition of relating history through stories is a central form of communication, especially between the old and the young.[47]

Refugees Immigrating to the United States

. . .

"My parents are both from Iran. They immigrated to this country about forty years ago. I am first generation. Growing up in this country has made me very grateful for what I have. Being Iranian/ American has not been easy. People do not know how to take you at first. As a child I was constantly teased and singled out. As a teenager, the revolution in my parents' country made life very awkward. I was ashamed to tell people I was Iranian."

—S. S., class of '93

. . .

Refugees are immigrants who have been forced to leave their homes by events such as war, revolution, genocide, invasion, internal political upheaval, and famine. The refugee experience is usually very traumatic, involving events such as escape from physical danger or violence and the involuntary abandonment of one's home, extended family members and friends, and possessions.

Relocating in the United States, mastering a new language and culture, dealing with new employment and educational systems, and trying to maintain the family system within those changes is also traumatic. Almost always a significant shift in status occurs. Education and training qualifications often don't transfer smoothly, and parents who held respected positions at home may find themselves professionally displaced, with lower salaries and less satisfying work.

Sources of Misunderstanding

· · ·

"With this being such a 'diverse campus,' everyone, all races, all cultures . . . we have to congregate with our 'like kind' to recap the things that are thrown at us constantly on a day-to-day basis. You need to weed out the negative and focus on the positive so that when you go back into that large group where everyone is different you will be more open-minded and willing and able to accept the individuals as they are and who they are."

—A. J., class of '92

· · ·

Often, programs and facilities developed primarily for minority groups have been misperceived as unwarranted special attention. These programs serve an important purpose for students entering predominantly white institutions. Many colleges, for instance, offer specialized preorientation programs for people of color. As explained in the previous chapter, a safe and welcoming campus climate is necessary for all students, but predominantly white campuses are often less than "at-home" environments for women of color. Some subtle indicators send out this message every day. For example, women of color may encounter a limited number of role models in high-level positions on campus, pictures of alumni may show few, if any, people of color, and the types of hair care products sold in the campus store may not be suitable to their needs. Preorientation programs provide an opportunity to establish a peer support network before students are dispersed to living assignments throughout the campus. This is also an important time for women of color to meet and establish connections with faculty and staff mentors. Recognition of the need for a strong support system and the manner in which many preorientation programs seek to achieve it are similar to the principles and practices of other programs that prepare exchange students, athletic teams, and residence staff for their experiences.

Other misunderstandings surround developmental education programs on campus. Participation in these programs does not indicate lack of intelligence; rather, the programs are designed to help students develop the skills to compete academically. Highly intellectually capable students may, because of limited educational opportunities, have received unequal preparation in elementary and secondary schools. Denying them access to some higher education opportunities on the basis of such inequality only compounds the unfairness and continues the inequity that such students experienced in their precollege educations. Students may be admitted to a college with some inconsistencies in particular subject areas because their academic records are otherwise promising. Developmental education programs generally include instruction in English, mathematics, study skills, and writing. Most developmental education programs are open to students who meet this underpreparedness criterion regardless of ethnic background.[48]

Since most institutions reflect European American culture, the social climate on campus for other cultural groups may be more limited and may be less than comfortable. Many campuses therefore maintain cultural centers. Appropriately staffed and funded cultural centers provide a comfortable place for students of color to meet, socialize, network, and participate in programs. Cultural centers also expand the quality of campus life for the entire community and contribute to the college's mission of promoting intercultural understanding and acceptance.[49] The purpose of a cultural center reflects the climate on a campus: the more unwelcoming or unsafe the campus, the greater the need for the center to be a separate, safe space; the more supportive and safe the campus, the more energy can go into providing programs for the entire community.

White students, particularly those who are anxious to challenge themselves, may be eager to learn by interacting with people from different backgrounds. Their approaches are sometimes rebuffed. Some educational opportunities in ethnically mixed groups will be available to them, but they can also learn a great deal in white groups. There is safety in learning separately at times. Some advantages of whites learning about racism from and with other whites include being able to explore racist attitudes in a climate of trust, being able to focus on the meaning of being white and on developing a sense of white identity, and being able to learn without people of color having to teach or having to hear potentially painful things said as part of the learning process.[50]

ENCOUNTERING AND RESPONDING TO THIS ISSUE

As all of you from various cultural backgrounds live and work together, you will understandably differ in what's important to you and in the ways you've learned to communicate with others. Conflicts are bound to arise. Behavior that may be respectful in some cultures can be considered rude in others. Members of some cultural groups prefer to deal openly with problems while others are less comfortable with that directness. This may be reflected, for example, in a roommate conflict in which one person says when something is bothering her and assumes that the other will do the same, but the other person will only speak up if the situation gets unbearable. Some of you prefer to deal with anger by letting it out and moving on. Those of you who come from cultures in which the expression of anger is not culturally acceptable could find this kind of encounter difficult.

Lack of assertiveness may be misinterpreted as apathy. Those of you who are more assertive should recognize that not everyone wants to assert herself. Those of you who are less assertive need not judge yourself by others' standards. However, you might find it helpful to develop some appropriately assertive skills, especially for academic situations. Being able to be assertive doesn't mean you *have* to be assertive all the time.

People also have different degrees of comfort being open about themselves, talking about problems, and expressing emotion with others. Some of you could feel uncomfortable with a roommate or hallmate who tells you a lot about her very personal problems. Others of you may sense that a friend is upset and may feel frustrated if she prefers not to talk about it with you or with a counselor. Shared shower rooms and partial nudity may make you uncomfortable if you're from a home where physical modesty was emphasized. Open discussions about personal topics such as sexuality will feel comfortable for some and awkward and inappropriate for others. Respect the other person's right to deal with her emotions as she wishes. If the situation becomes stressful for you, it's appropriate to let the other person know that, without demanding that she necessarily change her behavior. What may be standard in the United States, such as casual physical contact, may be inappropriate in other cultures. If you know what something means to someone else, it will help you to adapt your behavior with that other person.

Priorities about time, appointments, and deadlines are another potential source of frustration. Everyone needs to be patient and to understand that, for instance, Pat will always be late or Kim will get annoyed if she has to wait more than ten minutes.

Some cultures stress the importance of respect for parents, and others emphasize independence. It may be hard for some of you to believe that your friend can speak so disrespectfully of her parent and for others of you to understand why your roommate lets her parents have so much influence over her decisions. Realize that a friend's decision to challenge her tradition or family's wishes may be much more difficult for her than you can possibly imagine.

Respect for parents is generalized to other authority figures in many cultures, so there are also differences in how formally or informally you each approach people in authority roles at your institution. When I worked in student affairs, I usually asked students to call me by my first name rather than to use "ms." or "dean." *I* was more comfortable with the informality. A number of students, often ones from different cultural backgrounds, preferred *not* to call me by my first name. After telling these students "you can call me Carol" a couple of times, I realized that I needed to let them call me what *they* were comfortable calling me and not insist on their adapting to my preference for informality.

Religion plays a strong role in some cultures, and male and female sex roles and gender expectations also vary. In colleges where less traditional roles and more lenient rules are encouraged, there can be internal stress and conflict for students testing out new ideas. Dating situations and other social choices are also complicated by religious beliefs and cultural gender-role expectations.

For International Students

Even if you were well adjusted at home, you are still likely to experience some problems adapting to your new environment. The change often evokes a feeling of loss of status and competence as you deal with a new language, customs, culture, etc. Develop a support system for yourself to maintain a sense of balance. Allow yourself to adjust at your own rate. You won't learn everything or feel at home right away. Recognize that if you feel depressed or unsuccessful, that's part of the transition pattern and it won't last forever. If possible, prepare for the transition by learning the language, researching the host culture, practicing how to deal with some anticipated situations, and spending time with people from the host culture and other students from your country who have spent time where you're going.[51]

Because you remain a citizen of your home country, some of your experiences on campus will be unique. Depending on the distance to your home and your financial resources, you may find yourself unable to return home very often. Some international students remain in the United States for all four years; others are able to return home only once a year. Prepare for that degree of separation. The paperwork and visas needed for travel can take time to process, so plan ahead if you're going home or anticipating any travel outside of the United States. Plan vacation visits with classmates and trips within the United States during college breaks—it can get depressing to stay on campus when almost everyone else is away. Even if it's just for a weekend or a day, try to get off campus during those times.

Depending upon the exchange rates and difficulties with transfers of funds out of some countries, finances can be complicated. U.S. federal financial aid policies also limit how much you can earn and where you can earn it. Check with the Financial Aid Office at your college for more information. Think also about how best to budget your funds. Leave sufficient time for money to reach you, and know what emergency resources are available to you on campus.

You may begin to feel torn between your life in the United States and the life to which you'll be returning at home. For some of you, going home creates another kind of culture shock stress, and decisions about the future may be difficult. One international student has called it the "crisis of identity" in which one is "precariously poised over the gap between the two cultures," having acquired new ways of feeling and responding to add to those instilled at home.[52]

Cultural holidays and celebrations that are very important to you may not receive the same degree of attention on your campus. Try to get together with others from your country to celebrate. At some colleges, such celebrations are opened up to the entire campus in order to share the holiday and educate others. For those holidays that are more solemnly observed rather than celebrated, it's important that others respect your needs. Seek out reasonable accommodations from the institution to allow you to observe your holidays, such as making arrangements with dining services if you need to break your Ramadan fast after scheduled meal hours.

WHERE TO LOOK FOR HELP

(See also this section in chapter 11.)

Help can come from many sources, as described in more detail in chapter 11. Those of you who are white should seek out white faculty and staff as much as possible to help sort through your thoughts, reactions, and feelings. On predominantly white campuses, there is generally a small number of faculty and staff of color, and their role as potential mentors for students of color is vital. They are also often asked to participate on many campus committees and task forces. With such significant demands on their time and energy, on top of teaching, publishing, and work commitments, they may be more limited in the amount of time they can give to other educational efforts. This is particularly an issue for those with families and for junior faculty members working toward tenure.

EDUCATING YOURSELF

Books: Nonfiction, Anthologies, Biographies, Poetry, Plays

Angelou, Maya. Any of her work.

Asian Women United of California, ed. *Making Waves: An Anthology of Writings by and about Asian American Women*. Boston: Beacon, 1989.

Bell, Derrick. *Faces at the Bottom of the Well: The Permanence of Racism*. New York: Basic, 1992.

Brislin, Richard W. *Cross-Cultural Encounters, Face-to-Face Interaction*. New York: Pergamon, 1981.

Cary, Lorene. *Black Ice*. New York: Vintage, 1992.

Chin, Frank, et al., eds. *Aiieeeee! An Anthology of Asian American Writers*. New York: Mentor, 1991.

Cole, Johnetta B. *Conversations: Straight Talk with America's Sister President*. New York: Doubleday, 1993.

Fleming, Jacqueline. *Blacks in College: A Comparative Study of Students' Success in Black and in White Institutions*. San Francisco: Jossey-Bass, 1984.

Fugard, Athol. Any of his plays.

Giddings, Paula. *In Search of Sisterhood: Delta Sigma Theta and the Challenge of the Black Sorority Movement*. New York: Morrow, 1988.

Green, Rayna. *Native American Women: A Contextual Bibliography*. Bloomington: Indiana University Press, 1983.

―――, ed. *That's What She Said: Contemporary Poetry and Fiction by Native American Women*. Bloomington: Indiana University Press, 1984.

Hsu, Vivian Ling, ed. *Born of the Same Roots: Stories of Modern Chinese Women*. Bloomington: Indiana University Press, 1981.

Hull, Gloria T., Patricia B. Scott, and Barbara Smith, eds. *All the Women Are White, All the Blacks Are Men, but Some of Us Are Brave: Black Women's Studies*. Old Westbury, NY: Feminist Press, 1981.

Hunter-Gault, Charlayne. *In My Place*. New York: Farrar, Straus, Giroux, 1992.

Hurston, Zora Neale. Any of her work.

Ione, Carole. *Pride of Family: Four Generations of American Women of Color*. New York: Summit, 1991.

Karenga, Maulana. *The African American Holiday of Kwanzaa: A Celebration of Family, Community, and Culture*. Los Angeles: University of Sankore Press, 1989.

Katz, Judy H. *White Awareness: Handbook for Anti-Racism Training*. Norman: University of Oklahoma Press, 1978.

Kingston, Maxine Hong. *The Woman Warrior*. New York: Vintage, 1977.

Kohls, L. Robert. *Survival Kit for Overseas Living*. Yarmouth, ME: Intercultural Press, 1984.

Lewis, Tom, and Robert Jungman. *On Being Foreign: Culture Shock in Short Fiction*. Yarmouth, ME: Intercultural Press, 1986.

Lorde, Audre. Any of her work.

Moody, Anne. *Coming of Age in Mississippi*. New York: Dell, 1980.

Moraga, Cherríe, and Gloria Anzaldúa, eds. *This Bridge Called My Back: Writings by Radical Women of Color*. 2d ed. New York: Kitchen Table/ Women of Color Press, 1983.

Morales, Aurora, and Rosario Morales. *Getting Home Alive*. Ithaca, NY: Firebrand, 1986.

Shange, Ntozake. *for colored girls who have considered suicide/when the rainbow is enuf: a choreopoem*. New York: Collier, 1989.

Smith, Barbara, ed. *Home Girls: A Black Feminist Anthology*. New York: Kitchen Table/Women of Color Press, 1983.

Smith, Lillian. *Killers of the Dream*. Rev. ed. New York: Norton, 1978.

Sone, Monica. *Nisei Daughter*. Seattle: University of Washington Press, 1979.

Stavley, Lois Mark. *The Education of a WASP*. New York: Morrow, 1971.

Takaki, Ronald T., ed. *Strangers from a Different Shore: A History of Asian Americans*. New York: Penguin, 1990.

Terkel, Studs. *Race: How Blacks and Whites Think and Feel about the American Obsession*. New York: Anchor, 1993.

Weatherford, Jack. *Indian Givers: How the Indians of the Americas Transformed the World*. New York: Crown, 1988.

Wilson, August. Any of his plays.

Novels

Alvarez, Julia. *How the Garcia Girls Lost Their Accents*. Chapel Hill, NC: Algonquin, 1991.

McMillan, Terry. *Waiting to Exhale*. New York: Viking, 1992.

Morrison, Toni. Any of her work.

Naylor, Gloria. Any of her work.
Tan, Amy. Any of her work.
Walker, Alice. Any of her work.

Articles, Pamphlets, and Papers

Elfin, Mel, with Sarah Burke. "Race on Campus." *U.S. News and World Report,* April 19, 1993.
Louis, Errol T. "Racism on Campus." *Essence,* August 1987.
Russell, Karen K. "Growing Up with Privilege and Prejudice." *New York Times Magazine,* June 14, 1987.
Sanoff, Alvin P., and Scott Minerbrook, et al. "Students Talk about Race." *U.S. News and World Report,* April 19, 1993.
Three Rivers, Amoja. *Cultural Etiquette: A Guide for the Well-Intentioned.* Indian Valley, VA: Market Wimmin, 1990.

Films, Videos, TV Shows, Plays

Alamo Bay. Conflicts erupt along the Texas Gulf Coast between local fishermen and Vietnamese refugees.
The Autobiography of Miss Jane Pittman. Black history in the United States from the Civil War to the Civil Rights movement is seen through the eyes of a 110-year-old ex-slave who lived through it all. From the book by Ernest Gaines.
Avalon. Explores the lives and experiences of an extended immigrant family seeking the American dream in Baltimore.
Black History: Lost, Stolen, or Strayed. Bill Cosby illustrates how media and the arts have distorted the contributions of African Americans. PBS video.
The Brother from Another Planet. A black alien escapes from his own planet and winds up in Harlem.
A Class Divided. An experiment in discrimination is experienced first by a third-grade class in Iowa and later by adult populations. PBS video.
The Colored Museum. Satires on ethnic stereotypes. Play by George C. Wolfe.
Come See the Paradise. An Irish American man and a Japanese American woman fall in love and are affected by World War II.
Crisis at Central High. A Little Rock, Arkansas, high school is integrated in 1957. Based on a true story.
Dances with Wolves. History, lives, and culture of members of the Sioux tribe are seen through their relationship with one soldier.
The Defiant Ones. Two escaped prisoners chained together, one black and one white, have to depend on one another to survive.
"A Different World." Presents life at a historically black college. TV series.
Dim Sum: A Little Bit of Heart. Explores a tense and affectionate relationship between a traditional Chinese mother and her daughter living a more modern life in San Francisco.

Do the Right Thing. Racial tensions build up and explode during a hot day in a New York neighborhood.

El Norte. A brother and sister escape persecution in Guatemala and come to America to try to realize their dreams.

Empire of the Sun. A young British boy living in Shanghai is interred in a prison camp when China is invaded by the Japanese at the beginning of World War II.

Eyes on the Prize (parts I and II). Documents the history of the Civil Rights movement. PBS series.

for colored girls who have considered suicide/when the rainbow is enuf. The lives and feelings of various African American women are expressed through poetry and movement. Choreopoem/play by Ntozake Shange.

From the Mississippi Delta. An African American woman rises from poverty, overcomes racism, and becomes a personal and professional success. Play by Endesha Ida Mae Holland.

Glory. The first black regiment fights for the North during the Civil War. Based on a true story.

A Great Wall. A Chinese American family visits its homeland and more traditional Chinese relatives.

Heat Wave. Many individuals are affected by the events leading up to the 1965 riots in the Watts area of Los Angeles. Made-for-cable movie.

Hester Street. A young immigrant couple struggles with retaining their old world ideals and adjusting to America.

"*I'll Fly Away.*" Depicts life in a southern town at the start of the Civil Rights movement. TV series.

In the Heat of the Night. A black detective from Philadelphia goes south and winds up working with a rural white sheriff to solve a murder.

Jelly's Last Jam. Explores the life of jazz musician Jelly Roll Morton. Play by George C. Wolfe.

The Josephine Baker Story. The African American entertainer and activist becomes a superstar in pre–World War II Europe. Made-for-cable movie.

Jungle Fever. Explores the impact of a cross-racial and cross-class relationship.

The Killing Fields. A *New York Times* correspondent and his Cambodian colleague are caught in the terror of the Khmer Rouge Revolution. Based on a true story.

King. Presents the life and work of Martin Luther King, Jr. Made-for-TV movie.

La Bamba. Ritchie Valens, a Mexican American farm laborer, rises to musical fame during the early days of rock and roll. Based on a true story.

Little Big Man. The development of the West and the treatment of Native Americans is seen through the eyes of the sole white survivor of Custer's last stand.

The Long Walk Home. The 1955 Montgomery, Alabama, bus boycott is experienced by a strong and committed African American woman and the white family for whom she works.

Malcolm X. Presents the life and death of the African American leader. From the autobiography by Malcolm X and Alex Haley.

The Mambo Kings. Two brothers flee Cuba and try to realize their dreams as musicians in the United States. Based on the novel *The Mambo Kings Play Songs of Love* by Oscar Hijuelos.

The Milagro Beanfield War. A Chicano handyman takes on a large developer in order to preserve his small New Mexican town and way of life. From the book by John Nichols.

Mississippi Masala. An interracial relationship develops between an African American man and an East Indian woman.

Murder without Motive: The Edmund Perry Story. Pressures overpower a black student at a predominantly white prep school. Made-for-TV movie based on Robert Sam Anson's book, *Best Intentions.*

Racism 101. Examines the "new racism" on today's campuses, including the University of Michigan and Dartmouth. PBS video.

Ragtime. A racist act in early-twentieth-century New York triggers a strong reaction from a man who refuses to take it anymore. From the book by E. L. Doctorow.

A Raisin in the Sun. A black family in Chicago in the 1950s strives to overcome bigotry and hatred to achieve their dreams. From Lorraine Hansberry's play.

Roots. Explores many generations of African American history. TV miniseries from the book by Alex Haley.

Separate but Equal. A legal battle and the deliberations of the Supreme Court result in the desegregation of schools in 1954. Made-for-TV movie.

A Soldier's Story. Racial hatred explodes in this murder mystery set on a southern army base. From the play by Charles Fuller.

Stand and Deliver. A dedicated math teacher inspires his students in a Mexican American community of Los Angeles to achieve mastery in calculus. Based on a true story.

Thunderheart. An FBI agent investigates a murder on an Indian reservation and explores his own Native American heritage. Based on a true story.

To Kill a Mockingbird. The children of a small-town southern lawyer learn about racism and values by watching their father stand up for his principles. From Harper Lee's book.

Voices of Sarafina. The courage of black South African adolescents living under apartheid is celebrated through interviews with cast members and scenes from the Broadway musical.

White Lie. The press secretary to a city mayor learns the truth about his real father's death and manages to forgive and let go of the past.

Whoopi Goldberg Live. A little African American girl learns to love herself in one segment of this live concert on video.

The Women of Brewster Place. Seven African American women living in a tenement fight for control of their own lives. Made-for-TV movie based on Gloria Naylor's novel.

Zebrahead. A white high school student in Detroit falls for the cousin of his African American friend.

■ THIRTEEN ■

Religion

The variety of religions observed and practiced on college campuses is greater than ever.[2] This is due in part to the increasing numbers of international students attending college in the United States; in part to the rise in the number of independent religious organizations; and in part to students searching for some focus and meaning in their lives.[3] Exposure to other religions, and to other new experiences, challenges, and ways of thinking at college can bring into question some of the religious beliefs with which you grew up. Searching, expanding your ideas, and reevaluating your faith is often a natural and healthy outgrowth of this.

. . .

"I feel that it is important for college women to feel that they can express and explore their religious beliefs while at college. I know that this is a time in my life when I am examining all my beliefs and values, and for me religion is an important part of that."

—L. H., class of '95

. . .

Terminology and Background Information: Some Different Religions

Religious beliefs are personally developed and held by each individual. Commitment and practice vary within all denominations. Some students are quite open and public about their beliefs, and others prefer to observe their faith more privately. There are also atheists, who don't believe in the existence of God, and agnostics, who believe that any ultimate reality such as God is unknown and probably unknowable.[4]

It's impossible to present in this chapter all the specifics about the major religions. I will, however, provide an idea of each and talk about how the values and practices of different religions exist and interact on college campuses.

Christianity

Christianity, the world's largest organized religion, began in Europe, the Middle East, and Northern Africa and now has followers all over the world. Christians accept Jesus as Christ the savior, consider the holy Bible as the word of God, and use the scriptures as the basis for their lives. Jesus's moral teachings reflect the law of love and using that love to help others. Within the Christian religion a number of different denominations or sects have developed over time. Although they have much in common, each of them has its own emphases, traditions, customs, and practices. Two of the major Christian divisions/branches are the Eastern Orthodox Church and the Roman Catholic Church. The Protestant branch includes numerous denominations—Lutheran, Presbyterian, Episcopalian, Methodist, Quaker, Mormon, Baptist, Unitarian Universalist, Pentecostal, the United Church of Christ, etc. There have been many discussions about achieving more unity among the various denominations and branches, and the term "ecumenical" is used to describe this goal and movement.[5]

Islam

The followers of Islam are called Muslims. The youngest of the world's major religions, Islam is also the second largest. Muslims live all over the world, including the United States and Southeast Asia. Islam is centered in the Middle East and Northern Africa, where there are large Muslim populations. The central tenet of faith for Muslims is the belief that the only God is Allah, Allah is one God, and Muhammad is his prophet. The Qur'an (Koran) is the primary source of Muslim beliefs. The two divisions within the Muslim faith are the Sunni sect, to which most Muslims belong, and the Shiah or Shiite sect. Shiites are dominant in Iran and are found in significant numbers in Iraq, Pakistan, and Lebanon. Sufism is a mystical movement practiced by members of both sects. The Nation of Islam, which is best known in the United States as the Black Muslims, is also called the World Community of Islam. The religion of Islam calls for its people to spread the faith to others.[6]

Hinduism

Hinduism is one of the world's oldest religions. It is the religion of 85 percent of the people of India. Hinduism stresses the doctrine of nonviolence and the belief that one must pass through many rebirths to reach salvation. Mahatma Gandhi was inspired by Hinduism in his work. Hinduism is not a single unified religion; it includes a variety of beliefs and practices. Many different gods and goddesses are worshipped, and they are often considered to be different facets and incarnations of one androgynous god/goddess, who goes by many names. Hindus accept all religions as unknowingly part of Hinduism, and they don't believe that any faith can claim to be the only true religion. The most important writings of the Hindu scripture are the Vedas, the Upanishads, and the Bhagavad Gita.[7]

Hinduism is also a social system, and the caste structure locks individuals into the caste or social class into which they were born. This has implications for job opportunities, dress, and rituals. Although public discrimination based on caste is now technically illegal in India, the effects are still felt. Among the sects growing out of Hinduism are Jainism and Sikhism.[8]

Buddhism

After Christianity and Islam, Buddhism, which originated in India, is the next-largest religion in the world. Buddhists believe that all life involves suffering, all life is change, meditation is the main path to enlightenment, and salvation can be reached in one's lifetime. Following his quest for truth, Siddhartha Gautama became known as the Buddha. His teachings became the core of Buddhist thought. The Tripitaka are the three categories of Buddhist scriptures. Buddhism developed into two main divisions—Theravada Buddhism, found in Southeast Asian nations, especially Sri Lanka; and Mahayana Buddhism, which spread northward into countries such as Tibet, Korea, Japan, and China. Zen Buddhism is an offshoot of the latter. It began in China and became a Japanese religion, with a significant following in the United States. Zen Buddhists practice a style of meditation that values seeing into one's own nature to attain wisdom.[9]

Confucianism and Taoism
Confucianism and Taoism are two other philosophy-religions of China. Confucianism emphasizes the ideas of Confucius—good-heartedness, concern for community order and public good, acting for the good of others, intelligence, justice, and courtesy. In contrast, Taoism, founded by Lao Tzu, stresses the individual and is at times seen more as a philosophy, or even as a form of magic, than as a religion. Taoist ideas were first collected in a volume entitled Tao Te Ching.[10]

Shintoism
Shintoism is the native religion of Japan. It presently serves primarily as an expression of patriotism and reverence for ancestors, stressing purity and celebrations. Popular festivals and traditional rituals are important means of expressing national pride.[11]

Judaism
I have chosen to talk about Judaism last in this section because I want to devote more space to this religion. Anti-Semitism, or the oppression of Jews, is still being felt on college campuses today, and therefore it is necessary to include information on Judaism itself and on the oppression of Jews.

Jews believe in one God. Of the Jewish scriptures, the most important part is the Torah, which is comprised of the five books of Moses in what is known to Christians as the Old Testament. The Torah contains laws of worship and daily life, as well as an ancient history of the Jewish people. The Talmud is a record of the conclusions of learned Jewish teachers concerning the interpretation of the scriptures and laws.[12]

Judaism is one of the oldest religions in the world. Jewish people, however, have suffered from persecution throughout history, spending much of their lives in exile. Christianity emerged as a sect of Judaism in the Roman Empire in the first century A.D., and the developing Christian churches tried to distance themselves from their Jewish roots.[13] Although Jesus was opposed by some groups within Judaism, he was executed by the Romans on the orders of the Roman procurator Pontius Pilate.[14] The Christian gospels written in the last part of the first century, however, tell the story of Jesus in a way that exaggerates Jewish culpability.[15] These accounts have become a permanent part of the Christian teachings and have laid the foundation for anti-Jewish feelings and persecution throughout history.[16] When the Roman Empire became predominantly Christian in the fourth century, Jews were given the choice of converting or being expelled. The pattern of Jewish oppression has occurred over and over since the Middle Ages. Jews have continually faced persecution and/or expulsion in one place, forcing them to move to some new place. Some Jews became visible agents of the ruling class after being invited to serve as bankers or moneylenders (occupations forbidden to Christians). While these Jews received some privileges, most Jews were only tolerated and were part of the economically and politically oppressed general population. Repeatedly, the Jews, rather than the ruling class, became the focus of resentment from the oppressed population. When this resentment would reach its peak, the ruling class would withdraw its protection of the Jews, and anti-Semitism would thus be encouraged. Violence would erupt and surviving Jews would either be expelled or forced to flee to another new land, where the cycle repeated itself. The history of Jewish oppression reached its peak with the extermination of six million Jews, one-third of the entire Jewish population, during the Holocaust of World War II.[17]

"Anti-Semitism" is the term used to refer to Jewish oppression. The term "Semite" had a broader scope in ancient times, but now refers chiefly to Arabs and Jews. However, Arabs experience oppression differently than Jews.[18] The term "anti-Semitism" originated in Christian Europe, where Jews were the only Semitic people living among the Christians, and thus "anti-Semitic" has come to mean anti-Jewish.[19] It's defined as hatred and bigotry directed against the Jewish people, coming from either malice or ignorance, intentionally or unintentionally.[20] Anti-

Semitism can take the form of stereotyping, verbal or physical harassment of Jews, scapegoating, graffiti, and the suppression or ignoring of
Jewish culture and experience.

Anti-Semitic acts have been on the rise on college campuses. There
are also more subtle ways in which derogatory attitudes about Jews are
expressed.[21] The Jewish American Princess stereotype and jokes are one
example of this trend. They portray Jewish women as self-centered,
materialistic, overly stylishly dressed, and very aggressive. Of course,
these behaviors and attitudes are not limited to one religious group, and
some people use the term "JAP" to refer to individuals who aren't
Jewish. However, using the label "Jewish" to define anyone in a demeaning way is another means for provoking hostility and directing it
toward Jews. Although some Jews use the term "JAP" about themselves
and one another, this is another example of internalized oppression,
which was defined in chapter 11. Regardless of who uses the term, it's
demeaning and destructive.[22]

. . .

"I remember one time, in the beginning of my freshman year, my
roommate and her friend were discussing two women who lived
on our hall who were Jewish, referring to them as spoiled and
stuck up. They knew full well that I too was Jewish, and acknowledging that I was not 'spoiled' or 'stuck up' they nodded in my
direction with a 'You don't act or look Jewish.' To them, this was
a compliment. At the time, I almost took it as a compliment—it
meant that they didn't think I was spoiled or stuck up. And yet,
the 'compliment' rang alarms for me. I couldn't express it then
because I was too ignorant, but now, after five years of educating
myself on oppression, assimilation, and discrimination, it's bla-
tantly obvious that was an offensive stereotype that they were
applying to all Jews."

—S. L., class of '90

. . .

ENCOUNTERING AND RESPONDING TO THIS ISSUE

One student from the class of 1993 describes discussions between roommates about religion. "They can sometimes be a tense experience," she
says, "and other times a pleasurable and rewarding one. It depends on

being prepared to objectively explain the basis of your faith and not to condemn or judge another's faith or lack of faith."

Philosophical and spiritual discussions about faith constitute one level of exploration. There are also practical considerations. In group living situations, those observing different religious beliefs and practices need to be able to do so in their living space. This requires understanding and acceptance by hallmates and roommates. For example, dietary restrictions on pork exist for Muslims and Jews. While some may not observe that restriction, it would be considerate not to assume that everyone eats pork when planning meals. Also, some holidays involve fasting, for example, Ramadan, Yom Kippur, Ash Wednesday, and Lent. Be respectful of your friends or roommates during these times.

Devout Muslims generally pray five times a day, usually at dawn, early and late afternoon, just after sunset, and at night. A Muslim hallmate or roommate will need privacy in order to pray. Washing the exposed parts of the body beforehand, dressing appropriately, and praying in a clean place are all part of the ritual.[23] Aware and accepting hallmates can make it more comfortable for another student to observe her faith as needed. Colleges should also provide alternate arrangements so students can express religious beliefs freely and appropriately.[24] This might mean, for instance, arranging for a move to another room where a roommate also rises at dawn, perhaps to a single room, or even waiving some policies to allow for a move off campus.

One area of religious teaching that may evoke some conflict involves the role of women. The women's movement has stressed the importance of gender equality and of women developing to their full potential. At some institutions, and in segments at many others, women are encouraged to assert themselves and to achieve. Reconciling divergent views and arriving at your own decisions about such issues are important processes. For women from some religious backgrounds, this creates inner conflict. The traditional role of Hindu women, for example, has been to stay home under the protection and control of men.[25]

I remember attending a panel discussion at a conference for Southeast Asian students held on my campus. The audience included many women and men from other colleges as well as from my own. I sat with some women I knew well. At one point, a male in the audience began to ask a question that expressed a traditional Hindu gender-role perspective. "Here we go," said one of the women sitting next to me. As several women then spoke up to challenge these traditional views, I could feel the tension level begin to rise in the room—not just between the men and women but also among the various women. Afterward, some of the women around me talked about how typical this kind of male attitude was in their culture. Some spoke about wanting to stay in the United States after they graduated so they could pursue careers they might not be able to pursue back home. Others talked about their determination to go home and work to change things so life for women could be different. Still others knew they would return to a more traditional Hindu lifestyle. All seemed to know that none of the paths would be easy.

A source of conflict between religious groups can result from the different meanings religions ascribe to the same words, actions, or symbols. For example, a swastika, drawn counterclockwise or left handed, was used as the Nazi party emblem, and this symbol obviously has negative associations for many. In the Hindu religion however, the clockwise or right-handed swastika is a symbol of sanctity and is present at Hindu prayers and marriages.[26]

Holidays

Misunderstanding about religious holidays can arise on college campuses. On Easter many students, as a matter of course, greet others with "Happy Easter," assuming that everyone celebrates this Christian holiday. This assumption puts a responsibility on the person receiving these well-intentioned wishes to either smile, say "thank you" and accept a greeting that is inappropriate, or correct the well-wisher ("Thanks, but I don't celebrate Easter") and risk seeming hypersensitive or offending the well-wisher. Students from the less-represented religions often feel invisible, for the majority holidays are known by most and may also receive institutional and media acknowledgment (as in Christmas vesper concerts or calling spring break "Easter Break").

Efforts to learn and respect others' holidays can be hampered by several factors. First, Christmas is often viewed as the major holiday. Sometimes groups designate December as the time to talk about all holidays. The timing of this well-intended gesture, however, sets this one Christian holiday up as most important. Similarly, when people try to include some celebration of Hanukkah to express a more balanced approach, the effort may be misplaced, for it equates the more minor Jewish holiday of Hanukkah with the major holiday of Christmas. A number of important holidays for other religious groups, especially Jews, take place in September and October. Thinking about and respecting the religious celebrations and observances of your hallmates and friends really needs to begin from the day you arrive at school.

Some holidays are joyous occasions to be celebrated and shared freely with friends from different faiths. Other dates are more solemn holy days to be observed alone or with a religious congregation. These are the religious experiences less appropriately shared with friends or celebrated in the residence hall. A "Happy _____" greeting is not appropriate for these more solemn holy days.

The specific dates of many religious observances and celebrations vary from year to year, for some cultures use a lunar calendar. Islamic festivals are based on a lunar calendar and almost all Jewish holidays begin at sundown on the day before the first full day of observance and end at sundown on the concluding day. Buddhist holidays are often celebrated on the weekend closest to the actual date of the holiday. Although months are indicated for the holidays listed below, the actual occurrence of those holidays in a particular year may occasionally fall early in the following month or later in the previous one.

Following the academic calendar, these are some religious holidays it might help you to know: [27]

Fall (September–November)
Rosh Hashana (September), the Jewish New Year, lasts for two days. These are important Jewish holy days that involve prayer, study, reflection, and repentance.

Yom Kippur (September or October), the Day of Atonement, is one of the most important Jewish holy days. It is a day of fasting and repentance.

Sukkot (September or October) begins five days after Yom Kippur. This joyous Jewish harvest festival lasts eight days. During that time a *sukkah* (booth or hut) is constructed to commemorate the temporary shelters used by Jews during their wanderings to Palestine.

Durga Puja (October) is the Hindu fall festival that honors the mother-goddess, Durga. Celebration takes place during the first ten days of the autumn month of Asvina.

Diwali (October or November) is a joyous five-day festival for Hindus. It combines a number of festivals to celebrate different gods and goddesses. In some areas Diwali marks the start of the Hindu new year. Each night little oil lamps are lit to illuminate the area around houses so that Lakshmi, the Hindu goddess of prosperity, can find her way to each home.

Reformation Day (October 31) commemorates the Protestant Reformation, leading to the establishment of the Protestant denominations of Christianity.

All Saints Day (November 1) is a Christian holiday that celebrates the memory of the early martyrs and saints of the church.

All Souls Day (November 2) is designated in the Roman Catholic tradition as a day to remember those who have died.

Winter (December–February)

Advent (late November–December) begins the Christmas season and includes the four Sundays preceding Christmas. This is a time of spiritual preparation, by Christians, for the birth of Jesus.

Bodhi Day (December 8) is a holiday in which Mahayana Buddhists celebrate Buddha's enlightenment. In Zen temples this is a time of intensive meditation and reflection on the Buddha's heroic quest for enlightenment.[28]

Hanukkah (late November and/or December) is a joyous eight-day Jewish holiday celebrating one of the oldest struggles for religious freedom. It commemorates the victory of the Jewish Maccabees after the Syrians sought to assimilate the Jews in 165 B.C.E. ("before the common era"—equivalent to B.C.). The holiday also celebrates the rededication of the Temple in Jerusalem and the miracle in which one day's worth of oil burned in the Temple for eight days. During Hanukkah candles are lit, special foods are eaten, and gifts are given.

Feast of the Immaculate Conception (December) is a holy day of obligation for Catholics honoring the conception of Mary, the mother of Jesus.

On *Christmas* (December 25) Christians (both Roman Catholics and Protestants) celebrate the birth of Jesus. There are special church services on Christmas Eve and Christmas Day, and the congregation thanks God for the gift of his son. Nativity scenes with models of Jesus, Mary, and Joseph recreate the nativity scene in the stable where Jesus is said to have been born in Bethlehem. Christmas is a time of gift giving and celebration.

The Feast of the Epiphany (January 6) is important to the Roman Catholic, Anglican, and especially Eastern Orthodox churches, but is not as widely observed by Protestants. It was originally a celebration to commemorate Jesus' baptism.

Makara Samkranti/Pongal (January) is a Hindu holiday that celebrates the harvest and offers thanksgiving. The goddess Makara is associated with this holiday.

Nirvana (February) is the Mahayana Buddhist commemoration of the death of Buddah and his final nirvana.

Purim (February or March) is a festive Jewish holiday celebrating the story of Esther, Jewish queen in Persia, who rescued the Jewish people from their oppressor, Haman, and his plot to destroy them.

Shrove Tuesday or *Mardi Gras* (February) is a traditional festive day during which all fancy foods are eaten to clear the house for the Christian season of Lent.

Ash Wednesday (February) marks the beginning of the Lenten season for Christians.

Lent (February and/or March) is a period of prayer and self-denial that lasts for forty days. It commemorates Christ's fast in the desert. Not all Christians observe Lent, but some will abstain from something they enjoy during that period.

Spring (March–June)

Holy Week (March or April), the week preceding Easter, is the most dramatic week in the Christian year, commemorating the final days in Jesus' life. *Palm Sunday,* the first day of Holy Week, commemorates the day Jesus and his disciples entered Jerusalem for the Passover celebrations. It is named after the palm leaves that the welcoming crowds threw on the road to make a path for Jesus. *Holy (Maundy) Thursday* commemorates the last meal Jesus ate with his disciples. *Good Friday* is a solemn day when Christians remember the crucifixion of Jesus. *Easter Day* is the most important festival in the Christian year. It marks the day Christ is believed to have risen from the dead and is a time for rejoicing and looking hopefully toward the future. Easter occurs on the first Sunday after the first full moon after the spring equinox.[29]

Orthodox Holy Week and *Orthodox Easter* (March or April) is celebrated by members of the Eastern Orthodox Church. This includes Greek, Serbian, Russian, and other Orthodox churches.[30]

Maha Shiva Ratri (March) is a Hindu festival honoring the god Shiva. It is observed through fasting, prayer, and meditation.

Ramadan (February, March, and/or April) is the holiest month of the Muslim year. This period commemorates the revelation of the Qur'an to the prophet Muhammad. It is usually the time for a pilgrimage to Mecca, recalling that event in Muhammad's life. Ramadan involves total fasting and abstinence during the daylight hours. It is observed during a lunar cycle, beginning and ending with a full moon. *Eid al-Fitr* marks the end of Ramadan, and the breaking of the fast. This is a three-day festival of feasting and celebration.

Holi (March or April) is a Hindu festival dedicated to the god Krishna. It celebrates the arrival of spring in northern India. This is a time of enjoyment after the harvest, and large bonfires are lit. Games and folk dancing also occur.

Passover (March or April) is a week-long Jewish holiday celebrating the exodus of the Israelites from Egypt and their journey from slavery to freedom. Passover is marked by special meals called "seders." Only nonleavened food, most notably matzoh, may be eaten.

Yom Hashoah (April) is an observance in remembrance of the six million Jews who were killed by the Nazis during the Holocaust.

Ramanavami (April) is a Hindu holiday celebrating the Rama, a mythical figure in Indian and Southeast Asian culture. The holiday is observed with fasting.

Buddha's Birth (April) is the Mayayana Buddhist celebration of the birth of the founder of the Buddhist faith.

Visakaha (May) is the Theravada Buddhist celebration of Buddha's birth, enlightenment, and death. This is the most sacred festival in Thailand. Houses are decorated and people go to their temples to make offerings and receive blessings. Celebrations generally end with candle-lit processions.[31]

Eid al-Adha (May) is a Muslim religious observance commemorating the Qur'an's story of the rescue of Ishmael from being sacrificed by Abraham. Solemn services are held at mosques, and worshippers commemorate the dead.

Ascension Thursday (forty days after Easter) is when Christians commemorate Jesus' ascension into heaven. This is a holy day of obligation for Catholics.

Feast of Pentecost (fifty days after Easter) is celebrated by Christians on the seventh Sunday after Easter. Christians celebrate the gift of the Holy Spirit.

Shavuot (seven weeks after Passover) is a celebratory festival that originally had agricultural significance. It also commemorates when Moses received the Torah and Ten Commandments at Mount Sinai.

Summer (June–August)

Muharram (June) begins the new year for Muslims according to the Islamic lunar calendar.

Janmastami (August) is a great Hindu night festival celebrating the life of Lord Krishna. Dance dramas at temples enact highlights from his life.

Maulid an-Nabi (August) commemorates the birth of the founder of Islam, the prophet Muhammad.

When people are far from home, as many students at college are, it means a lot to have their special days recognized. It's also important to find a balance that allows all religions to be respected, celebrated, and observed.

■ ■ ■

> Those who keep not a day
> may unite in the same spirit,
> in the same love, with those who
> keep a day;
> and those who keep a day
> may unite in heart and soul
> with the same spirit and life
> with those who keep not a day;
>
> but anyone who judges the other
> because of either of these
> errs from the spirit, from the love,
> from the life, and so
> breaks the bond of the
> unity . . .
>
> and here is the true unity,
> in the spirit,
> in the universal life, and not
> in an outward uniformity . . .
>
> —Isaac Pennington[32]

■ ■ ■

Cults

During the last fifty years there has been a rise in the number of independent religious organizations on campus. These tend to be fundamentalist Christian in nature and have an evangelical focus, seeking to convert others.[33] Some of these independent groups provide support, fellowship, Bible study, and discussions. Other groups, not necessarily Christian in nature, are more destructive, manipulating individuals and taking away their individuality and freedom of choice. The number of these groups, often called cults, is large and growing. It's estimated that there are anywhere from three thousand to five thousand cult groups in the United States today.[34]

Destructive religious groups usually have a divine leader who claims to have all the answers and a special relationship with God. These cults come to exercise total control over members' daily lives—taking away their personal choice and promoting emotional dependence on the cult and isolation from both the outside and the past, cutting members off from family and friends. Independence and critical thinking are prohibited, and members' finances are exploited, often to the benefit of the group leader. Members work more and more hours for the group, often to the detriment of their own educational goals.[35]

College campuses are a prime recruiting ground for cults that seek out the lonely and vulnerable. The transition into a college environment can leave new students feeling isolated and uncertain. Vulnerable students include those who are under heavy pressure, who are searching for an authority figure or for security, who lack self-confidence, who are hurt or affected by recent personal or relationship crises, and who are intelligent but naive and idealistic.[36]

Cult recruiters generally identify vulnerable people and approach them with great warmth and friendliness. They reach out in ways that respond to the loneliness. The recruiter may follow up by inviting the person to dinner or to a meeting, and once there she is warmly welcomed by a caring group of people. The person may later be invited to attend a retreat in a more isolated off-campus location. The camaraderie is then combined with a preaching of the cult's message, and the person is given little time alone. The cult's message will often include a claim to have all the answers—an attractive claim to someone in search of them.

Be wary of people who are excessively or inappropriately friendly or flattering, claim to have the answers to all of life's problems, and try to convince you to drop your religious affiliation for theirs, which they *know* is right for you. Use caution if you're approached and targeted when you have not already chosen to seek information or initiate dialogue. These groups recruit through guilt, and invitations to isolated weekend workshops or retreats often have vague goals or unnamed sponsors.[37]

Learning to say no to an invitation or to pressure is an important first step (see the earlier chapter on assertiveness). Anyone who persists in approaching you after you've clearly said that you're not interested is *harassing* you. Most colleges have policies about this sort of persistent solicitation. If you need help and support in saying no, talk with your R.A. or your professional residence hall staff. If you're concerned or have questions about the activities of any religious group on your campus, talk with a chaplain. S/he will know if the group is recognized by the institution. If it is, the chaplain can talk with the group about acceptable methods of approaching other students. If not, the chaplain should be made aware of the group's presence and should take action.

Most individuals are drawn to cults in search of a caring community. Seek those caring communities in places that encourage rather than discourage your individuality and growth.

WHERE TO LOOK FOR HELP

(See also this section in chapter 11.)

Religious groups are among the fastest-growing organizations on many campuses.[38] They provide forums for religious discussions and networks for meeting students with similar religious affiliations. You should find some or all of the following among the groups on your campus: Newman Association, Christian Fellowship, Episcopal Fellowship, Hillel, Ecumenical Campus Ministries, Baha'i, Muslim Students' Group, and Bible study groups. The value of interaction and discussion among different groups is also great, and some campuses have an interfaith council to provide and coordinate these opportunities.

Women's spirituality is another avenue open to you regardless of your religious affiliation. Retreats, programs, and a virtual explosion of new books are all designed to help women explore their full spirituality. Yoga and meditation programs may also be available. I had one friend who treasured the peace she recaptured each week from her Buddhist meditation group.

EDUCATING YOURSELF

Books: Nonfiction, Anthologies, Biographies, Poetry, Plays

Ali, Ahmed, trans. *Al-Qur'an: A Contemporary Translation*. Princeton, NJ: Princeton University Press, 1988.

Bender, Sue. *Plain and Simple: A Woman's Journey to the Amish*. San Francisco: HarperSanFrancisco, 1991.

Broner, E. M. *The Telling*. San Francisco: HarperSanFrancisco, 1993.

Harris, Maria. *The Dance of the Spirit: The Seven Steps of Women's Spirituality*. New York: Bantam, 1989.

Heschel, Abraham J. *God in Search of Man: A Philosophy of Judaism*. New York: Farrar, Straus, Giroux, 1976.

Hesse, Hermann. *Siddhartha*. New York: Bantam, 1982.

The Holy Bible. Preferably a "new" translation.

James, William. *The Varieties of Religious Experience*. New York: Collier, 1985.

Kaye-Kantrowitz, Melanie, and Irena Klepficz, eds. *The Tribe of Dina: A Jewish Women's Anthology*. Montpelier, VT: Sinister Wisdom Books, 1986.

Lao Tze. *The Wisdom of Lao Tse*. Edited by Lin Yutang. New York: Modern Library, 1979.

Lewis, C. S. Any of his works, especially *Mere Christianity*. New York: Collier, 1986.

Miller, Barbara Stoler, trans. *The Bhagavad-Gita*. New York: Bantam, 1986.

Mottahedeh, Roy. *The Mantle of the Prophet: Religion and Politics in Iran*. New York: Pantheon, 1986.

Neihardt, John G. *Black Elk Speaks*. Lincoln: University of Nebraska Press, 1988.

Plaskow, Judith. *Standing again at Sinai: Judaism from a Feminist Perspective*. San Francisco: HarperSanFrancisco, 1991.

Pogrebin, Letty Cottin. *Deborah, Golda, and Me: On Being Jewish and Female in America*. New York: Crown, 1991.

Rahula, Walpola. *What Buddha Taught*. Rev. ed. New York: Grove/Weidenfeld, 1987.

Ross, Nancy Wilson. *Buddhism: A Way of Life and Thought*. New York: Vintage, 1981.

Schneider, Susan Weidman. *Jewish and Female: A Guide and Sourcebook*. New York: Simon and Schuster, 1985.

Smith, Huston. *The Religions of Man*. New York: HarperPerennial, 1992.

Suhl, Yuri, ed. and trans. *They Fought Back: The Story of the Jewish Resistance in Nazi Europe*. New York: Schocken, 1987.

Suzuki, Shunryo. *Zen Mind, Beginners Mind: Informal Talk on Zen Meditation and Practice*. New York: Weatherhill, 1970.

Van Dyke, Annette. *The Search for a Woman-Centered Spirituality*. New York: New York University Press, 1992.

Waley, Arthur, trans. *The Way and Its Power: A Study of the Tao Te Ching and Its Place in Chinese Thought*. New York: Grove/Weidenfeld, 1988.

———. *Analects of Confucius*. New York: Vintage, 1989.

Watts, Alan W. *The Way of Zen*. New York: Vintage, 1989.

Weisel, Elie. Any of his work.

Novels

Godden, Rumer. *In This House of Brede*. New York: Viking, 1969.

Howatch, Susan. *Glittering Images*. New York: Fawcett Crest, 1988.

———. *Glamorous Powers*. New York: Fawcett Crest, 1989.

———. *Ultimate Prizes*. New York: Fawcett Crest, 1990.

L'Engle, Madeleine. *A Severed Wasp*. New York: Farrar, Straus, Giroux, 1983.

Potok, Chaim. Any of his work.

Articles, Pamphlets, and Papers

"Multicultural Resource Calendar" published annually by Amherst Educational Publishing, 30 Blue Hills Rd., Amherst, MA 01002.

United Ministry at Harvard. "Protect Yourself from Destructive Religious Groups: Don't Be Afraid to Say 'No.' " Cambridge, MA: Memorial Church, Harvard University, 1981.

Organizations for Information and Assistance

Cult Awareness Network
2421 W. Pratt Blvd.
Suite 1173
Chicago, IL 60645
312-267-7777
International Cult Education Program
129 East 82nd St.
New York, NY
212-439-1550

Films, Videos, TV Shows, Plays

At Play in the Fields of the Lord. A missionary tries to find converts in the Brazilian rain forest. From the novel by Peter Matthiessen.

Becket. Follows the stormy relationship between England's King Henry II and Archbishop Thomas Becket. From the play by Jean Anouilh.

The Chosen. A friendship develops between two very different orthodox Jewish boys. Based on Chaim Potok's book.

The Diary of Anne Frank. A teenage girl hides with her family to escape the Nazis. Based on her book.

Exodus. Presents the story of the early days of Israel, leading up to its being partitioned into the Jewish state by the United Nations. Based on Leon Uris's book.

Friendly Persuasion. A Quaker family is affected by the Civil War. From the book by Jessamyn West.

Gandhi. A view of India and its people is seen through the life of Mahatma Gandhi, who spent his life seeking freedom for that country.

Gentlemen's Agreement. A reporter poses as a Jew to do a story on anti-Semitism. From Laura Hobson's novel.

Holocaust. Explores how the Holocaust is experienced by both Jews and Germans. A TV miniseries based on the book by Gerald Green.

Homicide. A detective has to confront his own repressed Jewish identity while investigating an anti-Semitic murder.

Jesus Christ Superstar. The last days of Jesus are portrayed in rock opera form. From the play by Andrew Lloyd Webber and Tim Rice.

Judgment at Nuremberg. After World War II, high-level Nazis are tried for their war crimes during the Holocaust.

Mass Appeal. Conflict erupts between a popular older priest and a young seminarian full of questions and challenges. From the play by Bill C. Davis.

The Mission. An eighteenth-century Spanish Jesuit goes into the Brazilian jungle to convert the Indian population.

Places in the Heart. A suddenly widowed Texas woman uses her faith and spirit to keep her family's farm working and to help others in need.

Playing for Time. A Jewish woman imprisoned in a concentration camp during the Holocaust survives by leading an inmate orchestra. Made-for-TV movie based on a true story.

School Ties. A working-class high school football star is recruited by a fancy prep school where he encounters anti-Semitism.

Skokie. Holocaust survivors fight to prevent the Ku Klux Klan from marching in their suburban Chicago neighborhood. Made-for-TV movie based on a true story.

Tender Mercies. An alcoholic former country singer finds a new beginning with a young widow and her son. Also portrays rural southern Baptist life.

Witness. A Philadelphia policeman hides out in the nonviolent Amish country to protect a young boy who witnessed a murder.

Yentl. A young Jewish woman disguises herself as a man to gain entrance to the all-male yeshiva, in a quest for knowledge and wisdom. From the story by Isaac Bashevis Singer.

▪ FOURTEEN ▪

Sexual Orientation

A number of years ago, I went to see Harvey Fierstein's play, *Torch Song Trilogy*. It's a bittersweet play about a gay man in search of love and respect. I went by myself, and I recall having some uneasy feelings before I actually bought the ticket and went into the theater. I wondered what the audience would be like, what people might think about my being there, and how comfortable or uncomfortable I would be as I watched the play. Looking back now, I realize how my reactions reflected fears I had about gays, lesbians, and bisexuals—fears that came from my lack of knowledge, contact, and understanding.

Terminology

Sexual orientation is defined by an individual's attraction to members of the same sex, other sex, or both sexes. The term "orientation" is used by those who believe that "preference" implies that you can just as easily choose one lifestyle rather than another.

▪ ▪ ▪

> "We *are* lesbians; we don't decide to become gay. Sexual preference is not a choice. Although you can wear tinted contact lenses or dark sunglasses, you can't choose the color of your eyes. In the same way, we can hide our sexuality but we can't change it."
>
> —Anonymous, "We Are You,"[1]

▪ ▪ ▪

264

A *heterosexual* is a person who is attracted to, and forms primary emotional, physical, and/or sexual relationships with, persons of the other sex. A *homosexual* is a person who is attracted to, and forms primary emotional, physical, and/or sexual relationships with, persons of the same sex. *Gay* is the term most often used to describe homosexual men. The term is also acceptable to some lesbians and bisexuals, although others feel that women tend to become more invisible when included within the general term "gay." *Lesbian* is a term used to describe homosexual women. One student said that she prefers to use the term "lesbian woman" to emphasize that being a lesbian is only one part of her whole person.

Although "gay" is a preferred term, the phrase "gay lifestyle" tends to be a negatively loaded one. It has come to be used by some as an implicit criticism of more extreme public demonstrations by gays and as a way of generalizing that behavior to all gay men and women. The truth is that gay men and lesbians lead a variety of different lifestyles.

While much of society looks at sexual orientation as being either/or—you're either heterosexual or homosexual—a much wider range of sexual feelings and activity exists. *Bisexuals* are those attracted to both men and women, either at the same time or at different times.[2]

Heterosexism is a system of beliefs that implies that heterosexuality is "better" and thus discriminates against those of different sexual orientations.[3] The most common expression of heterosexism is the assumption that everyone is heterosexual. Invitations to "bring your boyfriend" can certainly make a heterosexual woman without a boyfriend feel like she should have one. For a lesbian or bisexual woman, it can make her feel not only as though she should have a boyfriend but also as though her girlfriend, if she has one, isn't welcome. Invitations saying "bring friends" or "bring your boyfriend or girlfriend" are more accepting of different sexual orientations.

Heterosexism permeates popular culture on TV, in the movies, and in the mass media. Couples are almost always heterosexual. Homosexual characters or relationships, if shown at all, are most often caricaturized or depicted as "deviant." In 1993 the comic strip "For Better or Worse" ran a five-week storyline in which a seventeen-year-old tells his friend and parents he's gay. Some newspapers in the United States refused to run this series.

Homophobia is the irrational fear or hatred of gay men, lesbians, and bisexuals.[4] This fear perpetuates heterosexism and sexism. It can range from discomfort at hugging a friend of the same sex to open hostility and violence toward lesbians, gays, and bisexuals. My uneasiness before going in to see *Torch Song Trilogy* is an example of a homophobic reaction.

Internalized heterosexism or *homophobia* occurs when gays, lesbians, and bisexuals accept the negative stereotypes, myths, and status attached to them by society. They demonstrate this acceptance by denigrating themselves and/or by living out stereotyped sex roles and behaviors expected of them, rather than by being who they are.[5]

. . .

"When the only people who know you're gay are the ones you're gaying with, that's called in the closet."
　　　　　—Harvey Fierstein, *Torch Song Trilogy*[6]

. . .

To be *in the closet* means to hide one's homosexual identity, often in order to keep a job, housing situation, friends, family, etc. Homosexuals who remain in the closet for the sake of survival can pay a price, however, for this creates other stresses. It requires constant lying, pretending, and being on guard. It can be hard to meet other lesbians and bisexuals, and those in the closet often feel distant and alienated from friends and family who they know don't *really* know them.[7]

Coming out is a process by which a lesbian, gay man, or bisexual informs others of his/her sexual orientation. It involves first affirming a homosexual or bisexual identity to oneself, and then deciding to tell other people or the public in general. Coming out is not a single event but a life-long process. In each new situation, an individual has to decide whether and how to come out. Often people are out to some, such as friends and siblings, and not to others, such as their boss and parents.

. . .

"Looking back at my process of coming out to myself I have to laugh. I basically knew since late high school that I had attractions to other women, but it took me until sophomore year in college to actually admit it to myself—believe me, there is a difference. The whole process can be mapped rather accurately and humorously by my chronology of 'crushes.' First I had a crush on a gay man. We went to the prom together. Then I had a crush on a heterosexual woman who had a serious boyfriend (they're now married). Then I had a crush on a heterosexual woman who didn't have a boyfriend. After that was the big jump to having a crush on a lesbian who was practically married to another woman. These were all safe crushes and they gave the part of my mind that wasn't quite ready to admit to homosexual feelings time to catch up to that part of my mind that already knew. By the time I was comfortable enough to explore my feelings, I found out that a woman I liked had a crush on me, and I felt comfortable enough with myself and my feelings to finally embark on a relationship with another woman."

—S. L., class of '90

. . .

Background Information

Over 40 percent of students entering college in 1991 agreed strongly or somewhat that it was important to have laws prohibiting homosexual relationships.[8] Attitudes on college campuses reflect biases in the larger society, where gays, lesbians, and bisexuals have no legal protection for their civil rights at the federal level or in forty-eight states. This means that they have little or no recourse for challenging being barred from jobs, harassed at work, dishonorably discharged from the military or ROTC, or discriminated against in housing, public accommodations, etc., on the basis of their sexual orientation. Without the legal recognition of marriages between members of the same sex, employee partner benefits such as health plans, pensions, tuition waivers, and bereavement leaves are not options. While some companies and institutions are beginning to offer partner benefits, there's still a long way to go before same-sex partners have equal rights. Gays, lesbians, and bisexuals have difficulty adopting children and have on occasion lost custody of their natural children because of their sexual orientation.[9]

Hate crimes toward lesbians, gays, and bisexuals have almost tripled in recent years. According to a study published by the National Gay and Lesbian Task Force in 1984, over 90 percent of those polled had experienced some form of victimization based on their sexual orientation.[10] Recent surveys of lesbian, gay, and bisexual students on several campuses report that

- 45–65 percent have been verbally insulted
- 35–58 percent fear for their safety

- 22–26 percent have been followed or chased
- 16–25 percent have been threatened with physical violence, and
- 12–15 percent have been sexually harassed or assaulted.[11]

The last few years have seen a growing activism among the gay population. Annual gay pride marches draw big crowds in many cities, there are more political-action groups, and a number of professional organizations include gay caucuses or gay task forces within their membership. The 1993 debate about lifting the ban on gays in the military has helped bring the question of discrimination against homosexuals onto the front pages. As more gay men, lesbians, bisexuals, and their allies fight for gay rights, perhaps the climate in this country will continue to change.

Background Information: Sexual Identity Development

Developing a sense of identity is considered a prerequisite for being able to form strong intimate relationships with others. Your sexual orientation is only one part—albeit an important part—of your total identity. There's also a difference between sexual identity and sexual behavior. You can identify with a particular sexual orientation without being sexually active. You can be attracted to someone without necessarily acting on that attraction. You can also engage in heterosexual or homosexual behavior without identifying yourself with that sexual orientation.

Heterosexual Identity Development

Sexual identification is described as coming to terms with what it means to be a man or woman in our society, and with the behaviors that are appropriate to those roles. Sex-role characteristics and early sexual attitudes are strongly influenced by parents, teachers, peers, and the media. Individuals often struggle to establish their own particular blend of masculinity and femininity within these social parameters.[12] The most well-known models of student and adult development are based on the assumption that all individuals are heterosexual.[13] Thus, achieving a solid sense of sexual identity for a woman is assumed to mean her becoming comfortable with her own female sexuality and being able to establish trusting and satisfying intimate relationships with men.

Homosexual Identity Development

The development of a homosexual identity is discussed in more detail here as it involves issues not included in the general models of adolescent and adult development. Due to societal norms, many homosexuals initially consider themselves to be heterosexual. The work of Vivienne Cass, described below, is one of the more extensive descriptions of a model of homosexual identity formation.[14]

In the *identity confusion* stage, the individual first becomes aware of homosexual thoughts, feelings, or behaviors. If she acknowledges or acts on these feelings, this can create conflict between the behavior and her perception of herself as a heterosexual. If she has negative feelings about how acceptable the behavior is, she's likely to go no further and to remain at this confusion stage. If she has positive feelings about the behavior, then she may move on to the next stage.

At the *identity comparison* stage, she begins to see herself as possibly having a homosexual identity. This can cause conflict if others around her have negative feelings about homosexuality. If she has difficulty handling this conflict, she may deny her homosexual feelings and perhaps dislike herself for feeling them. If she feels positive about her feelings, she may try to meet more homosexuals while still maintaining a public image of heterosexuality.

At the *identity tolerance* stage, she begins to tolerate her homosexual identity. As her self-image becomes more firmly homosexual, she may become more uncomfortable pretending that she's heterosexual. She may spend more time with others who are gay and may feel more powerful as she creates a new support system in the gay community.

. . .

"I think that knowing other people who are gay helps tremendously in coming out. . . . I certainly was not in contact with any while growing up in Oklahoma (although now I do know several). Going to Boston and finding *positive* gay role models rather than the mostly negative media stereotypes helped me immensely."

—C. H., class of '92

. . .

At the *identity acceptance* stage, a woman's contacts with the gay community allow her to feel that her homosexual identity is valued. As she feels more comfortable with that identity, a conflict surfaces about whether to come out to others. She may not feel safe coming out and may limit or avoid contact with heterosexuals she sees as unaccepting or threatening. She may also "pass," which means participating in the gay community while still presenting a heterosexual image to the rest of the world. The individual at this stage may come out selectively, and this can ease some of the conflict. This is often a comfortable long-term stage for many lesbians and gay men—having a secure gay life while also avoiding some of the discrimination and hostility they might experience if they were out to everyone.

At the *identity pride* stage, the individual experiences more intense conflict between how she sees herself and how others see her. She tends to feel frustrated, angry with, and alienated from heterosexual society. She may restrict her contacts as much as possible to the gay and lesbian community, valuing the homosexual world and devaluing the heterosexual one, perhaps becoming more separatist. In order to move to the next stage, the individual must experience some positive responses from heterosexuals.

At the *identity synthesis* stage, the individual begins to see similarities and differences between herself and both homosexuals and heterosexuals. She will probably have friends in both the gay and heterosexual communities. She may still feel some anger and frustration toward the heterosexual society, but those feelings are less overwhelming. Sexuality is seen as part of her total identity rather than the main focus.

Bisexual Identity Development

. . .

"A gay man once told me 'Get real. Admit that you are a lesbian. Stop being so wishy-washy and make up your mind.' Needless to say, I was offended."

—C. H., class of '92

. . .

There are a variety of routes through which bisexuals define their identity. Some have intimate relationships with both males and females at the same time; some have monogamous intimate relationships, sometimes with a man and sometimes with a woman; others are totally monogamous with one sex yet still define themselves as bisexual. Some bisexuals have a preference for one gender over the other, while others are equally attracted to both.[15]

It's difficult to generalize about bisexual identity development because of the great variance among bisexuals. For some, a bisexual identity is a stable one; they remain open to relationships with both sexes throughout their lives. For others it is a transitional identity—a phase for heterosexuals waiting to feel more comfortable before identifying as homosexual or for lesbians and gay men realizing that their sexual identity is more accurately defined as bisexual.[16]

Sources of Misunderstanding

· · ·

"You can't, in a matter of seconds, turn away from all the false information you have heard all your life. But you can make an effort to test it, to find out if it's really true."

—W. C., class of '93

· · ·

Many of our opinions are based on what we learn while growing up. It's natural to feel uncomfortable when you're confronted with people and situations that challenge this information. Faulty information can perpetuate myths that promote misunderstanding.[17]

"Homosexuality is not very prevalent. After all, I don't know any gay men or lesbians." It's estimated that approximately 10 percent of the population is exclusively or predominantly homosexual. Homosexual behavior has been found in all cultures and in every social, economic, racial, and religious group. You may not *know* that you know any bisexuals, gay men, or lesbians, but chances are you do. Whether they choose to tell you probably depends on how accepting and comfortable they think you'll be.

"We know what 'causes' homosexuality." So far no research has definitely established what determines sexual orientation or "causes" either heterosexuality or homosexuality. While there's often disagreement about the development of sexual orientation, research suggests that biological, familial, social, and cultural factors all contribute.[18] There is also increasing evidence that sexual orientation may be biologically determined.[19]

"Homosexuality is unnatural." Each culture tends to define what is "natural." Homosexuality is sometimes said to be unnatural by those who believe that the purpose of sex is reproduction. Most heterosexual

sex, however, is not procreative either. Both heterosexual and homosexual relationships consist of much more than sexual encounters. For those who identify as homosexual, it's a natural way of life.

"Homosexuality is immoral." Each individual must choose her own religious beliefs. Several texts in the Old Testament are often used to condemn homosexuality as a sin. Some clergy and other religious individuals choose to interpret them this way. Other clergy and theologians have begun to reconsider these teachings, concluding that sexual relationships should be judged in terms of love, support, and responsibility regardless of the gender of the people involved. They interpret the religious passages in question as a reflection of the social context and time in which they were written, and do not use them to condemn homosexuality today.[20]

"Homosexuality is a mental illness." In 1973 the American Psychiatric Association removed homosexuality from its list of disorders. In 1975 the American Psychological Association followed suit. Sexual orientation itself has been found to have no direct relation to the emotional stability of the individual. Problems may arise, however, from harassment, isolation, and social pressures.

"Homosexuals and bisexuals are promiscuous and have trouble maintaining long-term relationships." There is a wide range of sexual activity levels within all sexual orientations. A number of gay, lesbian, and bisexual long-term monogamous relationships are often invisible to others. Like many heterosexuals, some homosexuals are in nonexclusive relationships or have many relationships, and still others are rarely or never in intimate relationships. However, society's generally negative attitudes toward homosexuality can make it more difficult to maintain a gay or lesbian relationship over time, as can the fact that homosexual couples often don't receive the family, legal, and religious supports offered to heterosexual couples.

"All lesbians hate men and all man haters are lesbians." Lesbians don't necessarily hate men; they're lesbians because they find greater emotional and sexual satisfaction with other women. Many lesbians may be angry at heterosexual privilege and male power without hating individual men. Anger toward men can come from both homosexual and heterosexual women.

"Lesbians want to be men; gay men want to be women." Gayness is a celebration of one's gender, not a rejection of it. Transsexuals are

individuals who want to become members of the opposite sex, and very few transsexuals are gay.

"Gay men and lesbians are dangerous to children." This myth has been used to discriminate against gay men and lesbians and to keep them out of some jobs, such as teaching. However, the overwhelming majority of child molesters are heterosexual men.

"Gay men and lesbians do not make good parents and their children will grow up to be gay." Dr. Judd Marmor, former president of the American Psychiatric Association, has said that there is no evidence that heterosexuals are better parents than homosexual men and women. There's also no evidence that the children of gay people are more likely to be gay. Most homosexuals were born to, and raised by, heterosexual parents.[21]

"You can identify people as gay by the way they look, act, and dress." You can't. Sexual orientation isn't determined by how closely people fit sex roles and stereotypes. Some lesbians and gay men fit the physical stereotypes society has of homosexuals, but so do some heterosexuals. Most gay men and lesbians look and act very much like society's images of heterosexuals.

- - -

"Once, before a lecture, I was asked to wait for the 'gay male' who would come and escort me to the classroom. This proved awkward because he and I had not previously met. I didn't look like a lesbian to him and he didn't look like a gay man, so we missed each other and I had to find the classroom alone."

—Gail Sausser, "Hello, I Am a Lesbian"[22]

- - -

ENCOUNTERING AND RESPONDING TO THIS ISSUE

It is very difficult to accurately measure, through polls and surveys, behavior to which society attaches a label of good or bad.[23] You can expect, however, that roughly 10 percent of the population on your campus could be gay, lesbian, or bisexual.[24] That means that on a small campus of one thousand, at least one hundred students may be homosexual or bisexual; on a large campus of forty thousand, the numbers could be closer to four thousand. That's a pretty large, yet often invisible, minority.

Some people assume that there are more homosexual students at certain kinds of colleges, such as those emphasizing the arts, those in cities like New York and San Francisco, and women's colleges. While some homosexual students quite logically gravitate toward schools in areas with receptive climates, there are gay, lesbian, and bisexual students at all kinds of colleges and in many different locations. Lesbians, bisexuals, and gay men may, however, be more visible and vocal at schools where they feel safer to be who they are.

The college years are vital for all students in developing sexual identity and attitudes about sexual orientations. Most lesbians, gays, and bisexuals become aware of their sexual orientation during late adolescence or early adulthood, although they don't necessarily come out then. For many heterosexual students, college may be their first exposure to more openly gay, lesbian, and bisexual individuals. This can provide an important opportunity to challenge stereotypes.[25]

For Those Who Identify as Lesbians

Residential and Social Life

. . .

"I wasn't sure how my roommate would feel about living with a lesbian, but apparently it wasn't a problem, since we lived together during our sophomore year, also. Imagine worrying that your roommate's parents will insist that their daughter be moved out of an 'unhealthy' environment. Imagine worrying that the person you live with won't give you the chance to be a friend."

—W. C., class of '93

. . .

Residential living can create challenges for lesbians, gays, and bisexuals on campus. Residence halls are generally pretty densely populated spaces, and widespread assumptions of heterosexuality are sometimes problematic. Your most complex relationship will probably be with your roommate. You have no way, really, of knowing whether your roommate is homophobic, knowledgeable about different sexual orientations, open and accepting, related to someone gay, or even a lesbian or bisexual herself. The kinds of "getting-to-know-you" conversations that occur at first may give you a chance to get a better sense of where she's coming from.

As described in chapter 3, many colleges send out questionnaires to gather information to help them pair roommates and assign rooms. You may be understandably hesitant to come out on paper to strangers. There are, however, subtle ways to provide information that might help the college make your housing assignment. You could ask, for instance, to be placed in a nonhomophobic residence hall or with an open-minded roommate. Or you might ask for someone who is open to a variety of lifestyles. If there are questions about overnight guests, you could say you prefer no overnight male guests.

Lack of privacy can be an issue, as hallmates are often curious about others' friends, lovers, and social lives. If it feels more comfortable to do so, you could arrange to socialize outside your residence hall and maintain a low profile in your own hall. Some students firmly but nicely claim their right to privacy, and still others choose to be more open about their lives if they feel safe doing so. Some living situations will be more comfortable for you than others, and if it takes a change of room, or hall, to put you in a more supportive environment, ask your R.A. how to request a change.

Holding leadership positions on campus can create some conflict, especially if you are not out in the group in which you are a leader. You'll be more visible as a leader and could have some power and influence. There may be situations where you want to speak up about heterosexist policies or practices but feel uneasy doing so. Not speaking up may, in turn, leave you feeling frustrated or annoyed at yourself. You could also be subject to a variety of expectations, particularly from friends who know you are a lesbian or bisexual and want you to play a more active advocacy role. A staff or faculty member, or a trusted upperclass woman who understands your situation, can be a valuable resource to help you work through your feelings in these situations.

Coming Out

. . .

"There are some parts of coming out that are fantastic—you no longer have to worry about others finding out your 'secret' and you certainly don't have to use up so much emotional energy trying to hide it. However, coming out is something that should not be done lightly—it is something that once said, can't be taken back."

—J. L., class of '91

. . .

Deciding to come out is a very individual decision. No one else can tell you what to do. Think about the pros and cons of coming out to specific people, including the emotional cost to you of "staying in."

One 1991 graduate describes how being in the closet can put a strain on a relationship, especially when one partner is out or wants to come out and the other doesn't. She explains that always hiding the fact that you love and spend time with your girlfriend may, over time, cause problems. "Closeted couples," she goes on, "have difficulty talking to others about fights, problems, and joys within the relationship. One of the ways that you can learn and reassure yourselves is to talk to others and share experiences. That opportunity is lost to closeted couples."

The National Gay Task Force makes the following suggestions about coming out, especially to parents and family: [26]

1. Work toward being comfortable with your own gayness before coming out.
2. If you come out, do so because you're ready to, not because others push you.
3. Be aware of timing—wait until the other person isn't overwhelmed with other problems and concerns.
4. Don't come out during an argument.
5. Affirm first that you both care about one another and that the relationship is important to you.
6. Be prepared for surprise and anger. Avoid getting defensive.
7. Emphasize that you are still the same person.
8. Keep future lines of communication open.
9. Be informed, and have information and resources available to share with the other person.
10. Offer the other person the opportunity to meet some of your lesbian, gay, and bisexual friends.
11. Give the other person time to adjust. Don't expect immediate acceptance. P-FLAG—Parents and Friends of Lesbians and Gays—is a national organization that can help.
12. If you are rejected, don't lose your sense of self-worth. The rejection reflects more on the other person than on you.

13. Try to avoid having the other person learn about your homosexuality through a third party.

Remember that it will rarely be easy to come out, and it will not always go well, but it can also be an incredibly freeing experience, especially if you get a supportive response. You may also challenge others' views, stereotypes, and assumptions as they confront the fact that someone they know, care about, and respect is a lesbian.[27]

Dual Identities

. . .

"Why is it so hard for me to prove that my Blackness is genuine and so is my lesbianism? Being both simultaneously—and I should not have to be either separately. Doesn't that make sense? And are we not sisters? I wonder sometimes. The way I act should not be painful to me. The way I am should not be suppressed. Do you get the point? I'm tired of being two halves. I'm not just a Black woman. I'm not just a lesbian. I am a Black lesbian."

—Anonymous[28]

. . .

If you're a lesbian or bisexual who is also a woman of color, you may experience additional conflicts. Decisions for women of color to come out can be influenced by the cultural expectations in their ethnic community. The role of family and religion is central in most African American communities, and an African American lesbian choosing to come out there may find herself alienated from another important part of her life.[29] For Latina lesbians, the cultural emphasis on the family, gender roles, and Catholicism, which rejects homosexuality, can also lead to a loss of support within the Latina community. An Asian American who identifies as a lesbian may be seen as rejecting Asian cultural norms, values, and gender roles and as bringing shame to the family. She may decide to negate her lesbian identity in some situations, such as in her family or ethnic community.[30] At some institutions, support groups have been developed specifically for lesbians who are women of color and who face some of the same conflicts.

If you're an international student, you may encounter additional problems if you come out as a lesbian. What may begin to become a more comfortable sexual orientation in the United States may be more risky back in your home country.[31]

Relationships with Your Family

. . .

" 'So tell me,' her aunt Catherine said, 'what do you do now?' She would have liked to answer: I'm a lesbian now, and live with a woman named Mandy. Or—I belong to a lesbian writers collective and write articles for the local gay newspaper. She wished she could pull it off, smiling sweetly at Aunt Catherine the whole time. They didn't know what a real radical was, didn't realize she was quite harmless. She sighed and gave the correct answers about her job and education, all the things which did not really matter."

—Becky Birtha, "A Sense of Loss"[32]

. . .

Relationships with your family become more complex as you identify as a lesbian. If you are not out to your family, letters and conversations can be awkward if they assume that you're heterosexual and always ask if you've "met any nice men yet." Rather than waiting for your parents to direct the conversation with their assumptions about what's important, you can take the initiative and talk about the things that have been exciting for you on campus, including various people you've met. If they keep asking about men, and if meeting a nice man isn't one of your priorities, you might say something like, "I came here to get a good education, learn as much as I can, and meet lots of different people . . . and I am. That's what's important to me right now."

Family visits can create discomfort if your parents meet your friends, or if you are careful to have them *not* meet your friends. Some gay men and lesbians talk about having to go through their rooms to "straighten up"—get rid of gay and lesbian posters, books, etc.—before their parents arrive.

Holidays can be a difficult time for lesbians, gays, and bisexuals because of the emphasis on family gatherings. If you have come out but are not accepted within your family, it can be painful to have nowhere to go or to spend stressful time at home. If you're not out, going home means knowing that you will have to repress your identity. In some families partners aren't welcome under any condition; in others they're welcome only under certain conditions such as having her sleep in a separate room and telling other relatives that she is "just a friend." In others your partner may always be welcome and accepted as part of the family. Some lesbians establish a family feeling with other lesbians to make up for what they may be missing from their own family. Some have found that their families have gradually become more accepting, and still others divide up their holidays in order to fulfill family obligations and also meet some of their own needs.

For Those Who Identify as Bisexual

. . .

"The feeling that one is 'riding the fence,' or doesn't *really* belong to any group is an experience that bisexuals live with day to day."
—Student, class of '93

. . .

Bisexuals often describe themselves as proud to be open to all possibilities for loving relationships. It's often hard, however, to find a supportive community. Bisexuals tend to be seen as gay by the heterosexual population, and they are therefore subject to discrimination and homophobia. Some in the gay and lesbian community, on the other hand, may mistrust those who identify as bisexual, perhaps seeing this self-label as a choice that maintains some degree of heterosexual privilege.[33]

What's the climate like for bisexuals on your campus? Are bisexuals "invisible" on your campus or are they acknowledged in some ways? Is there an organization or are bisexuals, in name at least, included as part of the lesbian and gay community? Is there a mixture of social functions—some open only to women and others to both men and women? As you look at posters and advertisements for events, do you feel as though you'll have some choices? How inclusive of bisexuals is the gay and lesbian community, on and off campus?

. . .

"It was easy for me to come out as a lesbian, because it involved choosing one gender over another. But coming out as a bisexual woman later was really hard. My lesbian friends thought I'd defected to the enemy camp, and my straight friends couldn't understand why I kept seeing women. 'Aren't you one of us now?' Only my bi friends understood."

—S. A., class of '93

. . .

For Those Who Identify as Heterosexual

. . .

When You Meet a Lesbian Person:
Hints for the Heterosexual Woman

1. Do not run screaming from the room.[34]

. . .

The handout that starts this way is usually good for some tension-relieving chuckles at workshops. As much as we may want to see ourselves as open minded, many of us—heterosexual, bisexual, and homosexual—have grown up believing or internalizing homophobic thoughts.

Several years ago I ran a meeting in a residence hall where two students had found homophobic slurs written just outside their room. At that meeting, a number of the residents kept saying things like, "I'm not homophobic, but . . . ," then going on in ways that indicated that they didn't really understand what homophobia was. I was joined, at that meeting, by the president of the Lesbian Bisexual Alliance, and I remember mumbling to her at some point, "Do you want to tell them what homophobia is?" She did. She said to them, "I'm a lesbian and I'm also homophobic." For the first time that night people really stopped to listen. She went on to talk about how she felt and how she was working on her own homophobic feelings. I could almost feel people in the room exhale and start to relax. Her honesty seemed to allow them to let go of their need to vehemently deny their own homophobic fears.

The video, *A Conversation with Brian McNaught on Being Gay,* describes a world in which *heterosexuality* is unacceptable, and heterosexuals are ignored, ridiculed, denied human rights, and treated like second class citizens. Imagine . . . if to buy magazines like *Cosmopolitan* or *Glamour* you had to go to a specialty store . . . down a dirty ally. Imagine . . . "those" magazines are either hidden in the back of the store or you have to ask the clerk for them. And when you ask him, he gives you a disgusted look. Imagine . . . you're in love with a man but you can't hold hands with him publicly or kiss him good-bye when he leaves for class. Some of your closest friends may know about your relationship with this man, but they seem uncomfortable when you talk about him. They wish you wouldn't flaunt it . . . even though they talk about their girlfriends all the time. Imagine.

Homophobic feelings can make you afraid to get to know gays, lesbians, and bisexuals who are out or to attend an event about, or sponsored by, the lesbian, gay, and bisexual community. Probably the best way to work through fears and replace negative stereotypes is by greater contact and interaction with more lesbians, gays, and bisexuals. That contact ought to be a sincere effort to get to know individuals who happen to be gay, not simply because they're gay. This sounds like a "catch 22"—the way to get over your fear is to get to know the people you're afraid of. It may help to begin to think about *what* you're afraid of, and try to get a sense of how realistic those fears are.

When Friends Come Out to You

. . .

"I remember telling my friends (at school and at home) about my girlfriend. Each reaction was different—one friend cried, another embraced me, another asked questions. Yet the underlying message from them to me was the same. They loved me. And they wanted me to be happy."

—Student, class of '93

. . .

If a roommate, friend, or family member chooses to come out to you, she is obviously taking a risk and trusting you with something very important. She is probably feeling a bit scared and vulnerable and is wondering how you'll react. The experience of having a close friend come out may raise all kinds of questions for you. You may wonder why she didn't tell you sooner, or you may feel as though she betrayed you in some way by not being honest with you from the start. You may wonder if she's interested in you sexually, or whether the fact that you're so close says something about your own sexual orientation. You may also worry that you've said or done some things in the past that were insensitive to her. While initially it can be hard for you to hear your friend if she comes out to you, it's probably as hard or harder for her to do it.

Copyright © 1986 by Alice Muhlback, Art Works.

You may feel scared, uncomfortable, angry, supportive, flattered, or unsure of what to say or do next. Your friend may be hoping for acceptance, support, understanding, and assurance that your friendship won't be negatively affected. What's most important, if you are truly friends, is that you continue, over time, to talk about your feelings and reactions with one another and work through any problems.

Some people will come out to you in person. Others prefer to write a letter, giving you a chance to react in private before you talk face-to-face. Still others may drop some subtle hints to get some idea of how safe it may be.

Gay Male Friends

While the focus of this chapter has been on lesbians and bisexuals, as a heterosexual woman you may also get to know gay men. Women may be attracted to some of the qualities that they believe gay men have—sensitivity, humor, warmth, a willingness to express emotions, intellectual depth, and an interest in women as more than sex objects.[35] These qualities are stereotypes—some gay men will possess them and others won't—but gay men can provide intimate relationships without the sexual pressures often present in relationships with heterosexual men. If you are friends with a gay male, you should respect the fact that your friend's life as part of the gay male community may not always be able to include you.

For Those Who Have Not Identified Their Sexual Orientation

The process by which you establish your sexual identity and the pace at which you reach that decision are yours to control. College provides you with many opportunities to help you understand and explore different options. Some of that exploration is exciting, and some of it may feel uncomfortable, but the college environment provides more support and resources for working through your reactions than you're likely to find at other times in your life. Your process may result in recognizing a new identity or in reinforcing the one you currently hold, with the added benefit of making you more understanding and accepting of yourself and those who make different choices.

WHERE TO LOOK FOR HELP

(See also this section in chapter 11.)

Some women, once they come out to their families, find themselves in danger of losing financial as well as emotional support. While the Financial Aid Office is bound by federal guidelines and the process for being classified as an independent student takes time to establish, the office may help you explore your options. The Controller's Office, or whichever department handles billing, is the place to try to work out financial arrangements. If you feel uncomfortable having to discuss your situation in detail and coming out to so many different offices, you could identify someone in the administration whom you already know and trust to pave the way for you with the other offices.

Your spiritual life may also be affected if you identify as a lesbian or bisexual. A number of traditional organized religions tend to decry homosexuality and expect lesbians to "convert" to heterosexuality. Some denominations, however, particularly Quaker and Unitarian, are more welcoming, as are some particular congregations within other denominations. Some also have gay and lesbian subgroups. The Universal Fellowship of Metropolitan Community Churches is one alternative church serving gay men and lesbians.[36]

If your campus doesn't have a structured lesbian, gay, and bisexual program, there may be other offices or particular individuals on campus who provide some services and support. It may also be possible to start a group; generally this involves following whatever process your student activities office has established for beginning organizations. You can begin by planning or suggesting more inclusive activities without necessarily labeling them as such. For example, you might suggest that films such as *Desert Hearts* be included in the regular monthly film series, or that *The Times of Harvey Milk* be shown, followed by a faculty panel discussion. If you're uncomfortable on your own campus, another alternative is to find gay, lesbian, and bisexual organizations at other nearby campuses or in the local community.

EDUCATING YOURSELF

Books: Nonfiction, Anthologies, Biographies, Poetry, Plays

Alyson Almanac: A Treasury of Information for the Gay and Lesbian Community. Boston: Alyson, 1989.

Beam, Joseph, ed. *In the Life: A Black Gay Anthology*. Boston: Alyson, 1986.

Beck, Evelyn Torton, ed. *Nice Jewish Girls: A Lesbian Anthology*. Rev. and updated ed. Boston: Beacon, 1989.

Berzon, Betty, ed. *Positively Gay: New Approaches to Gay and Lesbian Life*. Updated and expanded. Berkeley, CA: Celestial Arts, 1992.

Birtha, Becky. Any of her books of short stories or poems.

Borhek, Mary V. *Coming Out to Parents: A Two-Way Survival Guide for Lesbians and Gay Men and Their Parents*. New York: Pilgrim, 1983.

Burke, Phyllis. *Family Values: Two Moms and Their Son*. New York: Random House, 1993.

Chambers, Jane. Any of her plays.

Chuney, C., A. Kim, and A. Lemeshewsky, eds. *Between the Lines: An Anthology of Pacific/Asian Lesbians*. Santa Cruz, CA: Dancing Bird Press, 1987.

Clark, Donald. *Loving Someone Gay*. Rev. and updated ed. Millbrae, CA: Celestial Arts, 1990.

Evans, Nancy J., and Vernon A. Wall, eds. *Beyond Tolerance: Gays, Lesbians, and Bisexuals on Campus*. Alexandria, VA: American College Personnel Association, 1991.

Faderman, Lillian. *Odd Girls and Twilight Lovers: A History of Lesbian Life in Twentieth-Century America*. New York: Columbia University Press, 1991.

Fairchild, Betty. *Now That You Know: What Every Parent Should Know about Homosexuality*. Rev. ed. New York: Harcourt Brace Jovanovich, 1989.

Fierstein, Harvey. Any of his plays.

Geller, Thomas, ed. *Bisexuality: A Reader and Sourcebook*. Novato, CA: Times Change Press, 1990.

Griffin, Carolyn. *Beyond Acceptance: Parents of Lesbians and Gays Talk about Their Experiences*. New York: St. Martin's, 1990.

Heron, Anne, ed. *One Teenager in Ten: Writings by Gay and Lesbian Youth*. Boston: Alyson, 1983.

Holoch, Naomi, and Joan Nestle, eds. *Women on Women, 2: An Anthology of American Lesbian Short Fiction*. New York: Plume, 1993.

Hutchins, L., and L. Kaahumanu, eds. *Bi Any Other Name: Bisexual People Speak Out*. Boston: Alyson, 1991.

Jay, Karla, and Allen Yany. *Out of the Closets: Voices of Gay Liberation*. 20th anniv. ed. New York: New York University Press, 1992.

Lorde, Audre. Any of her work.

McNaught, Brian. *On Being Gay*. New York: St. Martin's, 1988.

Marcus, Eric. *Is It a Choice? Answers to Three Hundred of the Most Frequently Asked Questions about Gays and Lesbians*. San Francisco: HarperSanFrancisco, 1993.

Miller, Neil. *In Search of Gay America: Women and Men in a Time of Change*. New York: HarperPerennial, 1989.

Monette, Paul. *Becoming a Man: Half a Life*. San Francisco: HarperSanFrancisco, 1993.

Moraga, Cherríe, and Gloria Anzaldúa, eds. *This Bridge Called My Back: Writings by Radical Women of Color*. 2d ed. New York: Kitchen Table/ Women of Color Press, 1983.

Near, Holly. *Fire in the Rain . . . Singer in the Storm*. New York: Morrow, 1990.

Nestle, Joan, and Naomi Holoch, eds. *Women on Women: An Anthology of American Lesbian Short Fiction*. New York: Plume, 1990.

Pharr, Suzanne. *Homophobia: A Weapon of Sexism*. Little Rock, AR: Chardon, 1988.

Plant, Richard. *The Pink Triangle: The Nazi War against Homosexuals*. New York: Holt, 1988.

Ramos, Juanita, comp. *Companeras: Latina Lesbians: An Anthology*. New York: Latina Lesbian History Project, 1987.

Sherrill, Jan-Mitchell, and Craig A. Hardesty. *The Gay, Lesbian, and Bisexual Student's Guide to Colleges, Universities, and Graduate Schools*. New York: New York University Press, 1994.

Thompson, Karen, and Julie Andrzejewski. *Why Can't Sharon Kowalski Come Home?* San Francisco: Spinsters/Aunt Lute Books, 1988.

Whitney, Catherine. *Uncommon Lives: Gay Men and Straight Women*. New York: New American Library, 1990.

Williams, Walter. *The Spirit and the Flesh: Sexual Diversity in American Indian Culture*. Boston: Beacon, 1988.

Novels

Alther, Lisa. *Other Women*. New York: Signet, 1985.

Brown, Rita Mae. *Rubyfruit Jungle*. New York: Bantam, 1983.

———. *Venus Envy*. New York: Bantam, 1993.

Flagg, Fannie. *Fried Green Tomatoes at the Whistle Stop Cafe*. New York: Random House, 1987.
Gardner, Nancy. *Annie on My Mind*. New York: Sunburst, 1982.

Articles, Pamphlets, and Papers

Bendet, P. "What Is behind the Anger and Fear Triggered by Homosexuality? A Report on Homophobia on American Campuses." *Rolling Stone*, August/ September 1986.
Doe, Jane. "I Left My Husband for the Woman I Love." *Ms.*, January 1988.
Kasindorf, Jeanie Russell. "Lesbian Chic: The Bold, Brave New World of Gay Women." *New York*, May 10, 1993.
Toufexis, Anastasia. "Bisexuality: What Is It?" *Time*, August 17, 1992.
Van Gelder, Lindsy. "Personal Politics: A Lesson in Straight Talk." *Ms.*, November 1987.

Periodicals, Presses, and Mail Order

The Advocate (national gay newsmagazine)
    6922 Hollywood Blvd.
    10th Floor
    Los Angeles, CA 90028
    213-871-1225
The Crossing Press
    P.O. Box 1048
    Freedom, CA 95019
    1-800-777-1048
Directory of Homosexual Organizations and Publications
    Homosexual Information Center
    115 Monroe
    Bossier City, LA 71111-4539
    318-742-4709
Ferrari's Places for Women: World Wide Women's Guide
    (published annually)
    Ferrari Publications, Inc.
    P.O. Box 37887
    Phoenix, AZ
    602-863-2408
Firebrand Books
    141 The Commons
    Ithaca, NY 14850
Gay Yellowpages (guides for different sections of the United States)
    Renaissance House
    P.O. Box 533
    Village Station, NY 10014
    212-674-0120

Lambda Rising, Inc. (bookstore with mail order service)
   1625 Connecticut Ave. NW
   Washington, DC 20009
   1-800-621-6969
Naiad Press, Inc.
   P.O. Box 10543
   Tallahasee, FL 32302
   904-539-5965

Organizations for Information and Assistance

Dignity, Inc. (Catholic)
   1500 Massachusetts Ave. NW
   Suite 11
   Washington, DC 20005
   202-861-0017
East Coast Bisexual Network
   c/o Boston Lesbian/Gay Service Center
   338 Newbury St.
   2nd Floor
   Boston, MA 02115
   617-338-9595
National Gay Alliance for Young Adults
   P.O. Box 190426
   Dallas, TX 75219
National Gay and Lesbian Task Force
   1734 14th St. NW
   Washington, DC 20009-4309
   202-332-6483
National Gay Youth Network
   P.O. Box 846
   San Francisco, CA 94101-0846
National Lesbian, Gay, and Bisexual Student Caucus
   815 Fifteenth St. NW
   Suite 838
   Washington, DC 20005
   202-347-USSA
Parents and Friends of Lesbians and Gays Federation (P-FLAG)
   Box 77605
   Washington, DC 20038
   202-638-4200
Universal Fellowship of Metropolitan Community Churches
   5300 Santa Monica Blvd.
   Suite 304
   Los Angeles, CA 90029
   213-464-5100

World Congress of Gay and Lesbian Jewish Organizations
  P.O. Box 18961
  Washington, DC 20036

Films, Videos, TV Shows, Plays

Before Stonewall. Chronicles the history of gay life and the Stonewall Riot in the late 1960s, which began the new gay liberation movement. PBS documentary.

Consenting Adult. A college student comes out to his family. Made-for-TV movie based on Laura Hobson's novel.

A Conversation with Brian McNaught on Being Gay. A discussion about what it means to be gay.

Desert Hearts. A repressed professor goes to Reno for a divorce and becomes involved with a free-spirited young lesbian.

Execution of Justice. Dramatically presents the events surrounding the trial of Dan White for assassinating Harvey Milk. Play by Emily Mann.

Lianna. A professor's wife leaves her husband for another woman.

My Two Loves. A widow struggles with her feelings toward both a man and another woman. Made-for-TV movie.

Personal Best. A female track-and-field athlete has a relationship with another female athlete and later with a man.

Pink Triangles. Explores the treatment of homosexuals in Nazi Germany. Documentary.

A Question of Love. A lesbian fights for custody of her son. Made-for-TV movie based on a true story.

Sunday, Bloody Sunday. A man and a woman are both involved with the same man.

That Certain Summer. A divorced gay father comes out to his teenaged son. Made-for-TV movie.

The Times of Harvey Milk. Documents the life and career of the first openly gay person elected to the San Francisco city council, and the city's response to his assassination.

Torch Song Trilogy. A gay man searches for love and respect. From the play by Harvey Fierstein.

Word Is Out: Stories of Some of Our Lives. Twenty-six gay men and lesbians talk about their lifestyles. Documentary.

FIFTEEN

Socioeconomic Class

· · ·

"Although I am on a budget, I sometimes feel myself wanting to possess the material things that other students have. When in Rome, you know? I think this happens because as a newcomer there is a terrible need to possess the symbols that supposedly make one part of the 'community.' However, once settled into the groove of things I started to develop my own identity. I found that I did not need to have the symbols that other students have to be part of the community because a community should accept you for who you are and not what you own."

—M. J., class of '93

· · ·

It's your first week on campus. Everywhere you go—in the residence hall or at classes and social events—you're meeting new people. And you're probably asking and answering the same kinds of questions over and over as you try to get to know one another.

So . . . where ya from? "Pittsburgh." "Virginia Beach." "About a mile from here." "Pakistan." "North of Chicago." "East L.A." "Idaho." "90210."

What's your major? "Business." "Government." "Art History." "Women's Studies." "Engineering." "Physical Education." "Are you kidding, I just got here!"

What'd you do this summer? "Interned in my mom's office." "Got a tan." "Camp counselor." "Waitressed." "Traveled." "Sold vacuum cleaners." "Took care of my little brothers." "Looked for a job." "Got a head start on my courses." "Hung out with my friends."

Play any sports? "Volleyball." "Bowling." "Tennis." "Softball." "I jog." "I ride my horse."

What does your dad do? "Fireman." "Teacher." "He's out of work right now." "President of a corporation." "He takes care of my sisters; my mom works." "Lawyer." "Bartender." "Surgeon." "Construction worker." "He doesn't have to do anything." "I don't know; he doesn't live with us."

What do you do for fun? "I don't know . . . hang out, I guess." "Shop." "Go to concerts." "Watch movies." "Go dancing." "Eat out." "Read." "Sports." "Who's got time for fun?"

Nice jacket, where'd ya get it? "L. L. Bean." "Army Surplus." "Banana Republic." "K-Mart." "Bloomingdales." "Sears." "My sister."

Terminology and Background Information

. . .

Harriet: I grew up in New York. My mother still lives on East 69th Street.
Paul: East 69th Street. You were a rich kid.
Harriet: No. Upper middle class.
Paul: Only rich kids know what upper middle class is.
          —Wendy Wasserstein, *Isn't It Romantic*[1]
. . .

Class is defined in terms of an economic hierarchy in which different levels enjoy different degrees of social and economic privilege.[2] *Privilege* comes from having social status and/or from having money. Privilege can give you more choices in life—choices about where you can go to school, social activities you can afford, clubs or organizations you can join, vacations you can take, nonpaying internships you can accept, and clothes and other possessions you can buy. Having choices gives you greater opportunities to learn and develop your talents and skills. Those opportunities can then give you more choices, and that's a privilege.

Resources in the United States are unevenly distributed; this affects the opportunities and choices available to different individuals. In recent years, the richest have tended to get richer and the poorest, poorer. Consider that from 1973 to 1987 the average income of the poorest fifth of the U.S. population dropped 11.8 percent, while in that same period the average income of the wealthiest rose 24.1 percent.[3]

Labels used for the different socioeconomic classes often get in the way of people seeing and treating one another as distinct individuals. Class differences cross all lines—gender, ethnicity, sexual orientation, religious affiliation—although some groups may be over- or underrepresented in some classes. Although it's hard to neatly categorize people into socioeconomic classes, criteria sometimes used to define upper-class status include owning property, a home, or a business and employing others rather than working for someone else. Yearly income and money from savings, investments, and property also reflect economic status. Social status is defined by family history, education, and occupation.

Economists generally consider the term "middle class" to cover about 60 percent of the population. The middle class has been described as people who have high school or college diplomas, family incomes of twenty to sixty thousand dollars (slightly higher in cities like New York and Los Angeles), and, more recently, almost as much indebtedness as income. Members of the middle class generally have a house in a suburb and two vehicles; one or two family members work full time.[4]

Income level is only one part of the picture, but the following 1989 U.S. census figures may give you a general overview of the breakdown, by annual income, for households in the United States:[5]

- Under $10,000   15.6%
- $10,000–$14,999   9.7
- $15,000–$24,999   17.9
- $25,000–$34,999   15.9
- $35,000–49,999   17.3
- $50,000–74,999   14.5
- $75,000 and over   9.0

Although terms such as "upper class," "middle class," "working class," "poor," etc., are often used by demographers, economists, and others to break the U.S. population down into socioeconomic groups, outward symbols are not always accurate representations of socioeconomic class. Some people appear to have the signs of a privileged life but may be living beyond their actual financial means. Others have more money yet don't possess the education, home, or occupation that gives them status in others' eyes. Several families can earn the same income but have different numbers of people to support. Different decisions are also made about how to use money—to save, to spend on possessions, to spend on education, to buy a home, to provide for older parents, on health care, etc.

Sources of Misunderstanding

Faulty assumptions contribute to the attitudes we learn about socioeconomic class and lead to misunderstanding. The myth of upward mobility, for example, rests on the idea that everyone can improve his/her socioeconomic position if s/he just works hard enough. The faulty assumption here is that if you work hard you can succeed and that, conversely, if you don't succeed, then you haven't worked hard and you deserve whatever you have or don't have.[6] As one recent graduate put it: "Some people can work very hard but just don't get paid very much."

Growing up believing in the myth of upward mobility can influence the way people feel about themselves. Working-class students who internalize this myth may unjustly believe that they're inferior and that they deserve their so-called place in life. As a result, they may resent those in "higher places." Some try to emulate upper-class students by dressing, talking, and acting like them. Others outwardly adopt these appearances while still retaining their own culture and values. Still other working-class students refuse to accept this myth and remain proud of who they are and of working hard for what they achieve. Others develop feelings of superiority about having had to work hard for everything they ever got.[7]

Some upper- and middle-class students who believe this myth develop a conscious or unconscious sense of superiority and learn to take much for granted. Without meaning to hurt others, they may assume that everyone has the same choices they do, and they judge others for not achieving more. Some feel guilty about what they have and get stuck in that guilt. Others with money and power choose to use their position and influence to expand opportunities for others.[8]

Class differences can arise as students are being advised and making decisions about where to attend college. Sometimes whether or not they strive for admission to particular schools may be based on how they see themselves and the expectations high school teachers have of them. Some teachers incorrectly equate class-related characteristics such as accent, appearance, and manner with being intelligent and a good student.[9]

. . .

"When I was in high school, I had an English teacher who told the students in class about the class and 'racial' differences of the school. He informed us that the kids from the Hill (the richer part of town) were all in Curriculum 1 and Honors classes (the 'smarter' part of the tracking system) and all the Metro students (students from Boston, mostly black) and students from the 'Lake' (working-class neighborhood) were all in Curriculum 2 classes. These students, he told us, were the troublemakers and they didn't care about their studies. At that time I contested his generalizations, which I had seen reflected in his teaching and discipline. His attitude aided in curbing many students (whom I saw perform well in other classes) from achieving their potential."

—L. S., class of '91

. . .

Another myth is that everyone has equal educational opportunities. That's not true. Some families can choose to send their children to private schools. The resources, class sizes, facilities, technology, and guidance at private schools are often quite different from those in public schools. Public school systems also vary greatly. Schools are substantially supported by local property taxes, and wealthy communities have more money to provide more resources and programs for students. Less money is spent on education in many less wealthy districts.[10] Some students are able to prepare for college entrance exams by taking SAT prep courses that cost money. Others need to work after school and on weekends, which cuts into their study time.

Another common myth is that expensive equals better—a false assumption that if something is expensive it *has* to be better. Several years ago I attended a discussion with faculty, staff, and students at the private liberal arts college where I was then working. The discussion focused on what people felt they would take with them from their educational and social experiences at this school. I was one of the few participants who had neither attended this college nor been associated with it for many years. As I listened to people praise the value of their experiences, I thought to myself that I could say many of the same things about my own undergraduate experiences at one of the branches of the State

University of New York. At that point I was feeling proud of my own education, which happened to have cost so much less.

The conversation eventually began to veer into excessive testimonials. This private institution was being praised as so unique that it was almost unimaginable that anyone could possibly have as valuable an experience anywhere else. I began to feel slightly hostile. As the tributes went on, I felt more and more uncomfortable and out of place. The implication, loud and clear, was that the expensive education *had* to be superior. As I let myself feel inferior, that feeling contributed to my silence. That silence seemed to reinforce the opinion being expressed—that I, who had gone to a public university, was not as intelligent, articulate, or assertive as everyone else in the room. I· knew that wasn't true, but I certainly acted as if it was that night. If you choose to go to a less expensive school, that doesn't mean your education will be worth less.

. . .

"My brother is attending a technical college now and will have benefits that I, with a B.A. from my college, am not guaranteed. He will have employment after graduation in a field which he enjoys."

—L. S., class of '91

. . .

ENCOUNTERING AND RESPONDING TO THIS ISSUE

Residential and Social Life

. . .

"One of my friends, who is very well off, spent an evening telling me how traumatized she had been in middle school because of money. I felt bad for her, realizing how cruel kids can be, but she does flaunt her money, talking about her two houses in the richest parts of California, the probability that she and her brother will both go to medical school, etc., and putting a price on everything."

—Student, class of '94

. . .

Your reactions to others come from what they say and also from how they say it—their attitude. A new acquaintance may, for instance say she's from Dallas. She may say it in a way that tells you she feels Dallas is the *only* place to live, or she may say it in a way that tells you she feels it's not necessarily better or worse than anywhere else. She may also go out of her way to play down the fact that she's from Dallas in order to avoid the stereotypes about people from Texas that she thinks others' hold.

Similarly, someone who waitressed during the summer may say it in an apologetic way, or she may express pride in her work and enjoy telling funny stories about her experiences. She may also avoid saying what she really did if she thinks others will judge her for being a waitress.

Students may initially get to know one another by their labels or symbols—so-and-so has a BMW, so-and-so works two part-time jobs, so-and-so's father is a plumber, so-and-so has a summer home on the Cape, or so-and-so's room has more appliances than a Sears showroom. The more they get to know each other as people, however, the less dominant class differences will become in relationships. When money and opportunities are not taken for granted or are not expressed in ways that make others feel uncomfortable, stronger relationships will develop.

There are many subtle assumptions and expectations that create unnecessary discomfort. For example, conversations that automatically start with the kinds of questions that started this chapter consciously or unconsciously create first impressions and label people on the basis of their class. Those who are the first in their families to attend college may feel uneasy with the assumption that "of course everyone goes to college." On the other hand, someone who has a building on campus named after her grandmother may feel uncomfortable if others assume that she gets special treatment by the college. Some students judge others' friends or girlfriends/boyfriends according to whether, and where, they go to school. Someone from a state university, community college, or technical college is sometimes spoken of differently than someone who attends a private four-year college.

. . .

"I was sitting in the living room during my junior year of college when a commercial for a particular university came on TV. Someone else in the room not from this region of the country made a derogatory comment about how she would never go to a school which advertises on TV. I was offended and immediately told her that it is a good university. Its advertising on TV was a benefit to many people who have internalized the belief that an undergraduate or graduate education is inaccessible to lower classes or nontraditional-age students."

—L. S., class of '91

. . .

Assumptions in relation to money have a strong impact. It may help to understand what kinds of comments can be embarrassing or hurtful to others. For example, someone may have plenty of money but may also have some genuinely tough times and pain in her life. Comments that dismiss her legitimate concerns—"What do you have to complain about?"—can hurt even more.

On the other hand, students often tell each other to "charge it" or "call home for more money" when that isn't an option for everyone. It can be awkward for a student to have to explain that she doesn't have credit cards or that her parents don't have money to send. Suggestions that assume that everyone can "chip in ten dollars for refreshments" or "lay out money for tickets to be paid back later" can put someone on a tight budget in an uncomfortable bind. Then, too, the phrase "I don't have the money" or "I can't afford it" means different things to different people and can create unnecessary tension.

. . .

"As someone who is from the lower to middle portion of the 'middle class,' I know that I don't resent people *because* they have more money than I do. I resent when they have a trust fund and have the nerve to say 'I have *no* money.' Or when I am debating what to do over the summer, trying to figure out what I can and can't afford to do, and someone will tell me, 'I can't really afford to go to Europe this summer but I'm going to anyway. It's such a great opportunity.' It's not the fact that they have the money to do these things that bothers me, it's the fact that they tell me they can't afford it and assume that my meaning of not being able to afford something (there simply is not money to do it), and theirs (it will be difficult and they will have to live off the money their parents send once a week) are the same."

—Student, class of '93

. . .

Socializing in ways that always cost money can be stressful if you're watching your expenses, but you can always find inexpensive ways to spend time. While some social activities cost money, such as a concert or a nice dinner out, other activities may cost nothing—campus-sponsored sports matches, lectures, hanging out with friends, watching TV, playing cards, or sledding. Campus student activities offices often have free or low-cost tickets available for community events, and you can also get student discounts at some places by showing your I.D. Some theaters and concert halls offer those who usher a chance to see the play or concert for free. With a little creativity, you can always find ways to have fun together without emphasizing money differences.

Other assumptions revolve around financial aid. Regardless of how much financial aid someone receives, everyone enrolled at the college has a right to be there and to receive the same education and services. Students sometimes question why someone on financial aid has a car or a computer or something else they would label a luxury. A car, for example, may be necessary for the student to commute to and from an off-campus job. Some possessions are necessary academic "tools" that the student has either chosen to get in place of something else or received as a gift. Every student should have comparable opportunities to achieve academically, and a word processor is one tool that can make anyone's schoolwork more manageable.

Extra or unexpected expenses often crop up at college. Many colleges, for example, charge students for damage done to their rooms, broken furniture, and extra cleaning. Where this damage occurs in hallways or common areas, the cost is often divided among all residents. Dues and fees to participate in some residential or social activities may be either required or optional. If they are optional, a student without the funds may not be able to participate in some activities or will need to set some priorities. If some dues or fees are required, and if they pose financial problems, there may be ways to request a waiver or work out a delayed or staggered payment plan. Asking for this puts the burden on the working-class student to identify herself. This can feel awkward. Students in positions of authority in the residence hall, student government, or club can help by taking the initiative to offer that option. This way it is seen more as a reasonable and accepted alternative rather than as some major exception to an iron-clad rule.

Work is another big issue for many of you who are paying or helping to pay your own expenses. You may work to help out with your bills or to earn spending money. Some of you need to work, often excessive hours, to pay basic college bills. You may also be sending money home to help your family. Work demands cut into the time you have available for studying, socializing, and extracurricular activities.

. . .

"When I decided to come here, I knew that it would be tough since I am paying out-of-state tuition. I am here totally on financial aid—loans, grants, and scholarships. This semester I am working *four* regular part-time jobs and I barely have enough to get by."

—L. M., class of '92

. . .

College Staff and the Off-Campus Community

One significant way in which class distinctions play out on campus is the manner in which students treat staff who work at the college. The assumption that staff exist only to serve you ignores the fact that workers are much more than just their jobs. The people who work, for example, in the dining halls, as secretaries, for security, for the physical plant, or at the library work hard and often get paid less than many other people on campus. They have jobs to do, and you can help by doing your share and cleaning up after yourself. Under stress, some students who would never snap at a faculty member, administrator, or peer take out their frustrations on staff members. This certainly perpetuates the false message that people in some roles or jobs are less deserving of respect. Take opportunities to talk to staff and see more of them than the job they do. All-campus events, picnics, celebrations, etc., may include staff and their families. If you attend religious services or volunteer in the community, or if you go out to eat or shop or dance in town, you may run into staff members in other contexts. All these opportunities can help you know them better. Staff members who feel respected and valued by both the institution and its students can be an important bridge between the college and the community.

It's important to respect the community around you. While you may want to party on a Thursday night and sing at the top of your lungs walking home, remember that the homes you pass along the way house families who must rise early the next morning. Littering the streets with trash and making fun of the town also communicate disrespect and can generate hostility in return.

Relations between students and permanent residents of the town, city, or neighborhood are complicated. The needs of one group may conflict with those of another, and priorities are sometimes different. When the college is sharing community space with lower-income residents, the contrast between the wealth of the institution and the lives of those who live around it can create strong feelings. It's important for colleges and communities to work together. Open campus events such as lectures, movies, and concerts provide opportunities for the community. Sometimes the college and off-campus groups work together on projects such as building a playground, repainting a shelter, or organizing a women's march. Individual students can also reach out to the community by tutoring elementary school children, volunteering in a shelter for the homeless, working on a rape hotline, or leading a girl scout troop.

WHERE TO LOOK FOR HELP

(See also this section in chapter 11.)

The Financial Aid Office on your campus is the first place to look for assistance. Remember that in determining your eligibility for federal programs, financial aid officers are bound by guidelines, and you'll need to fully complete all forms by set deadlines. Some forms need to be filled out by your parents, and if finances have not been openly discussed in your family, or if they are a source of discomfort, this will require some difficult but necessary communication. One mother approached it all with a sense of humor:

. . .

"And don't tell me about financial aid. I had high hopes for that until I started filling out the application form. Question 12 inquired whether I had, in addition to my present income and home furnishings, any viable organs for donations. Question 34 solicited an inventory of the silverware. Question 92 demanded a list of rock stars who could plausibly be hit with a paternity suit."
    —Barbara Ehrenreich, "Welcome to Fleece U." [11]

. . .

The Financial Aid Office can also help you identify other sources of funding—both need and nonneed based. Loans are available from a variety of places, such as corporations, employers, and organizations, so don't limit your search to the Financial Aid Office. Consult with a financial aid counselor to assure that you don't take out loans that will cause you great economic hardship as you pay them back in the years ahead.

There's generally someplace on campus where listings of available jobs are posted. Such listings may be in the Financial Aid or Student Work Office or on bulletin boards in the Student Center or in academic buildings. To assure yourself the most options, find out the timeline and process for applying for jobs. Off-campus jobs are posted on campus or in the college newspaper, or you can consult the local newspaper. Often short-term or "spot" jobs are available, such as babysitting. If you're an international student, there may be limitations on where you can work and earn money. Check with the Financial Aid Office to find out.

If possible, consider how your job choices can fit in with your academic commitments and total schedule. For example, some work-study jobs, such as evening receptionist or movie projectionist, will allow you to do some studying. Serving as a lab assistant, research assistant, or administrative office worker may complement your academic interests and experiences. Other jobs—working in a health food restaurant downtown, babysitting, or coaching track at the Y—may provide a good break from campus routine.

Perhaps the best way to learn about the effects of class differences on your attitudes and actions is to think about your own background and the early memories and messages you internalized about money and social position. The following questions may give you some direction in this process.[12]

1. How would you describe your class background?
2. What have been some difficulties for you coming from this background?
3. What have been some sources of strength for you coming from this background?
4. How have these factors affected your feelings of "belonging" at your college?
5. When was the first time you recognized that class differences existed? What were the circumstances and how did you feel at the time?
6. When did you first identify as a member of a particular class? What were the circumstances and how did you feel at the time?
7. Think about a time when you remember seeing someone treated

differently because of her/his particular economic or social status (both working class and upper class)? What were the circumstances and how did you feel at the time?

8. What messages do you remember getting when you were growing up about what it meant to be from a particular social or economic group? Where did you get the messages (family, school, friends, media)?

9. What assumptions/associations do you have about having money and not having money?

10. How comfortable/uncomfortable do you feel talking about money and why?

11. To what extent, if any, has your understanding of different economic or social groups changed over time? What or who was responsible for that change?

12. What can you do now to better understand people from different economic and social backgrounds?

If possible, talk about some of these questions with family and friends; this will open up some valuable conversations.

. . .

"Class has been sort of a hidden issue for me—nobody seems to talk about it, especially not on a personal level."

—R. C. S., class of '94

. . .

EDUCATING YOURSELF

Books: Nonfiction, Anthologies, Biographies, Poetry, Plays

Buss, Fran Leeper. *Dignity: Lower-Income Women Tell of Their Lives and Struggles.* Ann Arbor: University of Michigan Press, 1985.

Davis, Angela. *Women, Race, and Class.* New York: Vintage, 1983.

DeMott, Benjamin. *The Imperial Middle: Why Americans Can't Think Straight about Class.* New York: Morrow, 1990.

Ehrenreich, Barbara. *Fear of Falling: The Inner Life of the Middle Class.* New York: HarperPerennial, 1990.

Fuentes, Annette, and Barbara Ehrenreich. *Women in the Global Factory.* Boston: South End Press, 1983.

Olsen, Tillie. *Silences*. New York: Delta, 1989.

Ostrander, Susan. *Women of the Upper Class*. Philadelphia: Temple University Press, 1984.

Rubin, Lillian Breslow. *Worlds of Pain: Life of the Working-Class Family*. New York: Basic, 1990.

Stack, Carol. *All Our Kin: Strategies for Survival in a Black Community*. New York: Torchbooks, 1983.

Articles, Pamphlets, and Papers

Wolf, Naomi. "The Psychic Expense of an Elitist Campus." *Ms.*, October 1984.

Films, Videos, TV Shows, Plays

Baby It's You. A romance develops between high school students from different social classes in 1960s New Jersey.

The Breakfast Club. High school students from varying backgrounds get below the surface during eight hours of Saturday detention.

Breaking Away. Conflicts erupt between "townies" and Indiana University college students.

Crossing Delancey. An upwardly mobile Jewish woman in New York remains close to her grandmother on the Lower East Side.

Dirty Dancing. A cross-class romance blossoms at a Catskill resort in the early 1960s.

The Flamingo Kid. A teenager in Brooklyn in 1963 spends the summer working at a wealthy beach club on Long Island.

Goodbye Columbus. A working-class young man gets involved with a wealthy young woman. From the book by Philip Roth.

Little Man Tate. A young boy genius is torn between his working-class mother and the opportunities offered by a psychologist.

Metropolitan. Explores life among the wealthy New York debutante set.

Mystic Pizza. Three working-class young women experience the gap between "townies" and tourists in the seaside town of Mystic.

Norma Rae. A small-town mill worker in the South helps to unionize the workers.

Places in the Heart. A farm family struggles against foreclosure after the husband is killed.

Pretty in Pink. Another cross-class high school romance develops.

"Roc." Follows a working-class family in Baltimore. TV series.

"Roseanne." Follows a working-class family in Illinois. TV series.

Saturday Night Fever. A working-class man from Brooklyn becomes the disco dancing partner of a woman with higher aspirations.

Silkwood. A nuclear plant worker and union activist dies suspiciously while trying to expose safety violations at her plant.

Stanley and Iris. A relationship slowly develops between a widowed factory worker and the acquaintance she teaches to read.

Trading Places. Two men from different socioeconomic extremes trade places and discover new ways of life.

True Colors. A friendship between two men from different social classes begins in law school and goes through many conflicts.

White Palace. A romance develops between a wealthy young widower and a working-class woman.

SIXTEEN

Disabilities

. . .

"And I want to learn to communicate with you in whatever language we both can learn to speak."
—Mark Medoff, *Children of a Lesser God*[1]

. . .

In the last ten years the number of students with disabilities on U.S. college campuses has tripled, and 10.5 percent of all college students have some kind of disability.[2] Perhaps you'll find yourself living in the same residence hall as Ginny, a woman with congenitally underdeveloped limbs who travels around campus using a motorized cart. You might sing in the college choir with Alicia, who has a visual impairment and lives on campus with her guide dog, or maybe you'll play on an athletic team with Randy, who takes medication to control chronic depression. Your classmates could include Robert, a student with a learning disability who was on academic probation until he discovered the reason why and developed new study strategies. You might become good friends with Nina, the woman next door who uses a wheelchair and gets to activities held everywhere on campus—even in nonwheelchair-accessible locations, where you help lift her and her chair up the stairs.

Terminology

. . .

"First, there's 'impairment,' which is the actual physical disability. I had polio, and the impairment is the damage in my spinal column. 'Disability' is the effect of the impairment; for me, I can't use certain muscles. A 'handicap' is an obstacle that prevents you from doing what you want to do. When I come to a flight of stairs, *they* are the handicap."

—Gwyneth Ferguson Matthews, *Voices from the Shadows: Women with Disabilities Speak Out*[3]

. . .

Although the term "handicapped" is most often used by the federal government, the origin of that term is considered by many to be demeaning, for it originally applied to someone begging in the street, "cap in hand." Terms such as challenged and differently abled have also been used at times, although they're more often used by people who do not themselves have disabilities. Generally, the term *disabled* is preferred. While individuals may have disabilities that can create some real limitations, they're often more handicapped by others' attitudes and by physical barriers.[4]

The federal government defines a *disability* as a physical or emotional impairment that substantially limits one or more of a person's major life activities.[5] A qualified person with a disability is someone who is capable of doing a particular job or who would be capable of doing that job if some reasonable accommodations were made.[6]

Federal laws are guaranteeing students with disabilities more equal opportunities in colleges and universities. The Americans with Disabilities Act of 1990 provides an even greater foundation for students with disabilities to exercise their rights. This law prohibits discrimination in employment, transportation, public facilities, and telecommunication.[7] Colleges are required to provide reasonable accommodations necessary to allow a student with a disability to perform up to her capacity. This includes access to programs and activities, including a range of class offerings and use of technology such as TDD (telecommunications device for the deaf) telephones and computer labs. Students with disabilities have a legal right to expect these kinds of services.

Background Information: Types of Disabilities

It can be easy to distance yourself from what it means to have a disability if you think in extremes, focusing on permanent and visible situations such as paralysis, loss of limbs, or total hearing loss. There are actually varying degrees of all disabilities, for example, legal but not total blindness or early stages in a progressively developing condition such as multiple sclerosis. Temporary disabilities include breaking a leg in a car crash or recuperating after surgery. None of us really knows when something might happen to disable us in some way, either temporarily or permanently. In fact, most of us will probably develop a disability at some point in our lives, even if only as a result of growing older.

Motor or Mobility Impairments

Physical disabilities are also called motor or mobility impairments. Causes include conditions such as cerebral palsy, multiple sclerosis, muscular dystrophy, spina bifida, and accidents resulting in amputation or injury to the spinal cord. Some people are born without limbs or with other birth defects. Some individuals use a wheelchair, crutches, or braces; others don't need extra support or use it only occasionally. Physical disabilities are visible disabilities because they are generally obvious to those who are sighted.[8]

Visual Impairments

Visual impairments range from partial sightedness to limitations of visual field to legal blindness to total blindness. They may result from a medical problem, birth defect, brain damage, or nerve damage. Corrective lenses and magnifying devices are used to compensate for some visual impairments.[9]

Hearing Impairments

Hearing impairments range from those that are light, moderate, or severe to profound deafness. At the less severe levels, hearing aids can be used, and at the more severe levels individuals read lips or work with a sign-language interpreter. At the profound level, it's not possible to understand even amplified speech.[10]

Speech and Language Impairments

Speech and language impairments sometimes occur along with other disabilities such as cerebral palsy or hearing impairments. They may include language or linguistic disorders, articulation disorders, voice disorders, and stuttering.[11]

Health Impairments

Health impairments include chronic disorders such as epilepsy, diabetes, asthma, hemophilia, chronic fatigue syndrome, and heart conditions. Many of these impairments are not visible to others. Some can be controlled by regular use of medication.[12]

Mental Impairments

Mental impairments are often neglected in discussions of conditions that can limit a person's ability to function independently.[13] Society often unjustly judges those with chronic psychiatric conditions. Increasing numbers of students enter college having previously been hospitalized or treated for psychological conditions. Some students arrive on campus taking regular medication such as antidepressants. With appropriate treatment, often combining medication and psychotherapy, the vast majority of psychiatric disorders can be reasonably controlled.[14]

Learning Disabilities

The number of students entering college with learning disabilities is increasing faster than that of any other group with an impairment.[15] Ongoing work with diagnosing and classifying learning disorders has contributed to this increase. Many students don't identify their learning disabilities until they reach college, where the amount of work required may finally exceed their ability to compensate by using learning strategies successful in high school. Students with learning disabilities are intelligent students with a permanent processing disorder or style that affects how they take in, retain, and express verbal information.[16] Probably the best-known learning disability is dyslexia, which can affect reading, spelling, and written, oral, and organizational abilities. Students with learning disabilities may read slowly and have trouble understanding what they read. They may see some letters incorrectly, reverse the order of other letters, and not perceive or remember some parts of material read. Students with learning disabilities often do very well academically. The process takes longer for them, however, and is harder work. Learning requires a combination of support, understanding, skill building, and development of compensatory strategies. Diagnosis of the specific degree and form of the disorder is an important first step to planning strategies.

ENCOUNTERING AND RESPONDING TO THIS ISSUE

For Students Who Have Disabilities

· · ·

"When I first came to college I wanted desperately to 'fit in.' I was so grateful for being here I would not have dreamed of asking for any special considerations. I now feel I can be grateful for being here and still ask that my civil rights are met."

—Student, class of '95

· · ·

While your experiences adjusting to college will be similar to those of all students, you could also encounter some added emotional stresses. If you know more about what different colleges offer, this will help you choose one where those stresses will be more manageable. Find out as much as possible about the physical environment at the schools you're considering, the attitudes there toward students with disabilities, and the support services available at each. If it's possible for you to visit the campus, you can learn even more.

Consider also personal issues, such as your academic interests and background, physical and emotional health, daily living and social skills, and your ability to live independently.[17] Seriously evaluate what supports you need to succeed at college. There are three general levels of support services offered on college campuses. With *minimal support* you're expected to adapt to the environment and serve as your own advocate for the services and accommodations you need. There's probably no specific office to coordinate services for students with disabilities, although there may be a particular person designated as a contact. When *moderate support* is given, accommodations, advocacy, and referrals are provided by an office of services for students with disabilities (the exact name of the office varies from campus to campus). If there's no specific office, some staff member will be designated as the 504 coordinator (person responsible for coordinating the college's efforts to comply with section 504 of the 1973 Rehabilitation Act). You'll be expected to take the initiative to contact that person or office to talk about services you need. *Intensive support* offers specific programs and instructional services.[18]

As you consider your particular needs and how well they can be met at each college, think also about your own style of assertiveness. If you feel comfortable asking for what you need, you may be able to work without support services at a school or where students are expected to take the initiative and advocate for themselves. If you're uneasy about speaking up or want to conserve your efforts for your academics, you may feel more comfortable where there is more organized and intensive support.

■ ■ ■

"A student with a mobility impairment may be asked to come to the special needs office on several occasions to pick up necessary equipment. The additional trips to the special needs office can be physically exhausting. The same student may be asked to call other offices for repairs. S/he may have to call several offices before s/he can track down the right person for the equipment repair. This student may have to dial slowly with the use of pencils, each phone call taking five times as long as it would for the average person."
—H. C., class of '91

■ ■ ■

Decisions about whether to continue to live at home while attending college, live on campus, or move a distance away are important ones. If those who supported and assisted you until now, such as parents, siblings, teachers, and friends, have tended to do things for you, it could be difficult for you to live on your own and advocate for yourself at college. On the other hand, your earlier helpers may have encouraged you to learn to function more independently. If so, perhaps you developed the skills needed to identify resources and get what you need in a new place.[19] As you look at your past experiences of being on your own, think about ways that you might expand these, if necessary, before leaving for college.

Many institutions give you the opportunity to identify your disability; doing so lets you discuss accommodations with them before you make your final decisions about where to enroll. Investigate thoroughly how each school will respond to your needs before committing to attend one.

If you wait until you arrive, this could delay some services and also limit the options available to you. Understand that reasonable accommodation does not necessarily mean having everything exactly as you want it or having things done for you. You will have to follow through with some details and you may have to set priorities and make some choices.

Academic Life

You're at college to learn and perform as a student. If you need reasonable accommodations to help you work up to your potential, you have the right to ask for and receive them. Some of the academic services available to you could include

1. Assistance with registration—location of classes, scheduling, possibility of taking a part-time load, waivers for some types of courses.
2. Accommodations for taking tests—untimed tests or extensions, separate rooms for taking tests, oral instead of written exams, use of typewriter or word processor for tests.
3. Note takers in classes.
4. Sign-language interpreters.
5. Course books and materials on audiotapes or in Braille.
6. Orientation programs.
7. Referrals to testing, diagnostic, medical, and rehabilitation services.
8. Computing services.
9. Accommodations with instructors such as taping lectures.
10. Student reader/taping services.
11. Library services.
12. Physical education options.[20]

If your disability is a less visible one, such as a learning disability or chronic illness, the choice to identify it or not may be more difficult. Some people are hesitant to do so, fearing that other's attitudes or preconceptions will hurt or limit them in the future. Identifying your disability to an office of services for students with disabilities or a 504 coordinator doesn't require you to accept particular accommodations. You can go on record with the college as having a disability and then proceed however you had originally planned. Should you find later, however, that you want to request some accommodations, you can do so then without first having to begin the paperwork and process. Identifying your disability at the start is a safety net in case you need it later.

Residential and Social Life

Residentially and socially, there are a number of factors to consider, especially if you choose to live on campus. How accessible is the campus—ramps, restrooms, curb cuts, elevators, etc.? Are there parking spaces for students with disabilities and accessible transportation for those commuting? If you want to live on campus, are there residence hall rooms equipped to meet your needs and provide interaction with other students? Is equipment such as TDD telephones and visual/vibrating fire alarms available to you? If you have specific medically documented dietary needs, can food services meet them or can you get released from the meal plan to prepare your own meals?

Developing relationships with roommates, hallmates, and friends can be complicated if they aren't aware of your disability. You can discuss with the Housing Office whether or not you will have a roommate and if so, what they look for in pairing someone with you. If you do have a roommate, it will probably be your decision and your responsibility to tell her about yourself. It can be hard to open up to someone you don't know, especially if you have no clue about how she'll react.

Think about the advantages and disadvantages of telling those close to you on campus about your disability. The burden of keeping a secret can create stress. It could help if your friends know what you need and why. For example, you may want privacy to take your insulin shot, no distractions when you're studying, or the room uncluttered so you don't bump into things you can't see. It will help if they know what to expect and what not to worry about: for example, if your medication sometimes makes you sleep a lot, your friends need to know that's OK. They also need to correct faulty assumptions and to understand, for instance, that even though you have a hearing impairment, you can still feel the vibration of the music and love to dance.

For Friends of Students Who Have Disabilities

. . .

"I'm in a sorority and I recall two years ago when a woman who was partially deaf went through rush. I, as well as other women in my house, was concerned that I might have to talk to her for ten to fifteen minutes and would not know how to act. I was afraid that she wouldn't be able to read my lips. As it turned out, our apprehension was for nought, because she turned out to be a very outgoing and intellectual woman and the girl in my house who visited with her just made sure to speak directly to her."

—R. E., class of '92

. . .

Many of your interactions with students who have disabilities will naturally be influenced by your preconceptions and assumptions, especially if you haven't had much previous experience. Stereotypes of people with disabilities either demean them or exalt them as "superpeople," heroes. Both extremes distort the fact that, as with any other group, there are great differences among individuals. The books, films, and videos listed at the end of this chapter, for instance, portray a wide range of people, each of whom responds differently to her/his disability.

Language can also reinforce stereotypes. Here are some positive approaches you can use: [21]

1. Consider the individual a person *first,* and refer to her, for example, as a person who is blind rather than as a blind person.
2. If the disability isn't relevant to the conversation, there's no need to mention it.
3. Use the term "has" rather than "is" to express the connection between a person and a disability. For example, say "she has a learning disability" rather than "she is learning disabled." "Is" creates a stronger connection between the disabling characteristic and the core of the person, whereas "has" more accurately implies that the disability is only one of her many characteristics.
4. Avoid terms that suggest dependence and victimization. For example, refer to someone as "having" cerebral palsy rather than as being "a victim" of it, "afflicted with" it, or "struck down" by it.
5. Items such as wheelchairs and crutches are tools used in activities and can be described in an active way. Talk about someone "using" a chair or "walking" with crutches, for example, rather than as "being confined" to a chair or "on" crutches.
6. Most people with disabilities are not sick, and medical terms such as "patient" or "illness" aren't appropriate.
7. The word "special" may serve to isolate rather than bring people together. Use the term "accessible entrance" rather than "special entrance."

Suggestions like these can sound overwhelming and may leave you feeling uncomfortable and afraid to say or do the wrong thing. If you let that discomfort translate into avoiding those with disabilities, you'll lose the chance to know some wonderful people. You don't need to be perfect, just to make a genuine effort.

If you have a roommate, hallmate, or friend with a disability, learn as much as you can about her condition without expecting your friend to always educate you. Do, however, talk with your friend about her specific needs. If you're sharing a suite or room with a student who has a disability, she may require additional equipment such as a wheelchair or recording and transcribing machines. Some individuals need privacy to perform medical or personal-care tasks.

Bear in mind that people need to trust and feel comfortable with you in order to talk openly about themselves. They may be afraid of your reactions, fearing that you will pity them or doubt their abilities. You may also find that they get angry at times because they feel frustrated or unfairly treated, now or in the past. If can be difficult for you to hear that anger, whether or not it's directed at you personally, but listening can be an important step in building trust.

You may worry that offering assistance to a friend with a disability will result in her becoming dependent on you for more than you can give her. Don't assume that this will necessarily happen. If you're someone who tends to feel responsible for others' well-being, you may be drawn into taking care of the other person. Read the earlier chapters on code-pendency and assertiveness and recognize your limits and how to set them clearly. If you need help doing this, talk to an R.A. or another staff member. Developing nondependent relationships is the most productive goal to work toward.

A disability that others can't see can make for awkward and hurtful situations. Comments expressing doubt about the legitimacy of someone else's need are frustrating and painful for a student with a disability to hear. Don't question the validity of someone's condition. Accommodations aren't special advantages; they're an attempt to equalize opportunities and access.

· · ·

"I am closed head injured. This means my brain has been damaged. Many of my disabilities are slight or not very noticeable. My brain processing is slower and I take longer to calculate problems. My speech has changed slightly. Some tasks I can accomplish with no problems. With others I have many problems. I often wondered what I would have been like if this accident hadn't happened. When I speak to some classmates about my situation, such as the fact that I take an untimed test, other students want to act like the school is giving me something. This makes me angry. Some friends in the first year I returned used to say I was using this as an excuse."

—B. A., class of '92

. . .

Friends with disabilities often want to be part of social and extracurricular activities both on and off campus. Don't assume that they will not want to do something simply because you've never seen someone with that disability do it before. There may be a variety of ways that your friend can participate or that accommodations can be made. You can, for example, call ahead to see if a restaurant is accessible, find out if there will be a sign-language interpreter at the lecture, or arrange to get front-row seats so your friend can read lips. Spontaneous ideas— "Let's go swimming," "There's a new group playing downtown, let's check it out"—may require more preplanning by those with certain disabilities.

It may take time, patience, and effort on your part to include students with disabilities in your activities and in your life. That effort means a great deal, and the individuals involved can also greatly enrich your life. Consider the amount of time, patience, and effort they expend every day.

. . .

"One friend of mine always said no if someone asked her if she needed help. But if they asked if she would like help she might say yes. She felt she didn't *need* help, but sometimes it was nice to have some."

—Student, class of '95

. . .

There are specific things you can do to be helpful to individuals who have disabilities. It's alright to offer assistance, but respect the person's privacy. Don't offer help unless she clearly needs it or requests it. Then, ask if she would like help and how it should be given. Let the person

identify her problem and potential solutions rather than trying to anticipate what she needs. Physical limitations are not mental limitations. Get
beyond the outside appearances to what's really there.[22]

. . .

"The first thing I was ever able to understand was that everyone
was supposed to hear but I couldn't and that was bad. Then they
told me everyone was supposed to be smart but I was dumb. Then
they said, oh no, I wasn't dumb, only temporarily, but to be smart
I had to become an imitation of the people who had from birth
everything a person has to have to be good: ears that hear, mouth
that speaks, eyes that read, brain that understands. Well my brain
understands a lot, and my eyes are my ears; and my hands are my
voice; and my language, my speech, my ability to communicate is
as great as yours. Greater, maybe, because I can communicate to
you in one image an idea more complex than you can speak to
each other in fifty words."

—Mark Medoff, *Children of a Lesser God*[23]

. . .

The following suggestions can help you relate to individuals with specific
types of disabilities: [24]

Hearing Impairments
1. Look directly at the person.
2. Speak slowly, as she may read lips.
3. If there's a sign-language interpreter there, speak directly to the
   person, *not* to the signer.
4. If a particular word or phrase is not understood, try substituting a
   different one.
5. Speak in a normal tone of voice; don't shout.
6. Only sign if you're qualified to do so.
7. If other modes of communication are unsuccessful, try using a pad
   and pencil.
8. Move away from sources of noise such as TVs and air conditioners.
9. Don't stand with bright light behind you—glare makes it difficult
   for your face to be seen.
10. Avoid chewing gum, eating, or covering your mouth while speaking.

Visual Impairments

1. Speak directly to the person, using a normal tone.
2. When offering assistance, respect her response.
3. When giving directions, be specific.
4. Walk alongside and slightly ahead of her; let her hold your arm.
5. Avoid escalators and revolving doors.
6. Assist her on stairs by guiding her hand to the banister.
7. If she needs help sitting down, place her hand on the back or arm of the seat.
8. Don't just leave her in an open space when you enter a room; lead her to a side or some other landmark she can use as a point of reference.
9. If you have to leave her in a crowded or noisy place, let her know you're leaving.
10. If she has a guide dog, don't pet the dog. It's working.
11. Don't stand with a bright light behind you. Few people are totally blind and most are very sensitive to light.

Mobility Impairments

1. Talk directly to the person.
2. If she's using a wheelchair, only push her after asking if she would like help.
3. At curbs, ask the person using the wheelchair if she prefers to go up forward or backward.
4. When going down an incline, hold the handles of the chair so it doesn't go too quickly.
5. When going up or down more than one step, keep the chair tilted back at all times.
6. Learn the location of accessible ramps, restrooms, elevators, phones, water fountains, etc.

Cerebral Palsy

1. Talk directly to the person.
2. Give her your complete and unhurried attention if she has difficulty speaking.
3. Let her finish her own sentences, even if it takes some time.
4. It's all right to ask her to repeat something if you don't understand.

Learning Disabilities

. . .

"A greater amount of energy and time is needed to complete a learning assignment. The emotional impact of this additional burden cannot be understood by others and is often not shared because the person with the disability has a great need to achieve."

—H. C., class of '91

. . .

You probably won't know if a roommate, hallmate, or friend has a learning disability unless she chooses to tell you. Someone who has a learning disorder may approach classes, studying, and writing papers in ways that seem extreme to you. For her these are necessary strategies for getting the work done. Some students with learning disabilities need to plan and start assignments long before they're due and to read things over several times in order to fully understand them. Teasing a person for starting to study or write a paper early may embarrass someone who has to plan that way.

Work takes more concentrated effort and time for someone with a learning disability. She isn't studying "all the time" in order to do better than everyone else, but to feel like she's keeping up and doing the best she can. She could also have less time to spend socializing. While your friend may want to participate in activities, she needs to manage her time carefully and choose her priorities. Students with learning disabilities are more easily distracted by noise and visual "clutter" and need more solitude when they study. They may need TVs and music turned off, or only certain kinds of music in the background. Distractions in the hall, or by others in the room, don't necessarily fade into the background for them, and they often find quiet places elsewhere on campus rather than trying to study in the room.

WHERE TO LOOK FOR HELP

(See also this section in chapter 11.)

The office responsible for services for students with disabilities, or the designated 504 coordinator, will often serve as a liaison to other offices on campus or will direct you to the appropriate people. Try to meet staff who will be working with you from departments such as physical plant, food services, and security. In addition to on-campus resources, the Office for Services for Students with Disabilities will have off-campus referrals for equipment and personal services, including diagnostic testing facilities for learning disabilities. If you have a chronic health or emotional impairment, establish a relationship with staff at the Health and Counseling Services before, or right after, you arrive on campus. They can monitor any medication you're taking and work with you and your health-care providers from home to develop ongoing treatment plans.

EDUCATING YOURSELF

Books: Nonfiction, Anthologies, Biographies, Poetry, Plays

Browne, Susan, et al., eds. *With the Power of Each Breath: A Disabled Women's Anthology.* Pittsburgh: Cleis, 1985.

Cordoni, Barbara. *Living with a Learning Disability.* Rev. ed. Carbondale: Southern Illinois University Press, 1990.

Hoffa, Helynn, and Gary Morgan. *Yes You Can: A Helpbook for the Physically Disabled.* New York: Pharos, 1990.

Keller, Helen. *The Story of My Life.* New York: Bantam, 1990.

Mairs, Nancy. *Plaintext: Deciphering a Woman's Life.* New York: Harper and Row, 1986.

Mangrum, Charles T., and Stephen S. Strichart, eds. *Peterson's Guide to Colleges with Programs for Learning Disabled Students.* 2d ed. Princeton, NJ: Peterson's, 1988.

Matthews, Gwyneth F. *Voices from the Shadows: Women with Disabilities Speak Out.* Toronto: Women's Educational Press, 1983.

Ridenour, Dian, and Jane Johnston. *A Guide to Post-Secondary Educational Opportunities for the Learning Disabled.* Oak Park, IL: Time Out to Enjoy, 1981.

Saxton, Marsha, and Florence Howe, eds. *With Wings: An Anthology of Literature by and about Women with Disabilities.* New York: Feminist Press, 1987.

Scheiber, Barbara, and Jeanne Talpers. *Campus Access for Learning Disabled Students.* Washington, DC: Closer Look, 1985.

Simpson, Eileen. *Reversals: A Personal Account of Victory over Dyslexia.* Boston: Houghton Mifflin, 1979.

Thompson, Karen, and Julie Andrzejewski. *Why Can't Sharon Kowalski Come Home?* San Francisco: Spinsters/Aunt Lute Books, 1988.

Tweed, Prudence K., and Jason C. Tweed. *Colleges That Enable: A Guide to Support Services Offered to Physically Disabled Students on Forty U.S. Campuses.* Oil City, PA: Park Avenue Press, 1989.

Weiner, Florence, comp. *No Apologies: Survival Guide and Handbook for the Disabled, Written by the Real Authorities—People with Disabilities and Their Families.* New York: St. Martin's, 1986.

Women and Disability Awareness Project Staff. *Building Community: A Manual Exploring Issues of Women and Disability.* New York: Educational Equity Concepts, 1984.

Organizations for Information and Assistance

HEATH Resource Center, the National Clearinghouse on Postsecondary Education for Handicapped Individuals
One Dupont Circle
Suite 800
Washington, DC 20036
1-800-544-3284 (Voice/TDD)
202-939-9320 (Voice/TDD)
National Network of Learning Disabled Adults
808 West 22nd St.
Suite F-2
Scottsdale, AZ 85257
602-941-5112
U.S. Department of Justice, Americans with Disabilities Act Information Line
202-514-0301

Films, Videos, TV Shows, Plays

Children of a Lesser God. A romance develops between a teacher at a school for students with hearing impairments and a former student at the school. From Mark Medoff's play.

Coming Home. The Vietnam War affects an angry soldier who has come home with paraplegia, and the army wife/hospital aide who falls in love with him.

The Elephant Man. John Merrick, an Englishman with a physically deforming condition, searches for respect and dignity. From Bernard Pomerantz's play based on a true story.

Gaby. A woman born with cerebral palsy becomes a successful writer. Based on a true story.

The Heart Is a Lonely Hunter. A man with hearing and speech impairments plays a significant helping role for many different people around him. Based on the book by Carson McCullers.

If You Could See What I Hear. Presents the story of the college years of singer Tom Sullivan.

"Life Goes On." Features a major character with Down's syndrome. TV series.

Love Is Never Silent. A young woman has a complex relationship with her parents, who have hearing impairments. Made-for-TV movie.

Mask. A bright, funny teenage boy refuses to let his disfiguring condition interfere with his life. Based on a true story.

The Miracle Worker. Helen Keller, though deaf and blind, first learns to communicate as a child. From William Gibson's play based on a true story.

My Left Foot. Explores the life of Christy Brown, a painter and writer able to use only his left foot. From the book by Shane Connaughton and Jim Sheridan, based on a true story.

Ordinary People. A high school student deals with, and works through, his emotional difficulties. Based on the novel by Judith Guest.

The Other Side of the Mountain, Parts 1 and 2. Jill Kinmont, a competitive skier, learns to live again after being paralyzed in an accident. Based on a true story.

Passion Fish. After an accident leaves her paralyzed, a soap opera actress returns to her home in Louisiana where she is pushed by her personal nurse to get her life together.

A Patch of Blue. A friendship develops between a sheltered young woman who is blind and the man who reaches out to her.

Positive Images: Portraits of Women with Disabilities. Shows the full lives of three women with disabilities. Documentary.

The Promise. A man takes responsibility for his brother, who has a mental illness. Made-for-TV movie.

Rain Man. A man travels across the country with his newly discovered older brother, who has autism.

"Reasonable Doubts." Follows the life and work of an assistant district attorney in Chicago, who happens to be deaf. TV series.

Whoopi Goldberg Live. One segment of this video depicts a woman with a physical disability falling in love and gaining the self-confidence to dance in public.

SEVENTEEN

Size and Appearance

. . .

"Everything has its beauty but not everyone sees it."

—Confucius

. . .

I'll always remember those 2 A.M. surprise fire drills in college. We would stumble out of the building in various degrees of consciousness and dress. The people who had been up late studying or hanging out looked pretty much like they always did. Other women had obviously been awakened out of a sound sleep. Their eyes were still half-closed, they wore sweat pants and t-shirts or flannel nightshirts, and sometimes their shoes didn't match. No makeup or styled hair here. No flattering clothes either. Fire drills were one of the great social equalizers. Many women want to look different in some way:

- "I wish I had your hair."
- "I hate my thighs."
- "I bet she never had a zit in her life."
- "I look like a twelve-year-old boy next to her."
- "Everything I eat goes right to my hips."

The connection between how we look, how we *think* we look, and how we feel about ourselves is a powerful one. It affects what we allow ourselves to ask for, strive for, and expect.

. . .

"Being an overweight college woman, I feel insecure about attending college parties. At these parties I feel as though I can only dance with or 'land' the undesirables. I do many times feel attractive, but only for a fat person. I am also always on diets, hoping one day I will be able to wear tight-fitting clothes and short skirts. I believe it mostly comes down to self-esteem."

—P. A., class of '92

. . .

Terminology

Body image is defined as "a picture of the body as seen through our mind's eye." It's an image that feels real even if it's not. Others' assessment of our physical attractiveness is often quite different from our own critical evaluations of ourselves. Our *visual body image* is what we see when we look at ourselves in a mirror; our *mental image* is how we think about our appearance; and our *historical image* has been shaped, over time, by the praise and criticism we've received from others.[1]

Fattism is an irrational prejudice based on physical characteristics. It equates being large sized with negative traits such as gluttony, laziness, lack of self-esteem, and other emotional problems.[2] This prejudice also leads to discrimination based on weight.

Looksism or sizeism links some qualities to society's standard of attractiveness and other characteristics to its standard of unattractiveness. Comments about short people having short personalities and thin people having wonderful, happy lives are examples. Those who fit more of the media's standards for attractiveness are also unfairly labeled. Consider the "bimbo" label: if you're beautiful you can't be very bright. Or you might be tagged as "stuck up" or aloof.

The fear of being perceived as not attractive enough can also affect those who are considered beautiful, since they may eventually have to confront fears about losing that beauty.[3] Buying into myths that make you feel attractive at one point in time may leave you dependent upon those qualities for your self-esteem. This makes you more vulnerable to losing that self-esteem when your appearance changes.

. . .

"Large women being motherly or Buddhalike or 'happy jolly people' has always annoyed me just like calling a media-perfect woman an ice cold bitch or ice queen. I may be the above but I hate being stereotyped. It is not a direct result of my size."

—L. S., class of '91

. . .

Objectification is defined as looking at people as objects and treating them that way. Women are objectified when attention is focused solely on their appearance to the exclusion of other characteristics. This is dehumanizing.[4]

The movement to confront discrimination and oppression based on size has been called by names such as *size acceptance, size awareness, size rights,* and *fat liberation.* This movement is over twenty years old, but many of its terms and ideals are still not well known. As a result, size discrimination is not taken as seriously as other forms of discrimination. Regardless of what we call objectifying attitudes and behaviors, however, the fact remains that they unfairly judge and mistreat people solely on the basis of their size.

Background Information

Physical attractiveness, or beauty, is something we learn about from the day we're born. Perhaps the most powerful force behind standards of beauty is the popular media. Women especially have been taught to measure themselves against often unreasonable standards of attractiveness. These standards are pretty narrow. How many women do you know who are naturally "thin, shapely or muscular, white, able-bodied, smooth-skinned, young, and glamorous" and whose breasts are whatever size is "in" that year?[5]

Women are particularly plagued by unreasonable standards of weight. Life-insurance tables have been used for many years to classify acceptable weight levels for different heights. Several times I've stood on public scales and been puzzled by the fact that I weighed more than the chart said a woman who was 5'10" should weigh, and yet I looked and felt fine. Recent research has shown that the ideal individual body weight is actually at least ten pounds higher than the medical charts suggest.[6] The obsession with weight in the United States has a powerful, often controlling effect on many women. Nineteen out of twenty American women think they're larger than they really are, even when they're at their "normal" weight, and 75 percent of college women are dieting.[7]

Some women develop dangerous eating disorders in efforts to manage their body image and weight. Chapter 5 explores the issue of eating disorders in more detail.

A number of other physical attributes form our concept of attractiveness and its effect on the quality of our lives. Extremes in height are one such physical attribute. Very short or very tall women often feel awkward. Short women may feel lost in a crowd when they really want to stand out, and tall women may feel they stick out when they only want to fit in. Hair color and style are another attribute. One example is the idea that "blondes have more fun." How many women color their hair to become blondes in hopes of having more fun? How many natural blondes wonder if there's something wrong with them because they're *not* having more fun?

When I was growing up, I always referred to my hair as dirty blonde—I guess it sounded better than light brown. As the gray started coming in a few years ago, I mentioned to my sister that I guessed I wasn't dirty blonde anymore. She just laughed and said, "Carol, you were never any kind of blonde."

Self-image—the way you see yourself—can affect self-esteem—how you feel about yourself. If you believe all the hype and messages about what you "should" look like and you don't look that way, you may falsely assume you're less of a person. Or you may buy products— usually expensive—and undergo processes—often uncomfortable and sometimes dangerous—to help you achieve those looks.

Acne and complexion problems are a natural part of adolescence. Yet over and over we hear that a bad complexion translates into having no social life. If, however, we use some medicated cream, special soap, or supercleaning lotion, we'll be rid of our blackheads and pimples overnight, and then we'll be on the road to being the most popular person in school. Is it really this simple? Cosmetic surgery—facelifts, tummy tucks, breast implants, nose jobs, liposuction—is another example of an industry that thrives on people's insecurities.

Dieting is a multibillion-dollar business that benefits from society's emphasis on appearance. Seventy-six percent of women are dieting for cosmetic reasons, while 80 percent of men are dieting for health reasons.[8] Americans spend thirty-two to thirty-nine billion dollars a year on diet programs.[9] Only 2–5 percent of the population, however, actually loses weight permanently.[10]

In addition to pressures from the diet and fashion industry, which affect all women, large-sized women are also oppressed by jokes, snickers, and comments from others. They have more difficulty finding jobs and getting promotions, and rarely do they see images of themselves on TV and in the movies, except as comic characters or sad ones. Large-sized women are often judged (and perhaps judge themselves) harshly, being told, or believing, that their weight is the cause of everything that goes wrong in their lives.[11]

. . .

"When I embark on any new romantic or career venture, there is for me always the same bottom line. Namely, I will assume that, no matter what happens, no matter how deeply I fall in love or how successful the project, if anything goes wrong it is because I prefer buttered rolls to bran flakes for breakfast. That is, the stock market almost crashed because I refuse to do aerobics. Or: I don't have fear of intimacy, my date has fear-o-flesh. O.K., maybe I'm exaggerating a little. But the paranoia, the impulse to blame everything on excess tonnage, is undeniably real."
—Wendy Wasserstein, "To Live and Diet" [12]

. . .

Large-sized women are not expected to be active and sexual and are often subjected to unfair and critical assumptions from health-care providers. They may be given a lecture and diet instead of receiving treatment and preventative care like other patients.[13] While most people could probably lose *some* weight by changes in their diet and the quality of their food choices, to a great extent heredity and metabolism determine size.[14] Assumptions from medical personnel that it's a woman's fault that she's large sized and that it's more of a psychological problem than a physiological state can be traumatizing to the patient looking for unbiased health care.[15]

Differences in weight and size constitute the area that is most riddled by misinformation and involves the greatest amount of fear, preoccupation, and discrimination. For this reason, I am focusing specifically on large-sized women at several points throughout this chapter. Bias against those who are large sized is often a socially acceptable form of prejudice.[16] In our culture, large-sized women are subjected to attitudes and treatment that are unacceptable by any standards of personal respect. Size oppression is beginning to be labeled as a civil rights issue, and it also overlaps with other forms of oppression: [17]

- *Sexism.* Women are more often the victims of size discrimination than men.
- *Racism.* People from some ethnic groups have a genetic predisposition toward large size.
- *Classism.* Large-sized people are underemployed and aren't hired or promoted as often as average-sized people.
- *Ageism.* Most women gain weight as they age. In some jobs, such as that of flight attendant, there may be weight standards for continued employment—even if ability to do the job is not affected by size.

Large-sized people are sometimes denied access to public accommodations such as transportation and restaurants. The 1990 Americans with Disabilities Act is a civil rights law that has addressed the question of access for those with disabilities. How can we justify not providing similar rights for large-sized people?

Sources of Misunderstanding

Many of our attitudes about large-sized people are based on faulty assumptions and misinformation that lead to misunderstanding.

"Large people eat more than thin people." Evidence shows that, as a group, large-sized people generally eat no more than thin people. People are more likely to be large if they have a history of dieting or a genetic predisposition to be a larger size and shape.[18]

"People who are large can lose weight if they really want to; it's their own fault they're big." There is evidence to suggest that we're each genetically programmed to keep within a natural weight range. What is referred to as setpoint theory describes a bodily system for weight regulation that maintains appetite, metabolism, and body fat. Dieting conflicts with the setpoint mechanism. When a large-sized person diets, she doesn't lose as much weight as a thinner person; the larger person's metabolism slows, her appetite increases, and calories are used more efficiently.[19] Frequent attempts to diet may only serve to increase the setpoint range.[20]

"Being large is unhealthy." There is no general correlation between weight and health; it increases the risk of some diseases and decreases the risk of others.[21] Many health problems attributed to obesity may actually be a result of erratic dieting and the stresses of living in a society that discriminates against large-sized people.[22] Studies indicate that

those who are large sized but not obese actually have the best chance of surviving to old age, with those who are model thin having the least chance.[23]

"Large people can't possibly be in shape." It's possible to be fit and large at the same time. Large-sized women can and do participate in a variety of sports and other activities.

"Large people have a hard time establishing intimate relationships." Many large-sized people are involved in successful intimate relationships with partners who are attracted to them. There's evidence that 5–10 percent of the population is attracted to large-sized people, but the social stigma attached to dating them keeps some from acting on that attraction.[24]

"Dieting helps you become thinner and that's good for you." Within five years of any weight loss, 95–98 percent of the dieters regain those pounds and may even gain additional ones.[25] Erratic dieting—taking off weight, regaining it, taking it off again, regaining it again—is bad for your health, both physically and psychologically.[26] It may actually be healthier to be ten to fifteen pounds above the ideal body weight for your height than to experience the health risks of erratic or "yo-yo" dieting.[27]

ENCOUNTERING AND RESPONDING TO THIS ISSUE

For All Women

Competition between women is part of the beauty myth, and some people's initial impressions of you are based on your outward appearance.[28] The degree to which the environment at your college, and in your residence hall, stresses the importance of physical appearance can affect how you feel about yourself, *if you let it.* If the emphasis is on how you look rather than on who you are, try to focus on those other qualities. Often, it is the more vocal people who determine the subject of conversation. Chances are, there are others around who would prefer to talk about something else. Look for them. Seek out friends and partners who accept you as you are rather than try to change you.

Learn to accept your body, even if it is sometimes a difficult process. Susan Kano, in her wonderful book *Making Peace with Food: Freeing Yourself from the Diet-Weight Obsession,* suggests several ways of developing more positive body awareness. Think about how you *feel* rather than how you *look.* If you currently weigh yourself often, stop. If you currently look at yourself in the mirror often, stop. If you avoid *ever* looking at yourself in the mirror, take some time to look at and admire yourself. Think about your body in a more instrumental way, in terms of how it functions and works for you, rather than in a decorative way, in terms of how it looks in comparison to others' standards of beauty. Learn about your sexuality and appreciate it, and wear clothes that are comfortable for you.[29]

What you think and say to yourself can often affect how you feel about yourself. Your thoughts are within your power to control. You can feel good about yourself, be optimistic, and be able to put criticism in perspective. Other ways of thinking make you feel less positive about yourself. You can change self-defeating thoughts by replacing negative thoughts with more reasonable messages.

Extreme thinking, or evaluating everything as either all good or all bad, for example, can hurt you. There's no middle ground with this kind of thinking: if you can't describe yourself as looking great, then you think you must look awful. Not hearing compliments, or rejecting them, or making unreasonable demands on yourself and how you "should" look will also keep you from recognizing and appreciating your strengths. Avoid feeling responsible for things that really are beyond your control, and don't take them personally. For example, should you really feel like a personal failure because you were one of the 95–98 percent who could not keep weight off permanently? Don't jump to conclusions or assume that it must be something about you that's causing something unpleasant to happen (e.g., your roommate moving out). Some personalities just don't click as roommates, and that's not necessarily one person's fault—no matter what she looks like! Avoid believing that what you feel inside (uncomfortable at a party) is an accurate reflection of what's happening in the outside world (everyone else at the party thinks you look terrible). Maybe it's just a really lousy party! Finally, avoid exaggerating or justifying a big reaction to a small event, for example, feeling that your social life is ruined forever because you don't have a date for Spring Weekend.[30]

Residence-hall life gives you the opportunity to get beyond appearances with people. When you live together so closely, you eventually get to see one another as you really are, including what you look like in the morning, when you're sick, and after staying up all night studying. During my junior year, I remember pulling an all nighter to study for finals with several other women in my hall. One was a woman I didn't know very well. I had always thought of her as *much* more sophisticated and attractive than I. We really seemed to hit it off that night, and I was pleasantly surprised. The next day I passed her in the snack bar as I was coming from my exam and she was going to hers. I was wearing a sweatshirt and jeans that were so dirty they could have walked to the test by themselves. (Actually, they might have done better than I if they had taken the exam!) She was wearing a suit and turban hat. We'd both been up all night, but she looked like she was on her way to a job interview. As we passed one another I said, "How can you look so good?" Out of the corner of her mouth she mumbled, "I always try to look good when I feel like hell." From then on I knew that no matter how we each looked on the outside, there were times when we felt very much the same inside.

Acceptance by desirable groups such as sports teams, sororities, and performance groups is sometimes affected by biases about size and appearance. Is your hair a certain length—long and silky, short, permed? Do you wear certain outfits—painters pants, designer skirts? Are you judged on these kinds of criteria? These biases can put you on an emotional roller coaster unless you're anchored by a strong sense of your own worth as a person.

Learn to feel good about yourself as you are. It's a more constructive use of your energy than striving for some unreasonable goal. Take time to reflect on the personal messages you grew up with about size and appearance. How did your experiences in high school contribute to your internalized feelings? Identify these messages, recognize the manipulation, and replace them with new and more constructive messages.

· · ·

"I really felt more free when I wasn't so concerned about appearance, size, and all those externals—but it did come with the growing process, and when I finally started to believe that I was a good person inside—why does it take us so long to accept this? We need to hear it more and have it more reinforced—not in the coddled sense but in an empowering sense."

—O. L., class of '89

· · ·

For Large-Sized Women

The following suggestions are offered for living successfully in a discriminatory world if you are truly large sized and are staying that way, either by choice or by genetic makeup:[31]

1. No matter what anyone says, you have a right to go anywhere you want to go and do whatever you want to do.
2. If someone makes rude remarks, you can feel hurt, and you can also respond.
3. If you go somewhere and find the aisles too narrow or the chairs too small, you have a right to request that accommodations be made. If you don't feel comfortable making such a request, find an ally to speak up for you.
4. You have the right to feel comfortable and to wear clothes that make you feel that way.
5. You don't have to try to look smaller. Be big and proud. You have the right to take up the space you need.

Identify your interests and which projects you will enjoy and try to shift the focus of your attention onto those and away from appearance. People who are enthusiastically involved in some task often generate great respect from others. They become known as "the woman who organized the recycling project" or "the chair of curriculum committee" or "that singer in choir who did the great solo," rather than "that big woman who lives on the second floor."

For Friends of Large-Sized Women

If you have a roommate, friend, or acquaintance who is large sized, help to create an environment that is supportive for her. Avoid encouraging her to diet; the facts presented earlier in this chapter indicate how unhealthy dieting can actually be for many women.

Avoid talking about your own weight issues with a friend who is large sized. It can be difficult for a woman who is large to hear a relatively thin friend ruminate about needing to lose ten pounds. Talk about other aspects of one another's lives. When you communicate that physical appearance is someone's most important feature, this reinforces the unhealthy bond between appearance and self-esteem. It's one thing to compliment someone about a variety of characteristics, *including* her appearance; it's another to focus exclusively on it. Large-sized people don't often get positive feedback on their appearance, and offering it when it's warranted can make a difference in someone's feelings about herself. Phrase compliments in terms of looking "great" or "relaxed" rather than saying that someone looks "so skinny." The former puts more emphasis on the person while the latter emphasizes her size.

Try to make your residence hall room a comfortable space for large-sized people. It's probably more comfortable for them to use a sturdy chair without arms than to lounge on the bed or sit on the floor.[32] These same accommodations ought to be remembered if you're planning social or educational events, activities, or meetings. Let people wear what they're comfortable wearing. If you tell everyone to "wear blue jeans" to a party, for instance, this may be awkward for a large-sized woman who is much more comfortable, and looks just as attractive, in a casual skirt.

WHERE TO LOOK FOR HELP

(See also this section in chapter 11.)

Many campuses offer courses, workshops, and programs aimed at helping women develop positive feelings about themselves. Wellness programs, perhaps offered through Health Services, Physical Education, or Student Affairs, are a wonderful resource. If your institution has a nutritionist, either through the Health Service or the Food Service, seek her/him out also.

Exercise is another important part of your life. However, exercising with large numbers of people is not comfortable for everyone. Some activities, such as swimming, may be done individually. Some colleges have sections of physical education courses specifically designated for large-sized women. Off-campus health clubs provide opportunities, but again they may not be comfortable environments for everyone. Some clubs may be particularly geared for large-sized women. It can be fun to exercise and share physical activities with others, especially if they respect your right to control your own exercise program.

NAAFA—the National Association to Advance Fat Acceptance— is a primary resource that offers support, educational materials, and opportunities to become involved in human rights activism related to size oppression. Sizeism has been a socially sanctioned prejudice for a long time, and this may limit the knowledgeable resources available to large-sized women on your campus. You may need to play a role in educating some staff.

The attitudes of staff in health and counseling services are especially important. A document entitled "Declaration of Health Rights for Fat People" can be given to your doctor and added to your health file for reference by anyone who treats you. Contact NAAFA (see resources section) for more information. If you encounter a practitioner who makes erroneous assumptions or judgments about you because of your weight, you certainly have the right to correct those assumptions, challenge those judgments, and even to seek a different health-care provider.

EDUCATING YOURSELF

Books: Nonfiction, Anthologies, Biographies, Poetry, Plays

Bennett, William, and Joel Gurin. *The Dieter's Dilemma: Eating Less and Weighing More.* New York: Basic, 1983.

Boston Women's Health Book Collective. *The New Our Bodies, Ourselves.* Updated ed. New York: Simon and Schuster, 1992.

Brown, Laura, and Esther Rothblum, eds. *Overcoming Fear of Fat.* Binghamton, NY: Harrington Park Press, 1989.

Chernin, Kim. *The Obsession: Reflections on the Tyranny of Slenderness.* New York: HarperPerennial, 1982.

Craft, Christine. *Too Old, Too Ugly, and Not Deferential to Men.* New York: Dell, 1989.

Ehrenreich, Barbara, and Deirdre English. *For Her Own Good: 150 Years of the Experts' Advice to Women.* New York: Anchor, 1989.

Ernsberger, Paul, and Paul Haskew. *Rethinking Obesity: An Alternative View of Its Health Implications.* New York: Human Sciences Press, 1987.

Freedman, Rita. *BodyLove: Learning to Like Our Looks—and Ourselves.* New York: Harper and Row, 1988.

Hutchinson, Marcia Germaine. *Transforming Body Image: Learning to Love the Body You Have.* Trumansburg, NY: Crossing Press, 1985.

Kano, Susan. *Making Peace with Food: Freeing Yourself from the Diet-Weight Obsession.* Rev. ed. New York: HarperCollins, 1989.

Millman, Marcia. *Such a Pretty Face: Being Fat in America.* New York: Norton, 1980.

Olds, Ruthanne. *Big and Beautiful: Become the Big, Beautiful Person You Were Meant to Be.* Washington, DC: Acropolis, 1982.

Roberts, Nancy. *Breaking All the Rules: Feeling Good and Looking Great, No Matter What Your Size.* New York: Penguin, 1987.

Steinem, Gloria. *Outrageous Acts and Everyday Rebellions*. New York: Holt,
Rinehart, and Winston, 1983.
Wolf, Naomi. *The Beauty Myth: How Images of Beauty Are Used against
Women*. New York: Morrow, 1991.

Magazines

New Attitude (quarterly newsletter)
NAAFA Feminist Caucus
P.O. Box 163
Northampton, MA 01060
Radiance: A Magazine for Large Women
P.O. Box 30246
Oakland, CA 94604
510-482-0680

Organizations for Information and Assistance

Boston Women's Health Book Collective
240 A Elm St.
Somerville, MA 02144
617-625-0271
National Association to Advance Fat Acceptance (NAAFA)
P.O. Box 188620
Sacramento, CA 95818
916-443-0303
NAAFA Fat Feminist Caucus
P.O. Box 163
Northampton, MA 01060

Films, Videos, TV Shows, Plays

Bagdad Cafe. A woman leaves her husband and finds a home at a cafe in
Nevada.
A Bunny's Tale. As a journalist, Gloria Steinem works undercover as a bunny at
the Playboy Club. Made-for-TV movie from her story in *Outrageous Acts
and Everyday Rebellions*.
Dogfight. Some Marines in the 1960s have a contest to see who can bring the
most unattractive date to a party.
Eating. A group of women talk about food and life.
Foodfright. Women present skits and songs about body image and food. Video
of the musical, cabaret-style stage performance.
Georgy Girl. A woman demonstrates the truth that beauty comes from the heart.
Hairspray. Parodies old teen movies.

Killing Us Softly and *Still Killing Us Softly*. Shows how the advertising industry objectifies women's bodies. Documentaries.

Roxanne. Updates the Cyrano de Bergerac story.

Sugar Baby. A large-sized woman doesn't have to diet to get the man of her dreams. German movie remade as a TV movie called *Babycakes* in the United States.

■ EIGHTEEN ■

Age

❧

• • •

"I have a lot of respect for those who put their life on hold to go back to school. A good friend of mine is thirty-one or thirty-two, raising a child, working part-time, and going to school full-time. I don't know how she does it. I feel overwhelmed working part-time, going to school full-time, and trying to support myself."

—H. B., class of '93

• • •

In August 1986, I was waiting to meet the student head resident staff due to arrive on campus for their training. Late that morning I received a telephone message that one of the head residents would be delayed a day or two because her daughter was in the hospital . . . giving birth to the head resident's first grandchild!

The student, now also a proud grandmother, arrived on campus a day later. A woman in her fifties who had raised a family almost singlehandedly, she had returned to college several years earlier and lived on campus in a traditional residence hall. Now she was completing an academic major in philosophy and working with me during her senior year as a head resident for approximately seventy traditional-aged students.

Terminology and Background Information

Returning adult students are defined as those over twenty-four or twenty-five years old and/or those who enter college after having had their education interrupted.[1] The average age of adult students is from thirty-six to forty.[2] In 1989, over 21 percent of all full-time college students and almost 67 percent of all part-time college students were of nontraditional age.[3] By the mid-1990s, it's estimated that more than half of the students in higher education will be of nontraditional age.[4]

Among these returning students are those who have worked full-time, some who are married, some who have children, some who are divorced, and those who attended college earlier. Some returning students enroll in regular degree programs. Others choose external degree programs requiring limited on-campus attendance and the potential for credit to be granted for previous experience and learning.[5]

Adult learners used to be seen as people with leisure time who took courses primarily for their own personal enrichment.[6] Today's adult students return for a variety of reasons—to prepare for a career or career change, to begin an academic path that will continue through graduate or professional school, or to update their job skills.[7] Increasing numbers of returning students include single-parent heads of households, single women interested in career advancement, students from underrepresented ethnic groups, and those from lower-income backgrounds.[8]

Returning adult students have some distinctive characteristics that influence their approach to college. They generally arrive more highly motivated and with a strong sense of purpose. They've returned for specific reasons and often have particular goals to achieve. They prefer applying skills and knowledge to concrete situations rather than concentrating on abstract concepts, and they tend to be self-directed in most situations. Returning students have a variety of life experiences, including balancing multiple roles, that can be a strong learning resource. A woman who has raised three children, for instance, can bring great practical knowledge to a course on child development.[9]

A student entering or returning to school at an older age will experience academic life differently than a high school graduate who goes directly on to college. These differences help explain how college life affects returning adult students. First, returning students may have to balance their classwork with other priorities such as a partner, children, job, and community responsibilities. They may have to arrange convenient class schedules, child care, and transportation. Being a part-time student also limits financial aid opportunities. Adult students often have to cut back on work hours or withdraw from community involvement, which can result in a loss of economic and/or social status. Their primary role changes from mother or businesswoman or laborer to student. Adjusting to that new role can be difficult and may evoke confusion and even guilt. Returning students have often been out of the traditional academic setting for a number of years. Many lack confidence in their skills and in their ability to compete with traditional-aged students and readjust to the formal educational structure. They often minimize, or fail to recognize the value of, their knowledge, abilities, and experience. This anxiety can affect self-image. The experience of starting over, after perhaps having felt successful in other roles, can be disorienting.[10]

Adult women in higher education often return to school knowing what they want to learn and why, and appreciating the benefits of a college education. Many traditional-aged students don't have this same perspective, simply because they have not had the life experiences that are necessary to focus them in this way. There's nothing inherently "better" about either approach. It's important for students of all ages to consider what they can offer to one another. Gloria Steinem notes that because so many older women have returned to college, the campus is becoming a major place for establishing connections between genera-tions of women.[11]

ENCOUNTERING AND RESPONDING TO THIS ISSUE

For Returning Adult Students

. . .

"The worst homesickness 'case' I remember was from an adult student; she'd come in dragging her feet behind her long face to tell me how much she missed her grandkids."

—T. J., class of '89

. . .

Divorce, children leaving home, a job change, moving, or an unsatis-fying, "going nowhere" job—all can prompt a return to school. The transition will probably affect your view of yourself and the world, your relationships with family and friends, and your daily routines and responsibilities.[12] There's bound to be some confusion and vulnerability as you work to adapt in each of those areas. One way to bridge the gap between your present and new environments is to familiarize yourself with the new community before making the change. Take advantage of any "open house" days at the campus. If possible, attend some activities or events there or spend an afternoon or evening at the library or in the Student Center. If the college you'll be attending is not near your current home, try to do the same with a similar school nearby. Ask your prospective school to put you in touch with some current adult students, and talk with them about the environment.

You probably *will* experience some discomfort. This is entirely natural. The impact of the transition depends on the degree to which it alters your life. The more it does so, the more coping resources you will need and the longer the adaptation process may take.[13] If you make a well-thought-out decision that you need and want to go back to school, the transition will be easier to deal with than if you have to return to school because, for instance, your job is terminated and you can't find another. The more similar the student role is to the roles you're leaving, the less abrupt the transition is likely to feel. If you're moving from a supervisory position in business, for example, you could have a harder time. The more positive past experience you've had with similar transitions, the easier the change should be. If you started college earlier and it was a negative experience for you the first time, perhaps you will bring some anxieties and fears with you. Remember that you're a different person now, and this is a new opportunity. The transition could also be more difficult if there are stresses in other areas of your life such as your children, sick parents, finances, or housing.[14]

. . .

"Financially, it is wise to divest yourself of as many debts as possible before you begin. I plan on paying off my credit cards before going back to grad school. Going to school with debts owed is an additional burden at an already stressful time."

—P. P., class of '84

. . .

A strong and varied support system is important in making a successful transition. If you have a partner and/or family, their encouragement and understanding is crucial. Perhaps once they see you in your new role as a student, they'll recognize and appreciate what that change means for you. The support of your more extended family also helps. It's possible that not everyone will be as excited about your academic experiences as you are. Also, some family members or friends could be uneasy with your changes or even prefer not to see you change for a variety of reasons. This is an issue that needs to be worked out among you. At times you may have to make some difficult choices.

· · ·

"It is important to recognize that personal relationships will change a great deal. The amount of time taken away from family and friends takes its toll on all. There may be some relationships that will falter or go bad."

—P. P., class of '84

· · ·

The term "convoy" is sometimes used to describe systems of support.[15] A convoy is like a buffer of vehicles that travel along with you as you make a trip, helping you feel less alone. A convoy ranges from the most stable presences in your life, such as family and closest friends, to those more likely to leave the picture as your world changes, such as work colleagues and neighbors. Sometimes your convoy is physically present; at other times, you carry it in your head and heart and connect to it by phone and letters. Theirs are the voices you hear when you're trying to work something out. Before you make your transition, take time to identify the more stable parts of your convoy and plan how you will connect to them in the future.

Different people provide you with different kinds of support. Some provide love and affection, others make you feel valued, some are great in a crisis, some give you important information, and others challenge you.[16] Some people provide a variety of things, and others offer only one thing that you may not receive from anyone else. As you make your transition, find new supports to supplement those that become less accessible for you.

Residential and Social Life

· · ·

"Seek out friends of all ages, but especially seek other adult students. I am amazed at the loneliness a person can experience until they meet that first person with whom they can share experiences.

Unfortunately some nontraditional students feel they should not take time for fun and they miss a lot."

—H. D., class of '92

. . .

It's important to build new friendship networks among your adult peers, especially if you're feeling a bit out of place at college. It helps to know that others feel the same way. Consider that many of you are juggling a variety of roles and responsibilities and also feel anxious about studies. New friendships build slowly as people struggle with priorities and managing their time.

Some opportunities for involvement with the institution will help you feel more a part of the college. They also give you a chance to meet and cultivate relationships with a wider variety of people, including other students, faculty, and staff. Find people with similar interests such as student government, academic clubs, theater, twelve-step groups, and intramural athletics. Experiment and take some chances if there's something you really want to do. For example, why not try out for the softball team if you have the time and love to play and compete? Recognize that you have wonderful and important life experiences to bring to any group.

Look also for opportunities to meet students who live on campus and share meals or time with them in the residence halls or at other campus facilities. Get to know various buildings on campus so you feel comfortable in different places. Make the campus feel like *your* campus too. Those of you living at home or off campus and commuting will probably find that it takes more effort to "connect" if you choose to. The effort, though perhaps awkward initially, is worth it in the long run.

. . .

"When I returned, I realized at the end of first semester that I was not very happy. I had focused so much on my academics that I had let my personal life go. I had isolated myself and was very lonely. It's easy to do. Don't let your own life go for the sake of grades, etc. It is important to be good to yourself."

—P. P., class of '84

. . .

If you don't plan to live at home, you'll need to check out the housing options for returning adult students. Perhaps your college provides on-campus residence facilities. Living on campus eliminates the pressure on you to keep up an apartment, prepare your meals, and deal with commuting. It provides more opportunities to meet a variety of people and develop a support system. Living on campus can also put you much closer to classes and extracurricular activities that you might be less likely to attend if you had to travel back to campus for them. If you want a more "traditional" college experience, living on campus is one option to explore.

On the other hand, living on campus can be a difficult adjustment if you're used to having your own apartment or house and if you prefer not to have to adapt to the living habits of others. Also, living on campus, where the emphasis is on youth, may feel uncomfortable. Activities, priorities, and noise levels are set by the traditional-aged population. Some colleges offer separate space such as a particular building, or floor within a building, or suites for adult students.

If you don't have a permanent home elsewhere, be aware of on-campus policies about residence halls closing when the college is not in session. Would you need to find another place to live during these periods, such as over the summer and during vacation breaks? Co-ops, apartments, and group-living options may be possible alternatives, and sometimes faculty on sabbatical look for house sitters.

For Friends of Returning Adult Students

We grew up with certain images of what college students are like. As the student population changes, our expectations need to change accordingly. Several years ago, on the first episode of the TV show "A Different World," when Denise Huxtable met her college roommate, she was initially surprised, curious, and uncomfortable living with Jaleesa, an adult student who had returned to school. As Denise eventually got to know Jaleesa as a person, she got past her stereotyped first impressions and grew to appreciate her.

Returning adult students will probably be in classes with you, and you may also find yourselves in the same living environment. Think about your own feelings, beliefs, attitudes, and assumptions about adult students. I'm often struck by the messages greeting cards send out about age—take a look at them in the store sometime. They equate age with declining health, depleted sex drive, a lack of activity, and a general state of being "over the hill." And yet many of the older women and men at college are precisely the opposite.

· · ·

"Many students assume that I'm a mother . . . furthermore, they think I'm *their* mother. This has happened quite a bit and it's brought up some mixed feelings in me, because there are some students that can't get beyond that. And there are others who have. I have to say my classroom experiences, without exception, have been positive as far as friendship goes. And there have been some very rare but wonderful moments when we've transcended that generation gap."

—H. M., class of '92

· · ·

Some adult students *may* remind you of your mother, but responding to them as if they *were* your mother or were even *like* your mother isn't fair to either of you. There's much you can learn from them, just as there's much they can learn from you. There will certainly be great variety among adult learners, just as there is variety among your traditional-aged peers. You may relate well to some adult students and not to others. Get to know them as individuals.

Often returning students take smaller course loads because of their outside commitments, and sometimes traditional-aged students express resentment about their doing so well because they "only take two or three classes." Some traditional-aged students react to adult students' eagerness in classes without understanding how much they want to be there; how important school is to them; and often what they've had to sacrifice, put on hold, or juggle in order to be a student.

Some returning students are anxious about being in a formal classroom again. Reach out in friendship, extend academic support, and perhaps offer chances for them to become involved on campus. Decisions about time commitments are often more complicated for adult students. If they aren't always able to accept invitations, don't assume they're necessarily rejecting you.

WHERE TO LOOK FOR HELP

(See also this section in chapter 11.)

· · ·

"Students should not be afraid or embarrassed to ask for help. Most faculty and staff recognize that the lives of older students can be very complicated and are usually more than willing to flex or help the student find solutions. Pride tends to prevent students from asking for help."

—P. P., class of '84

. . .

In order to reduce some of the initial anxiety about returning to school, some institutions offer a reentry course or, during the first semester, have sections of some classes set aside for returning adult students. These alternatives can build peer support; focus on common problems of the adult learner; provide smaller classes, with faculty who choose to work with adult students; and provide conveniently scheduled classes, often back to back.[17]

Consult the Financial Aid Office for possible sources of economic help. This office can provide information about qualifications and processes for seeking federal loans, aid from employers, aid from professional organizations and businesses, and assistance from social services.

The health and counseling services may offer help with issues of particular concern to returning adult students—dealing with older parents, chronic illness, divorce, and parenting. Remember to take care of

Doonesbury copyright G. B. Trudeau. Reprinted with permission of *Universal Press Syndicate*. All rights reserved.

yourself, especially if others in your family still need or expect you to provide for them.

EDUCATING YOURSELF

Books: Nonfiction, Anthologies, Biographies, Poetry, Plays

Apps, Jerold. *The Adult Learner on Campus.* New York: Cambridge, 1988.

Aslanian, Carol, and Henry Brickell. *Americans in Transition: Changing Reasons for Adult Learning.* New York: College Board, 1980.

Baruch, Grace, Rosalind Barnett, and Caryl Rivers. *Lifeprints: New Patterns of Love and Work for Today's Women.* New York: Signet, 1983.

Belenky, M. F., et al. *Women's Ways of Knowing: The Development of Self, Voice, and Mind.* New York: Basic, 1988.

Bianchi, Anne. *Smart Choices.* Princeton, NJ: Peterson's, 1990.

Calyx Editorial Collective. *Women and Aging: An Anthology by Women.* Corvallis, OR: Calyx, 1986.

Doress, Paula Brown, Diana Laskin Siegal, and the Midlife and Older Women Book Project in cooperation with the Boston Women's Health Book Collective. *Ourselves, Growing Older: Women Aging with Knowledge and Power.* New York: Simon and Schuster, 1987.

Haponski, William, and Charles McCabe. *New Horizons: The Education and Career Planning Guide for Adults.* Princeton, NJ: Peterson's, 1985.

Hawes, Gene. *The College Board Guide to Going to College while Working: Strategies for Success.* New York: College Board, 1985.

Knowles, Malcolm. *The Adult Learner: A Neglected Species.* 4th ed. Houston, TX: Gulf, 1990.

Lennox, Joan H., and Judith H. Shapiro. *Life Changes: How Women Can Make Courageous Choices.* New York: Crown, 1990.

Schlossberg, Nancy. *Counseling Adults in Transition: Linking Practice with Theory.* New York: Springer, 1984.

———. *Overwhelmed: Coping with Life's Ups and Downs.* New York: Dell., 1991.

Siebert, Al, and Bernardine Gilpin. *Time for College: When You Work, Have a Family, and Want More from Life.* Portland, OR: Practical Psychology Press, 1989.

Articles, Pamphlets, and Papers

Yudkin, Marcia. "I Thought I Was a Terrific Teacher until One Day . . . " *Ms.,* October 1987.

Films, Videos, TV Shows, Plays

Educating Rita. A bored English professor is challenged and renewed by his tutorials with a working-class adult student. From the play by Willy Russell.

Harold and Maude. A young man fascinated by death meets, and is rejuvenated by, a free-spirited 79-year-old woman.

The Heidi Chronicles. A woman's choices during the sixties, seventies, and eighties reflect the changing times and her personal growth. Play by Wendy Wasserstein.

The Women's Room. A woman returns to college after marriage, children, and a divorce. Made-for-TV movie from the book by Marilyn French.

Notes

INTRODUCTION

1. Cherríe Moraga, "The Welder," in *This Bridge Called My Back: Writings by Radical Women of Color,* 2d ed., ed. Cherríe Moraga and Gloria Anzaldúa (New York: Kitchen Table/Women of Color Press, 1983), 219–20.

1. ARRIVAL: INDEPENDENCE, FREEDOM, AND RESPONSIBILITY

1. Ellen Goodman, *Keeping in Touch* (New York: Summit, 1985), 56.
2. Kent M. Weeks, "The Buckley Amendment and College Students' Parents: Limitations and Allowances," in *Working with the Parents of College Students,* ed. Robert D. Cohen. New Directions for Student Services Series, no. 32 (San Francisco: Jossey-Bass, 1985), 17–20.
3. Weeks, "Buckley Amendment," 17–20.
4. M. Lee Upcraft, John N. Gardner, et al., *The Freshman Year Experience* (San Francisco: Jossey-Bass, 1989), 2.

2. FAMILY TIES

1. Susan Forward with Craig Buck, *Toxic Parents: Overcoming Their Hurtful Legacy and Reclaiming Your Life* (New York: Bantam, 1989), 168.
2. Maureen E. Kenny, "College Seniors' Perceptions of Parental Attachments: The Value and Stability of Family Ties," *Journal of College Student Development* 31 (1): 39.
3. Diana K. Conklin, Norman W. Robinson, and Vincent J. D'Andrea, "The Parent-Student-University Relationship," *Journal of College Student Psychotherapy* 2 (1–2): 7–8.

4. Wendy Wasserstein, "My Mother, Then and Now," in *Bachelor Girls* (New York: Knopf, 1990), 20.
5. Harold H. Bloomfield and Leonard Felder, *Making Peace with Your Parents* (New York: Ballantine, 1983), 9.
6. Forward with Buck, *Toxic Parents,* 242–45.
7. Wasserstein, "Big Brother," in *Bachelor Girls,* 83–84.
8. J. S. Peck and J. R. Manocherian, cited in Frederick G. Lopez, "The Impact of Parental Divorce on College Students," in *Dealing with Students from Dysfunctional Families,* ed. Robert I. Witchell. New Directions for Student Services Series, no. 54 (San Francisco: Jossey-Bass, 1991), 19.
9. Frances L. Hoffman, "Developmental Issues, College Students in the 1990s," *Journal of College Student Psychotherapy* 4 (2): 4–5.
10. Lopez, "Impact," 20–29.
11. Timothy M. Rivinus and Marguerite Chadwick, "Can Parents Help Their Children with Substance Abuse?" *Journal of College Student Psychotherapy* 2 (1–2): 132.

3. ASSERTIVENESS AND CONFLICT RESOLUTION

1. Lynn Bloom, Karen Coburn, and Joan Pearlman, *The New Assertive Woman* (New York: Dell, 1975), 21–22.
2. Numbers 1–10 from Bloom, Coburn, and Pearlman, *Assertive Woman,* 32–50. Numbers 11–15 from Manuel Smith, *When I Say No, I Feel Guilty* (New York: Bantam, 1975), 47–71.
3. Student Affairs Office, "Feedback Guidelines" (Smith College, Northampton, MA, handout).
4. Bloom, Coburn, and Pearlman, *Assertive Woman,* 100–120.

4. TAKING CARE OF YOURSELF

1. Fred Leafgren and Dennis Elsenrath, "The Role of Campus Recreation Programs in Institutions of Higher Education," in *Developing Campus Recreation and Wellness Programs,* ed. Fred Leafgren. New Directions in Student Services Series, no. 34 (San Francisco: Jossey-Bass, 1986), 3–5.
2. B. Hettler, cited in Leafgren and Elsenrath, "Recreation Programs," 6–7.
3. Wendy Wasserstein, "The Body Minimal," in *Bachelor Girls* (New York: Knopf, 1990), 24.
4. Carol Otis and Roger Goldingay, *Campus Health Guide: The College Student's Handbook for Healthy Living* (New York: College Board, 1989), 51–52.
5. Otis and Goldingay, *Campus Health,* 52.
6. Otis and Goldingay, *Campus Health,* 42.
7. Sandra Smith and Christopher Smith, *The College Student's Health Guide* (Los Altos, CA: Westchester, 1988), 116–18.
8. Otis and Goldingay, *Campus Health,* 42.

9. Lori W. Turner, et al., *Life Choices: Health Concepts and Strategies*. 2d ed. (St. Paul, MN: West, 1992), 102–12.

10. Turner, *Life Choices*, 103.

11. Otis and Goldingay, *Campus Health*, 10.

12. Turner, *Life Choices*, 150.

13. Otis and Goldingay, *Campus Health*, 7–10.

14. Gregory S. Blimling and Lawrence J. Miltenberger, *The Resident Assistant: Working with College Students in Residence Halls*, 2d ed. (Dubuque, IA: Kendall/Hunt, 1984), 267–68.

15. Blimling and Miltenberger, *Resident Assistant*, 268–75. Also Otis and Goldingay, *Campus Health*, 274–77.

16. Christine Dunkel-Schetter and Marci Lobel, "Stress among Students," in *Crisis Intervention and Prevention*, ed. Harold L. Pruett and Vivian B. Brown. New Directions for Student Services Series, no. 49 (San Francisco: Jossey-Bass, 1990), 19–20.

17. Otis and Goldingay, *Campus Health*, 246–47.

18. Dunkel-Schetter and Lobel, "Stress," 28.

19. Otis and Goldingay, *Campus Health*, 254–55.

20. Smith and Smith, *Health Guide*, 267–68.

21. Vera Robinson, cited in Smith and Smith, *Health Guide*, 22–23.

22. Susan Forward with Craig Buck, *Toxic Parents: Overcoming Their Hurtful Legacy and Reclaiming Your Life* (New York: Bantam, 1989), 226.

23. Forward with Buck, *Toxic Parents*, 227–28.

24. William W. Kates, "Depression Definitions, Clinical Picture and Precipitants" (handout).

25. Otis and Goldingay, *Campus Health*, 278–79.

26. Turner, *Life Choices*, 62.

27. Brent Q. Hafen and Brenda Peterson, "Preventing Suicide" (Brigham Young University, Provo, UT, handout). Also Blanche McHugh and James R. Rooney, "A Matter of Life and Death: Strategies and Resources for Suicide Intervention" (Northern Illinois University, DeKalb, IL, booklet).

28. Herbert Brown, "Recognizing and Helping Others Who May Be Suicidal," *Medical Forum*, October 1981, 3–4.

5. EATING DISORDERS

1. Michele Siegel, Judith Brisman, and Margot Weinshel, *Surviving an Eating Disorder: New Perspectives and Strategies for Family and Friends* (New York: HarperPerennial, 1988), 36.

2. H. Mitzi Doane, *Famine at the Feast: A Therapist's Guide to Working with the Eating Disordered* (Ann Arbor, MI: ERIC Counseling and Personnel Service Clearinghouse, 1983), 13–16.

3. American Psychiatric Association, *Diagnostic and Statistical Manual of Mental Disorders*, 3d ed. (Washington DC: American Psychiatric Association, 1987), 65–67.

4. American Psychiatric Association, *Diagnostic*, 66.
5. Patricia A. Neuman and Patricia A. Halvorson, *Anorexia Nervosa and Bulimia: A Handbook for Counselors and Therapists* (New York: Van Nostrand Reinhold, 1983), 10–11.
6. Siegel, Brisman, and Weinshel, *Surviving*, 19.
7. Neuman and Halvorson, *Anorexia*, 45–55.
8. Doane, *Famine*, 12–17.
9. Vivian Meehan, "Cover Letter" (National Association of Anorexia Nervosa and Associated Disorders, Highland Park, IL, informational packet, 1989).
10. Neuman and Halvorson, *Anorexia*, 22–23.
11. Carol L. Otis and Roger Goldingay, *Campus Health Guide: The College Student's Handbook for Healthy Living* (New York: College Board, 1989), 288. Also Sandra Smith and Christopher Smith, *The College Student's Health Guide* (Los Altos, CA: Westchester, 1988), 325.
12. Maryland Association for Anorexia Nervosa and Bulimia, "Is Someone You Know Dying to Be Thinner?" (Maryland Association for Anorexia Nervosa and Bulimia, Baltimore, MD, brochure).
13. Doane, *Famine*, 20.
14. Doane, *Famine*, 65–66.
15. Lori W. Turner, et al., *Life Choices: Health Concepts and Strategies*, 2d ed. (St. Paul, MN: West, 1992), 160–61.
16. Otis and Goldingay, *Campus Health*, 288.
17. Doane, *Famine*, 67–68.
18. Neuman and Halvorson, *Anorexia*, 74.
19. Katherine Byrne, *A Parent's Guide to Anorexia and Bulimia* (New York: Holt, 1987), 95–101.
20. National Association of Anorexia Nervosa and Associated Disorders, cited in Neuman and Halvorson, *Anorexia*, 48.
21. Otis and Goldingay, *Campus Health*, 302–3.
22. Doane, *Famine*, 51–52.
23. Susan Hurwit, excerpt from "Eating and Identity: A Preventative Program on Eating Disorders," reprinted in the *Anorexia Bulimia Care Newsletter*, March 1988.
24. Byrne, *Parent's Guide*, 45–46.

6. ALCOHOL AND DRUGS

1. Sandra Smith and Christopher Smith, *The College Student's Health Guide* (Los Altos, CA: Westchester, 1988), 200–211.
2. Lillian Donnard, "Alcohol" (Community Counseling and Resource Center, Cockeysville, MD, 1981, brochure).
3. Donnard, "Alcohol."
4. Donnard, "Alcohol."
5. John M. Cavendish, "Colleges Must Protect Their Students from Drug

Abuse While Preserving Their Right to Freedom and Growth," *Chronicle of Higher Education,* November 25, 1987, B1.

6. University of Maryland, "Alcohol" (University of Maryland, College Park, MD, handout).

7. "Student Usage of Illegal Drugs Declines," *Smith College Sophian,* February 11, 1993. Also Bill Frischling and Jeff L. Kart, "Drug Usage Drops on Campus, yet the Crisis Remains," *U: The National College Magazine,* March 1993, 12–13.

8. Mary Crystal Cage, "Probability That Students Will Drink to Become Intoxicated Found to Rise," *Chronicle of Higher Education,* June 10, 1992, A28.

9. John Stossel, "Blitzed, Ripped, and Wasted," "ABC News 20/20," May 7, 1993.

10. University of Maryland, "Alcohol."

11. Donald W. Steele, "Managing Alcohol in Your Life" (Steele Publishing and Consulting, Mansfield, MA, 1986, booklet).

12. Smith and Smith, *Health Guide,* 207–11.

13. Lindsy Van Gelder, "Dependencies of Independent Women," *Ms.,* February 1987, 38.

14. J. S. Rudolf, "Special Problems of Women Alcoholics," reprinted in Barbara Yoder, *The Recovery Resource Book* (New York: Fireside, 1990), 66.

15. Women's Alcohol and Drug Education Project, "Facts about Women, Alcohol, and Drugs," adapted in Yoder, *Recovery,* 71.

16. Massachusetts Department of Public Health, "Facts on Women, Alcohol, and Alcoholism" (Massachusetts Department of Public Health, Boston, MA, handout).

17. Massachusetts Department of Public Health, "Facts."

18. Stephanie S. Covington, cited in Rudolf, "Special Problems," 67.

19. Marian Sandmaier, cited in Rudolf, "Special Problems," 66.

20. Massachusetts Department of Public Health, "Facts."

21. Covington, in Rudolf, "Special Problems," 67.

22. Women's Alcohol and Drug Education Project, "Facts."

23. Dennis Hevasi, "Two Princetonians Sentenced to Jail for Liquor at Eating Club Party," *New York Times,* May 26, 1988, B9.

24. Gregory S. Blimling and Lawrence J. Miltinberger, *The Resident Assistant: Working with College Students in Residence Halls,* 2d ed. (Dubuque, IA: Kendall/Hunt, 1984), 166–67. Also Steele, "Managing." Also verbal communication from various students.

25. R. Jessor and S. Jessor, cited in Blimling and Miltenberger, *Resident Assistant,* 162.

26. Timothy M. Rivinus, "Introduction," *Journal of College Student Psychotherapy* 2 (3–4): 3–4.

27. Timothy M. Rivinus, "Alcohol and Drug Abuse in College Students," *Journal of College Student Psychotherapy* 1 (4): 14–17.

28. Yale University, "Abusing Alcohol? Drugs? Worried You Might Be? I'm Here to Help," *Yale Weekly Bulletin and Calendar,* September 12–19, 1988, 2.

29. Timothy M. Rivinus and Marguerite M. Chadwick, "Can Parents Help Their Children with Substance Abuse?" *Journal of College Student Psychotherapy* 2 (1–2): 128.
30. Health Education Office, "Women and Alcohol Project Fact Sheet" (Smith College, Northampton, MA, 1989, handout).
31. Rivinus, "Introduction," 4.
32. Vernon E. Johnson, *Intervention: How to Help Someone Who Doesn't Want Help* (Minneapolis: Johnson Institute, 1986), 54–55.
33. Johnson, *Intervention*, 61–87. Also Health Education Office, "Women and Alcohol." Also Western Massachusetts Primary Prevention, "Steps in Confronting a Problem Drinker" (Western Massachusetts Primary Prevention, Northampton, MA, handout). Also Jim Wuelfing, "Guidelines for Approaching Someone about Alcohol Abuse" (Adcare Hospital, Worcester, MA, handout).
34. Robert L. DuPont, "The Counselor's Dilemma: Treating Chemical Dependence at College," *Journal of College Student Psychotherapy* 2 (3–4): 59.

7. CODEPENDENCY

1. Barbara Yoder, *The Recovery Resource Book* (New York: Fireside, 1990), 216.
2. Melody Beattie, *Codependent No More: How to Stop Controlling Others and Start Caring for Yourself* (New York: HarperPerennial, 1987), 35–47. Also Anne Wilson Schaef, *Co-Dependence: Misunderstood–Mistreated* (New York: HarperPerennial, 1986), 41–65.
3. Beattie, *Codependent*, 35–47. Also Schaef, *Co-Dependence*, 41–65.
4. Beattie, *Codependent*, 35–47. Also Schaef, *Co-Dependence*, 41–65.
5. Beattie, *Codependent*, 35–47. Also Schaef, *Co-Dependence*, 41–65.
6. Yoder, *Recovery*, 219.
7. T. Magoon, cited in Robert I. Witchel, "The Impact of Dysfunctional Families on College Students' Development," in *Dealing with Students from Dysfunctional Families*, ed. Robert I. Witchel. New Directions for Student Services Series, no. 54 (San Francisco: Jossey-Bass, 1991), 10.
8. Claudia Black's descriptions summarized in Molly Malone, "Dependent on Disorder," *Ms.*, February 1987, 54–55.
9. Sharon Wegscheider-Cruse, *Choicemaking for Co-Dependents, Adult Children, and Spirituality Seekers* (Pompano Beach, FL: Health Communications, 1985), xii.
10. Yoder, *Recovery*, 217. Also Robert Subby, cited in Yoder, *Recovery*, 217. Also Wegscheider-Cruse, *Choicemaking*, 6–8.
11. Yoder, *Recovery*, 217. Also Subby, cited in Yoder, *Recovery*, 217. Also Wegscheider-Cruse, *Choicemaking*, 6–8.
12. Yoder, *Recovery*, 217. Also Subby, cited in Yoder, *Recovery*, 217. Also Wegscheider-Cruse, *Choicemaking*, 6–8.
13. Yoder, *Recovery*, 217. Also Subby, cited in Yoder, *Recovery*, 217. Also Wegscheider-Cruse, *Choicemaking*, 6–8.

14. Schaef, *Co-Dependence,* 68.
15. Claudia Black, cited by Jo Anne Bishop in Bob Sipchen, "Children of Alcoholics Battle Trauma as Adults," *Los Angeles Times,* September 24, 1985, sec. 5.
16. David Suchman and Elizabeth Broughton, "Treatment Alternatives for University Students with Substance Use/Abuse Problems," *Journal of College Student Psychotherapy* 2 (3–4): 138.
17. Witchel, "Impact," 9.
18. Veronica Shoffstall, reprinted in Yoder, *Recovery,* 222.
19. Yoder, *Recovery,* 219.

8. SEXUALITY

1. Fred Bronson, *The Billboard Book of Number One Hits,* 3d ed. (New York: Billboard, 1992), 28.
2. Summary of work by Dr. Alfred Kinsey, in Equity Institute, *Training of Trainers Follow Up* (Equity Institute, Emeryville, CA, 1991, booklet).
3. Karen Johnson and Tom Ferguson, *Trusting Ourselves: The Sourcebook on Psychology for Women* (New York: Atlantic Monthly Press, 1990), 315.
4. Paula Brown Doress and Peggy Nelson Wegman, "Working toward Mutuality: Our Relationships with Men," in *The New Our Bodies Ourselves,* updated ed., Boston Women's Health Book Collective (New York: Simon and Schuster, 1992), 158.
5. Doress and Wegman, "Mutuality," 163.
6. Lesbians Revisions Group, "Loving Women: Lesbian Life and Relationships," in Boston Women's Health Book Collective, *Our Bodies,* 183.
7. Doress and Wegman, "Mutuality," 159.
8. Doress and Wegman, "Mutuality," 167.
9. Doress and Wegman, "Mutuality," 174–75.
10. Johnson and Ferguson, *Trusting Ourselves,* 167–68.
11. Johnson and Ferguson, *Trusting Ourselves,* 167–68.
12. Lesbians Revisions Group, "Loving Women," 185.
13. Gloria Steinem, "Words and Change," in *Outrageous Acts and Everyday Rebellions* (New York: Holt, Rinehart, and Winston, 1983), 153.
14. Beverlie C. Sloane, "Partners in Health" (Columbus, OH: Merrill, 1986), 8.
15. Wendy Sanford with Nancy P. Hawley and Elizabeth Mcgee, "Sexuality," in Boston Women's Health Book Collective, *Our Bodies,* 204.
16. Sanford, "Sexuality," 213–14.
17. Johnson and Ferguson, *Trusting Ourselves,* 303–4.
18. Sandra Smith and Christopher Smith, *The College Student's Health Guide* (Los Altos, CA: Westchester, 1988), 162.
19. Douglas Daher, Carlos Greaves, and Alice Supton, "Sexuality in the College Years," *Journal of College Student Psychotherapy* 2 (1–2): 118.
20. Smith and Smith, *Health Guide,* 162.
21. Sloane, "Partners," 16–17.

22. Jane Hiatt and ETR Associates, "Birth Control Facts" (Network Publications, Santa Cruz, CA, 1985, brochure).
23. Sloane, "Partners," 35.
24. Christina Waters, "Talking with Your Partner about Birth Control" (Network Publications, Santa Cruz, CA, 1984, brochure).
25. Jill Wolhandler, with Ruth Weber, Trude Bennett, and Dana Gallagher, "Abortion," in Boston Women's Health Book Collective, Our Bodies, 359.
26. Sloane, "Partners," 42–43.
27. Wolhandler, et al., "Abortion," 369–70.
28. Carol L. Otis and Roger Goldingay, Campus Health Guide: The College Student's Handbook for Healthy Living (New York: College Board, 1989), 226.
29. Mary Crowe with Judy Norsigian, "Sexually Transmitted Diseases," in Boston Women's Health Book Collective, Our Bodies, 308.
30. Center for Population Options, cited in Reginald Fennell and Chonda Walden, " 'Three for Free' Encourages Responsible Sexual Health Decision Making," Journal of College Student Development 32 (5): 466.
31. "VD? STD? Who, me?" (Private Line, Kenilworth, IL, 1991, brochure).
32. Dr. Leslie Jaffe, written communication to the author, 1992.
33. "VD? STD?"
34. "VD? STD?"
35. "VD? STD?"
36. "VD? STD?"
37. American Council for Healthful Living, "Common Sexually Transmitted Diseases" (American Council for Healthful Living, Orange, NJ, 1988, brochure).
38. Smith and Smith, Health Guide, 175.
39. Mary O'Donnell, cited in Lawrence Biemiller, "Health Experts Assail College for Wasting Opportunity to Lead AIDS-Education Drive among Students," Chronicle of Higher Education, September 23, 1987, A37–38.
40. Joseph Triggs and Diane McDermott, "Short-Term Counseling Strategies for University Students Who Test HIV Positive," Journal of College Student Development 32 (1): 17.
41. Smith and Smith, Health Guide, 192.
42. Smith and Smith, Health Guide, 178.
43. Jaffe, written communication.
44. Women's AIDS Network, "Women and AIDS" (San Francisco AIDS Foundation, San Francisco, CA, 1987, brochure).
45. Jaffe, written communication.
46. Sharon Ybarra, "Women and AIDS: Implications for Counseling," Journal of Counseling and Development 69 (3): 285.
47. Women's AIDS Network, "Women and AIDS."
48. Ybarra, "Women and AIDS," 286.
49. Richard P. Keeling, "AIDS on the College Campus: ACHA Special Report" (Task Force on AIDS of the American College Health Association, Rockville, MD, 1986, report), ix.

50. American College Health Association Task Force on AIDS, "AIDS . . . What Everyone Should Know" (American College Health Association, Rockville, MD, 1987, brochure).
51. American College Health Association, "AIDS."
52. Peter Adair, Janet Cole, and Veronica Selver, "Absolutely Positive," on PBS television program "Point of View," November 1991.
53. Smith and Smith, *Health Guide*, 193–94.
54. Wolhandler, et al., "Abortion," 361–62.

9. SEXUAL HARASSMENT

1. Billie Wright Dziech and Linda L. Weiner, cited in Vita C. Rabinowitz, "Coping with Sexual Harassment," in *Ivory Power: Sexual Harassment on Campus,* ed. Michele A. Paludi (Albany: State University of New York Press, 1990), 104.
2. Louise Fitzgerald, cited in Rabinowitz, "Coping," 104.
3. Massachusetts General Laws, Chapter 151C, sec. 1(e), adapted by Office of Affirmative Action, "In Academic Setting" (Smith College, Northampton, MA, handout).
4. S. Tangri, M. Burt, and L. Johnson, cited in Michele A. Paludi, Marc Grossman, et al., "Myths and Realities," in Paludi, *Ivory Power,* 7–8.
5. Bernice Sandler, cited in A. Gibbs and R. B. Balthrope, "Sexual Harassment in the Workplace and Its Ramifications for Academia," *Journal of College Student Personnel* 23 (2): 158.
6. Derived from work by Catharine MacKinnon and F. Till, cited in Louise F. Fitzgerald, "Sexual Harassment: The Definition and Measurement of a Construct," in Paludi, *Ivory Power,* 22–34.
7. From work by MacKinnon and Till, cited in Fitzgerald, "Definition," 33.
8. Kathryn Quina, "The Victimizations of Women," in Paludi, *Ivory Power,* 93–95.
9. R. Whitmore, cited in Sabrina C. Chapman, "Women Students," in *The Freshman Year Experience,* M. Lee Upcraft, John N. Gardner, et al. (San Francisco: Jossey-Bass, 1989), 289.
10. Kathy Hotelling, "Sexual Harassment: A Problem Shielded by Silence," *Journal of Counseling and Development* 69 (6): 497.
11. Rabinowitz, "Coping," 105.
12. Darlene C. DeFour, "The Interface of Racism and Sexism on College Campuses," in Paludi, *Ivory Power,* 48–49.
13. Sexual Harassment Panel of Hunter College, "The Student in the Back Row: Avoiding Sexual Harassment in the Classroom," in Paludi, *Ivory Power,* 283–85. Also Advisory Committee on the Status of Women, "Summary: Assessing Sexual Harassment and Public Safety: A Survey of Cornell Women" (Cornell University, Ithaca, NY, 1987, report), 1–2.
14. Mary Koss, "Changed Lives: The Psychological Impact of Sexual Harassment," in Paludi, *Ivory Power,* 78.

15. Fitzgerald, et al., cited in Sue Rosenberg Zalk, "Men in the Academy," in Paludi, *Ivory Power*, 142.
16. Middlebury College, "Concerning Sexual Harassment" (Middlebury College, Middlebury, VT, brochure).
17. Rabinowitz, "Coping," 107.
18. Montana Katz and Veronica Vieland, *Get Smart! A Woman's Guide to Equality on Campus* (New York: Feminist Press, 1988), 64.
19. Billie Wright Dziech and Linda Weiner, *The Lecherous Professor: Sexual Harassment on Campus* (Boston: Beacon, 1984), 122–24.
20. Rabinowitz, "Coping," 106–8.
21. Rabinowitz, "Coping," 112–13.
22. Bernice Sandler, "Writing a Letter to the Sexual Harasser: Another Way of Dealing with the Problem" (Project on the Status and Education of Women, Association of American Colleges, Washington, DC, 1983, report).
23. Quina, "Victimizations," 95–96.
24. Koss, "Changed Lives," 73–75.
25. Helen Remick, et al., "Investigating Complaints of Sexual Harassment," in Paludi, *Ivory Power*, 196–97.
26. Remick, et al., "Investigating," 198.
27. Remick, et al., "Investigating," 196–98.
28. Sandra Shullman and Barbara Watts, "Legal Issues," in Paludi, *Ivory Power*, 258.
29. National Association for Women in Education, *About Women on Campus* 1 (2): 5.
30. Shullman and Watts, "Legal," 260–61.
31. Jean O'Gorman Hughes and Bernice R. Sandler, "Peer Harassment: Hassles for Women on Campus" (Project on the Status and Education of Women, Association of American Colleges, Washington, DC, 1988, report), 2–5.
32. Hughes and Sandler, "Peer Harassment," 4–5.
33. Hughes and Sandler, "Peer Harassment," 1–3.
34. Hughes and Sandler, "Peer Harassment," 5–6.
35. Hughes and Sandler, "Peer Harassment," 6.
36. Hughes and Sandler, "Peer Harassment," 3.

10. SEXUAL ABUSE, RAPE, AND PERSONAL SAFETY

1. Jodie Foster, Academy Awards acceptance speech, 1989.
2. "Editors Notes," in *Responding to Violence on Campus*, ed. Jan-Mitchell Sherrill and Dorothy G. Siegel. New Directions for Student Services Series, no. 47 (San Francisco: Jossey-Bass, 1989), 1.
3. Ellen Bass and Laura Davis, *The Courage to Heal: A Guide for Women Survivors of Child Sexual Abuse* (New York: HarperCollins, 1988), 234–35.
4. Karen Johnson and Tom Ferguson, *Trusting Ourselves: The Sourcebook on Psychology for Women* (New York: Atlantic Monthly Press, 1990), 402.
5. Robert I. Witchel, "College-Student Survivors of Incest and Other Child

Sexual Abuse," in *Dealing with Students from Dysfunctional Families,* ed. Robert I. Witchel. New Directions for Student Services Series, no. 54 (San Francisco: Jossey-Bass, 1991), 64.

6. Witchel, "Survivors," 64.
7. Bass and Davis, *Courage,* 21–22.
8. Robin Warshaw, *I Never Called It Rape: The Ms. Report on Recognizing, Fighting, and Surviving Date Rape* (New York: HarperPerennial, 1988), 2.
9. Looking Up, "Looking Up: Ending the Silence on Child Sexual Abuse" (Looking Up, Augusta, ME, brochure).
10. Ellen Goodman, "The Double Standard," in *Keeping in Touch* (New York: Summit, 1985), 284–85.
11. C. L. Muehlenhard and M. A. Linton, cited in Nancy Greene Cerio, "Counseling Victims of Perpetrators of Campus Violence," in Sherrill and Siegel, *Responding to Violence,* 60.
12. E. J. Kanin and S. B. Parcell, cited in Johnson and Ferguson, *Trusting Ourselves,* 393.
13. N. M. Malamuth, cited in Johnson and Ferguson, *Trusting Ourselves,* 393.
14. J. M. Makepeace, cited in Linda P. Rouse, "College Students and the Legacy of Spouse Abuse," in Witchel, *Dysfunctional Families,* 59.
15. Rouse, "Legacy," 52.
16. Rouse, "Legacy," 52–53.
17. Susan Morrow and Donna M. Hawxhurst, "Lesbian Partner Abuse: Implications for Therapists," *Journal of Counseling and Development* 68 (1): 58.
18. L. E. Walker, cited in Morrow and Hawxhurst, "Lesbian Partners," 59.
19. Ralph L. Rickgarn, "Violence in Residence Halls: Campus Domestic Violence," in Sherrill and Siegel, *Responding to Violence,* 34–35.
20. Bass and Davis, *Courage,* 20.
21. Witchel, "Survivors," 67–72.
22. Bass and Davis, *Courage,* 42–43.
23. Carol Mithers, "Incest and the Law," *New York Times Magazine,* October 21, 1990, 44 ff.
24. Bass and Davis, *Courage,* 48–52. Also Witchel, "Survivors," 67–72.
25. Warshaw, *Never Called,* 13.
26. Warshaw, *Never Called,* 1.
27. Warshaw, *Never Called,* 1.
28. Warshaw, *Never Called,* 8–10.
29. Project on the Status and Education of Women, "The Problem of Rape on Campus" (Association of American Colleges, Washington, DC, report), 2.
30. Project SORT, "Rape, Sexual Assault, and Sexual Harassment" (Towson State University, Towson, MD, pamphlet), 2.
31. Students Together against Abusive Relationships, "Early Warning Signs and What You Can Do to Help Friends and to Help Yourself" (Smith College, Northampton, MA, handout).
32. Massachusetts Coalition of Battered Women Service Groups, "Ten Common Questions about Domestic Violence" (Massachusetts Coalition of Battered Women Service Groups, Boston, MA, handout).

33. Massachusetts Coalition, "Ten Questions."
34. Students Together against Abusive Relationships, "Early Warning Signs."
35. Elie Axelroth, "Retrospective Incest Group Therapy for University Women," *Journal of College Student Psychotherapy* 5 (2): 92.
36. Witchel, "Survivors," 66–67.
37. Witchel, "Survivors," 74.
38. Bass and Davis, *Courage*, 184–86.
39. Bass and Davis, *Courage*, 321–44.
40. Bass and Davis, *Courage*, 219–20.
41. Warshaw, *Never Called*, 57.
42. Health Education Office, "Rape Trauma Syndrome" (Smith College, Northampton, MA, handout).
43. Health Education Office, "Syndrome."
44. Health Education Office, "Syndrome."
45. Health Education Office, "Syndrome."
46. Project SORT, "Rape." Also Warshaw, *Never Called*, 162–65.
47. Project SORT, "Rape." Also Warshaw, *Never Called*, 162–65.
48. Project SORT, "Rape." Also Warshaw, *Never Called*, 162–65.
49. Aileen Adams and Gail Arbarbanel, "Sexual Assault on Campus: What Colleges Can Do" (Santa Monica, CA: Rape Treatment Center, Santa Monica Hospital Medical Center, 1988, report), v.
50. Warshaw, *Never Called*, 121–29.
51. Eileen N. Wagner, "Campus Victims of Date Rape Should Consider Civil Lawsuits as Alternatives to Criminal Charges or Colleges' Procedures," *Chronicle of Higher Education*, August 7, 1991, B2.
52. Warshaw, *Never Called*, 121–29.
53. Warshaw, *Never Called*, 158–61.
54. Rape Crisis Center, "A Note to Those Closest to Rape Victims: Families, Spouses, and Friends" (Rape Crisis Center, Washington, DC, 1974, newsletter).
55. University of Massachusetts Counselor/Advocates against Violence against Women, et al., "Rape and Sexual Assault: Prevention and Treatment" (University of Massachusetts, Amherst, MA, pamphlet). Also R. R. Gonzalez, "Date Rape: Developing a Prevention Strategy" (Hampshire County Rape Information and Prevention Project, Northampton, MA, pamphlet). Also "Rape: A Handbook of Preventative Measures" (Family Planning Council of Western Massachusetts, Northampton, MA, pamphlet). Also Jean O'Gorman Hughes and Bernice R. Sandler, "'Friends' Raping Friends: Could It Happen to You?" (Project on the Status and Education of Women, Association of American Colleges, Washington, DC, 1987, report), 6. Also Robin Warshaw, "How to Identify a Date Rapist," *Woman*, May 1990, 28.
56. Warshaw, *Never Called*, 32.
57. Warshaw, *Never Called*, 135.
58. "Codes and Classes on Sex Offenses Draw Praise," *New York Times*, April 12, 1992, 53.

11. LIVING IN A DIVERSE ENVIRONMENT

1. "The American University and the Pluralistic Ideal" (Brown University, Providence, RI, 1986, report), ix.
2. *Webster's New Collegiate Dictionary* (Springfield, MA: Merriam, 1977), 68.
3. Nancy Schniedewind and Ellen E. Davidson, *Open Minds to Equality* (Englewood Cliffs, NJ: Prentice Hall, 1983), 87.
4. Joanne Salus, comp., "A Common Thread: Shared Heritage through Diverse Cultures—an Introduction to the Asian American Experience" (University of Massachusetts Center for Social Issues/Housing Services, Amherst, MA, 1988, booklet).
5. Equity Institute, "A Report On: An Introductory Program on Multicultural Awareness" (Equity Insititute, Emeryville, CA, 1988, booklet), 6.
6. Fletcher Blanchard, presentation given at Multicultural Organizational Development Seminar, Smith College, Northampton, MA, 1988.
7. Daniel Goleman, " 'Useful' Modes of Thinking Contribute to the Power of Prejudice," *New York Times*, May 12, 1987, C1 and C10.
8. Thomas Pettigrew, quoted in Goleman, "Prejudice," C10.
9. Student Affairs Office, "Definitions, Specific Manifestations of Oppression, and Preferred Terms" (Smith College, Northampton, MA, 1989, handout).
10. Equity Institute, "Introductory Program," 6.
11. Student Affairs Office, "Definitions."
12. Donald R. Atkinson, George Morten, and Derald Wing Sue, *Counseling American Minorities: A Cross-Cultural Perspective,* 3d ed. (Dubuque, IA: Brown, 1989), 7.
13. Equity Institute, "Training of Trainers Intensive Program" (Equity Institute, Emeryville, CA, 1991, booklet), 7.
14. Mitsuye Yamada, "Invisibility Is an Unnatural Disaster: Reflections of an Asian American Woman," in *This Bridge Called My Back: Writings by Radical Women of Color,* 2d ed., ed. Cherríe Moraga and Gloria Anzaldúa (New York: Kitchen Table/Women of Color Press, 1983), 36–37.
15. Arthur Levine, "Who Are Today's Freshmen?" in *The Freshman Year Experience,* M. Lee Upcraft, John N. Gardner, et al. (San Francisco: Jossey-Bass, 1989), 15–16.
16. U.S. Bureau of the Census statistics, cited in *One-Third of a Nation: A Report on Minority Participation in Education and American Life* (American Council on Education, Washington, DC, 1988), 2.
17. Census, *One-Third,* 2.
18. Laura F. Rothstein, "Campuses and the Disabled," *Chronicle of Higher Education,* September 4, 1991, B3 and B10.
19. Gerald L. Stone and James Archer, Jr., "College and University Counseling Centers in the 1990s: Challenges and Limits," *Counseling Psychologist* 18 (4): 543.
20. Michele N-K Collison, "Judge Cites First-Amendment Protection in Over-

turning Suspension of Fraternity," *Chronicle of Higher Education,* September 4, 1991, A45–46.

21. Nilanjana Dasgupta, written communication to the author, 1990.

22. Carole L. Johnson, presentation given at Multicultural Organizational Development Seminar, Smith College, Northampton, MA, 1988.

23. Amoja Three Rivers, *Cultural Etiquette: A Guide for the Well-Intentioned* (Indian Valley, VA: Market Wimmin, 1990), 20.

24. W. Terrell Jones, "Perspectives on Ethnicity," in *Evolving Theoretical Perspectives on Students,* ed. Leila V. Moore. New Directions in Student Services Series, no. 51 (San Francisco: Jossey-Bass, 1990), 69.

25. Jacqueline Fleming, *Blacks in College* (San Francisco: Jossey-Bass, 1984), 2.

26. Fleming, *Blacks,* 1–2.

27. Martin Niemoller, "In Unity," University Fellowship of Metropolitan Community Churches, August/September, 1978, quoted in Schniedewind and Davidson, *Open Minds,* 222.

28. Equity Institute, "Training of Trainers."

29. Felice Yeskel and Charmaine Wijeyesinghe, "Responding to Heterosexism on Campus" (DiversityWorks, Pelham, MA, 1990, booklet).

30. Judy H. Katz, *White Awareness: Handbook for Anti-Racism Training* (Norman: University of Oklahoma Press, 1978), 11–12.

31. Douglas Biklen and Robert Bogdan, "Media Portrayals of Disabled People: A Study in Stereotypes," reprinted in Equity Institute, "Training of Trainers."

32. "Suggested Roommate Intervention Strategy" (American College Personnel Association Workshop, 1989, handout).

33. Dick Scott, "Working with Gay and Lesbian Student Organizations," in *Beyond Tolerance: Gays, Lesbians, and Bisexuals on Campus,* ed. Nancy J. Evans and Vernon A. Wall (Alexandria, VA: American College Personnel Association, 1991), 118–21.

34. Office of Human Relations, "Against Racial Harassment" (University of Massachusetts, Amherst, MA, brochure).

35. Holly Near, *Fire in the Rain . . . Singer in the Storm* (New York: Morrow, 1990), 139–40.

36. Audre Lorde, *Sister Outsider: Essays and Speeches* (Trumansburg, NY: Crossing Press, 1984), 118.

12. ETHNICITY AND CULTURE

1. Eric V. Copage, *Kwanzaa: An African-American Celebration of Culture and Cooking* (New York: Morrow, 1991), xiii–xxiv.

2. Donald R. Atkinson, George Morten, and Derald Wing Sue, *Counseling American Minorities: A Cross-Cultural Perspective,* 3d ed. (Dubuque, IA: Brown, 1989), 3–4.

3. Michael Guillen speaking on the ABC-TV news special, "Prejudice: Answering Children's Questions," April 25, 1992.

4. L. Wirth, cited in Atkinson, Morten, and Sue, *Counseling American Minorities, 8.*

5. Gloria Steinem, "If Men Could Menstruate," in *Outrageous Acts and Everyday Rebellions* (New York: Holt, Rinehart, and Winston, 1983), 337.

6. P. I. Rose, cited in Atkinson, Morten, and Sue, *Counseling American Minorities, 4–5.*

7. R. Linton, cited in Atkinson, Morten, and Sue, *Counseling American Minorities, 5.*

8. Paul Pederson, *A Handbook for Developing Multicultural Awareness* (Alexandria, VA: American Association for Counseling and Development, 1991), 55.

9. Atkinson, Morten, and Sue, *Counseling American Minorities, 6.*

10. *Webster's New Collegiate Dictionary* (Springfield, MA: Merriam, 1977), 733.

11. Atkinson, Morten, and Sue, *Counseling American Minorities, 7.*

12. Jewelle Taylor Gibbs and Larke Nahme Huang, "A Conceptual Framework for Assessing and Treating Minority Youth," in *Children of Color: Psychological Interventions with Minority Youth,* Jewelle Taylor Gibbs, Larke Nahme Huang, et al. (San Francisco: Jossey-Bass, 1989), 10.

13. Joan Lester, "What Happens When the Myths Are Found to Be Untrue," Equity Institute, Emeryville, CA, October 1, 1987, essay, 2.

14. Joseph G. Ponterotto, "Racial/Ethnic Minority Women Students in Higher Education: A Status Report," in *Affirmative Action on Campus,* ed. Joseph G. Ponterotto, Diane E. Lewis, and Robin Bullington. New Directions for Student Services Series, no. 52 (San Francisco: Jossey-Bass, 1990), 46.

15. Deborah King, "A Guide to Racial and Ethnic Identity: Preferred and Disfavored Terms" (SOAR conference at Dartmouth College, Hanover, NH, 1988, handout).

16. Janet E. Helms, "Toward a Theoretical Explanation of the Effects of Race on Counseling: A Black and White Model," *Counseling Psychologist* 12 (4): 153–64. Also Robert T. Carter, "The Relationship between Racism and Racial Identity among White Americans," *Journal of Counseling and Development* 69 (1): 46–50. Also W. Terrell Jones and Art Constantino, "Agent of Oppression Group Awareness" (Equity Institute, Emeryville, CA, handout).

17. W. E. Cross, Jr., "The Thomas and Cross Models of Psychological Nigrescence: A Review," *Journal of Black Psychology* 5: 13–31. Also W. Terrell Jones and Art Constantino, "Target Group Awareness" (Equity Institute, Emeryville, CA, handout). Also Atkinson, Morten, and Sue, *Counseling American Minorities,* 35–46. Also Helms, "Effects of Race," 153–64.

18. W. S. Carlos Poston, "The Biracial Identity Development Model: A Needed Addition," *Journal of Counseling and Development* 69 (2): 153–54.

19. Courtland C. Lee, "Promises and Pitfalls of Multicultural Counseling," in *Multicultural Issues in Counseling: New Approaches to Diversity,* ed. Courtland C. Lee and Bernard L. Richardson (Alexandria, VA: American Association for Counseling and Development, 1991), 13–16.

20. Gerardo M. Gonzalez, "Cuban Americans: Counseling and Human Development Issues, Problems, and Approaches," in Lee and Richardson, *Multicultural Issues,* 161.
21. King, "A Guide."
22. History summary from W. Terrell Jones, "Perspectives on Ethnicity," in *Evolving Theoretical Perspectives,* ed. Leila V. Moore. New Directions in Student Services Series, no. 51 (San Francisco: Jossey-Bass, 1990), 65.
23. Jewelle Taylor Gibbs, "Black American Adolescents," in Gibbs, Huang, et al., *Children of Color,* 184–86.
24. A. Hilliard, cited in Lissa J. Van Bebber, "Integrating Diversity into Traditional Resident Assistant Courses," in *Cultural Pluralism on Campus,* Harold E. Cheatham, et al. (Alexandria, VA: American College Personnel Association, 1991), 96–97.
25. King, "A Guide."
26. King, "A Guide."
27. Joanne Salus, comp., "A Common Thread: Shared Heritage through Diverse Cultures—an Introduction to the Asian American Experience" (University of Massachusetts Center for Social Issues/Housing Services, Amherst, MA, 1988, booklet).
28. Satsukie Ina Tomine, "Counseling Japanese Americans from Internment to Reparation," in Lee and Richardson, *Multicultural Issues,* 92.
29. Jodine Mayberry, *Recent American Immigrants: Koreans* (New York: Watts, 1991), 9.
30. Donna Nagata, "Japanese American Children and Adolescents," in Gibbs, Huang, et al., *Children of Color,* 81.
31. Tomine, "Counseling Japanese Americans," 94.
32. Derald Wing Sue, "Ethnic Identity: The Impact of Two Cultures on the Psychological Development of Asians in America," in Atkinson, Morten, and Sue, *Counseling American Minorities,* 104–5.
33. Larke Nahme Huang and Yu-Wen Ying, "Chinese American Children and Adolescents," in Gibbs, Huang, et al., *Children of Color,* 36–37. Also Tomine, "Counseling Japanese Americans," 93.
34. Imogene C. Brower, "Counseling Vietnamese," in Atkinson, Morten, and Sue, *Counseling American Minorities,* 133–34.
35. Ponterotto, "Racial/Ethnic," 54–56.
36. Fali Chothia, "Other Cultures, Other Ways: Why Can't Everyone Be like Us?" (Center for the Orientation of Americans Going Abroad, Olney, MD, booklet), 5–14.
37. King, "A Guide."
38. King, "A Guide."
39. Patricia Arrendondo, "Counseling Latinas," in Lee and Richardson, *Multicultural Issues,* 143.
40. King, "A Guide."
41. Oscar Ramirez, "Mexican American Children," in Gibbs, Huang, et al., *Children of Color,* 227–29.
42. Ramon A. Laval, Efrain A. Gomez, and Pedro Ruiz, "A Language Minority:

Hispanic Americans and Mental Health Care," in Atkinson, Morten, and Sue, *Counseling American Minorities,* 244–46.

43. Roger D. Herring, "Counseling Native American Youth," in Lee and Richardson, *Multicultural Issues,* 38.

44. Herring, "Native American," 37.

45. Jones, "Perspectives," 67–68.

46. Frances Everett, Noble Proctor, and Betty Cartmell, "Providing Psychological Services to American Indian Children and Families," in Atkinson, Morten, and Sue, *Counseling American Minorities,* 60–67.

47. Everett, Proctor, and Cartmell, "American Indian," 57–60.

48. Jeanne L. Higbee, "The Role of Developmental Education in Promoting Pluralism," in Cheatham, et al., *Cultural Pluralism,* 77–79.

49. Lawrence W. Young, Jr., "The Minority Cultural Center on a Predominantly White Campus," in Cheatham, et al., *Cultural Pluralism,* 46–47.

50. Judy H. Katz, *White Awareness: Handbook for Anti-Racism Training* (Norman: University of Oklahoma Press, 1978), 27.

51. Thomas Coffman, cited in Pederson, *A Handbook,* 59.

52. Devika Choudhuri, written communication to the author, 1989.

13. RELIGION

1. Ntozake Shange, *for colored girls who have considered suicide/when the rainbow is enuf* (New York: Collier, 1989), 63.

2. John Butler, "An Overview of Religion on Campus," in *Religion on Campus,* ed. John Butler. New Directions for Student Services Series, no. 46 (San Francisco: Jossey-Bass, 1989), 15.

3. Ann Marie and Donald Coleman, "Student Life and the Global Community," in Butler, *Religion,* 69–70. Also Karen Levin Coburn and Madge Lawerence Treeger, *Letting Go: A Parents' Guide to Today's College Experience* (Bethesda, MD: Adler and Adler, 1988), 56.

4. *Webster's New Collegiate Dictionary* (Springfield, MA: Merriam, 1977), 23.

5. Sister Loretta Pastva, *Great Religions of the World* (Winona, MN: Saint Mary's Press, 1986), 195–223.

6. Pastva, *Great Religions,* 173–92. Also Christopher Barlow, *Today's World: Islam* (London: Batsford Academic and Educational, 1983), 48–49.

7. Pastva, *Great Religions,* 71–84.

8. Pastva, *Great Religions,* 71–84.

9. Pastva, *Great Religions,* 87–102.

10. Pastva, *Great Religions,* 111–18.

11. Marcus Bach, *Major Religions of the World* (Marina del Ray, CA: DeVorss and Co., 1959), 84.

12. Pastva, *Great Religions,* 147–70.

13. Charles Patterson, *Anti-Semitism: The Road to the Holocaust and Beyond* (New York: Walker, 1982), 8.

14. Lewis M. Hopfe, *Religions of the World,* 4th ed. (New York: Macmillan, 1987), 338–39.
15. Patterson, *Anti-Semitism,* 8–9.
16. Patterson, *Anti-Semitism,* 8–9. Also Hopfe, *Religions,* 338–39.
17. Larry Goldbaum, "Notes on the Cycle of Jewish Oppression and the Meaning of the Holocaust," in Equity Institute, "Training of Trainers Intensive Program" (Equity Institute, Emeryville, CA, 1991, booklet).
18. Deborah Kutonplon, et al., "Overcoming Oppression in Groups" (University of Massachusetts Student Center for Educational Research and Advocacy, Amherst, MA, 1987, booklet).
19. Goldbaum, "Cycle."
20. Student Center for Educational Research and Advocacy and the Office of Human Relations, "Anti-Semitism: What Is It, What You Can Do about It" (University of Massachusetts, Amherst, MA, brochure).
21. Francine Klagsbrun, "JAP: The New Anti-Semitic Code Word," *Lilith: The Jewish Women's Magazine* 17: n. p.
22. Sherry Chayat, "JAP-Baiting on the College Scene," *Lilith: The Jewish Women's Magazine* 17: n. p.
23. Pastva, *Great Religions,* 181.
24. George W. Jones, "Knowing the Legal and Political Opportunities," in Butler, *Religion,* 41.
25. Pastva, *Great Religions,* 80.
26. Sonali Shah, "Swastika Creates Controversy," *Smith College Sophian,* October 9, 1989.
27. Amherst Educational Publishing, "The Multicultural Resource Calendar, 1993–1994" (Amherst, MA: Amherst Educational Publishing, 1993). Also Office of the Chaplains, "Religious Holidays, 1990–91" (Smith College, Northampton, MA, handout).
28. John Snelling, *Buddhist Festivals* (Vero Beach, FL: Rourke, 1987), 40.
29. Nancy Martin, *Religions of the World: Christianity* (New York: Bookwright, 1986), 38.
30. Pastva, *Great Religions,* 207–10.
31. Snelling, *Buddhist Festivals,* 19.
32. Isaac Pennington was one of the founding Quaker fathers.
33. Butler, "Overview," 9–10.
34. James Rudin and Marcia Rudin, *Prison or Paradise: The New Religious Cults* (Philadelphia: Fortress, 1980), 15. Also Marcia Rudin, personal communication to the author, April 2, 1993.
35. Office of the Chaplains, "Protect Yourself from Destructive Religious Groups!" (Smith College, Northampton, MA, brochure).
36. Pastva, *Great Religions,* 233–34.
37. Office of the Chaplains, "Protect Yourself."
38. Ernest L. Boyer, *College: The Undergraduate Experience* (New York: HarperPerennial, 1988), 187.

14. SEXUAL ORIENTATION

1. Anonymous, "We Are You," *Smith Alumnae Quarterly*, Summer 1991, 5.
2. Heidi Levine and Nancy J. Evans, "The Development of Gay, Lesbian, and Bisexual Identities," in *Beyond Tolerance: Gays, Lesbians, and Bisexuals on Campus*, ed. Nancy J. Evans and Vernon A. Wall (Alexandria, VA: American College Personnel Association, 1991), 16–18.
3. Felice Yeskel and Charmaine Wijeyesinghe, "Responding to Heterosexism on Campus" (DiversityWorks, Pelham, MA, 1990, booklet).
4. Yeskel and Wijeyesinghe, "Responding."
5. Yeskel and Wijeyesinghe, "Responding."
6. Harvey Fierstein, *Torch Song Trilogy* (New York: Gay Presses of New York, 1981), 120.
7. Yeskel and Wijeyesinghe, "Responding."
8. Alexander Astin, "Attitudes and Characteristics of Freshmen," *Chronicle of Higher Education*, August 28, 1991, 14.
9. Kathy Obear, "Homophobia," in Evans and Wall, *Beyond Tolerance*, 41–42.
10. Obear, "Homophobia," 46.
11. Obear, "Homophobia," 46.
12. Arthur W. Chickering, *Education and Identity* (San Francisco: Jossey-Bass, 1969), 83.
13. Arthur Chickering and Erik Erikson, cited in Nancy J. Evans and Heidi Levine, "Perspectives on Sexual Orientation," in *Evolving Theoretical Perspectives on Students*, ed. Leila V. Moore. New Directions for Student Services Series, no. 51 (San Francisco: Jossey-Bass, 1990), 50.
14. Cass's model described in Evans and Levine, "Perspectives," 52–54.
15. Raechele L. Pope and Amy L. Reynolds, "Including Bisexuality: It's More Than Just a Label," in Evans and Wall, *Beyond Tolerance*, 206.
16. Sharon Sumpter and Julia Salazar, "Myths/Realities of Bisexuality" (Holistic Therapy, Hollywood, CA, handout).
17. All of the myths and misunderstandings, unless otherwise noted, are from Sexual Orientation Services Committee, et al., "Straight Talk about Homosexuality" (University of Massachusetts, Amherst, 1986, brochure).
18. Dr. Judd Marmor, cited in Nancy J. Evans, "Introduction: Why We Need This Book," in Evans and Wall, *Beyond Tolerance*, xvi.
19. John Money, cited in Kathleen Y. Ritter and Craig W. O'Neill, "Moving through Loss: The Spiritual Journey of Gay Men and Lesbian Women," *Journal of Counseling and Development* 68 (1): 9. Also Natalie Angier, "Report Suggests Homosexuality Is Linked to Genes," *New York Times*, July 16, 1993, A1 and A12.
20. Sarah Babb, "Commonly Held Incorrect Beliefs" (Akron Newsletter, Akron, OH, handout).
21. Equity Institute, "Myth/Fact Sheet" (Equity Institute, Emeryville, CA, handout).

22. Gail Sausser, "Hello, I Am A Lesbian," in *Lesbian Etiquette* (Freedom, CA: Crossing Press, 1986), 53.

23. Felicity Barringer, "Measuring Sexuality through Polls Can Be Shaky," *New York Times,* April 15, 1993.

24. Vernon A. Wall and Nancy J. Evans, "Using Psychosocial Development Theories to Understand and Work with Gay and Lesbian Persons," in Evans and Wall, *Beyond Tolerance,* 35.

25. Evans and Levine, "Perspectives," 50–51.

26. National Gay Task Force, "About Coming Out" (National Gay Task Force, Washington, DC, handout).

27. Jamie Washington, "ADODI Retreat" (ADODI, Baltimore, MD, 1991, booklet). Also National Gay Task Force, "Coming Out."

28. Anonymous, " . . . In," *New Current,* Smith College, April 1987, 28.

29. Darryl K. Loiacano, "Gay Issues among Black Americans: Racism, Homophobia, and the Need for Validation," *Journal of Counseling and Development* 68 (1): 21.

30. Connie S. Chan, "Issues of Identity Development among Asian-American Lesbians and Gay Men," *Journal of Counseling and Development* 68 (1): 16–17.

31. Natalie S. Eldridge and David C. Barnett, "Counseling Gay and Lesbian Students," in Evans and Wall, *Beyond Tolerance,* 158.

32. Becky Birtha, "A Sense of Loss," in *For Nights like This One: Stories of Loving Women* (San Francisco: Frog in the Well, 1983), 39.

33. Pope and Reynolds, "Including Bisexuality," 207.

34. Lesbian Bisexual Awareness Workshop, "When You Meet a Lesbian Person" (Smith College, Northampton, MA, handout).

35. Catherine Whitney, *Uncommon Lives: Gay Men and Straight Women* (New York: New American Library, 1990), 43.

36. Ritter and O'Neill, "Moving through Loss," 9–10.

15. SOCIOECONOMIC CLASS

1. Wendy Wasserstein, "Isn't It Romantic," in *The Heidi Chronicles and Other Plays* (San Diego: Harcourt Brace Jovanovich, 1990), 100.

2. Barb Jensen, "They Must Be Made of Something Different: Class, Classism, and the Lesbian Movement," *Lesbian Inciter,* n. d.

3. The House Ways and Means Committee, March 1989, cited in "Class: The American Caste System?" *Prism* 4 (4): 12.

4. Peter T. Kilborn, "The Middle Class Feels Betrayed, but Maybe Not Enough to Rebel," *New York Times,* January 12, 1992, sec. 4.

5. *U.S. Bureau of the Census Statistical Abstract of the United States: 1991,* 111th ed. (Washington, DC: U.S. Bureau of the Census, 1991), 449.

6. Nancy Schniedewind and Ellen Davidson, *Open Minds to Equality* (Englewood Cliffs, NJ: Prentice Hall, 1983), 13–14.

7. Schniedewind and Davidson, *Open Minds,* 13–14.

8. Schniedewind and Davidson, *Open Minds,* 13–14.

9. Benjamin Demott, "The Myth of Classlessness," *Prism* 4 (4): 18.
10. Schniedewind and Davidson, Open Minds, 133.
11. Barbara Ehrenreich, "Welcome to Fleece U.," in *The Worst Years of Our Lives: Irreverent Notes from a Decade of Greed* (New York: Pantheon, 1990), 216.
12. From exercises and workshops developed by the Equity Institute and by the Student Affairs Office at Smith College.

16. DISABILITIES

1. Mark Medoff, *Children of a Lesser God* (New York: Dramatists Play Service, 1980), 29.
2. Laura F. Rothstein, "Campuses and the Disabled," *Chronicle of Higher Education,* September 4, 1991, B3 and B10.
3. Gwyneth Ferguson Matthews, *Voices from the Shadows: Women with Disabilities Speak Out* (Toronto: Women's Educational Press, 1983), 126–27.
4. Douglas Biklen and Robert Bogdan, "Media Portrayals of Disabled People: A Study in Stereotypes," reprinted in Equity Institute, "Training of Trainers Intensive Program" (Equity Institute, Emeryville, CA, 1991, booklet).
5. Brenda G. Hameister, "Disabled Students," in *The Freshman Year Experience,* M. Lee Upcraft, John N. Gardner, et al. (San Francisco: Jossey-Bass, 1989), 340.
6. Massachusetts General Laws, chapter 15 1B, S 1(16).
7. Maryland Governor's Office for Individuals with Disabilities, "Americans with Disabilities Act of 1990 (ADA) Resource Guide" (Maryland Governor's Office for Individuals with Disabilities, Annapolis, MD, handout).
8. Ellen Barnes, Carol Berrigan, and Douglas Biklen, *What's the Difference? Teaching Positive Attitudes toward People with Disabilities* (Syracuse, NY: Human Policy Press, 1978), 134–35.
9. Barnes, Berrigan, and Biklen, *What's the Difference?* 154–56.
10. Barnes, Berrigan, and Biklen, *What's the Difference?* 122–24.
11. Barnes, Berrigan, and Biklen, *What's the Difference?* 149–51.
12. Barnes, Berrigan, and Biklen, *What's the Difference?* 117–19.
13. The Research and Training Center on Independent Living, "Guidelines for Reporting and Writing about People with Disabilities," 3d ed. (University of Kansas, Lawrence, 1990, brochure).
14. American Psychiatric Association, "Let's Talk about Mental Illness" (Association on Handicapped Student Service Programs in Postsecondary Education, Columbus, OH, 1990, newsletter), 1–2.
15. Staff update from HEATH, cited in Thomas P. Byrne and Alice LoCicero Crawford, "Some Theoretical and Practical Issues in Counseling the Learning Disabled Student," *Journal of College Student Psychotherapy* 5 (1): 75.
16. Research and Training Center, "Guidelines."
17. Barbara Scheiber and Jeanne Talpers, *Campus Access for Learning Disabled*

Students: A Comprehensive Guide (Washington, DC: Closer Look, 1985), 38–39.

18. Scheiber and Talpers, *Campus Access*, 41–44.
19. Diane E. Woods, "Needs of Disabled Students: Help Asking and Help Giving," in *Disability: The College's Challenge*, ed. J. P. Hourihan (New York: Teachers College Press, 1980), 34.
20. Judith J. Albert and James S. Fairweather, "Effective Organization of Post-secondary Services for Students with Disabilities," *Journal of College Student Development* 31 (5): 446. Also Special Needs Office, "Special Needs Services for the Differently Abled" (Smith College, Northampton, MA, booklet).
21. Equal Access Committee, "Guidelines for Sensitive Use of Language" (Vanderbilt University, Nashville, TN, brochure). Also Robert G. Hadley and Martin G. Brodwin, "Language about People with Disabilities," *Journal of Counseling and Development* 67 (3): 148–49.
22. New York State Office of Advocate for Disabled, "What Makes Disabled People Disabled?" (New York State Office of Advocate for Disabled, Albany, NY, brochure). Also Equal Access Committee, "Guidelines." Also Woods, "Needs of Disabled," 39–40.
23. Medoff, *Children*, 65.
24. New York State, "What Makes." Also National Information Center on Deafness (Gallaudet College, Washington, DC, bookmark).

17. SIZE AND APPEARANCE

1. Rita Freedman, *BodyLove: Learning to Like Our Looks—and Ourselves* (New York: Harper and Row, 1988), 8.
2. L. Louderback, cited in Susan Kano, *Making Peace with Food: Freeing Yourself from the Diet-Weight Obsession*, rev. ed. (New York: HarperPerennial, 1989), 48.
3. Wendy Sanford, "Body Image," in *The New Our Bodies, Ourselves*, updated ed., Boston Women's Health Book Collective (New York: Simon and Schuster, 1992), 23.
4. Kano, *Making Peace*, 40.
5. Sanford, "Body Image," 24.
6. Judith Stein, cited in Sanford, "Body Image," 26.
7. Karen Johnson and Tom Ferguson, *Trusting Ourselves: The Sourcebook on Psychology for Women* (New York: Atlantic Monthly Press, 1990), 364.
8. Carrie Hemenway, "Fuel for Dispelling the Myths," *Radiance* 7 (1): 12.
9. Hemenway, "Fuel," 12.
10. Carrie Hemenway, "Dispelling Common Myths about Large-Sized People" (NAAFA Fat Feminist Caucus, Northampton, MA, handout).
11. Sanford, "Body Image," 27.
12. Wendy Wasserstein, "To Live and Diet," in *Bachelor Girls* (New York: Knopf, 1990), 111–12.
13. Sanford, "Body Image," 27.

14. Kano, *Making Peace,* 16–17.
15. Carrie Hemenway, written communication to the author, 1992.
16. Kano, *Making Peace,* 48.
17. "Support Your Fat Sisters" (NAAFA Fat Feminist Caucus, Northampton, MA, handout).
18. Hemenway, "Common Myths."
19. Freedman, *BodyLove,* 89. Also Johnson and Ferguson, *Trusting Ourselves,* 368–72.
20. Hemenway, "Common Myths."
21. Kano, *Making Peace,* 13–14.
22. From research compiled by Paul Ernsberger and Paul Haskew, *Rethinking Obesity* (New York: Human Sciences Press, 1987) and Willim Bennett and Joel Gurin, *The Dieter's Dilemma* (New York: Basic, 1983), cited in Hemenway, "Fuel," 12.
23. Kano, *Making Peace,* 14.
24. Hemenway, written communication.
25. Hemenway, "Fuel," 12.
26. Freedman, *BodyLove,* 86–88.
27. Johnson and Ferguson, *Trusting Ourselves,* 372.
28. Naomi Wolf, *The Beauty Myth: How Images of Beauty Are Used against Women* (New York: Morrow, 1991), 12–14.
29. Kano, *Making Peace,* 52–55.
30. Freedman, *BodyLove,* 38–44.
31. L.A. Radical Feminist Therapy Collective, cited in Johnson and Ferguson, *Trusting Ourselves,* 377.
32. Carrie Hemenway, "Creating a Size-Friendly Practice/Workplace" (NAAFA Fat Feminist Caucus, Northampton, MA, handout).

18. AGE

1. Barbara Copland, "Adult Learners," in *The Freshman Year Experience,* M. Lee Upcraft, John N. Gardner, et al. (San Francisco: Jossey-Bass, 1989), 303.
2. S. M. Molstad, cited in Gay Holliday, "Addressing the Concerns of Returning Women Students," in *Facilitating the Development of Women,* ed. Nancy J. Evans. New Directions for Student Services Series, no. 29 (San Francisco: Jossey-Bass, 1985), 62.
3. U.S. Department of Education statistics, cited in LuAnn Krager, Robert Wrenn, and Joan Hirt, "Perspectives on Age Differences," in *Evolving Theoretical Perspectives on Students,* ed. Leila V. Moore. New Directions for Student Services Series, no. 51 (San Francisco: Jossey-Bass, 1990), 38.
4. College Entrance Examination Board, cited in Copland, "Adult Learners," 303.
5. William C. Haponski and Charles E. McCabe, *New Horizons: The Education and Career Planning Guide for Adults* (Princeton, NJ: Peterson's, 1985), 55.

6. Holliday, "Addressing Concerns," 62.
7. Patricia M. King and Barbara A. Bauer, "Leadership Issues for Nontraditional-Aged Women Students," in *Empowering Women: Leadership Development on Campus,* ed. Mary A. Danowitz Sagaria. New Directions for Student Services Series, no. 44 (San Francisco: Jossey-Bass, 1988), 77.
8. Holliday, "Addressing Concerns," 62.
9. M. S. Knowles, cited in Copland, "Adult Learners," 306.
10. King and Bauer, "Leadership Issues," 78–79.
11. Gloria Steinem, "Why Young Women Are More Conservative," in *Outrageous Acts and Everyday Rebellions* (New York: Holt, Rinehart, and Winston, 1983), 216.
12. Nancy K. Schlossberg, *Overwhelmed: Coping with Life's Ups and Downs* (New York: Dell, 1989), 5–7.
13. Schlossberg, *Overwhelmed,* 5.
14. Nancy K. Schlossberg, *Counseling Adults in Transition* (New York: Springer, 1984), 70–77.
15. R. L. Kahn and T. C. Antonucci, cited in Schlossberg, *Overwhelmed,* 55–63.
16. Lawrence M. Brammer and Philip J. Abrego, "Intervention Strategies for Coping with Transitions," *Counseling Psychologist* 9 (2): 28.
17. Copland, "Adult Learners," 310.

Index

68–69; thoughts and feelings of, 66–67
Suicide attempts, 69
Suicide gestures, 69
Support systems, 11, 218, 339; for commuting students, 13–14; to cope with stress, 62; for international students, 239; for minority students, 204, 208, 217, 219, 236; religious, 260; for returning adult students, 338–40, 341, 343
Survivor, xi, 167
Survivors of Incest Anonymous, 191
Swastika, 253
Syphilis, 136. *See also* STDs

Take Back the Night marches, 191
Taoism, 249. *See also* Religious diversity
Telephones, sharing, 13
"Ten Little Indians," 205
Therapy. *See* Counseling
Thomas, Clarence, 148, 149, 155
Time management, 9, 58–60; categories of time, 58–59; maximizing discretionary time, 59; minimizing interruptions, 59–60; schedules, 55, 59–60; sources of help, 70; and students with learning disabilities, 317
Times of Harvey Milk, The, 284
Title IX of the education amendments of 1972, 147, 158–59
Title VII of the Civil Rights Act of 1964, 147
Torch Song Trilogy, 264, 266
Townsend, Robert, 123
Trudeau, Garry, 214
Tutors, 15
TV shows. *See suggestions at end of specific chapters*
"20-20," 93–94
Twain, Mark, 28
Twelve-step programs, 105, 119, 219. *See also names of individual groups*

University Fellowship of Metropolitan Community Churches, 283
University of Massachusetts, 219
University of Michigan, 201
University of Wisconsin, 201
Upward mobility, myth of, 292

Vacations: and adult children of alcoholics, 115; and changing relationships with parents, 27–28; and changing relationships with family, 29; and incest survivors, 177; and international students, 240; and returning adult students, 341
Values: challenges to, 11, 22–23, 200, 215–16, 246–47, 277; decision making, 8; of the dominant culture, 229; of parents, 23
Van Derbur Atler, Marilyn, 191
Victim. *See* Survivor
Videos. *See suggestions at end of specific chapters*
Violence, cycle of. *See* Cycle of violence
Violence, sexual: campus crime statistics, 188–89; effects of feeling vulnerable to, 169; sources of help, 188–91; taking action against, 191; and transition to college, 165–66; vulnerability to, 166
Virginity, 131; and rape, 184
Volunteer work. *See* Community service

"Wake Up Little Susie," 122
Wasserstein, Wendy, 26, 29, 55, 290, 325
Weight, obsession with, 56–57, 78–79, 323–24. *See also* Anorexia nervosa; Appearance; Attractiveness; Bulimia; Dieting; Eating disorders
Wellness, 54–55, 140–41; sources of help, 70. *See also sources of help under specific topics*
Williams, Montel, 210
Wolfe, George C., 64
Women's centers. *See sources of help under specific topics*
Women's colleges: and leadership opportunities, 45; meeting men at, 45
Work. *See* Jobs
Writing counselors, 15

Yale University, 98
Yamada, Mitsuye, 199
Yamaguchi, Kristi, 75
"Yo-yo" dieting, 327

Zen Buddhism, 249. *See also* Religious diversity